Managing AFS®

The Andrew File System

ISBN 0-13-802729-3

90000

9 780138 027292

Managing AFS®
The Andrew File System

Richard Campbell

Prentice Hall PTR
Upper Saddle River, NJ 07458
http://www.phptr.com

Library of Congress Cataloging-in-Publication Data

Campbell, Richard.
   Managing AFS: the Andrew File System / Richard Campbell.
      p.   cm.
   Includes bibliographical references and index.
   ISBN 0-13-802729-3 (paper : alk. paper)
   1. File organization (Computer science) 2. AFS (Computer file)
   3. Electronic data processing--Distributed processing. I. Title.
   QA76.9.F5C36 1998   97-43581
   005.4'367682--dc21   CIP

Editorial/production supervision: *Jane Bonnell*
Cover design director: *Jerry Votta*
Cover design: *Design Source*
Cover illustration: *Sally Wern Comport, courtesy of The Stock Illustration Source*
Copyeditor: *Mary Lou Nohr*
Composition: *FASTpages*
Manufacturing manager: *Alexis R. Heydt*
Acquisitions editor: *Paul W. Becker*
Editorial assistant: *Bart Blanken*
Marketing manager: *Dan Rush*

Printed in the United States of America
10 9 8 7 6 5 4 3 2 1

ISBN 0-13-802729-3

Prentice-Hall International (UK) Limited,London
Prentice-Hall of Australia Pty. Limited, Sydney
Prentice-Hall Canada Inc., Toronto
Prentice-Hall Hispanoamericana, S.A., Mexico
Prentice-Hall of India Private Limited, New Delhi
Prentice-Hall of Japan, Inc., Tokyo
Pearson Education Asia Pte. Ltd., Singapore
Editora Prentice-Hall do Brasil, Ltda., Rio de Janeiro

Contents

Preface

INTRODUCTION

This book describes the implementation, administration, and use of Transarc Corporation's AFS®, the Andrew File System. This distributed system has several attributes which make it ideally suited for use in organizations trying to manage the constantly growing amount of file data needed and produced by today's operating systems and applications.

Even though most of the academic emphasis on AFS concerns its performance and semantics, much of the benefit of the system derives from its integrated approach to administration. The ability of AFS to support many more clients per server, to decrease network loads, to provide location-transparent access to data, and to automatically fail over to replica sites is reason enough to investigate the system. But the collection of tools supplied to administrators which provides behind-the-scenes control of the distributed system is equally important.

Over the last decade, AFS's use has steadily increased so that by now many hundreds of sites around the world are full-fledged members of an on-line, global, distributed file system. These sites tend to be quite large because AFS is particularly optimized to support the file storage needs of thousands of users. Yet given the ever-increasing sales of computers and their voracious disk appetites, mature solutions to medium- and large-scale computing sites will be needed by more and more people.

AUDIENCE AND SCOPE

When you purchase AFS, you'll receive several manuals that come with the package. This book is not a replacement for serious reading of that official documentation. There are a multitude of options for almost all processes and utilities in the AFS command suite. Rather than catalog each argument, I hope to provide the reasons behind some of the design decisions which otherwise may appear arbitrary or counterintuitive.

How and why the AFS clients and servers work as they do is the scope of this book. The following chapters describe the newer features of the system and highlight the latest advances with some explanations of their purpose; they do not describe the precise syntax or option to every possible command. For that, you can use the manual set supplied by Transarc, the developer of the commercial AFS product.

The examples and suggestions for managing AFS are shown using the standard UNIX® command-line interface; the AFS server programs are available only for UNIX servers, so knowledge of basic UNIX commands and operations is a prerequisite for using the system.

If you've used NFS® or NetWare™ before and have managed desktops, file servers, and disks, you may be wondering what all the fuss is about; after all, these services have been around for years. But AFS is designed quite differently from these other file systems for reasons that make sense but take some explaining.

There's no simple linear way to discuss the mechanisms to manage and use AFS because most parts of the system are dependent on each other. I will try to create some order out of this interdependence at the risk of using some terms that are not fully described until later. For example, access control lists—used to detail who can access which files—are mentioned early on but are not defined until the middle of the book. The definition isn't required in the early stages, as long as you can trust that eventually the specifics will be explained.

Structurally, we'll begin with a broad overview and gradually introduce more and more detail, moving from the central servers to the distributed client desktops.

CONTENTS

The first two chapters describe AFS in general terms.

Chapter 1 provides a general overview of the benefits of AFS, why it was developed in the first place, its particular design and drawbacks, and information about Transarc. Administrators, managers, and users will gain an understanding of the system from Chapter 1.

Chapter 2 introduces much of the technical vocabulary of AFS and describes its client/server architecture, including the caching protocol and file server organization. Here, the architecture described in Chapter 1 is put into concrete terms of the protocol used by clients and servers.

The next four chapters are devoted to the administrative specifics required to install and run an AFS cell.

Chapter 3 discusses basic server management by itemizing the processes, operations, and systems that make the servers work, with special emphasis on the internal distributed database protocol. These issues are of concern when setting up an AFS cell.

Chapter 4 discusses AFS volume management issues, the very heart of AFS administration. While AFS is primarily thought of as a protocol by which client workstations access file data, the system's real value is in its support for large-scale administration. This chapter describes how AFS volumes are administered to create the global file namespace, to provide access to replicated data, and to provide users with on-line access to a backup version of their files.

Chapter 5 describes client configurations and includes suggestions for optimizing desktop access to AFS. The chapter also introduces the package client administration tool as well as two products that allow PCs to access AFS— Transarc's port to Windows NT™ and Platinum Technology's PC-Enterprise™.

Chapter 6 describes the user authentication process, management of the Kerberos database, and the use of standard MIT Kerberos, versions 4 and 5.

Chapter 7 details the user and developer view of AFS, including logging in to AFS, access controls, group management, and the slight differences in file system semantics. There's also a brief description of how PC users manage their AFS files with Transarc's NT port. Users not interested in administration and management can refer to this chapter for examples of how to use AFS.

Chapter 8 focuses on Transarc's built-in archiving system, ad hoc volume dump tools, and mechanisms to save other critical configuration data. It also includes information on integrating AFS with commercial backup systems.

Chapter 9 returns to the subject of overall administration, with more information on AFS server administrative responsibilities, insights into the Kerberos authentication system, providing access for NFS clients, issues regarding the installation of third-party software, and comments on a few of the public and commercial AFS administrative tools now available.

Chapter 10 continues the subject of management with a discussion of AFS's debugging and monitoring tools. The chapter focuses in depth on advanced issues of administering UNIX-based AFS servers.

Chapter 11 describes large-site administration and presents four case studies of successful use of AFS by global or otherwise interesting sites.

Chapter 12 concludes the book with some thoughts on how to evaluate and begin using AFS at your organization, and what alternative file systems are up to. Managers and administrators will gain a greater appreciation for the potential scope of an AFS implementation project.

Appendix A is a command-by-command description of the major AFS tools including all subcommands. As you read through the book, you can refer to this appendix for a reminder of the purpose of any commands. This listing also includes information on the precise authentication required to run each command.

TYPOGRAPHIC CONVENTIONS

System operations are shown as command-line input and output, such as:

```
$ fs mkm alice   user.alice
$ fs lsmount alice
'alice' is a mount point for '#user.alice'
```

For people unfamiliar with UNIX, $ is the standard UNIX Bourne shell prompt. Following UNIX convention, when you have logged in as the superuser or root, the shell prompt is #. These command sequences were executed on a Sun® workstation running the Solaris™ operating system with AFS version 3.4a and pasted into the text of this book. Output from AFS commands on other systems should be identical apart from dates and other ephemeral data; output from standard UNIX commands may differ more or less depending on your particular desktop operating system. Liberal use is made of standard programs such as date, touch and shell output redirection to demonstrate file creation. The cat program is often used to demonstrate that the files in question were created successfully.

The hypothetical organization used as an example throughout the examples, HQ, and its domain name, hq.firm, were non-existent at the time this book was written.

ACKNOWLEDGMENTS

In writing this book I am indebted to the software engineers who put AFS together, first (and still) at Carnegie Mellon University and later at Transarc Corporation; to the computing community which has freely shared experiences and workarounds; to the University of Michigan's Center for Information Technology Integration, where some of my best friends work and play; and to the Union Bank of Switzerland for their support. Many people in these groups helped review this book; over the years, I've learned much about AFS, but their dedicated oversight, support, and occasional drinks at corner tables in smoky bars have made this a much better book. Among them, I'd like to thank John Brautigam, Bill Doster, Ted Hanss, Peter Honeyman, Tony Mauro, Tom Menner, Anne Perella, Jim Rees, Dave Richardson, Lyle Seaman, and Mike Stolarchuk.

I'd also like to thank the staff at Prentice Hall who have guided my first effort at book-length writing from conception to publication.

And one nonacknowledgment: While I know many people from Transarc and have happily used and administered AFS over the course of many years, this book is not a product of Transarc Corporation. Certain members of Transarc's staff, past and present, have helped me with the myriad system details, but the content and any errors in the book are mine alone. Notes and additional information on AFS can be found at my web site, http://www.netrc.com.

TRADEMARK ACKNOWLEDGMENTS

AFS and Encina are registered trademarks of Transarc Corporation. All AFS command names, options, and their output are copyrighted by Transarc Corporation; they are used in this book with Transarc's permission.

Acer Fast File System and OpenServer are registered trademarks of Santa Cruz Operation, Inc.

ADSM, AIX, AS/400, Journal File System, MVS, OS/2, and RS/6000 are registered trademarks of International Business Machines, Inc.

Alpha AXP, DEC, DECstation 2100, 3100, 500, Digital Unix, and Ultrix are a registered trademarks of Digital Equipment Corporation.

Amiga is a registered trademark of Amiga International, Inc.

Apollo, HP, and HP-UX 9000 Series, are registered trademarks of Hewlett-Packard Company.

Appleshare and Macintosh are registered trademarks of Apple Computer, Inc.

BoxHill is a trademark of BoxHill Systems Corporation.

## CHAPTER 1

Architectural Overview

Let's allow the devil's advocate to begin: People and applications have been using distributed file systems for several years. The total cost of hardware and especially disk drives has been plummeting for the last decade and looks like it will continue to do so. Computers are sharing data through local-area and wide-area networks now more than ever. Files, sounds, still and moving pictures, and interactive forms and games are being delivered through the World Wide Web, in some cases directly to consumer's television sets. So why do we need yet another file system?

There are two immediate responses: One, files may not be the sexiest of media, but they are where the overwhelming majority of information we come into contact with is stored. And two, there are still plenty of problems with the current implementations. Do any of the following scenarios apply to your systems?

- A desktop is attached to a remote server that stores production applications, but the network is down so the user can't run anything.
- A desktop user is having a problem with an application. After searching though the local disk, the user discovers some outdated system binaries.
- A new project team has been hired and they'll need their own server because the current server and network are already overloaded.
- An important new application is available, but you can't run it because you can't find it on your current server.

- Your project has run out of shared disk space. Administrators will have to wait until evening to shut down the machine and add a disk. They're grumbling because they've stayed late for several consecutive nights just to add more disk drives to other servers.
- You want to share a file with a new employee but uncertainties about Internet use prevent both of you from sharing the easy way. Finally, you give up, copy the file to a floppy, and walk over to the new employee's computer.
- You want to share a file with the entire organization. You send an e-mail to the administrators asking them to copy the file to a general directory. You're not sure when this file will ever become generally available.
- A user accidentally deleted their mail folder. It will take several hours of an administrator's time to retrieve this file from backup tape.
- A new employee joins the company. After finally getting an ID and home directory, she finds that this information has not been propagated to some of the systems she'd like to use.
- A user is moving to an office on another floor for a few days. How will he find his home directory on a different desktop? How much network traffic will this connection generate?
- A user is moving permanently to a new floor or office. The administrators schedule another late shift so they can copy over her files and update the location maps.

And consider if the above problems are happening in the office across the street. Or across the country.

Most users are happy enough with distributed system technologies if they can just get connected and perform some function. The richness of the AFS solution is not just that it enables the easy sharing of information, but that it also builds a management infrastructure that supports ever-increasing sharing without a similar increase in costs. It's not just a way to share a file; it's a way for an organization to control its distributed file services.

The benefits of AFS include:

- High scalability because of protocol efficiencies
- Ease of sharing via its single namespace
- Reliable access to replicated data
- Centralized administration model based on distributed services
- Improved security model for access and group management

- Superior support for dataless clients and desktops of different architectures

These features are not a random collection of tricks stuffed into a single package. They are the result of a conscious effort to build a sustainable distributed file system that can support medium- to large-scale enterprises. Whereas other file system products have evolved to fill a market, AFS was engineered to solve a set of problems—the kinds of problems, as you can see, that affect most organizations today.

BEGINNINGS

As with many UNIX products, the AFS developers were university researchers who were charged with providing solutions to their users. In this case, the campus was Carnegie Mellon University in the early 1980s, the researchers worked for the central computing center, and the problem was how to easily share file data between people and departments.

CMU was looking to alleviate the difficulties departments encountered as individuals dealt with disk drives, file locations, duplicate data, and service outages. The group wanted to provide central storage for file resources such that the entire campus, some thousands of workstations and users, could have access to the same files. This wish raised many issues: How many servers would be needed? Could the network traffic be supported with the existing LAN and WAN infrastructure of the day? With so many files, how would users navigate the file namespace? How many administrators would be needed to manage the system? What about failures?

Few technologies were available to help with these issues and most were proprietary to a particular vendor's operating system. Sun's Network File System stood apart from the rest in that it was bundled on many different platforms and the implementation was available for study.

But CMU soon found inefficiencies with the NFS architecture: For typical systems of the time, only a few dozen clients could be supported; there was no systematic security system; because clients could mount practically anything, anywhere they wanted, the same files would wind up with different names on different clients, or worse, no two clients ever saw the exact same set of files. And with the small memory-only cache, certain benchmarks that performed many reads and writes of file data to and from the servers failed to complete at all at certain loads.

More importantly, the CMU researchers recognized that the costs attributed to enterprise file management include not only the hardware and software that store and deliver the data but also the administration costs to oversee and manage these processes. In short, the strengths of NFS—its small scale and flexibility—proved to be its weakness. This was not the architecture to solve the problems CMU had identified.

Luckily, the University was in the habit of undertaking serious computing research projects with an eye toward using those same systems in production at their campus—the Andrew Message Service for multimedia mail and the Mach operating system are two of the more notable examples. So, the center decided to engineer their own system, one that could handle either a small or large site without the hefty increases in the number of systems and support staff otherwise necessary. This new system became known as the Andrew File System, or AFS. (The eponymous name recognizes both Andrew Carnegie and Andrew Mellon, the primary benefactors of CMU).

To create AFS, the researchers made several key assumptions, foremost being the decision to exploit the increasingly powerful processing capacity of the desktop computers themselves. In the modern era of computing, the disparity between server and client power is diminishing; why not take advantage of often underused clients to help take the load off the disk servers and networks? The designers rigorously examined any way to reduce network protocol packets and server processing. In all cases, the semantics of the file system operations were to be kept as close as possible to local behavior, but certain optimizations might be adopted if the changes made sense in a distributed system.

Because CMU is an academic institution, its security needs may appear to be less than those of other companies; however, with the constantly changing user population and the relatively open campus environment, the problems of inappropriate access to data are perhaps greater than in many other organizations. A new security model would have to be implemented; one that used the public WAN but relied on cryptographically secure communications to authenticate the identities of users. The inherently untrustworthy desktops would never confirm a user's identity; only the trusted AFS security servers could do that.

Another goal was to build complete location transparency into the system: operators should be able to manage the storage devices without having to concern themselves with manually updating desktop configurations. Any changes to server configurations or the ultimate physical location of a set of files should be automatically noticed by interested desktops without manual intervention by administrators or users. And as administrators and users manipulated the file system, clients must have guaranteed access to the latest data.

A key factor in the design of AFS was the result of the latest file system research. It turned out that even in a distributed organization involved in intensive software development, file access patterns were not random. Overwhelmingly, files were opened and read through from beginning to end. And though software development means writing files and creating new executables, files are still read three times more often than they are written. Further, usage of the file system shows high locality of reference: files that were read recently are far more likely to be read again. And finally, these files were most often quite small, only tens to hundreds of kilobytes.

These results of file system studies suggested that aggressive caching of files by clients would prove successful in reducing server load. The designers of AFS decided to fully embrace client-side caching with quite a large disk cache and a guaranteed consistency model. While this made the AFS servers and clients more complicated to engineer, the hypothesis was that the servers would be able to support a large campus environment without a significant investment in specialized hardware or networks.

BENEFITS OF AFS

The first version of AFS was completed in 1984. The results were impressive: versus NFS, the savings in protocol efficiencies permitted from five to ten times as many clients per server and reduced network traffic some two-thirds. And, even better, this capability also translated into faster client response times.

The earliest versions comprised user-made processes named Venus and Vice, names which live on in a few places in AFS. In the version 2 release of AFS in 1986, these pieces were placed inside the operating system itself for even better performance.

After a few revisions, AFS became the primary file storage system at CMU. Significantly, because it was designed to meet the real-world needs of a large, distributed organization, the system implements many policies directly rather than presenting a toolkit for administrators to build their own system. These policies allow fewer operations staff to support larger number of clients and users; again, this was a specific design goal, and the designers weighed a variety of design choices to achieve these high levels of scalability.

Figure 1-1 is a high-level view of the components that make AFS work. At the top is a typical desktop client computer that caches all information from the system onto its local disk; on the right are the various servers that respond to requests to fetch and store data.

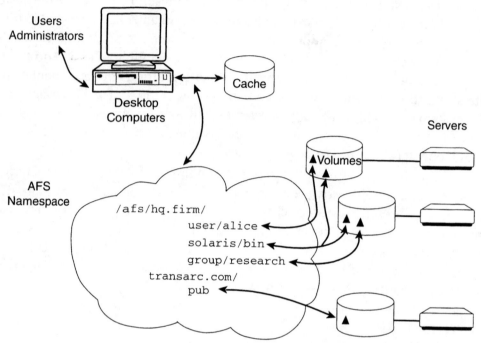

Figure 1-1   The AFS Architecture

The most interesting part of this architecture is the central AFS file namespace. While all the file and directory names in the namespace are related to physical data on the servers, the names are visible in a single, abstract, enterprisewide, and consistent directory structure. The servers perform all their work in concert to provide a seamless file namespace visible by all desktops and all users. Any changes to the namespace—any new files or changed data— are publicized to clients immediately without per-client administration.

We've seen how client caching can reduce network traffic and server load. The hard part of caching is determining when cached data is invalid. In AFS, a server manages all invalidation processing by tracking which clients are using which files. When one AFS client writes a new copy of a file to a server, the server promises to call back all other workstations that have cached that file, with a brief notice to disregard that piece of cached data on subsequent requests.

Caching reduces client/server traffic enormously. When, for example, a client runs a Perl script, the Perl executable program must be read and used. In AFS, this use automatically causes the program to be cached. Now, for every new Perl script run ever after, the client is able to use the cached version.

Because it uses its local copy, not a single packet is put on the network and the server is not interrupted to satisfy requests for commonly used data.

When a new version of the Perl executable is inevitably installed, the server storing the program will call back all clients it knows have cached the program and give them an explicit indication that the file has been updated. On the next execution of this program, the client will realize that the local copy is out of date and quickly fetch the newer version from the server.

Compare this mechanism with a caching Web brower: browsers also store recently accessed files in a cache, but the browser has no idea if or when that data becomes out of date. The browser must either contact the server on each access and check if a new version of the page has been installed—a check which adds additional network traffic and interrupts the server—or it must blindly assume that the page is not going to be updated for some period of time, in which case, the user may see out-of-date data until the client sees fit to check the server again. The AFS model incorporates proactive notification of new versions to all interested clients. Chapter 2 goes into more detail on how this protocol works and scales to large numbers of clients.

The fact that servers must keep track of which clients are reading what files is indeed a burden. And in AFS, a few optimizations are in place to reduce the complexity of tracking all that data and recovering from failures. But the one-time cost in developing a complex consistency model is more than offset by the day-in-day-out savings in server processing time and network load. These consistency guarantees are not constructed simply to provide the same view of the file system to all clients but to support large caches with a minimum load. AFS clients can cache their data in either kernel memory or on local disk, the latter often leading to cache sizes of several hundred megabytes. This scheme represents several hundred megabytes of data that will not be thrashing across the network or be redundantly accessed.

Next, the NFS architecture of allowing clients to mount server file systems practically anywhere in their local namespace permits great flexibility, but in large enterprises, the problem is not that users need or want to create their own directory structures but that users can't find data that is supposed to be shared globally. This problem is solved by integrating file location discovery with the file access protocol.

In Figure 1-1, you can see that a client contacts the cached, abstract namespace first. Directions to the actual storage locations of the files and directories are stored in the namespace itself; only after a client discovers these hints will that client contact a server directly to download the desired data. AFS maintains a database mapping named collections of files and their locations; as clients enter new subtrees supported by new collections, they contact the database servers, discover the new locations, and then contact the appropriate file server to fetch the correct data.

Conventionally, applications enter the AFS namespace by changing to the directory named /afs. As applications navigate through that well-known directory name, clients are regularly discovering location hints and determining the actual names of the servers and disk locations of the files. That location information is also cached, just as file data is, to reduce future requests to a minimum.

The huge benefit for you as an administrator (and therefore, eventually, users) is that as the locations of files are manipulated because of system housekeeping needs, the file and directory namespace remains the same. Those clients that have accessed a specific part of the file tree are called back with new location information, and any further need for file or directory information is satisfied from the new servers and disks. You don't need to run any lengthy or extraneous commands to push out this information to clients; clients inherently have access to the entire distributed file system by asking where data is and then fetching the data as one integrated operation.

Because all clients navigate the same file namespace, all changes to the files or directories are visible to all clients all the time. No extra administration need be done on a client to access different parts of the /afs file tree: everything under that directory is consistently visible to all clients at all times.

Also, besides being stored on physical disks, files are stored in logical containers called *volumes*. These collections of file subtrees, normally invisible to users, are the unit of administrative control in AFS. Typically, a package of related files is stored in a single volume—a user's home directory, the common binaries for an architecture, a version of a production application. An administrator can apportion a chunk of physical disk to a new volume and then assign the volume to represent a subtree of the AFS namespace, much as a disk partition controls a piece of a UNIX or PC file system.

These connections between path names and volumes allow administrators to enlarge any area of the namespace at will without undue concern about the location of each set of files. And through the technology out of which volumes are built, you can move a volume's files from server to server without the user ever seeing an interruption of service.

Moreover, you can make snapshots of a volume's data available in the file system; users themselves can trivially retrieve yesterday's files rather than requesting a tape retrieval of every accidental deletion.

Best of all, you can replicate volumes. Typically, replication is done for system or other production binaries such as the Perl executable or other widely used programs of data which are infrequently updated. This replication, like most AFS administration, can be performed in the background, behind the scenes, invisible to the user population, and yet used to provide a highly available system. Here, "highly available" implies a higher level of reliability and failure recovery than is otherwise available.

When clients need access to replicated file data, all locations that have been administered to contain copies of the file are returned to the client machine. In Figure 1-1, you can see that the files underneath /afs/hq.firm/ solaris/bin are apparently stored on each of two different disks. As the client accesses a file in that directory, if there is any sort of outage, such as a network problem or server crash, the client simply goes to the next server on its list. This on-line fail over has proven of critical importance to institutions that have installed AFS. And the easy availability of reliable access to important data reduces the need for more additional expensive fault-tolerant servers and redundant networking.

Note that the fail over mechanism is how clients manage to find access to critical data. Equally important is the capability added by the CMU engineers for administrators to replicate the data in the first place. Again, to compare this with NFS, nothing in the NFS protocol manages failures. Even when you've managed to repoint a client at a new NFS server following some disaster, you have got no guarantee that what you're pointing at is an exact copy of the data—if you're lucky, someone might have managed to manually copy the right files at the right time between systems. The AFS system gives you an integrated, centrally controlled capability to manage replication of file data.

For the most part, you perform all these procedures on-line, transparently to users. For example, AFS administrators routinely move a user's home directory from one system or disk to another during the middle of the day with virtually no interruption of service. You can decommission entire file servers by moving their file data to another machine, with no one the wiser. System administration does not have to be performed during off-hours, neither in the middle of the night nor on weekends.

AFS supports these procedures by centralizing the administrative databases but this does not mandate another level of bureaucracy that will encourage inefficiences. Note from the figure that the first-level administrative interface is through a simple AFS desktop client. Because the centralized mechanisms are available via a client/server command suite, with the most common tasks available as simple one-line commands, AFS allows administrators greater flexibility and power in the management of the system.

As an example, say a single-disk drive has crashed with the only copy of a user's home directory on it. AFS permits you to quickly restore that directory subtree to another disk in the file system; you can then easily connect the new location of that subtree to the old directory name, and all clients will automatically—and invisibly to users—begin to contact that new location whenever that subtree is accessed.

Given all of this centrally controlled information of file locations, server systems, and namespace management, it stands to reason that the internal databases used by AFS are of primary importance. To reduce the risks of depending on this data, the databases used by AFS are also replicated and clients can automatically fail over between the available database servers as needed. These databases are not based on any commercial relational database system; they are custom-built for AFS clients and servers and use their own caching, replication, and read/write protocol. The collection of these database and file servers and their clients is called an *AFS cell*.

Yet another problem faced by CMU was that of secure user authentication. The engineers looked to the Kerberos security system, designed at the Massachusetts Institute of Technology around the same time and for many of the same reasons. In a campus computing environment, an essentially unknown number of desktops are found in every nook and cranny; it is therefore unsafe to trust any of the desktops' claims about a user's identity—desktop operating systems can be too easily subverted. By storing user's secret keys in a secured database, an encrypted protocol can prove users' identities without passing those secrets around the network in the clear. Once identified, all file system transactions use this authenticated credential to check access control. The AFS system builds on this model by efficiently replicating the Kerberos servers to increase their reliability.

One part of traditional UNIX systems that has never proven adequate in large enterprises is group access to files. The UNIX permission bits allow a single group to be given a combination read/write/execute control over a specific file. The main problems with this permission system are that artificial names must be created to enable that single group to have the correct membership. And group membership has normally been controlled only by the superuser. Both features greatly reduce the effectiveness of UNIX groups.

AFS provides three solutions to managing file accesses. Each directory can have a list of access controls entries with each entry containing either a user identity or a group name. So, multiple groups with different permissions can easily be accommodated. Also, the permissions allowed are extended from the usual read and write to include insertion, deletion, listing of files in the directory, file locking, and administration of the permissions themselves. Lastly, individuals can create and maintain their own groups (according to a strict naming scheme), so that group membership administration can be delegated away from the operations staff. This ability drastically reduces the administration complexity and increases the security of the file system by encouraging accurate access controls based on natural organizational groupings of users.

Seeing as how the set of AFS servers includes replicated Kerberos database servers, it is natural for standard AFS practices to mandate that the servers be kept in physically secure locations. That security consideration could be a drawback to administration procedures, but the AFS administration command suite is written to enable operators to manage all server operations from their desktops without resort to remote login. This client/server approach is natural, given the distributed nature of the system, but makes even more sense when most administration functions are operations performed on the single, global namespace. Because all changes to the namespace are visible to all clients instantaneously, administrators perform many of their day-to-day tasks by manipulating the namespace rather than by executing commands on server systems using some backdoor into the file data.

As an example of how the use of AFS depends on manipulation of the namespace, let's examine how to provide distributed file system support for clients of different architectures. In NFS, if you wanted a single, well-known file name to be used for access to the Perl executable, say, `/usr/local/bin/perl`, you could load the Solaris binaries on one file server under the name `/export/solaris/local/bin/perl` and the AIX™ binaries at `/export/aix/local/bin/perl`. Each Sun and IBM client would then have to be configured so that it mounted the correct server path name at its local path of `/usr/local/bin/`.

In AFS, the client operating system includes a hook in the internal name lookup function such that any use of the path name element `@sys` is automatically translated—on a per-client basis—into a string of characters dependent on the client's architecture. An IBM AIX version 4.1 desktop would translate /afs/@sys/bin into /afs/aix_41/bin; a Sun desktop would translate the same string as /afs/sun4m_53/bin. The Perl executable could therefore be loaded into the architecture-specific directory and the local path /usr/local/bin could be set up as a symbolic link into the AFS path /afs/@sys/bin. Any access to /usr/local/bin/perl would then be directed to the appropriate executable no matter which desktop performed the lookup.

The point of this example is that support for multiple client architectures has been transformed from an administrator's laborious management task into the simple creation of a single directory with a special name, @sys. While the Perl executable may be managed by administrators, any other set of files which are machine-dependent can be managed by individual developers or users. AFS decentralizes what was previously an administrator's chore into a simple path name cliche that can be implemented by anyone.

The combination of all of these benefits—scalability due to caching, single namespace, reliable data access, reduced administration overhead, security, and support for heterogeneous, dataless clients—ultimately allows us to move much of our local data from desktop clients onto AFS servers. With a high degree of confidence, we can rely on the AFS central management model with its highly available data access characteristics to support practically cheap desktop clients—clients that need almost no backing up because all interesting data is stored in the AFS system. Disks on desktops can be used to store mostly ephemeral data such as temporary files, swap space for many large processes, print and mail spool areas, and, of course, a file cache.

These desktops are called dataless because they have a disk but no interesting data is stored on them; instead, only transient data or copies of distributed data are kept local. Compare this configuration with either a diskless machine, which has no hard drive attached, or a diskfull system, which has a large disk on which are stored critical applications and other data that may or may not be available to others. Diskless machines produce a large amount of network traffic and server load because they have small caches; diskfull systems require resource-intensive per-client administration.

To effectively support dataless clients, you need a protocol which reduces network traffic as much as possible, and just as important, the protocol must have built-in fail over so that access to production data is available all the time. Even today, the only protocol which integrates these characteristics is AFS.

Another way to consider the utility of AFS is to take a very high level view of a generic computing system. In the broadest view, a traditional computer consists of a processing unit, storage, and I/O. Storage is normally of two types, transient or persistent, with the former usually implemented by volatile electronic memory and the latter by disks. In both cases, a hierarchy of caching is performed to increase performance and functionality.

For memory, a typical PC has small, fast memory on the CPU chip itself, a large off-chip cache, a much larger local memory system, and finally, a very large area of disk for temporary data. The objects stored in memory are usually the data associated with active processes, and all processes on a machine exist in a single namespace (the names are usually just the process identification number). The important point for us is that the entire complex memory hierarchy is managed automatically by the operating system. Neither users nor the processes themselves are involved in location administration. The result is seamless integration of different levels of storage with overall improved performance and low cost.

Objects stored on disk are predominantly files in a hierarchical namespace. The difference here is that the namespace and the storage devices are mostly managed manually. When no network is available, users themselves must move data from machine to machine. And often, even when a distributed file system is available, it may be that shared files and programs are stored there but the files are copied locally by innumerable custom-built scripts. This is cache management by direct manipulation.

AFS provides a way to automatically manage file storage by making local disks merely a cache for a true, enterprisewide, persistent, shared, distributed data space. Almost all aspects of the local cache are managed mechanically, using policies optimized for the general cases but that do not degrade in the large scale. Unlike the case of processes in memory, the benefit of a persistent file space is that the global set of files can be managed independently of the local desktops, but with the knowledge that any changes will automatically be visible on all desktops.

Let's recap our initial list of problems and some of the solutions provided by AFS.

- Desktops can reliably use applications that are stored on replicated servers.
- Desktops can use system files and binaries efficiently even when the files are stored remotely because, overall, the caching protocol gives near-local disk performance.

- New users do not require additional server systems because the servers and networks are doing much less work.
- All users can get to the same set of files through the single available namespace. Replication permits this data to be located close to the users who need it most without hindering use of the data by other users.
- There's far less concern about running out of disk space; as long as one disk is available on a server anywhere in the enterprise, an administrator can logically expand the namespace at any point to include that data space. Alternatively, sections of the namespace can be transparently moved around the system to disks with extra space available while users are on-line.
- Sharing files is simplified because all files in AFS are shared equally by everyone. With an integrated Kerberos authentication system and discrete access controls throughout, this sharing can be restricted or opened up as needed.
- Snapshots of yesterday's file contents are efficiently saved and are easily made available, eliminating the majority of file restoration requests.
- User identities and group information are efficiently propagated throughout the enterprise by means of a consistent distributed database model, just as file data itself is available to every desktop whenever it has changed.
- A user's move to a new floor normally requires no changes to any configurations. Because of the caching protocol used, the smallest amount of data possible will be transmitted between the servers and desktop.
- If users are moving permanently, it is easy to move their home directory and any other data with which they are closely associated to servers nearer their new desktop. Such a data move is done purely as a networking optimization; no path names are changed, and all desktops continue to see the same file namespace.
- Caring for remote systems is easy because the distributed administration model permits operators to manage and monitor servers throughout the enterprise from their own desktops.

So, what's the downside? Though AFS solves many administrative and user issues, it raises other, different problems. Only the market can tell you whether the cure is better than sickness; while this system has been overshadowed in some respects by other commercial products, the last decade has seen significant growth in the use of AFS.

GLOBAL FILESYSTEMS

After AFS's success at CMU in the mid-80s, other universities grew interested in using the system. This collaboration was encouraged through the use of AFS itself as a means for distant sites to share information. The network protocol on which AFS is built is based on a robust, hand-crafted remote procedure call system capable of efficient transfer of file data while surviving potentially lossy WAN links. This protocol enables many organizations to access their remote cells as well as other AFS sites in a truly Internet-based and globally scalable distributed file system. Today, a typical AFS client well connected to the Internet has several dozen institutions and organizations with which it can share files—not through special-purpose file copy programs, hardcoded addresses, or browsers—but simply by changing directories and opening files, all with Kerberos-authenticated access controls.

Table 1-1 shows a small selection of cells with which a well-connected client can securely share files. This listing is effectively the visible top-level directory structure as seen on an AFS client. These entries are independent domains of AFS use, not individual machines, and each represents a handful to tens of servers, from 100 to 10,000 users, and thus, in total, literally terabytes of file data.

Although this list seems to suggest that the majority of sites are academic institutions, there are actually somewhat more commercial sites using AFS than schools. The reason that few companies are listed is simply that zealous security concerns cause most for-profit organizations to place their AFS site behind a network firewall. As long as you're using Kerberos authentication and access controls correctly, a cell is completely secure; but even so, an administrative mistake can still present a security risk.

In any case, you can see several corporations that are using AFS to solve global connectivity needs. Also visible are several organizations that have implemented multiple AFS cells rather than constructing a single, large cell. There is no ultimate limit to the size of a cell; in practice, the size of a cell depends more on internal politics and budgeting than it does on any technical limitations.

With their success, many of the original design team left CMU in 1989 to form Transarc Corporation, which packaged the old Andrew File System into "AFS." At this time, the commercial AFS product name is a registered trademark of Transarc and is no longer an acronym, so it is proper to speak of the AFS file system. The first commercial release was version 2.3. As of 1997, the

Table 1-1   A Selection of Publicly Accessible AFS Cells

AFS Cell Name	Organization
transarc.com	Transarc Corporation
palo_alto.hpl.hp.com	HP Palo Alto
sleeper.nsa.hp.com	HP Cupertino
stars.reston.unisys.com	Paramax (Unisys), Reston, Va.
vfl.paramax.com	Paramax (Unisys), Paoli Research Center
ibm.uk	IBM UK, AIX Systems Support Centre
afs.hursley.ibm.com	IBM Hursley, UK
zurich.ibm.ch	IBM, Zurich
ctp.se.ibm.com	IBM, Chalmers, Sweden
stars.com	STARS Technology Center, Ballston, Va.
telos.com	Telos Systems Group, Chantilly, Va.
isl.ntt.jp	NTT Information and Communication Systems Labs.
gr.osf.org	OSF Research Institute, Grenoble
ri.osf.org	OSF Research Institute
wu-wien.ac.at	University of Economics, Vienna, Austria
cern.ch	European Laboratory for Particle Physics, Geneva
ethz.ch	Federal Institute of Technology, Zurich
urz.uni-heidelberg.de	Universitaet Heidelberg
uni-hohenheim.de	University of Hohenheim
desy.de	Deutsches Elektronen-Synchrotron
lrz-muenchen.de	Leibniz-Rechenzentrum Muenchen Germany
mpa-garching.mpg.de	Max-Planck-Institut fuer Astrophysik

Table 1-1   A Selection of Publicly Accessible AFS Cells *(continued)*

AFS Cell Name	Organization
ipp-garching.mpg.de	Max-Planck-Institut Institut fuer Plasmaphysik
uni-freiburg.de	Albert-Ludwigs-Universitat Freiburg
rhrk.uni-kl.de	Rechenzentrum University of Kaiserslautern
rrz.uni-koeln.de	University of Cologne, Computing Center
urz.uni-magdeburg.de	Otto-von-Guericke-Universitaet, Magdeburg
rus.uni-stuttgart.de	Rechenzentrum University of Stuttgart
caspur.it	CASPUR Inter-University Computing Consortium, Rome
le.caspur.it	Universita' di Lecce, Italia
infn.it	Istituto Nazionale di Fisica Nucleare, Italia
cc.keio.ac.jp	Keio University, Science and Technology Center
sfc.keio.ac.jp	Keio University, Japan
postech.ac.kr	Pohang Universtiy of Science
nada.kth.se	Royal Institute of Technology, Sweden
rl.ac.uk	Rutherford Appleton Lab, England
pegasus.cranfield.ac.uk	Cranfield University
cs.arizona.edu	University of Arizona, Computer Science Dept.
bu.edu	Boston University
gg.caltech.edu	Caltech Computer Graphics Group
cmu.edu	Carnegie Mellon University
andrew.cmu.edu	Carnegie Mellon University, Campus
ce.cmu.edu	Carnegie Mellon University, Civil Eng. Dept.
theory.cornell.edu	Cornell University Theory Center

Table 1-1   A Selection of Publicly Accessible AFS Cells *(continued)*

AFS Cell Name	Organization
graphics.cornell.edu	Cornell University Program of Computer Graphics
msc.cornell.edu	Cornell University Materials Science Center
northstar.dartmouth.edu	Dartmouth College, Project Northstar
afs1.scri.fsu.edu	Florida State Univeristy, Supercomputer Institute
iastate.edu	Iowa State University
athena.mit.edu	Massachusetts Institute of Technology, Athena
media-lab.mit.edu	MIT, Media Lab cell
net.mit.edu	MIT, Network Group cell
nd.edu	University of Notre Dame
pitt.edu	University of Pittsburgh
psu.edu	Pennsylvania State University
rpi.edu	Rensselaer Polytechnic Institute
dsg.stanford.edu	Stanford University, Distributed Systems Group
ir.stanford.edu	Stanford University
ece.ucdavis.edu	University of California, Davis campus
spc.uchicago.edu	University of Chicago, Social Sciences
ncsa.uiuc.edu	University of Illinois
wam.umd.edu	University of Maryland Network WAM Project
glue.umd.edu	University of Maryland, Project Glue
umich.edu	University of Michigan, Campus
citi.umich.edu	University of Michigan, IFS Development
lsa.umich.edu	University of Michigan, LSA College
math.lsa.umich.edu	University of Michigan, LSA College, Math Cell

Table 1-1   A Selection of Publicly Accessible AFS Cells *(continued)*

AFS Cell Name	Organization
cs.unc.edu	University of North Carolina at Chapel Hill
utah.edu	University of Utah Information Tech. Service
cs.washington.edu	University of Washington Comp Sci Department
wisc.edu	University of Wisconsin-Madison, Campus
anl.gov	Argonne National Laboratory
bnl.gov	Brookhaven National Laboratory
fnal.gov	Fermi National Acclerator Laboratory
ssc.gov	Superconducting Supercollider Lab
hep.net	US High Energy Physics Information cell
cmf.nrl.navy.mil	Naval Research Laboratory
nrlfs1.nrl.navy.mil	Naval Research Laboratory
nersc.gov	National Energy Research Supercomputer Center
alw.nih.gov	National Institutes of Health
nrel.gov	National Renewable Energy Laboratory
pppl.gov	Princeton Plasma Physics Laboratory
psc.edu	Pittsburgh Supercomputing Center

current release is 3.4a and, at the time of this writing, version 3.5 is being pre-pared for release at the beginning of 1998.[1]

As of 1997, about a thousand sites are running AFS. While this might seem small compared to the total number running NetWare or NFS, remember

---

1.   By the way, the SCO Corporation's UNIX operating system, OpenServer™, also has an AFS file sys-tem: this is the Acer® Fast File System and is a local disk file system only. Also, the Apple® Macin-tosh® file system and the Amiga File System are occasionally referred to as AFS. Don't confuse these file systems with Transarc's distributed file system.

that the AFS sites typically have clients numbering an order of magnitude or two more. And, though AFS started off in academia, now over half of the sites are commercial organizations. More significantly, because AFS sites can securely connect their file systems, the global, Internet-based AFS shared file system has the greatest number of clients and servers, the largest amount of data, and the broadest geographic range of any on-line distributed file system. In fact, the T-shirts at the AFS user group symposiums declare the revolutionary phrase: "One world, One filesystem."

As for the stability of the firm, in 1994, Transarc was purchased by IBM. There appears to be no pressure from IBM to force Transarc to change its support model or favor one system vendor over another. Ports and enhancements are still scheduled according to the needs of the AFS market; IBM profits when Transarc makes money and not by forcing support for any particular piece of hardware. In general, this means that Sun and IBM servers and Sun desktops dominate the support schedule.

In the early 90s, Transarc—at that time still an independent company—collaborated with IBM, DEC, HP, and Bull in the solicitation by the Open Software Foundation for a new set of standard components of a distributed computing environment: a remote procedure call system from Apollo™ (now owned by HP), a domain name server and X.500 directory service from DEC, a distributed time service, and a major revision of AFS by Transarc.

These pieces of products were put together by the OSF and packaged as DCE and DFS. While AFS is a proprietary protocol maintained by a single company (though with extensive support through its collaboration with academic research institutions), DCE and DFS are maintained by a multivendor consortium. The long-term prospects for DCE/DFS are therefore potentially greater than AFS, but the larger installed base of AFS cells (as of 1997), its simpler administrative model, and lower initial costs make it an attractive alternative. Some of the similarities and differences between AFS and DFS are described in Chapter 12.

However, before trying to guess who will win the file system shakeout, note that there is no reason for any organization to support only a single protocol. In fact, for most, supporting only one protocol is impossible because of certain software packages which, for one reason or another, are wedded to some semantic behavior of a particular protocol. But, just as Fortran, COBOL, and C source code produce executables that can all run side-by-side on the same desktop, so too can multiple file systems be supported. Use of AFS at an organization does not imply a big-bang event, where one day file data comes from one set of disks and the next day it all comes from AFS servers. Distributed file systems can be complementary, especially during a migration phase, where different classes of data—home directories, development areas, and production binaries—can be moved to the most appropriate location.

Certainly, NFS and NetWare are still being used at most sites that are using AFS. And other protocols will be used for other kinds of data; SQL for databases, HTTP for the Web, etc. As an organization employs these differing protocols, users and developers will vote with their data to find the best fit between their requirements and the underlying functionality. Chapter 11 includes some case studies that describe large and small sites which have found AFS to be indispensable and cost effective.

DRAWBACKS

If all this sounds too good to be true, rest assured that there are several issues you should carefully examine before moving wholeheartedly into AFS. Most obviously, this is a proprietary technology. Only Transarc Corporation produces fully supported ports to vendor hardware. Table 1-2 lists the ports currently available; this set of machines probably accounts for well over 90 percent of the installed base of UNIX workstations. Transarc has done a fair job of keeping up with new releases of these operating systems, but their porting schedule depends on satisfying their current customers first

You might note in this list that the internal Transarc system name does not always coincide with the operating system release number, as with Sun's operating system 4.1.3, which is supported by AFS version sun4m_412. The reason is simply that Transarc doesn't always have to recompile their binaries to support a new operating system release. Check with Transarc if your system is not listed; some earlier versions are available. Naturally, they'll port it to anything for the right price.

On the other hand, one reason for the continued improvements to the system is that Transarc makes the source available for a very reasonable price. Many sites, educational institutions especially, have been able to go over the code and find exactly where problems occur with new operating system releases or other resource contentions. And ports to unsupported systems, such as NetBSD or Linux on Intel™-based hardware, have been produced by other individuals and made available from Transarc's Web site. (In this respect, the AFS community feels much more like an open standard consortium than, say,

Table 1-2 Supported Hardware/OS Ports of AFS

Vendor	Operating System, Hardware Type	AFS System Name
Digital Equipment Corporation		
	Ultrix 4.3, DECstation 2100, 3100, or 5000 (single processor)	pmax_ul43 (3.4)
	Ultrix 4.3a or 4.4, DECstation 2100, 3100, or 5000 (single processor)	pmax_ul43a (3.4)
	Digital Unix 3.0, Alpha AXP	alpha_osf30 (3.4)
	Digital Unix 2.0, Alpha AXP	alpha_osf20 (3.4)
	Digital UNIX 3.2-3.2a, Alpha AXP	alpha_osf32
	Digital UNIX 3.2c-3.2d, Alpha AXP (**)	alpha_osf32c
	Digital UNIX 4.0-4.0b, Alpha AXP	alpha-dux40
Hewlett-Packard		
	HP-UX 9.0, 9.0.1, 9.0.3, 9000 Series 700 (**)	hp700_ux90
	HP-UX 9.0. 9.0.2, 9.0.4, 9000 Series 800 (**)	hp800_ux90
	HP-UX 10.01, 9000 Series 700 (**)	hp700_ux100
	HP-UX 10.01, 9000 Series 800 (**)	hp800_ux100
	HP-UX 10.10, 9000 Series 700 (**)	hp700_ux101
	HP-UX 10.10, 9000 Series 800 (**)	hp800_ux101
	HP-UX 10.20, 9000 Series 700 and 800 (**)	hp800_ux102
IBM		
	AIX 3.2, 3.2.1-3.2.5, RS/6000	rs_aix32
	AIX 4.1.1, 4.1.3-5, RS/6000 (**)	rs_aix41
	AIX 4.2, 4.2.1 RS/6000 (**)	rs_aix42
NCR		
	NCR UNIX 2.0.2 and 3.0	ncrx86_30
Silicon Graphics		
	IRIX 5.2	sgi_52 (3.4)
	IRIX 5.3	sgi_53

Table 1-2 Supported Hardware/OS Ports of AFS *(continued)*

Vendor	Operating System, Hardware Type	AFS System Name
Silicon Graphics *(continued)*		
	IRIX 6.1 (**)	sgi_61
	IRIX 6.2 (**)	sgi_62
	IRIX 6.3 (**)	sgi_63
	IRIX 6.4 (**)	sgi_64
Sun Microsystems		
	SunOS 4.1.1-4.1.3, Sun 4 (non-SPARCstations)	sun4_411 (3.4)
	SunOS 4.1.1-4.1.3, Sun4c kernel	sun4c_411
	SunOS 4.1.2, 4.1.3, 4.1.3_U1, Sun4m kernel (**)	sun4m_412
	SunOS 5.3, Sun 4 (non-SPARCstations)	sun4_53 (3.4)
	SunOS 5.3, Sun4c kernel (**)	sun4c_53
	SunOS 5.3, Sun4m kernel (**)	sun4m_53
	SunOS 5.4, Sun 4 (non-SPARCstations)	sun4_54 (3.4)
	SunOS 5.4, Sun4c kernel (**)	sun4c_54
	SunOS 5.4, Sun4m kernel (**)	sun4m_54
	SunOS 5.5-5.5.1, all kernels (**)	sun4x_55
	SunOS 5.6, all kernels (**)	sun4x_56
Microsoft Windows		
	NT 3.51, 4.0, x86 only	i86_nt

** including multiprocessors
(3.4) AFS 3.4 only; no new releases planned

DFS.) And for systems that are still unsupported, it is possible for a client to use NFS, NetWare, or other protocols to access a gateway machine that is a client of AFS, thereby providing access to the AFS file namespace.

Another issue is the fundamental architecture: CMU wanted to provide centralized file services for a large, distributed campus, and AFS is the result. If your organization cannot provide management support for centralized file services or if your particular division is extremely small, then AFS just won't work too well. For a department with a half-dozen workstations and a single file server, AFS is probably overkill. Of course, as the department inevitably grows, AFS becomes more attractive. And some day, someone will point out that all of the individual departments are reinventing the same administrative wheel as maps and disks and software and users are installed and maintained on dozens of independently managed servers. If an organization is structured around small-scale, decentralized servers, AFS in and of itself won't reduce the hardware and administrative overhead.

Indeed, effective use of AFS requires a lot of reengineering not simply of technology but of the enterprise. While the system comprises distributed components and takes advantage of the price, performance, and functionality of modern computing, it seeks to recentralize and coordinate file storage. For example, the system encourages a small number of AFS administrative domains, potentially just one. In this domain, there is a single repository of security information. Rather than have multiple, independently managed servers each with their own set of users, this single domain will have just a single set of users—all the members of an enterprise, each uniquely identified. Implementing this is mostly a political question.

For organizations that wish to use AFS to provide good centralized file services, the biggest risk is the education of the operations staff. It will do no good to centralize file services if only one or two people know how the system works. Nowadays, it is customary to hire administrators who are already fully versed in NFS or NetWare. To get the best results from AFS requires systematic training, probably from Transarc, for all of your staff. And the education doesn't stop there, for users will have to have a smattering of AFS knowledge, such as the issues described in Chapter 6—access controls, authentication, group management, and those few commands (such as disk space usage) that don't work as expected in the AFS file namespace.

The most contentious aspect of AFS has to do with its imperfect mapping of local file behaviors, expected by certain applications, to its distributed system interfaces. Naturally, as applications have been developed over the years, many of them have been optimized for the characteristics of the local operating and disk system. For these few applications, either local or other distributed file systems may have to be supported for some time.

Certainly, some application data files should be stored in specialized file systems; as one good example, high-powered databases will still need their own raw disk surfaces and server hardware with which to implement their own distribution and replication architecture. For another example, certain UNIX files, such as block or character device files and named pipes, don't have established semantics in a distributed world and are unsupported in AFS; these too, remain wedded to their local machine.

And it is not difficult to find home-built or third-party applications that depend on looser, UNIX-style authentication models that simply do not translate well into a strictly authenticated Kerberos system. Many jobs in a UNIX environment are started up by `cron` or `rsh` and need to write file data. If those files are to be managed by AFS, their access will be controlled by Kerberos-authenticated identities, identities which standard UNIX tools have trouble obtaining or sometimes forget. Lack of support for these applications is rarely a show-stopper, but it is often an important issue; many power users are especially bothered by this problem as they've come to accept the weak distributed security model of both UNIX and PC systems. With the strong, mutual authentication guarantees of Kerberos, old mechanisms based on untrustworthy desktops are no longer valid.

Though Transarc is in the file storage business, their backup and archiving system is a little rudimentary though comprehensive. It certainly does the job of reliably saving and restoring file data and internal AFS meta-data when and as needed. But it is certainly not as flexible or graphically enticing as most of the third-party backup systems available. By now, several companies have begun to integrate AFS support with their archive products—to back up both the file data and the AFS volume structures. Besides these, several other techniques have been developed by the AFS community to use Transarc's tools or home-grown hacks to provide additional functionality; Chapter 7 discusses some of these.

Because AFS is complex and its installation needs to be optimized for each enterprise, much like any other database system, Transarc does not supply a free demo of AFS downloadable from the Net. It may sound as though Transarc would miss sales opportunities, but given the complexity of the system, it's all too easy for a customer to miss the point and reject AFS out of hand. (Of course, this book should help to some extent to describe what it is that AFS can do for an organization and will certainly provide tips on how to use the system effectively.) But so far, Transarc wants to be in the loop on the sales call to provide a human point-of-contact and to guide potential customers to success.

All of these issues are significant and should be examined when you investigate AFS and Transarc. But studies have shown and extensive use of the system has demonstrated that AFS is a powerful, successful product that can provide demonstrably better distributed file system performance and efficiencies to many organizations.

To those who believe that AFS is too expensive in a world where disk drives become cheaper every month: Understand that other distributed file systems bundled with machines may be free, but the on-going administration costs quickly outstrip any imagined advantages. The costs of file storage are not simply the dollars spent on hardware but on the investments needed to control the ever increasing amount of data needed by programs, data, and developers. Disks are cheap, but the data stored on them is of paramount importance to most organizations and therefore justifies the use of appropriate technologies to keep the system usable. Certainly the risks of data loss and unavailability are far more important than choosing protocols based solely on purchase price.

OTHER SOURCES OF INFORMATION

The best source of the information on AFS is Transarc itself:

Transarc Corporation
The Gulf Tower
707 Grant Street
Pittsburgh, PA 15219 USA
phone: 412-338-4400
fax: 412-338-4404
e-mail: information@transarc.com or afs-sales@transarc.com
Web: http://www.transarc.com/

A complete set of hardcopy documentation is shipped with a product purchase. The latest release of the system, version 3.4a, comes with the following manuals:

- *AFS System Administration Guide*—Detailed chapters covering the architecture, behavior, common practices, and use of all of the AFS commands. Not quite exhaustive; some information is to be found only in the *Reference Guide*.
- *AFS Command Reference Guide*—An alphabetical listing of each command and every option.

- *AFS Installation Guide*—How to get AFS up and running at your site. Somewhat confusing for the first-time AFS administrator; contains platform-specific sections in between architecture-independent sections.
- *AFS User's Guide*—Information on AFS needed to help user's navigate the enhanced features of the file system.
- *Release Notes*—Not only lists the latest fixes and workarounds but also describes new functionality not included in the main documentation.

Transarc is converting all of their documentation to the Web HTML standard, shipping on-line copies with their product and even permitting viewing of the available text from their Web site. The AFS manual set should be done, as we say, real soon now.

Source code for the entire system is available at a reasonable price. This is not quite the luxury it seems: When you need to write custom management tools that interface with the AFS kernel modules or client/server RPCs, using the source is the best way to quickly complete the job. While the documentation tries to describe the interfaces, the examples are difficult to follow—it is wiser and almost essential to cut'n'paste code from Transarc's own utilities to quickly produce your own specialized programs.

While the source code is not free, Transarc has permitted certain client binaries created from it to be distributed. Over the years, enterprising individuals have ported the AFS client code to some of the other UNIX ports now available. Currently, you can find client executables for the Linux and NetBSD UNIX variants available for free to any AFS site; though Transarc appears to encourage client proliferation, they'll still want to charge you for their AFS servers.

There is quite of bit of free code and other documentation in Transarc's public area of their FTP site: `ftp://ftp.transarc.com/pub`.

Here, a variety of subdirectories with information, source code, and scripts help you to understand and administer AFS. Some programs are almost essential to investigating odd client behavior; others have been devised and contributed by other AFS sites and administrators.

Transarc also publishes a technical journal that it mails to each site. Besides highlighting upcoming product features, it usually contains a description of a customer's AFS cell configuration. Such examples are useful in confirming certain cell designs you may have questions about.

Questions and comments regarding AFS can be directed to a public mailing list for general discussion of problems and solutions. When sent to `info-afs@transarc.com`, the message goes to all subscribers. Currently, the list processes just one or two mail messages a day and the postings are usually informative. You can subscribe to this mailing list by sending a message to `majordomo@transarc.com` with the sentence `subscribe info-afs` as the body of the message. Getting off the list is similar; just insert "unsubscribe" in the body. Make sure you send the message to `majordomo` and not to the list `info-afs` as a whole.

For several years Transarc hosted an AFS User's Group conference. With the expansion of the Transarc product line to incorporate DCE, DFS, and the Encina™ transaction monitor, the conference focus has been broadened to embrace these DCE technologies as well as AFS. Held once a year, usually in the early spring, this conference brings together some of the DCE and DFS implementors from various vendors, as well as many third-party software publishers and commercial users of the system.

And of course, other information is available on the Internet, including a Frequently Asked Questions document, to which there is a pointer at the Transarc Web site.

SUMMARY

This chapter presented an overview of the benefits of AFS. Actually achieving these benefits depends on a careful implementation plan. Such a plan must not only construct a technological infrastructure that correctly supplies AFS's advantages to the desktop, but also must incorporate the computing culture at any given organization.

Typically, sites that embark on a migration of file services into AFS undergo growing pains as they invent new administration practices and unlearn habits caused by the vagaries of their previous infrastructure. Once the migration is in full swing, a critical point is quickly reached where the benefits of the new system are self-evident. For users, the change amounts to learning to navigate a slightly different file-naming convention; for administrators, ease of use and maintainability of AFS makes them wonder why they took so long to make the move in the first place.

As the details of AFS are described, we will often compare AFS to NFS or NetWare. The point is not to start a war of words over which is better but simply to discuss the different implementations and how those designs reflect the initial goals of the products. There's no denying that NFS is the best NFS around. And as far as it goes, it is functional and extremely useful. But it is not the only distributed file system available.

The next chapter provides a detailed look at the technology and protocol that make up AFS clients and servers. After that, the following chapters return to a somewhat more general view of administration practices and use of the system.

AFS Technology

T he ultimate goal of AFS is to present a coherent view of a file namespace. The simplest way to imagine this view is as a cloud of information to which desktop clients can read and write data. Such a view, as in Figure 2-1, is the vision of many distributed systems, but AFS manages to achieve this goal with a high level of fidelity. As the figure suggests, users can easily navigate through a set of files and directories without regard to the actual locations of the data. Through caching, accesses will generally be quite speedy but will never return outdated data to the user. And with well-administered replication, important pieces of the production system (such as the topmost directory levels) will be resilient to failures.

After a short period of use, most users will find that they expect file access to work this way—all file data should be available to them no matter where the users are located in the enterprise. Indeed, the phrase, "No matter where you go, there you are" has been adopted as the unofficial AFS slogan. This truism holds because users do not see any storage locations: the file namespace is not composed of server names, addresses, or protocol identifiers, nor is any extra syntax needed for file use in AFS. Everything looks like a normal set of directories and files, or folders and documents, or however your desktop usually depicts file data.

This image doesn't come about by magic, of course. Many processes and systems are engineered to work together to promote this view. Luckily, each piece is relatively simple to understand; it's the relationship between the pieces that can be hard to grasp.

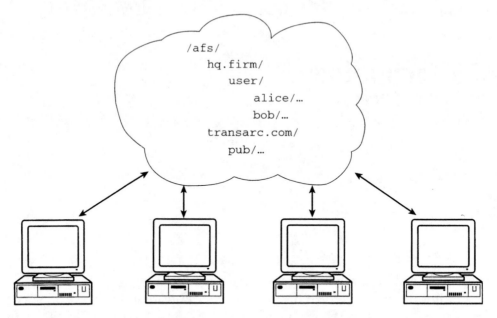

```
/afs/
    hq.firm/
        user/
            alice/...
            bob/...
    transarc.com/
        pub/...
```

Figure 2-1   A User's View of AFS

The first step is to recall some of the design principles of AFS, especially the goal of supporting thousands of clients. The best mechanism to help a small number of servers handle that kind of scale is to off-load as much work as possible onto the client: let the client cache as much file data as possible and help flush out-of-date content. For this shift in responsibilities to work, AFS clients and servers must be carefully configured.

In this chapter, we briefly run through the configuration files, processes, servers, and network traffic which compose the AFS system. This technology walkthrough should serve to demystify AFS and illuminate some of the internals of the system.

CLIENT CONFIGURATION

The first step to connecting a desktop to AFS is to get the code that implements the client side into the operating system where it belongs. For some UNIX systems, Transarc supplies a module (really just an object file) that must be statically linked into the operating system kernel. For other systems, the object file can be dynamically loaded into the kernel either with a vendor-supplied tool such as Sun's `modload` or, if no tool is available, Transarc's own `dkload`.

Besides this kernel module, a sufficient cache area must be available. These days, with new machines delivered with 1- or 2-gigabyte internal disks, there should be no excuse for small cache sizes, but it is possible to run AFS with only 10 megabytes of cache on disk or even in memory. Various studies have shown that upwards of 70 megabytes of memory are needed to make the system effective, though now, it is common to have 200 megabytes or more of cache.

The physical location of the cache on disk and in the local file system namespace is immaterial. One of the few configuration files used by the startup process, /usr/vice/etc/cacheinfo, defines the name of the cache directory. To ensure that the kernel cache manager always has control of the cache area, create a separate disk partition for the cache.

As you'll see, there are a few artifacts of previous versions from the CMU days still in AFS. One of these is the vice directory name, which refers to the earliest release of the system. What's important to note is that when we mention files in /usr/vice/, we are invariably discussing the client portion of AFS.

Another key configuration file is /usr/vice/etc/CellServDB, commonly called the CellServDB file. This file lists, in a fairly strict format, the important servers that manage file location mappings and other information. A *cell* is the AFS term for this collection of cooperating server systems. It is the domain of administrative control of the system. As staff administer AFS, most commands are not sent to a specific server; they are simply relayed automatically to one of the main servers listed for the cell, and the changes are seamlessly propagated to the other servers to preserve the illusion of a single distributed system.

Actually, the need for the CellServDB file is the oddest aspect of AFS. In the middle of a rigorously distributed system, surrounded by servers that are constantly working to provide location independence and a single virtual namespace, we're faced with this static file that must be administered and installed on every client desktop. And even worse, the lines listing each server contain the raw IP addresses of the servers.

The reason for this anomaly is historical: at the time of AFS's design no good directory services were available, no well-established mechanisms for storing and looking up the information needed by AFS clients. Some source code licensees have modified their AFS system to use the Domain Name System for this lookup, but Transarc has yet to incorporate those changes into their product. The good news is that not all servers in an organization need to be listed in the file, only those servers keeping file location and authentication information. As such, the file data changes very infrequently.

The last configuration file is /usr/vice/etc/ThisCell, which contains just the single name of the local, default cell.

Finally, the directory upon which the AFS system will be mounted, /afs, must be created before the client daemons start up.

When you have prepared these three configuration files and one directory, set aside a cache area, and integrated the supplied module into the client's kernel, you can now run the daemon process afsd, which executes some new system calls to start up the kernel's management of AFS. This daemon delivers the relevant data from the configuration files to the operating system. In regular usage, the module loading and daemon startup occur during the early phases of client booting. Once afsd returns, leaving behind a few daemon subprocesses, /afs is accessible.

READING DATA

When a user process first attempts to read the /afs directory, the client kernel recognizes that the data is managed by AFS and uses the just-loaded kernel module algorithms to get at the files. In this scenario, since the data has not been previously cached, the client contacts one of the listed servers in CellServDB and requests information on the location of the file server for the root AFS directory. That location is cached, a given file server is accessed, the data returned, and the contents of the directory are also cached. If the user process that accessed /afs was a directory listing program, the contents are returned and listed on the screen. Figure 2-2 shows graphically how files are fetched when they are not already in the client cache.

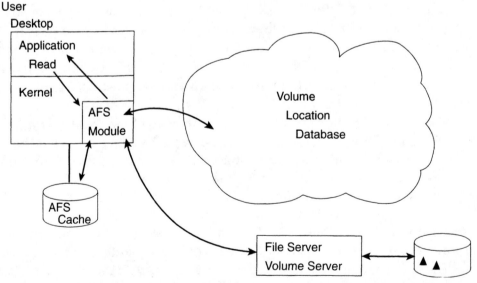

Figure 2-2   How Clients Read Data: First Access

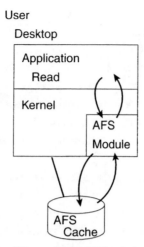

Figure 2-3   How Clients Read Data: Subsequent Accesses

Now that this client has cached the location information and entries for the top-level directory, any other process subsequently accessing /afs can use the cached data. Neither the servers nor the networks will be bothered by redundant requests for this now-cached data. And because the cache is stored on disk, it will remain valid across client reboots. See Figure 2-3.

The process of finding and caching data is the same for directories or folders as for files. In the earliest versions of AFS, a client would read in the entire contents of a file at once. Now, a client reads file data from the server in chunks of 64 kilobytes. As an application needs to access successive bytes of a file, the client's operating system makes requests of the server to return 64-kilobyte chunks of the file; as each chunk is received, the kernel stores the chunks on disk and passes the data to the application. (The chunk size is variable and can be increased to take advantage of faster networks.)

As with other true distributed file systems, neither applications nor users are aware that the file accesses need to traverse a network and be resolved by a remote machine. Application programs—editors, mail readers, data filters, or games—all simply use the native operating system's file read and write system calls. The system itself is configured to perform any work necessary to get the data to or from the application by way of any distributed protocol.

The hard part of distributed file systems comes when applications on multiple clients have previously read data that another client has just changed. It is here that AFS distinguishes itself. Once a client has requested file data, the file server remembers that that client has cached data about that file. The server further promises the client that if the file is changed by any other user or process, the server will contact the client, notifying it that newer data is available.

In AFS, the term *callback* means both the promise made by the server to a single client that it will contact it when the file is written to by another client, as well as the protocol request itself. Clients know that whenever a file is read, and therefore cached locally, a callback promise has been automatically registered by the server of that file. Therefore, the client kernel can confidently return the cached data to any other process up to the moment when it actually receives the callback notification. Before that moment, if the server hasn't called back with a message invalidating the file data, the client knows the data hasn't changed on the server.

As other clients read the file, the server keeps track of each of them as well. When any client writes data into the file, the data is sent to the server and the server sends a message to all clients in its callback list to tell them that subsequent users of that file data must refetch the data from the server. Figure 2-4 shows that after a new version of a file has been written back to the server by the desktop machine client-one, the server has sent a callback message to all clients, such as client-two, that had previously cached a now-outdated version of a file.

A client that receives the callback message needs only to note that the cached data is now invalid; the new file data is not transferred until needed. When a user on client-two requests that file data the next time, the fetch operation proceeds much as in Figure 2-2. The only difference is that, while the file data has been invalidated in the cache, the file's location information is still valid. Hence, the subsequent fetches will occur slightly faster than the initial fetch because no location queries will need to be processed.

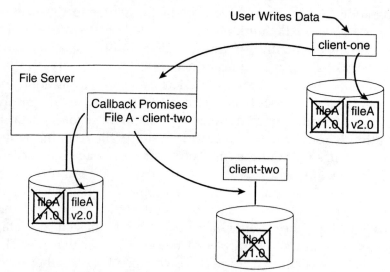

Figure 2-4   Server Callback and Client Cache Invalidation

The effect of this protocol is the seamless retrieval of the most up-to-date data for every file or directory access. Most of the time, that retrieval will come from the local disk cache and as such, the response will be almost as quick as if the data was stored locally through some manual mechanism. If either the data isn't cached or the client was explicitly informed that its version of the data is out of date, then the more recent version will be retrieved from the server.

So far, we haven't talked about security. The traditional local authentication model of UNIX does not work for distributed clients unless all clients trust each other. For a wide-ranging enterprise, whether it is two separate offices, a campus, or global company, this model is far too trusting. AFS uses the Kerberos authentication protocol, whereby all identities must be validated by a known, trustworthy security server; cryptographically secured credentials can then be exchanged so that users' identities can be associated with all file requests. In addition, desktops are assured that they are contacting the real AFS servers at an organization.

Most importantly, AFS does not trust a user's regular UNIX identity, not even the superuser root. Anyone able to compromise a desktop in an AFS-based organization will not get universal access to AFS data. In addition, only administrators who can prove their identity to the trusted Kerberos servers are permitted to run various operational commands. Because of the sensitivity of the secrets stored by the Kerberos servers, access to them must be strictly controlled.

WRITING DATA

The process of writing data from a client to the server is one place where the AFS designers introduced an optimization that slightly changes traditional UNIX write semantics. Normally, for processes on the same machine, the last process to write some data to an area of a file wins; that is, a process reading data from a particular area of a file will be given the last data written there, no matter which process wrote it. A UNIX kernel supports this behavior even though, behind the scenes, it is keeping some data in a small memory buffer waiting for an opportunity to write it to disk.

CMU desired to make file sharing possible, but, given the rarity of simultaneous read and write sharing of files, they decided to relax the "last writer wins" semantic for distributed processes, such as any two users running applications and reading and writing the same file at exactly the same time. Instead, for distributed processes using AFS, the last process to save or close the file wins. This means that as one application on one machine is writing data to a file, it is being stored on that machine's local disk only. A second client requesting and reading the file will not see any intermediate writes of data by the first client. When the writer is done with the file and issues the close system call, all the file data is finally sent to the server system at which point a callback message is sent to signal that a whole new version of the file is available.

This optimization allows servers to concentrate on storing whole, consistent versions of files. Rather than keeping track of all writes to any ranges of bytes in the file and sending messages about ranges that have changed, servers limit their involvement to telling clients when completely new versions of the file are available. Clients, therefore, aren't told of every change to a file as it is made by some other client but are informed only when the entire file has been modified.

The reason this behavior works in practice is simply because almost no UNIX tools or applications depend on multiple access to open files being written by multiple processes. It is a compromise that happens to work. Like the lack of any consistency guarantees in the NFS protocol, which works only because clients occasionally and on their own initiative check the server for new versions, the AFS architecture was an experiment. In practice, both systems work well in day-to-day environments.

Most importantly, the good news is that for processes on the same workstation, the UNIX behavior of "last writer wins" is preserved: as a process writes data to a file, another process on the same client reading that file will see each range of bytes as soon as it is written. So, in the very few cases where it is important to see this behavior, locate the writers and readers on the same system.

Where this causes a problem is in poorly written UNIX software that does not check for errors from the operating system when executing the close system call. Because AFS is a distributed system, it is possible (though rare in practice) to have some problem occur while the written data is being sent to the server. Perhaps the network failed or the server hardware failed; whatever the problem is, the client kernel signals the failure with an error code returned by close. If checked, the application can issue the close until successful or take some other action to save the data.

These changes to UNIX single-site semantics were not made arbitrarily; they were made because the potential for improving the performance and efficiency of the system outweighed the rareness of distributed processes sharing write access to files. Over the years, it's been clear that the overwhelming majority of users and UNIX software run oblivious to the change. And for very large files that need different performance characteristics, an option is available to side-step this delayed write.

Some more optimizations to this protocol are discussed in Chapter 5 on client administration. Though these optimizations are introduced to improve performance even further, they do not change the protocol model.

As far as directory updates go, the only mechanism for modifying entries in a directory is the atomic system calls to create or delete a file or subdirectory. These requests are therefore sent directly to the AFS file servers. However, just like file data, clients that have cached AFS directory data are given callback promises by the relevant file server. As directories are updated, the changes are immediately available to any and all interested clients.

SERVER CONFIGURATION

Clients are fairly robust systems that, in practice, require little administration. AFS servers take a bit more work to set up because servers must process several tasks—location information queries, file data requests, authentication activity, group management, and more. The fact that so many kinds of data are managed by the system makes AFS administration somewhat challenging. As far as clients are concerned, the AFS data and metadata simply come from the integrated set of servers.

For administrators, the previous depiction of a file system "cloud" with no location dependencies now gives way to a physical set of servers and disks. The behind-the-scenes view, as in Figure 2-5, seems to show a perfectly ordinary set of hardware. At the lowest levels of AFS administration, there's little to do but employ the usual amount of labor to install and keep running the servers that provide the file data and that keep track of the location information.

Just like an AFS client, a file server must have a module loaded into its kernel. As supplied by Transarc, the client and server modules are actually the same file. The location of the module on the server is conventionally the /usr/afs directory tree (as opposed to /usr/vice, where client-side information is stored).

Next, a file server will naturally have several disks dedicated to AFS service. Unlike NFS, AFS servers always manage whole disk partitions, that is, they do not export arbitrary parts of their local file namespace. Furthermore, each of the AFS server's partitions must be mounted at well-known names in the server's root directory: /vicepXX, where XX is any one or two letters of the

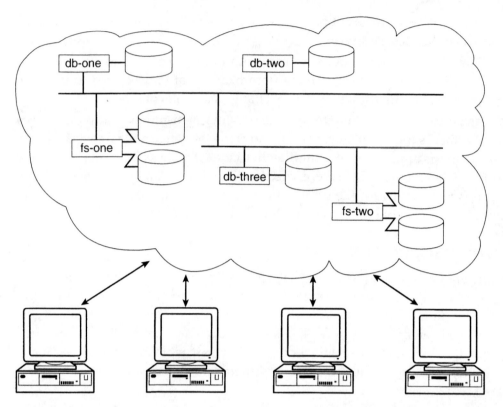

Figure 2-5   Administrator's Physical View of AFS

alphabet from /vicepa to /vicepz and /vicepaa to /vicepiv, for a total of 256 possible partitions, commonly called the vice partitions. As the AFS file service process starts, it scans the server's table of mounted physical disks and assumes control of these vice partitions.

It so happens that an AFS server uses the vendor's native file system format inside the vice partitions, so the basic disk set up process for a server is unchanged. Each vice partition should have a standard UNIX file system created on it. This will install several blocks of information into the low levels of the disk indexing system. Some operating systems use the newfs or mkfs utility to do this installation, but it is possible to have these partitions serviced with software-based striped or mirrored file systems or even to use RAID disks.

However, inside a vice partition, there is little evidence that AFS is storing files, directories, and access control lists. Recall that one design point of AFS is that there is one, single, ubiquitous namespace. The important consequence of this design is that once the AFS servers take control of the vice partitions, the only way to access file data is through the /afs directory. If you're working on an AFS file server, there is no built-in mechanism to read files and directories in the AFS namespace by examining the vice partitions. Happily, the kernel module loaded on servers can also be used to start up the client-side daemons that provide access to the canonical namespace.

Most day-to-day administration tasks are not concerned with each and every file in the server. Instead, a collection of files and directories are logically contained in an AFS volume.

Today, it seems as if every vendor uses the word "volume" and every use means something different. In particular, Sun's Solaris system uses "volume" to mean removable media; in IBM's AIX system, "volume" means a logical section of disk space; and in NetWare, it means a physical section of the server's disk that can be mapped onto a PC client's drives. In this book, we will refer only to AFS volumes: a container of files and directories. In a sense, it is a logical disk partition; volumes can be created and connected to the AFS namespace much like a disk can be partitioned and mounted at a directory name. As a volume is accessed by a client, the client sees the files and directories that have been placed there just as a workstation accessing different disk partitions sees only its file and directories. Volumes are the unit of administrative control for the file system.

The server's vice partitions are the physical storage location for volumes. Typically, a partition will store many volumes; an individual volume can be as small as desired or as large as a partition. (The size limits of disk partitions are dependent upon the vendor's operating system software.) Conventionally, volumes are kept to under a couple of hundred megabytes in size just for convenience. Because AFS administration consists to a large degree in manipulating sets of volumes, it is nice to have large volumes to reduce their numbers, but once the volumes grow too large, it is difficult to move them around, find temporary places to put them, or store them on archive media in one shot.

Inside a volume you can store any number of files and directories. In normal use, a single volume contains a subtree of related files: a user's home directory, the source to a programming project, a set of binaries for a particular hardware platform, some Web HTML files, etc. When created, each volume is given a short name by an administrator. For no really good reason, the names can effectively be only 22 characters long.

After its creation, a volume will be connected to the AFS namespace. Any volume from any partition on any server can be connected to any directory name under /afs. Because these connections imply modifications to the namespace, clients will always see the most up-to-date set of connection directories just as they always see the latest file data. And in fact, the connections appear exactly like regular directories.

The action of making the connection is actually called an AFS mount, but in UNIX this word has heavyweight connotations of a process that must be carried out on all clients, as NFS mounts or Novell® mappings are done. A key concept for understanding how AFS clients and server work is this: Clients don't mount volumes—they access files in AFS by finding out where volumes are stored and then getting data from that volume's server. As a result, there is just a single, ubiquitous file namespace supported by AFS.

The administration view can now be better described as a virtual world of volumes and the location database which tells where each volume is physically stored. Figure 2-6 suggests how administrators deal with AFS; once the hardware has been configured and is smoothly running, day-to-day administration involves creating and manipulating the volume containers. With the AFS toolset, such manipulation is easy, permitting the administrator to create and move home directory volumes or to replicate collections of system binaries as needed.

We can now more fully explain the original example of reading the /afs directory. It so happens that this topmost directory is a connection to a well-known volume named root.afs. The first time a client traverses this directory a query will be sent to find out which particular server is storing that volume's data. Once discovered, the location information is, of course, cached, and then a request is sent to the specified file server to retrieve the directory's contents.

Once the location of the root.afs volume and then the contents of the /afs directory have been downloaded from the proper servers, this information is cached on the client's local disk. Future accesses to this same information will follow a similar local path, but because the data is available in the cache, the client will immediately respond to the application's request. When using cached data, the client will not need to use any network or server resources at all. When someone changes the contents of the /afs directory, the client will be notified that its cache is now invalid.

As more files and directories are traversed, a client will continue to retrieve the data from the current volume's file server. Just as on a UNIX desktop, where path name elements are resolved in the context of the current disk partition (or the current drive letter on PCs), AFS files are retrieved from the current volume.

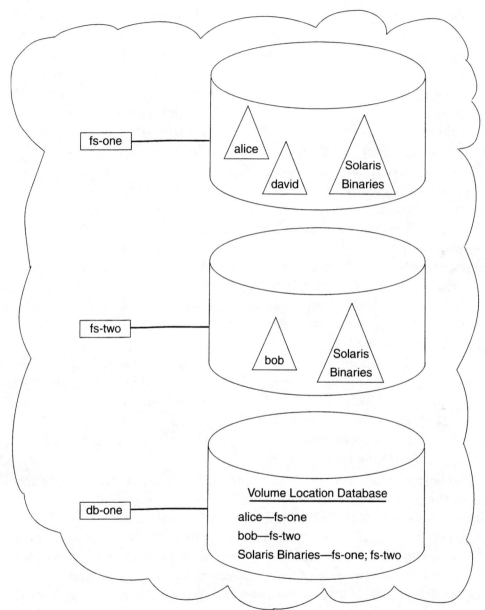

Figure 2-6 Administrator's View of Volumes and Location Database

Eventually, a client will discover that some directory leads to a different volume. Again, the behavior is akin to how a normal UNIX workstation traverses local files and partitions. As a process traverses the directory structure, the kernel assumes that file data is stored in the same partition as the parent directory. At some point, a process will traverse a new volume connection: this traversal causes a quick lookup of the new volume's location with subsequent file accesses being directed to the appropriate server and partition.

The key concept is that all workstations are forced to see the same file namespace because the connections between all volumes are stored in the namespace itself. A corollary is that any volume not connected to some path name cannot have its file data read by a client because there is no path that would cause the client to seek out the volume's location.

Most other network file systems rely on a map of names and locations which must be loaded into a running system. Even when this operation is automated, it is still performed on a client-by-client basis and depends on consistent maps being delivered in a timely fashion to each desktop. In AFS, half of the map—the published volume name—is stored along with the file data in the namespace itself. The other half of the map—the specific location of the volume's data—is available from reliable and replicated database servers. Just as with file data, if the location information ever changes, clients that have cached the data will check it so that upon the next reference, the new location information will be retrieved.

For another example, let's assume that a new user has joined our organization. We'll first create a new volume for the user on a specific server and partition and name the volume user.joe, a typical style of naming for user volumes. This creation step makes the physical space available on the server, and initializes the location information in the databases but does not make the volume available in the file namespace.

The next step is to connect that volume to some directory. The only argument to this connection command is the volume name, user.joe, and the directory name, say, /afs/home/joe. Once the connection is made, all clients immediately see the new directory name /afs/home/joe. If they had previously cached the /afs/home directory listing, they would now have received a callback from the server saying that the directory had changed. When asked to list the directory again, they would have to request the new data from the server, which would respond with the new contents, which now include the directory joe.

As any client traverses into the /afs/home/joe directory, the client senses that it has crossed into a new volume. It therefore contacts the AFS database server to find the location of the volume data and then contacts whichever server holds the contents of the volume to get at Joe's home directory. This process works exactly the same for all clients in the organization—in fact, for all AFS clients on the Internet. Every client traverses the shared namespace by finding volumes in a cell and reading data from the designated servers.

To implement this protocol, AFS gives each file in the cell a file identification number (FID). A FID is an identifier consisting of a volume number, a file number, and a *uniquifier* or version number. In AFS, the FID performs a function similar to a UNIX file's inode number, helping the system to get to the file. When examining a directory and discovering a file's FID, a client will extract the volume number and query the AFS databases to discover the location of that volume if it is not already known. Once the volume is located, the client will request the uniquely identified file from the indicated server.

By this method, AFS maintains the illusion of a single namespace. Clients access the correct file servers by using the namespace and querying the AFS databases automatically. In NFS terms, it's as if the automount maps were somehow hidden inside the directory names. AFS administration consists first of behind-the-scenes volume management, and second, modification of the file namespace, of which there is only a single and guaranteed consistent copy.

Access to the AFS files of another enterprise can be had as easily and securely as access to the local files. Conventionally, underneath the /afs root, connections are made to dozens of other sites as needed. A company such as Transarc would add their own cell as a connection to the path /afs/transarc.com. Joe's home directory, mentioned above, would normally be located at /afs/transarc.com/home/joe and once logged in, he could access files in other cells by changing to directories such as /afs/umich.edu or /afs/cern.ch. As the first Internet-ready file service, AFS has been delivering files across the global wide-area network for almost a decade. (In fact, when source code to the AFS system is purchased, the unpackaged files include regular UNIX symbolic links to Transarc's AFS cell in Pittsburgh for easy access to the latest releases of the code.)

VOLUME MANAGEMENT

Now that we've created some volumes and attached them to form the beginnings of an AFS namespace, we can start using some of the powerful management tools of the system.

One method used to control the use of the AFS file system is to put a cap on the amount of data that can be stored in a volume. To help limit a user's natural desire to fill up all available disk space, each volume has a data quota. Administrators can set this quota to any practical size or disable it. Typically, users' personal volumes might be set to a quota of 100 megabytes so that at a certain point, they will be unable to add more than that amount of data to their home directory. In this way, although one user might not be able to download a large GIF picture because her volume quota is full, the other users of that disk partition won't suffer from the shared disk becoming full.

With quotas on volumes, administrators can parcel out their available disk partitions to users and developers and be assured that important areas of their file tree will always have space available.

In normal usage, users will little know or care about the underlying volumes to which their file reads and writes are occurring. But there are some aspects, such as quotas and access controls, which are significantly different from the behavior of users' local file systems, and an organization should introduce users to these issues carefully.

When users have managed to fill up a disk's volumes with file data, an administrator may need to add more disks to the system and move some users' home directories from one disk to another. AFS manages the complete volume move operation with a single, short command. With a simple instruction to the system, the administrator can move a volume from one server or disk to another on-line and transparently to the user. The command takes care of moving the entire set of files, notifying clients that the files have moved and informing the cell of the new location of the volume. No downtime is needed to stop users from accessing the volume as it is moved, all AFS services are running all the time, and, in fact, the user will likely not notice that the files have been moved at all.

By reducing off-hours administration, this operation can likely pay for AFS itself. Assume some new hardware needs to be installed on a file server. Rather than waiting for a weekend, throwing users off the system, and bringing the machine and file access to a halt, staff can instead move all volumes on a system to sibling servers in the days before needed maintenance. By the time the server must be halted, no file data is being stored on the system and there is, therefore, no downtime to file access.

Replication of important volumes of file data is a similarly straightforward operation. Given a volume containing files that should be always available to clients, some stock trading applications, for example, an administrator can inform the cell's central databases that the volume will be copied over to a set of other servers and disks. The administrator defines this collection of replication sites as needed.

Once a directory subtree has been filled with the latest versions of a software package, the underlying, original volume is then released to its read-only replication sites. Releasing causes the AFS servers to copy over all the changed data to each of the replication sites. For files that are new or changed, the entire file is copied; for files to be deleted, only the new directory entry is sent in order to cause the file to be erased. The collection of replicas is therefore guaranteed to consist of exact copies, file for file and byte for byte, of all data in the master, read-write volume. The administrative cycle thus consists of installing and testing a set of files in a given volume and then releasing the changes to the replica sites.

This replication provides highly available access to the file data and automatic load-balancing as clients choose randomly among the available servers. But note that this replication is for read-only data—AFS replication does not support read-write redundancy or mirroring. Administrators must still provide stable storage, such as RAID or disk mirroring, to enhance the availability of read-write data, such as home directories or project source.

Because an AFS client normally gathers information about which server stores which volume as it traverses the cell's namespace, discovering replica sites is easy. If a volume has only a read-write site, its single location is returned; if the volume has been replicated, the client will be given the complete list of replica servers. When data needs to be read from a replicated volume, the client will pick one of the multiple replication sites from which to request file data. Because all sites contain the same data, it won't matter which replication site is chosen. And thus, if there is a machine outage, network partition, or disk disaster that affects data access to one server, the client can serenely skip to the next site on its list and request more file data from one of the other available servers.

SERVER PROCESSES

To make all of this magic work, AFS servers run a number of processes, each of which manages, sometimes alone and sometimes in concert with other processes, pieces of the data that make up the cell.

The first processes that concern us are `fileserver` and `volserver`; these two programs keep track of and deliver file data and volume data in response to specific client requests. They have direct responsibility for the data that is stored in all the `vice` partitions on a server.

The next set of processes to consider are the database services that enable volume location data, group membership information, and authentication secrets to be reliably accessed by clients. By running multiple instances of the these programs on different servers, AFS ensures that all clients will be able to retrieve data from the system in spite of most system outages. The processes, `vlserver` for volume locations, `ptserver` for protection group membership, and `kaserver` for Kerberos authentication data, do not need to be as widely distributed as stock file servers because their data changes less frequently.

These processes maintain their information by using a database protocol called Ubik.[1] This protocol has been heavily optimized to store and disburse the specific data needed to maintain an AFS cell. Because any database process can potentially fail, each particular database periodically elects a master to which all write operations are sent. After the master writes the database to stable storage, the master updates the slave databases with the changes. All of these operations are invisible to users of the AFS file service but must be monitored and supported by administrators.

In practice, most organizations separate their server computers into file servers, which run the `fileserver` and `volserver` processes, and database servers, which run `vlserver`, `ptserver`, and `kaserver`. Thus, administration of one machine (e.g., when adding disks to a file server) affects as few services as possible.

Naturally, keeping track of which machines should run which servers is a small chore for the administrators. Like much of AFS, this very practical concern was solved by engineering. A special program was written which runs on each AFS server machine and maintains a simple table of processes that are to be started. This is the basic overseer server, `bosserver`. Administration of servers consists of properly authenticated individuals running an application, `bos`, which connects to the overseer on a specific server in order to start, stop, create, or delete a certain AFS service. This overseer not only controls the existence of other processes, but it notices if a service crashes and restarts it if necessary. In such a case, it even rotates the log files and moves the core dump (if any) to a safe location for shipment to Transarc.

---

1.   Ubik is named after the science-fiction novel by Philip K. Dick. The novel takes place in a world where corporate psychics are nullified by anti-psi humans, where the dead are placed in cryonic storage yet are still available for consultation, and where the apparently living need periodic rejuvenation from Ubik—a handy aerosol spray available in a variety of ever-changing packages and which, as the name suggests, is ubiquitous in time and space. Use only as directed. Do not exceed recommended dosage.

File backup is handled by another database service, buserver, and an application, backup that uses the configuration information stored in this database to dump and restore data to external media on a per-volume basis. As this activity is done, the backup database keeps track of when each volume was archived, permitting recovery operations to be easily managed.

One concern of the designers was to ensure that all server machines ran the correct versions of all of these server processes and that the common configuration data was consistent among them. So they added a final set of update processes—upserver and upclient—to propagate binaries from assigned master machines for each architecture or to copy configuration files from a central master to all other servers. To install a new version of AFS, you simply install the new binary or configuration files onto a master machine and the system will pull down the new files onto the update clients. At regular intervals, the basic overseer restarts the server processes; at this time any new executables will be started or new configuration data will be read and used.

Finally, consistent time services are needed by clients when they access shared file data; the Kerberos protocols need these services, too. AFS provides an implementation of a distributed time service by which all machines at a site can keep the same standard time. This particular implementation is optional and can be replaced with other public versions of network time services if desired but having consistent time kept by all systems in a cell is critical to correct performance of AFS.

NETWORK PROTOCOL

For all of these network requests and data transfers, AFS clients and servers use a homegrown wire protocol called Rx. Rather than a heavyweight, connection-oriented protocol such as TCP, AFS needs a transport layer that can manage many small RPC requests and answers but that approaches streaming transfer rates for large data movement.

Rx uses the UDP transport layer directly because of its lightweight characteristics. Though UDP is usually thought of as an unreliable protocol, Rx adds a layer of timeouts and packet management of its own to create a robust and reliable system. To decrease the costs of connection set up even further, multiple file accesses by the same user on the same client are multiplexed over a single Rx circuit.

Because the design goal of AFS was to support a distributed campus environment with many LANs connected by slower links into a wide-area network, the Rx protocol has undergone many engineering iterations. (The previous version of CMU's protocol was called, simply, R; the design of Rx is a prescription for some of R's problems.) The current version uses several techniques from other protocols, such as negotiation of maximum transmission unit, exponential backoff of retransmissions, and quick round-trip time estimation, all to ensure that reading and writing of AFS files and database responses would be quick and reliable even under network duress.

As with other protocols, such as TCP, Rx numbers each packet so that lost data can be tracked. Packet sizes start at 1500 bytes and increase when run across media with a larger maximum transmission unit, such as FDDI. Acknowledgments are required after every two packets of the normal Rx window of eight packets. Unlike Sun RPC, only the unacknowledged packets need to be retransmitted. There is a two-second retransmission timeout interval; keep-alives stop a connection from being dropped due to inactivity.

Rx is a complete RPC system available to any developer and includes rxgen, a utility which translates an interface definition file into client and server stub code. These stubs can marshall and unmarshall data as needed; they use the Rx protocol to transmit and receive procedural requests with enforced at-most-once semantics (i.e., a procedure is guaranteed to either finish once or not at all).

In practice, few developers outside of Transarc will use Rx. But each AFS process, such as the file, authentication, or volume location server, uses one or more Rx interfaces as the formal boundary between themselves and any client applications. Since one of the client applications happens to be the desktop operating system, Rx has also been crafted to behave well in either the kernel or user space.

One important feature built in to Rx is its extensible support for security modules. When building a specific server, the programmer can choose which of many authentication systems should validate the connections. For most AFS connections, the Kerberos authentication module is used. All Rx transmissions are, therefore, authenticated. To forestall the potentially high cost of connections and authentication steps, each connection can host multiple channels of data exchange. This optimization permits servers to process thousands of open channels as they support large-scale enterprises.

The maturity of Rx and its success at handling different WAN and LAN conditions are demonstrated when you peruse file systems from AFS sites across the world. Though bandwidth can sometimes be low, connectivity to remote cells is routinely successful. Not only Rx, but the entire architecture of AFS—the cell domain, internal database management, and the caching of all distributed data—contributes to this success.

AFS EXTRAS

AFS desktops are more than capable of accessing multiple file systems, such as when communicating with a site's legacy NFS servers. In addition, an AFS client can re-export the AFS namespace (or a portion thereof) via the NFS protocol to other NFS clients. Thus, any machine for which AFS ports from Transarc are unavailable can still get to AFS files. This intermediary is called a *translator* or *gateway* because it receives NFS client requests and turns them into AFS client requests. As the AFS/NFS gateway accesses the AFS cell, the files read will be cached on the gateway's local disk. Generic downstream NFS clients cannot perform disk caching on their own, but multiple NFS clients accessing the same gateway can reuse files that the gateway has previously cached; this capability helps spread out the server load if the cache hit ratio is high enough.

One imperfection in this process is that the users of the NFS clients must perform extra authentication steps to permit the gateway system to properly access restricted areas of AFS data.

SUMMARY

These then are the programs, configuration files, clients, servers, and databases that constitute AFS. To be sure, the complexity of all of these systems working together is somewhat overwhelming. In reality, administrators need to deal with only a few pieces of the AFS puzzle at any one time.

Clients are mostly self-sufficient and require only a few small, static configuration files. As long as the client remains connected to the network, nothing more is needed to gain access to organization's or the Internet's AFS systems. Because of the caching algorithms installed in the client kernel, reading and writing files from any desktop in the enterprise is efficient and presents a minimum load to the network or servers.

While clients cache data retrieved from the network, the AFS servers take care to note who's reading what; when any information changes, each client is informed of the change so that the next read will fetch the more current data.

This callback guarantee gives the file servers some extra work to do, but in the long run, this work is far less than that needed to service requests from clients without large caches. The state information stored by AFS servers does make them more complicated, but it is that state information which makes the entire system more efficient, and users see higher performance from their desktops.

In their zeal to achieve the highest efficiencies, the designers of AFS chose to change distributed write semantics. Processes on multiple machines will see different data at different times than if the processes were all located on the same desktop. In practice, these concessions are not noticeable by users. The distributed semantics provided by AFS represent reasonable compromises, which in turn enable a system of a given size to support orders of magnitude more clients.

Like clients, AFS servers are relatively robust systems that require just a bit of care. Once the various processes and databases are up and running, most administration consists of volume manipulation and backing up data; these tasks are not much different from tasks for any other local machine. The big difference is that, with the ability to manage file data with drastically limited downtime and on-line failover to replicated volumes, a small administration staff can handle a much larger group of users and data.

With the integration of Kerberos services, not only can access controls be refined, but group administration can be delegated to the users themselves. And remote system management can be based on strong authentication rather than on blind trust between distant systems.

Depicting AFS as a file system cloud demonstrates the ubiquity of the system and the simplicity of connecting to the service. Perhaps a better analogy would be to a consumer utility provider—the water supply or the electric company. After a single hookup is made, services are constant, reliable, and affordable. As with telephone services, you simply expect that a single phone line will be able to connect you to any other phone in the world. AFS is like that; the worldwide community of AFS sites shares files without any special browsers or other applications. As far as they are concerned, "No matter where you go, there you are."

In the next three chapters, we'll dive into real administration operations. First, we'll set up a cell including all of the AFS services, then we'll begin to construct the AFS namespace of volumes, directories, and files, and then we'll set up standard clients.

Setting Up an AFS Cell

AFS cells consist of server machines acting in concert to provide file services to client workstations. No preferred architectures or numbers of servers are defined by the system; a cell's servers could be a single computer or dozens of relatively independent systems strewn about an enterprise. It is only important that all the servers know about each other, one way or another. From the first server installed with AFS software, the cell infrastructure will evolve, with specialized systems supporting a selection of the various AFS services.

As you learn about how an AFS cell is brought to life, you might be surprised at the number of programs and commands used to operate the system. At first glance, there seem to be too many. But AFS is not just a system for the delivery of files; it is a way for an enterprise to manage all distributed file data, to securely manage user identities, to provide flexible authorization policies for file access, to archive data in a manner consistent with the additional functionality of the system, to oversee all AFS server processes, and to distribute new versions of server executables. It should not be expected that these services could be provided with only one or two programs.

In general terms, three kinds of programs are used to make the different servers and disks accomplish these goals:

- Server programs—Long-running daemons that execute on the file server: such as `bosserver`, `kaserver`, `volserver`, or `fileserver`

- Operational commands—Programs run by administrators to manipulate the system: `fs`, `vos`, and `kas`

- Client cache management—The client itself and some utilities to modify its behavior: `afsd`, `fs`

We'll look at each of these kinds of processes over the next few chapters. Here, we'll go over the server processes in detail with an emphasis on how they are initialized in a brand-new cell. It may be fruitful to read this chapter once now, and then return to it after reading further chapters that introduce other operational aspects of the system.

PRELIMINARY DECISIONS

There are a few questions that you must answer before starting installation. First and foremost is the choice of an AFS cell name. This name is used throughout the system, in server databases, as a key used to encrypt Kerberos information, on each client machine to define its default cell location, etc. As such, changing a cell's name should be treated as a moderately difficult task. The fact that it can be done (as described later) is no reason not to pick a good cell name in the first place.

That said, your organization could purchase a site license for the product. Not only will the license eliminate regular additional costs as more servers are brought on line, but it will permit you to create test cells as needed. With a test cell, you can train new administrators in your standards and practices of cell support, including installation. Because AFS allows centralized control of an enterprisewide file server, it is difficult to test new software releases of operating systems, or AFS itself, as well as new hardware configurations or disk hardware, within your production cell. With a test cell, you can experiment freely so choosing your first cell name decision can be less traumatic.

If you do not choose to set up an ongoing test environment, you should still envision the initial AFS installation as an experiment, with the software configuration to be thrown away after evaluation. In this case, no individual decision will haunt you for your career. The first installation will seem a bit magical; once you understand the AFS terminology and mechanics, you'll see why each operation is performed in its particular order—you'll even be able to optimize the installation. The second installation will go much more quickly and (it is hoped) you will configure the system more confidently.

When choosing your final AFS cell name, keep in mind the possibility of publicizing that name to a larger audience. Many organizations rely on the strong authentication model of AFS and allow their cells to be visible in an Internet-wide file sharing namespace. The conventional directory structure has cell names as the subdirectories directly underneath `/afs`. To keep that directory organized and to encourage unique cell names worldwide, we recommend that your cell name be based on your organization's DNS name. For example, Transarc's cell is called `transarc.com` and can be found at `/afs/transarc.com`, the University of Michigan's cell is at `/afs/umich.edu`, IBM in Switzerland at `/afs/zurich.ibm.de`, and the Fermi National Accelerator Lab at `/afs/fnal.gov`. The dot characters in the name do not have any meaning to AFS as they do to DNS; there is no integration of cell names with DNS at all. Nor is there any internal hierarchical namespace for cells. The dots just suggest a hierarchy whereas in reality the cell namespace is flat. The similarity of cell names to DNS names is just a convention of the AFS community.

If you can guarantee that your site will never, ever have its cell visible to the outside world, you could, of course, name your cell practically anything. But given the explosive use of the Internet, that's an unwise bet to make. And, even though, for clarity, a cell's name is often included in the directory structure, you are free to invent new directory structures to hide the cell name from users.

As your organization grows, you'll likely wind up with multiple cells either just for testing, for political reasons, or even just large-scale geography. A reasonable practice, therefore, is to use your organization's registered DNS name as the starting point for your cell and then to add one (or more) levels to indicate status or geographic subdivisions, such as `test.hq.firm`, `prod.hq.firm`, or `main.new-york.hq.firm`. While shorter is better (for typing's sake) additional sublevels can help administrators coordinate very large scale AFS sites. Many firms have cells in several dozen cities worldwide; each cell is given a country and possibly a city sublevel to make administration procedures more predictable and simpler to construct.

After we look at more AFS administration practices, you'll see that the actual cell names chosen can be mostly hidden behind a variety of other names through symbolic links and additional mount points.

HARDWARE REQUIREMENTS

Neither AFS server nor client software puts a great stress on system resources. Though distributed file servers regularly service hundreds of clients, it is not necessary for specialized hardware platforms, clusters, or appliances to be used with AFS. All that is needed is a modestly configured server computer, typically just a high-end workstation. One advantage of this configuration is that as a server runs out of steam in a few years with the addition of ever greater numbers of clients and gigabytes of disks, you can move the old server workstation to a user's desktop and install a new computer in its place. This waterfall model extends the depreciation lifetime of an organization's hardware and can greatly reduce the overall costs of the computing infrastructure.

For reasons outlined later, it is beneficial to run the servers that provide access to the database of volume location, authentication, group, and backup information separate from the file servers. And, as access to the database should be highly available, we recommend you have at least three separate servers to provide this service. These servers will also need some extra disk space to hold their databases. With workstations being shipped these days with at least 2 gigabyte internal disks, the concern over disk space is not quite as critical as it was in the early days of AFS.

Although you could dedicate three or so systems to AFS database servicing, no minimum or maximum numbers of file servers are required. Clearly, it will be useful to have at least a handful to provide reliable data access and to have that access spread around, relatively close to various desktops. But AFS has been proven to support, depending on actual access patterns, upwards of several hundred clients per modest server with the clusters of clients located over a small-city-sized WAN. A single AFS cell can easily scale from one to tens of thousands of desktop users, so there's no need for most organizations to have multiple production cells at a single site.

Other considerations could warrant such multiplicity; if the WAN links between buildings are particularly unreliable or the geography quite large, more than one cell can be a good idea, especially during the initial pilot project. And large organizations often suffer from bureaucratic or political issues that can best be solved by creating one administrative cell for each division. There's certainly nothing wrong with such a topology; but while it is easy to navigate and work in more than one cell, there are effectively no AFS tools with any built-in support for multicell administration.

As for concrete specifications for an individual server system, only a small amount of local disk space, about 18 megabytes, is needed for storage of the server binaries, and less than 1 megabyte for clients. Servers also need some local disk storage for possible server process core files and for storage of log files.

Clients and especially servers use RAM for many internal data structures; therefore, the more the better, but there's no need, as far as AFS is concerned, to go over 32 megabytes for clients or 64 megabytes for servers. Servers will benefit from more RAM only if the organization is particularly large, say, over 1,000 users.

More important is disk space used by clients as caches and by servers as file storage. For the latter, you can add up to 256 partitions to be used by AFS to a single file server. That number accounts for the naming convention used by the volume server as it starts up to discover what disk space it controls: it assumes it controls any partition mounted at a directory name that begins with /vicep and followed by a through z or aa through iv. As we'll see when we examine volumes in closer detail, all AFS needs from a file server is a native file system installed on the vice partitions. In the past, this requirement limited the amount of data that could be installed on a server. Today, however, with virtual disks commonly available through hardware RAID or operating system enhancements such as Sun's DiskSuite™ or IBM's Journal File System™ (JFS), the potential data storage for a single system is enormous.

Note that as the partitions are fairly normal local file systems, administrators can create and delete files and directories in them. This practice doesn't harm AFS at all, but it is not how one manages AFS. When you take a look at the files that are written to a vice partition, you'll be surprised to see hardly any visible file activity.

For clients, a piece of the local disk must be devoted to AFS caching. In this regard, the bigger the better, but there are diminishing returns especially for anything over 100 megabytes. However, again, given the large internal disks shipped by many manufacturers, it is hard to resist the temptation to give 200-300 megabytes to the cache manager. Though initial startup of the client is delayed as the manager creates the large number of cache files, there are ways around this delay. Eventually, as you migrate more and more locally installed files into the AFS namespace, it is good practice to store on the client disks only transient data, such as the cache, temp files, swap, and spool files.

INSTALLATION OVERVIEW

The installation procedure creates a running cell on a single machine to which you can introduce additional server machines and clients. A running cell consists of several cooperating processes, which must be started one at a time in a particular order. Once initiated on one server, they can be started on others, providing resiliency to the system as a whole. Achieving this level of flexibility takes some doing, especially when you are attempting to eliminate any security exposures.

After initial installation, you will have constructed a single machine that runs a management process, the security database, the protection database of group information, the volume location process, and the file server. Several pieces of information, such as the first security credential and the first volume, need to be created during this phase. To finish, the client daemon is started so that the administrator can access the cell's file system to begin regular AFS management.

Figure 3-1 shows how these processes relate to one another and what data each controls. As more servers are installed, you can choose which processes run on which machines.

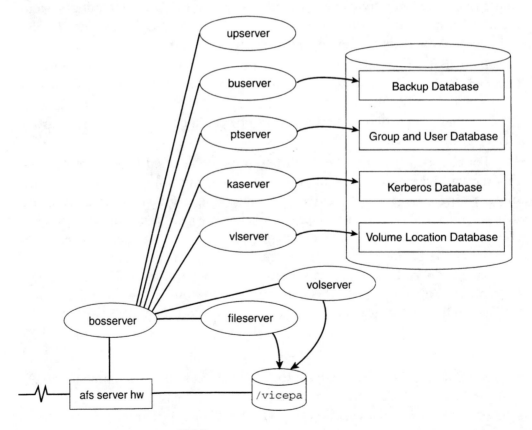

Figure 3-1   Processes on an AFS Server

Because this first machine is necessarily a file server, make sure to set up a few desired disk partitions and mount them at directories named /vicepa, /vicepb, etc.

Later, when we discuss volume internals, it will be clear that although the vice partitions use the native file system layout, there are a few differences which the vendor file system check program, fsck, would report as errors and attempt to correct. At this stage in the installation, you must copy Transarc's AFS fsck into place in the expected system location, such as /usr/etc/fsck. This version will perform as usual for non-AFS partitions but will do the appropriate lower-level checks only in vice partitions.

To continue the installation, load Transarc's AFS module into the kernel. The module is usually just an object file, libafs.o, which contains the algorithms and data structures that implement the AFS file system. You load the file into the kernel either by using Transarc's dynamic kernel loader or the vendor's own tool or by building a new kernel statically link-edited with the module. These procedures are slightly different for each architecture and are outlined in detail in Transarc's AFS installation manual.

In terms of administration overhead, both loading mechanisms require that a binary file (either the module or a new version of the kernel) be copied onto each server. Either way, the server's kernel will have a new system call to start up AFS kernel threads, a new file system (usually installed as part of a kernel vnode layer), and other hooks.

Now that the system hardware and software are ready, start the AFS services. All servers begin by running an overseer process, bosserver. This service manages all other AFS jobs on the server. Administrators normally control AFS through a client program bos which sends instructions to the overseer process on a particular server rather than logging in to a machine and manually manipulating a specific process.

As with the overseer process, each subsequent AFS service is managed by a server program that is contacted via a protocol request sent by a custom-built client program. (In the case of the file server, the control program is the client kernel as it reads and writes files.)

Before you continue, note that it is important to perform the installation tasks in one pass because regular authorization checking is turned off. You may want to disconnect from the network or disable logins to ensure that the system is secure and that no unauthorized reading or writing of data can occur. Once the installation is complete and the system is up, there is strongly controlled access to all critical data. However, it will still be important to restrict access to servers as much as possible, and especially so for the Kerberos security servers themselves.

Next, you will configure the cell name with a special subcommand of the `bos` administration command. This command sends a data packet to the `bosserver` process so that the server can create the configuration file `/usr/afs/etc/ThisCell`, which stores the local cell name; the server also automatically configures the file `/usr/afs/etc/CellServDB`.

The server's `CellServDB` file is similar to the client's. It is a text file in which the names and addresses for the cell's database servers are stored. This step of the installation process ensures that a correctly formatted version of the file is created.

The Kerberos server, `kaserver`, is the next job created; this starts up authentication services. Immediately, you'll add two privileged identities to the security database. The first is a name to be used initially for AFS management. This shared administrator's name can be any name you'd like: `admin`, `afsadmin`, or `celladmin` are common choices. The second identity which must be created is `afs`, the principal which acts as a service key for the AFS processes themselves. Be sure to remember (and don't write down) the passwords for these two principals. Later on, you can add administrator privileges to other identities.

When the cell is finally running, you'll need to authenticate as one of the AFS administrator identities to perform system management. To authenticate, you'll use the `klog` program, much like a regular log-in program, to confirm your AFS identity against the Kerberos system. The installation process outlined here only stores the administration name in the Kerberos databases; you must also add this name to your password file or map. This way, any files or directories created in AFS by an administrator will have their ownership information displayed correctly. Keeping the password maps and the AFS Kerberos databases synchronized for all user identities is an on-going concern.

One benefit of AFS is that users of client workstations mutually authenticate themselves with the AFS file servers: once authenticated, a server can trust the user's identity and the users can trust that they are talking to the cell's true file servers. This authentication can happen only when the Kerberos servers store secrets both about the users (their password) and about the AFS servers (the service key). It is critical to the security of the AFS system that the Kerberos servers be trusted and that their integrity never be violated. To increase the safety of the `afs` service key, you should change its secret password regularly to forestall efforts to crack it.

If your site is already using Kerberos based on the MIT distribution, you do not need to install Transarc's server, but you will probably have to take care of small inconsistencies between the two implementations. Some of these issues are discussed in Chapter 6.

With the `afs` principal defined, you can now extract a Kerberos service ticket and install it on the file server. This ticket is essentially a new secret password, usable only on this server, which authenticates the server to Kerberos. You extract this ticket with another `bos` command, which stores the ticket in a special file, `/usr/afs/etc/KeyFile`. Occasionally, access problems to AFS are a result of corruptions to this key file; we examine the failure mode and fixes in Chapter 10.

Only after Kerberos has started can the protection database containing group membership information be initialized. Administrative control of most AFS procedures is permitted via a few mechanisms, one of which is membership in the group `system:administrators`. This group is automatically created as you start up the protection server process, `ptserver`. The next step is to add the administration name defined previously into the protection database and to add it to the membership list of the `system:administrators` group.

Once the security infrastructure is in place, you can run the processes that make up the file system proper:

- The volume location server, `vlserver`—This server process allows AFS clients to determine which server holds a given volume's file data.
- The backup database server, `buserver`—This server tracks the backup schedule, the volumes archived at a given time, and the backup media sites. In Chapter 7, we'll see how this database stores information on our archive jobs.
- The file server processes—These are three related processes: `fileserver`, to store and retrieve file data, `volserver`, to manage volumes, and `salvager`. The `salvager` is not a long-running server like `fileserver` or `volserver` but is available to scan the file server's disks to recreate any lost file or volume data on the disk if the other two processes crash.

Now, you can create the first AFS volume. Nominally called `root.afs`, this volume name is assumed by clients to be connected to the directory named

/afs. To create the volume, you use the vos command suite. This command controls most aspects of AFS volume existence and is perhaps the commonest command run by an administrator. It is discussed in detail in the next chapter.

Finally, you can set up two optional services. The first is the update server, upserver, which allows for easy updating of servers' AFS binaries and configuration files. It is critical that all servers in a cell are running exactly the same version of all AFS processes and have exactly the same data in the few static ASCII configuration files. To that end, you can use Transarc's update system to propagate changes among the servers themselves.

The upshot is that new configuration files need be installed on a single machine and new binaries installed on a single machine per architecture. The update server system will perform all transfers between the masters and slaves and ensure that the new data or programs are installed in a methodical manner without any disruption of distributed file service.

The second optional service, runntp, is a process to start up synchronization of the local clock. Both Kerberos and the distributed database servers use timestamps for controlling their operations. If you're not running any of the publicly available network time protocols, you can use the system that Transarc supplies.

Your first server will now be running all the AFS server processes outlined in Figure 3-1, and the first, topmost, volume has been created.

To complete the AFS installation, you'll next install the client software. It may seem odd to think of client software being installed on a server, but AFS is a rigorously architected client/server system. All access to file data must use the AFS protocol to reach the correct server processes which return the data; so even on an AFS server, the only way to get at the files is by using the AFS client software. One reason for this requirement is that it increases the security of the system: even the root superuser on an AFS server must be properly authenticated before being able to read or write data. Before we discuss client set up, let's examine the server processes in more detail.

THE BASIC OVERSEER

Thinking back to the original motivation of the AFS designers, it is easy to imagine their dismay when faced with monitoring all the services they had just written. Like most of AFS, this practical need for a monitoring tool was satisfied with the creation of the basic overseer server, bosserver. This server process manages much of the installation and other administration tasks of the system. Rather than logging in to a remote server and manipulating jobs manually, the administrator can use a simple command-line client program, bos. The primary purpose of bosserver is to start up, track, and restart any server processes that fail.

Once the AFS server jobs have been defined, all that is required to begin services after a reboot is to load the kernel module and begin bosserver. These two actions are the only ones that need be added to a system's startup scripts, such as /etc/rc.local.

Naturally, bosserver has been written to handle the special cases needed by AFS servers. But this job control system is actually somewhat flexible and can be used to manage other processes needed for server administration. These other jobs are controlled through a configuration file named /usr/afs/etc/BosConfig. The data is formatted in a simple ASCII-based language which you can edit by hand, but the bos program is the preferred means to communicate with a bosserver changes to configuration information or to start and stop services.

A bos job consists of a unique name, a program name and invocation arguments, a job type (e.g., simple, fs, or cron), and optionally a program to be run when the job terminates. During the installation, you created three simple jobs: kaserver, ptserver, and vlserver. Each of these is "simple" in that each is a single process which is expected to run forever and does not depend on any other process. The unique name for these jobs is based on the server name; the program name is the full path of the executable. If you'd like, simple jobs can be used to manage long-running servers of your own devising.

The fs type of job is a custom job which only the AFS file server programs should use. Its unique name is normally fs and the program name is a set of three path names for the fileserver, volserver, and salvager programs. The basic overseer understands that the first two programs are expected to be long-running processes and that if either exits, special processing may be needed. In particular, if volserver crashes, bosserver restarts it without further ado; but if fileserver crashes, then bosserver will stop volserver and run salvager to restore some file system state. After salvager has run, bosserver restarts fileserver and then volserver.

During installation, no cron jobs are created. These jobs are short-lived programs defined to run at regularly scheduled times. By running out of the bosserver system, administrators can take advantage of the bos tool to monitor their operation.

In addition to these per-job pieces of data, all jobs includes two overall configuration items: restart times and a time to turn over new binaries. These and other more advanced server management facilities are described in more detail in Chapter 10.

FILE SERVICES

File services are ultimately provided by three processes on each file server. Of these three, two are always running, and the third runs only to clean up after a failure. Because of this dependency, bosserver has a single job that controls the startup of the file services or the initiation of cleanup followed by the two long-running processes.

The aptly named fileserver is the first of the two long-running processes; it delivers or stores file data to or from client systems. Although a file server will usually hold a great deal of data in multiple vice partitions, only a single fileserver process is run per server.

Besides communicating with clients, this process also queries the protection server to check the permissions of a user's read or write request. For other queries or administration, the fs command can check or change access controls, volume connection points, or quotas. (As an aside, yes, overloading the name "fs" to signify both a kind of basic overseer job and a command suite is potentially confusing.)

A similar process, volserver, runs continually on each file server to make or destroy volumes, coordinate entire volume dumps or restores, and moves volumes from one server to another. Don't confuse this process with the volume location server, vlserver, which manages the database of volume locations. As with fileserver, there is only one volserver process per file server no matter how many volumes or partitions are on the machine.

The final process in an fs job is salvager. This process is similar to the portion of the native file system check program, fsck, which checks for consistency of directory and file names and linkages. In this case, salvager understands the connectivity between volumes, files, and access control lists. It is normally not running at all but is started up when a failure is detected.

The detection method is triggered by the existence of a sentinel file. When the fileserver process starts normally, it creates a file /usr/afs/local/ SALVAGE.fs; when the fileserver exits normally (such as during a graceful AFS shut down), it deletes the file. Hence, if the file exists before bosserver runs fileserver, then fileserver must have exited abnormally, potentially leaving the volume structures in an inconsistent state. In this case, bosserver runs salvager to check and restore the volumes structures.

Naturally, this file can be created manually if ever a salvage of vice partitions is deemed necessary, but there is also a separate bos command to start a salvage if needed.

As previously mentioned, there is no explicit configuration file to describe which partitions are controlled by the fs job processes. AFS assumes control of any disk partition mounted at a name beginning with /vicep. Although ordinary UNIX tools can be used to create or delete files in these vice directories without harming the rest of the AFS data, such usage is not recommended.

For the curious, inside the vice partitions are volume headers, visible as 76-byte files named Vnnnnnnnn.vol, where nnnnnnnn is the volume identification number. As volserver starts, it scans the disk to find all volumes available and attaches them, that is, it validates their integrity and acknowledges ownership of them.

These volume header files contain data which points to more volume information stored in the vice partition; the root directory entries, and thereby, the rest of the file data for the volume. All of the file, directory, and access control data is stored in standard inodes and data blocks in the vice partition file system, but none of this data is given a regular, user-visible file name.

As users store data, fileserver assigns each file a FID or file identification number. Unlike file handles in NFS, which are different on each server, FIDs are enterprisewide identifiers that can be used to discover where the file is stored anywhere in the system. Each FID is composed of a 32-bit volume identity number, a 32-bit vnode or file number, and a 32-bit uniquifier or version number. Once a client has used the volume identifier to find the server that stores the file, the file and uniquifier numbers are sent to the fileserver process. This process then searches through AFS data structures maintained in the operating system to directly point to the location of the file data in the vice partition.

Although the inodes and data blocks in the vice partition are standard, their connections and lack of visible names will cause the vendor's file system check program to believe that there are numerous problems with the internal system state. If the vendor fsck program is run, it will attempt to fix these problems and thereby undo some of the state that was being used by fileserver and volserver. For this reason, during the installation process you must replace the normal fsck program with Transarc's version. That version will work correctly on the vendor's regular UNIX file systems as well as do the right thing with the `vice` partitions.

Because AFS servers spend much of their time processing data and updating disks, they should be gracefully shut down before the system is rebooted. You use `bos` to shut down any or all AFS processes on any server. It is especially important to perform this action on any servers holding read-write file data or the master site for the database processes. There are a variety of recovery mechanisms for systems that crash; these are discussed in Chapter 10.

DATABASE SERVICES

The other main jobs run on AFS central machines are the database services. Separate databases store authentication information, group memberships, volume location information, and historical data about volume archives. Each database type can be replicated among a few servers; these replicas permit the data to be available in the face of server or network failures.

Although each database server process is independent of the others, most AFS commands assume that each database server listed in `CellServDB` will be running all four of the database processes: the volume location server, the authentication server, the protection server, and the backup server.

The *volume location server*, `vlserver`, keeps track of every volume in the cell. For each named volume, up to three versions are potentially available: a master read-write, a few read-only copies, and a backup or snapshot. For each of these volumes, `vlserver` stores information about the server and partition in which it is stored, its size, creation and update time, and other data. Volumes are manipulated by `vos` commands, which will update both the volume location database as well as the actual volume on disk. For example, the volume creation command adds an entry to the volume location database and also contacts a specific volume server to create the actual volume data. The `vlserver` is also contacted by clients to find out where data is stored. The location information is stored in the *volume location database*, often abbreviated as VLDB; do not confuse this with other literature that uses that acronym to mean very large database.

The *authentication server*, `kaserver`, is an almost-standard Kerberos version 4 server. Interestingly, the original CMU `kaserver` was the first Kerberos server written according to the MIT specification. Its database stores all the encrypted user passwords and server keys. Users interact with the server through modified login programs or a separate program, `klog`, to become authenticated and retrieve a Kerberos ticket-granting ticket. Administrators will use AFS's `kas` command suite to add or delete users and change passwords.

The *protection server*, `ptserver`, stores access control information, user name and IDs, group names and IDs, and group membership mappings. The `fileserver` process queries this server to determine access permissions. Administration of user IDs, groups, and group membership is performed through the `pts` command which queries the server's information in the *protection database*.

The *backup server*, `buserver`, tracks and stores data used by Transarc's archival system. The administrative command `backup` defines full and incremental dump schedules and archives sets of volumes as a unit. As dumps are made, `buserver` keeps a complete database of which volume sets were dumped to what media at what time.

Each of these four database processes stores the actual data on the server's local disk under the `/usr/afs/db` directory. The data is accessed via two files per database: their suffixes are `.DB0` and `.DBSYS1`. The `.DB0` file holds the database entries themselves while the `.DBSYS1` file holds a log of add or update operations which are being applied to the database. If certain errors occur, this log can be replayed to bring the database file into a coherent state. In addition to backing up AFS file data, you must archive these database files to storage in order to have complete disaster recovery procedures.

SERVER MACHINE TYPES

While AFS is composed of a number of services all acting together, it is not necessary for every server to run every service. This is not to suggest that random combinations of processes are supported; Transarc (and their documentation) distinguishes between the following types of servers:

- File servers—These systems run the `bosserver` `fs` job (consisting of `fileserver`, `volserver`, and `salvager`) and therefore are known to have `vice` disk partitions. It is common for a cell to have a dozen or so file server machines.
- Database servers—These systems run the processes that maintain AFS databases. As mentioned, for reliability you'll probably want to run more than one database server. It is expected that each database server is running all of the database processes that you require. Typically, this means that each will run `vlserver`, `kaserver`, `ptserver`, and `buserver`.

- System control machine—This single server is so named because it is the
  distribution point for systemwide data, such as the AFS service key file.
  This and other textual configuration data must be synchronized across all
  AFS servers. This data can be propagated automatically by making all
  other servers clients of the update process on the system control machine.
  By design, the configuration data which must be propagated is all stored
  in the single directory, /usr/afs/etc.
- Binary distribution machine—Just as systemwide configuration data must
  be the same everywhere, so too must the binary releases of the server programs themselves be the same. Of course, each different machine architecture must have its correct executables. So, for each server's hardware and
  operating system version, there should be one binary distribution
  machine; the other similarly configured systems will be clients of this
  binary distribution master. Again, by design, the binary files of concern to
  the system are all stored in one directory, /usr/afs/bin.

Naturally, a single machine may be performing several of the above roles.
But many sites choose to run their database services on machines separate from
their file server machines. As we'll see as we explore file and volume operations, AFS file servers are quite independent machines—neither clients nor the
databases need any prior knowledge of the identity of the AFS file servers prior
to using them. It is therefore a simple operation to administer a file server system without affecting the cell's operation as a whole. On the other hand, AFS
database servers must be known to each client in a cell and must be known to
each other, thus requiring somewhat more careful administration practices.
While it is easy to bring down a file server to, say, add a disk, with a predeter-
mined amount of service outage, bringing down a database server may affect
the cell in less predictable ways. Hence, isolating the file and database functionality onto their own machines provides a more manageable environment.

While file servers and database servers are often segregated, one of them
will almost certainly be the system control machine, propagating its configuration data to all other servers. Likewise, this machine may as well be the binary
distribution machine for any other servers of the same architecture.

As an example (and, indeed, in examples throughout the book), we will be
administering computers at a firm named "HQ." Its domain name is hq.firm,
which will be therefore be the name of its AFS cell. Our firm has many clients
and many gigabytes of files to be managed, so we've set up their servers as
depicted in Figure 3-2.

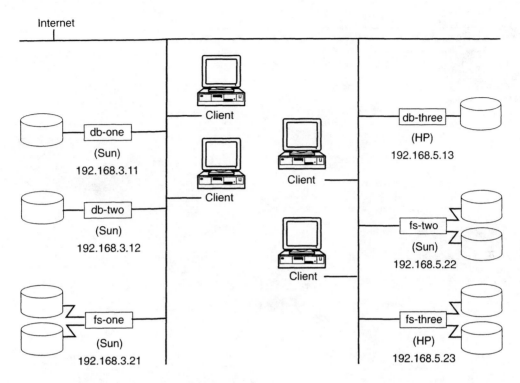

Figure 3-2   The Machine Topology at hq.firm

According to the suggested practice, we have installed separate servers for database and file services. (Note: It is not necessary to give the machines as dull a set of names as is done in our example; we chose these names to make clear which server should be listed as an argument to example commands in the rest of the book. It is possible with DNS to give such names as aliases to your real server; this practice may make writing scripts or teaching the system to others easier.)

Of the servers, db-one is the system control machine and also the binary distribution machine for all Sun servers—db-two, fs-one, and fs-two. db-three is the binary distribution machine for other HP® servers, of which there is only one, fs-three. Finally, fs-one, fs-two, and fs-three are simple file servers.

Table 3-1 summarizes the exact services and daemons that are running on each system.

Table 3-1   Server Types and Running Processes

Machine	Server Type	Configured Processes
db-one	database server	`bosserver, kaserver, vlserver, ptserver`
	system control	`upserver` (for `/usr/afs/etc`)
	binary distribution	`upserver` (for `/usr/afs/bin`)
db-two	database server	`bosserver, kaserver, vlserver, ptserver`
	system client	`upclient` (of db-one `/usr/afs/etc`)
	binary client	`upclient` (of db-one `/usr/afs/bin`)
db-three	database server	`bosserver, kaserver, vlserver, ptserver`
	system client	`upclient` (of db-one `/usr/afs/etc`)
	binary distribution	`upserver` (for `/usr/afs/bin`)
fs-one	file server	`bosserver, fileserver, volserver`
	system client	`upclient` (of db-one `/usr/afs/etc`)
	binary client	`upclient` (of db-one `/usr/afs/bin`)
fs-two	file server	`bosserver, fileserver, volserver`
	system client	`upclient` (of db-one `/usr/afs/etc`)
	binary client	`upclient` (of db-one `/usr/afs/bin`)
fs-three	file server	`bosserver, fileserver, volserver`
	system client	`upclient` (of db-one `/usr/afs/etc`)
	binary client	`upclient` (of db-three `/usr/afs/bin`)

Because a single server machine can be running more than one process for more than one purpose, we'll use the server type names with care: db-one is an AFS server, which could be described as a database server, a system control machine, or a binary distribution machine, depending on the circumstance; fs-three is a file server and a client of the binary distribution system.

Also note that these names are descriptive only. Given an arbitrary cell, the only way to determine what roles a machine is taking is by examining the output of the bos status command and reading which services it is performing at that moment. Knowing that a machine serves a specific purpose does not rule out other uses for that machine; the system control machine is probably also a database server and perhaps a file server as well.

ADDING MORE MACHINES

Once you've completed the somewhat tedious startup configuration of the first machine, adding further servers is much more straightforward. To install a new file server, you must first copy the program files to the system. Given that a few vice partitions have been set up, all that is required is to start the bosserver and initialize the fs job and the two upclient jobs: one for the system configuration data and one for the binary programs.

Additional file servers are this simple because they do not communicate with each other; they only need to know the addresses of the database servers. Other than that, the only configuration information that identifies a file server to the rest of AFS is the volume location database, which stores pointers to the machines and partitions that store a given volume.

A new database server is a little more complex, mainly because all other servers and clients in the cell need to be told about the existence of the new server. After copying over the program files, start bosserver and initialize it with the four database jobs—vlserver, kaserver, ptserver, and buserver—and also an upclient job to periodically retrieve new configuration data.

To let all other AFS servers know of the new database server, add its name and address to the /usr/afs/etc/CellServDB file on the system control machine. The upserver and upclient jobs that were set up previously will copy over this changed file to all other AFS servers. In a few minutes, all other servers in the cell will have the new file.

At this point, you must manually restart the database jobs on the other database servers. When they restart, they will read the CellServDB file and contact the listed servers, including the new server, and begin communication to determine which site is to be the master site. The new database processes will quickly discover that they do not have a copy of the databases and will request a transfer of the data. The election and internal management of this process is handled by the Ubik algorithm, described in the next section.

AFS client machines also need to be informed of the new database server. Running clients need to be explicitly told that a new server exists; the server should also be added to client's CellServDB file. It is simple to write a script to check for a new version of the CellServDB file in some well-known place and install it; you could even write a small daemon process to run on a client and listen for custom messages. Given that large AFS cells are regularly run with only three AFS database servers, the need to change such a server is a fairly rare occurrence. Yet, given the large number of potentially visible cells, somewhat frequent changes to the cell server database file must be made. And with no standard mechanism for distributing these changes from external sites to your site or to your client desktops, you'll have to develop homegrown solutions to keep your clients in synchronization with the AFS world.

UBIK

The database services are set up on multiple servers so that a client can send its queries to any available server. This configuration not only automatically spreads out the load (and the load is further reduced by client caching of the answers) but during outages permits a client to query successive database servers until it gets an answer.

The problem posed by running multiple instances of the databases is deciding where updates are to be sent and how to make sure that those updates are propagated to the other instances. Any solution should be able to manage circumstances when one or more of the database servers has crashed or is running but unable to communicate with the other servers.

In AFS, multiple database instances are synchronized through an algorithm named Ubik hard-coded into the server process. The algorithm's prime purpose is to enable the multiple instances to elect one of themselves as the master site to which all update requests are sent. When a single process handles all updates, the requests are inherently serialized. For example, a request to change a user's record could not be accepted at exactly the same time that the user is deleted from the system; if these two requests are serialized, then either the deletion occurs first, so that the request to change would fail, or the change would occur first, to be followed by the deletion.

Once changes are made at the master site, they must be reliably propagated to the other sites. To ensure that the propagation succeeds requires that the database instances communicate among themselves to discover and work around any outages. When all database processes agree that the new version of the database is ready, any of the instances is available to respond to read requests, such as queries for a volume's location or which users belong to which groups. Compare this scheme to a file server's fs job which performs its work with no interaction with any other file server's processes.

There are, of course, many ways to provide replicated read access to this kind of data. The advantage of Ubik over other database technologies is that during system or network outages, a majority of surviving database processes can elect a new master, so that updates to the database can still be accepted and maintained correctly despite the failure. The ability of the master site to automatically move itself to a new site during network outages enables the AFS databases to be highly available for both read and write operations.

In Ubik terms, the master is called the *synchronization* or *sync* site, and the other sites, which hold read-only replicas of the database, are called *secondaries*. When an update to a database is received from an administrator's program, it is logged to the sync site's disk and then propagated to all of the secondaries. If less than a majority of secondaries responds that the update succeeded, the sync site aborts the update and tells the administrator that the request failed.

Every time an update is successfully applied to the sync site, the update is immediately propagated to all other secondaries and the database version number is incremented. The sync site and the secondaries regularly check to make sure that the latest version of the database is used for replying to requests. If a secondary has been unavailable due to a network outage and has missed an update or two, once the network is repaired, the secondary will notice that its database has an older version number than that which is available on the sync site and so will request a transfer of the more up-to-date version.

To determine which system is the sync site upon startup, all database processes examine their local /usr/afs/etc/CellServDB file to find the other AFS database machines. An individual server will check to see which of these machines are reachable on the network and then will decide to vote for one. This choice is made by selecting the available server with the lowest numerical IP address; a purely arbitrary but easily calculated algorithm. What is important is that because the voting preferences are well known, all observers (and administrators) will know that the election represents a stable, and, under normal circumstances, repeatable situation.

To be elected sync site, a server has to receive a majority of votes, that is, a majority of the number of servers listed in the CellServDB file for this cell. If three servers are listed in the CellServDB file, the sync site must receive at least two votes. To help make a majority when there are an even number of servers, the lowest-addressed site gets to break the tie in its favor.

In a normally functioning cell, the lowest-addressed database server will win all the elections for all of the database servers. That machine will receive 100 percent of the available votes and all servers will recognize that machine as the elected sync site. From then on, all requests to update any AFS database data will be directed to the sync site, which will accept the update and write the data to its disk before propagating the new record to the secondaries. In our example cell with three database servers, db-one has the lowest IP address and will win election as the Ubik sync site.

The sync site stays in touch with the secondary sites by periodically sending out a packet of information called a *beacon*. The beacon lets the secondary know that the sync site is still alive and represents a promise that, unless explicitly told of a record update, the database it holds will be valid until some number of seconds in the future, usually about 60 seconds. A new beacon will be sent out before the previous one expires.

When secondaries receive this beacon, they send a response back; this acknowledgement enables both secondaries and sync site to know that both are running well. If a secondary realizes a beacon has expired, it knows that some outage has occurred and therefore will begin a new election process. At some point, if a sync site crashes and another machine takes its place, then, when the original sync site reboots and joins in an election, it will retake the read-write mastery of the database. Although a site may win the election, it may realize that there is a higher-numbered version of the database on one of the secondaries. If so, it will transfer a copy from there to its own site, and then begin synchronization beacons with the remaining secondaries.

If a database process running as a secondary realizes that it has lost contact with the sync site, it is still permitted to respond to queries. This response is a potential problem because, if the sync site is still running but is hidden behind a network partition, the sync site's contents may change at any time. For the volume location database, an incorrect response does little damage; at worst, when told the incorrect name of a file server, the file read or write request will fail on its own. More problematic are incorrect answers to queries of the Kerberos and protection database instances. But as of AFS 3.4a, it was decided that in the rare event of a network partition, it would be better to permit read access to the databases, which would permit logins and access control lists to be checked, rather than refuse to answer such queries.

There are any number of ways for a collection of database servers to crash or lose contact with each other, and so it's important to understand that the Ubik algorithm running inside each database instance does its best to ensure that correct read-only data is available and that only one sync site will be available at any given time. A few selected examples should suffice to demonstrate how this works.

In a single-server system, the server will always be available, and will receive one vote—a majority—as it votes for itself as the lowest-addressed server. It is always available because if the machine crashes, there are no other databases which would compete in the election; either this system is available, in which case it is the sync site, or it will have crashed.

In a two-server system, there is the possibility that either the sync site or the secondary crashes or that they are both running but unable to communicate with each other over the network. Table 3-2 shows the possible scenarios: When both are running normally, the lowest-addressed server gets votes from each server and becomes the sync site.

When the highest-addressed server is running but doesn't hear from the other server, it will decide to vote for itself as the currently available server with the lowest address. But this adds up to only one out of two votes and so is not a

Table 3-2 Ubik Resiliency: Two-Server Scenarios

Machine Name	db1	db2
IP Address	a.b.c.1	a.b.c.2
Scenario	both machines running	
Votes For	db1	db1
Result	2/2	0/2
	sync	secondary
Scenario	running	crashed
Votes For	db1	—
Result	1.5/2	—
	sync	—
Scenario	crashed	running
Votes For	—	db2
Result	—	1/2
	—	secondary
Scenario	both running, but a network partition doesn't permit db1 or db2 to communicate with each other	
Votes For	db1	db2
Result	1.5/2	1/2
	sync	secondary

majority the highest-addressed server will never be the sync site and will remain a secondary. All that it can do is service read requests from the database and periodically attempt to begin a new election. When the original sync site reboots, it will win the next election and retake sync-site responsibilities.

On the other hand, if the lowest-addressed server cannot contact the other server, it will vote for itself, but because it knows that there are an even number of servers, it adds a half vote as the lowest numbered server in `CellServDB` and so gains a majority and remains the sync site. This situation occurs either if the secondary has crashed or if a network problem blocks transmissions between the two servers. If the secondary has crashed, upon reboot it will respond to a beacon from the sync site, it will realize that it has an old version of the database, and a copy of the current version will be transferred.

From these scenarios, you can see that two AFS database servers provide a small measure of load balancing but not much in the way of greater availability.

For more availability, a three-server system is preferred. In this case, all queries are split between three servers for load balancing. If the sync server crashes, the remaining two servers engage in an election and one of them will receive two votes as the lowest-available-addressed server; those two votes represent a majority of the original three machines, and so a new sync site will become available. Obviously, if one of the two nonsync sites crashes instead, the sync site will remain available. Thus, the Ubik protocol provides a mechanism for three servers (at a minimum) to always establish a sync site no matter which single machine crashes or becomes unavailable. In Table 3-3, several scenarios are worked out.

More interestingly, in the case of a network partition that leaves the sync site isolated from the other two servers, both sides of the partition will start up an election. The single sync site will vote for itself but will not get a majority of two or more votes and so will stop being a sync site; the other two sites will elect a new sync site between themselves and be available for updates from those clients on their side of the partition. When the network problems are resolved and a new election takes place, the original sync site will win the next election, and the newest version of the database will be transferred back to the original sync site.

The Ubik sync site election rules ensure that at no time will more than one active site be accepting updates to the database. At worst, no updates will be permitted, but client data queries can be answered. When a majority of servers

Table 3-3   Ubik Resiliency: Three-Server Scenarios

Machine Name	db1	db2	db3
IP address	a.b.c.1	a.b.c.2	a.b.c.3
Scenario	all three machines running		
Votes For	db1	db1	db1
Result	3/3	0/3	0/3
	sync	secondary	secondary
Scenario	running	crashed	running
Votes For	db1	—	db1
Result	2/3	—	0/3
	sync	—	secondary
Scenario	crashed	running	running
Votes For	—	db2	db2
Result	—	2/3	0/3
	—	sync	secondary
Scenario	crashed	crashed	running
Votes For	—	—	db3
Result	—	—	1/3
			secondary
Scenario	network partition: db1 and db2 can communicate with each other but not with db3		
Votes For	db1	db1	db3
Result	2/3	0/3	0/3
	sync	secondary	secondary
Scenario	network partition: db2 and db3 can communicate with each other but not with db1		
Votes For	db1	db2	db2
Result	1/3	2/3	2/3
	secondary	sync	secondary

is available, a new master read-write site can be elected. To ensure that all communication during an election is accurate, the election itself can last almost three minutes. During the election, neither updates nor queries can be processed.

Why not create more than three database servers then? The trouble with additional servers is that updates must be propagated to all secondaries. As the number of servers increases, the odds increase that some subset will crash or lose communication with the others. While the Ubik protocol manages this unavailability, it does put a stress on the system: updates must be sent to all servers, and elections may take place, new sync sites may be chosen, and database transfers may occur. Also, because the servers must send each other periodic beacons and votes, multiple databases add their own load to the network.

In general, three servers are recommended as optimum; this number can support thousands of clients and a few tens of file servers. Some sites have as many as five database servers, a few, up to seven. Beyond seven database servers, there simply isn't much experience available.

As can be seen, this architecture depends on the accurate a priori knowledge of database machine names. Each server needs to know the set of servers in its own cell, listed in `/usr/afs/etc/CellServDB`. And each client needs to know of all potentially available servers for all cells it will want to access, listed in `/usr/vice/etc/CellServDB`.

Client workstations will initially prefer one of the database machines as the system to which to send queries. The queries are satisfied immediately whereas the updates must be sent to the sync site for processing. If the preferred database machine becomes unavailable, a client will dynamically fail over and use one of the other database servers listed in the `CellServDB` file. When the preferred server becomes available again, the client will return to using it.

A program is available for querying the status of the Ubik algorithm running inside each of the database server processes. See Chapter 10 for information on diagnosing and repairing Ubik failures.

TIME SYNCHRONIZATION

Several AFS services insist that systems maintain synchronized time clocks. For security, the Kerberos authentication model relies on timestamps to help prevent replay attacks and to manage the expiration of user credentials. For the files themselves, it is important for the times seen by one client to make sense to other clients: it would be strange for one user to see that a file had been changed by another user, but that the file's modification time was several minutes into the future. In addition, the Ubik protocol uses timestamps to validate server votes and database version numbers.

In 1987, an Internet RFC was published which describes the Network Time Protocol (NTP). This is a mechanism by which many independent computers can agree on and distribute time information. The result of this protocol is that clocks on all functioning systems can agree with one another to within milliseconds of a reference timeframe.

Many AFS sites use the public domain version of NTP for their time services. Because this was not in wide usage when AFS was first released, the AFS product includes a version of NTP and integrates the protocol and programs with the rest of the system. If precise time services are already available, you can skip the following configuration information.

The general layout of NTP starts with one system in the organization getting its time reference from an external source. This external source can either be a quasi-absolute provider, such as a radio receiver set to the WWV U.S. time service or a GPS (Global Position Satellite) system receiver. A simpler reference can be had by using the NTP protocol to receive timestamp packets from another, trustworthy, computer on the Internet. Figure 3-3 shows the general layout of time distribution.

Alternatively, if you do not care about the accuracy of your timestamps, you can just rely on any reliable local computer and declare that that system's clock is the correct time for your organization.

Once your reference point is set up, you must assign a set of servers as the next stratum of timestamp support. In the AFS product, these servers are normally the same as the set of database servers. An enterprise needs only a handful of time servers spread around the network topology—a distribution which happens to match that of the AFS database servers.

From there, file servers will communicate with the time service daemons on the database servers using the NTP protocol to maintain precise local clocks.

Transarc's AFS comes with an NTP server daemon, `runntp`, which uses the synchronization protocol to keep the times accurate on AFS servers. Like other server processes, this daemon is managed by `bosserver`. Because timestamps are used by Ubik to coordinate elections and database versions, you should monitor this job as closely as you monitor any other AFS service. AFS clients query servers to set their clocks on their own, as discussed in Chapter 5.

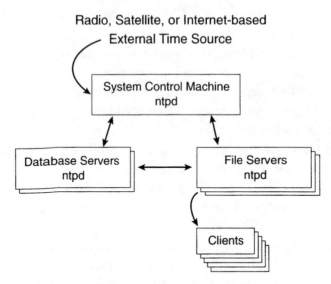

Figure 3-3   AFS Time Synchronization

SUMMARY

At first glance, there seem to be an overwhelming number of servers and databases needed to get AFS up and running. This is in stark contrast to, say NFS. But NFS is really just a wire protocol to tie together remote UNIX file systems; it accomplishes this goal quite successfully. But AFS's goals are to present an integrated file system service with improved reliability, security, and performance.

The beauty is that even with all of these new processes, command suites, and architectures, regular management of an AFS cell is easy and provides important functionality. Certainly the up-front costs are higher, but the continuing costs end up being much lower.

The basic overseer process is the biggest aid to managing the system. Through it, you can discover the jobs running on any of the servers in the cell. With the implementation of a client/server architecture for almost all services, management tasks can be executed from any administrator's own desktop, making it easy to quickly check on the status of a cell.

AFS file server machines tend to be fairly nondescript workhorses. As long as they have disks to manage, they tend to respond reliably to read and write requests. With the ability to replicate and move file trees off file servers, administrators can schedule maintenance during regular working hours with no disruption to any users.

The database services employ a built-in replication scheme with one significant advantage: when set up on at least three servers, the database processes can vote to elect a new master site in a well-defined manner. Not only does this make the vital AFS state information highly available, but it also enables changes to the data to be made even in the face of otherwise disastrous service outages.

These production-ready and mature technologies form the bedrock for the AFS services. With them, organizations can expand in size without the need for a constantly increasing administration or hardware budget. But the price for this scalability is in the up-front costs of education and training in the processes and mechanisms by which the servers provide the illusion of an integrated file system.

CHAPTER   4

AFS Volumes and Files

Now that we have initialized our cell and one or more AFS server machines, we can finally begin the process of creating and managing file data. In AFS, all file and directory data is stored in collections called volumes. When connected to the AFS namespace, a volume looks just like directory; a process or application can change directories into it and then create new files. In a sense, volumes are logical disk partitions and can be attached to names in the file system just like disks can. But while they may act like a logical partition, they are physical entities in the system. Much of an AFS administrator's life will revolve around volume management.

VOLUME OPERATIONS

During the initial set up of the AFS servers, the Transarc installation process makes sure that we create a first volume named root.afs. There are many naming conventions practiced by the AFS community, and having the first volume named root.afs is one of them. Volume names can contain up to 31 characters and can be constructed of any combination of lower- or uppercase letters, numbers, and the punctuation characters "-", "_", and ".". The only other restriction of volume names is that the name cannot be completely composed of digits because it would be indistinguishable from a volume identification number.

During the operation of certain volume commands, the server processes will automatically append certain well-known suffixes, such as .backup, or

.readonly. Because these processes silently truncate a volume name if it gets too long, it is wise to make sure that the names are meaningful and 22 or fewer characters long (22 characters plus 9 characters for .readonly makes 31 characters). In fact, the volume creation command will refuse to make a volume with a name longer than 22 characters.

To create a volume, use the volume operations command vos; most volume management uses this command suite. Remember that almost all management tasks are run from an administrator's desktop computer via client programs. These programs interact with the remote AFS services as needed and rely on the strong authentication provided by Kerberos.

In the command examples below, you'll notice that the shell prompt is $. The commands are not run by a UNIX superuser but, in general, by a regular UNIX user who has also authenticated with AFS as a member of the system administrator's group. The precise authentication level needed for each command is spelled out in detail in the AFS command reference manuals; administration authentication is discussed in Chapter 9 and a summary of privileges needed for each command is presented in Appendix A. For now, we can quickly get authenticated as an AFS administrator, an identity we created during the cell installation, via klog:

```
$ klog afsadmin
Password:
```

The basic command to create a volume looks like this:

```
$ vos create -server fs-one -partition /vicepa -volume example.vol
```

Before going any further, let's examine this command-line interface. Almost all of Transarc's commands follow a strict usage format. After the name of the command, in this case, vos, a subcommand specifies exactly which action is to be performed, in this case create to make a new volume. Most commands accept a help subcommand, which displays all of the subcommands available along with a brief sentence describing their use. To help find exactly which of possibly many subcommands is appropriate, an apropos subcommand searches the descriptive sentences to find matching items.

```
$ vos apropos new
create:   create a new volume
```

After the subcommand, you may need additional options and arguments. You can list the options for a particular subcommand with the `help` subcommand.

```
$ vos help create
vos create: create a new volume
Usage: vos create -server <machine name> -partition <partition
name>
-name <volume name> [-maxquota <initial quota (KB)>] [-cell <cell
name>]
[-noauth ] [-localauth ] [-verbose ] [-help ]
```

For more detailed information on the subcommands, see the on-line UNIX manual pages which should have been copied over during installation. Rather than collect all the text on all the subcommands into a single man page, Transarc has separated each subcommand into its own page. The naming convention used to read a page is to join the command and subcommand with an underscore, as in man `vos_create`.

While these manual pages contain in-depth usage suggestions, the command-line help text is the easiest place to find information on what operations a command can perform. Because of the internal coding conventions followed by Transarc, you can be assured that the output of a `help` subcommand presents exactly what subcommands and options are really supported.

Furthermore, the coding conventions allow you to omit option names, such as `-server`, if you give the corresponding argument in the same order as the options are printed in the help line. For the create subcommand, as long as the `-server`, `-partition`, and `-name` mandatory arguments are provided in that order, the option words themselves can be dropped. Omitting options is how most administrators run AFS commands on the command line. However, when writing shell scripts or other programs that use AFS commands, make sure to spell out all options in full just in case Transarc changes the order of options or adds new options that have similar prefixes.

One last abbreviation allows file server partitions to be abbreviated: because all partitions must begin with a prefix of `/vicep`, a partition named `/vicepa` can be abbreviated as `vicepa`, `a`, or even `1`, for the first possible volume.

In the following examples, the qualifying options are dropped and the partitions are abbreviated; the text will make the meaning of the various arguments clear. After all, most of the arguments are only going to be servers, such as fs-one or db-one, partitions, such as a or b, volume names, or path names. With this in mind, the above command would then be typed interactively as:

```
$ vos create fs-one  a  example.vol
Volume 536870937 created on partition /vicepa of fs-one
```

After the create subcommand, the arguments are a machine name, partition, and the volume name. This machine and partition must refer to an existing AFS file server machine installed as described in Chapter 3.

The response shows that the volume was created and displays the server and partition name as well as the volume identification number. This number is of little interest to general administration and, in this instance, only serves to confirm that AFS has indeed finished the work needed to create the volume.

Information about the volume can be extracted with the following command.

```
$ vos examine example.vol
example.vol                        536870937 RW           2 K  On-line
    fs-one /vicepa
    RWrite   536870937 ROnly        0 Backup        0
    MaxQuota        5000 K
    Creation     Sat Mar 29 09:14:37 1997
    Last Update Sat Mar 29 09:14:37 1997
    0 accesses in the past day (i.e., vnode references)

    RWrite: 536870937
    number of sites -> 1
       server fs-one partition /vicepa RW Site
```

The output of the volume examine command describes in a rather verbose and seemingly unstructured manner much of the internal bookkeeping information for this volume. The first line repeats the volume name, example.vol, and reports the identification number, RW, to indicate that the volume is a read-write volume, the current size, 2 kilobytes, and on-line indicating that the file and volume server are able to process read and write requests.

The next few lines are indented and show more detailed information about the volume. The second line prints the server and partition name; the third, the volume identification numbers for the read-write master volume, as well as placeholders for the currently nonexistent read-only replica and backup versions of the volume; the fourth, the maximum quota limiting the amount of data stored in the volume; the fifth and sixth lines are timestamps stating when the volume was created and last updated with data; and the seventh line attempts to show how many times during the previous day that file data in the volume was accessed.

The final stanza is really a small table which shows exactly how and where this volume is replicated. Because this volume has just been created, there is no replication information available: the table reports that only the read-write master volume is available.

As more of the AFS command suite is described, you may wonder why certain commands insist on including a volume's location information—a specific server and partition name—where other commands do not. In the volume creation command, location information is clearly necessary because the operation is designed to actually create a real AFS volume on server disks. This command manufactures a volume with a physical volume header on a particular server's disk partition and inserts this information into the volume location database, the VLDB.

On the other hand, the volume examine command needs no location information; the command queries the VLDB of one of the known database servers and prints out the information returned.

Now that the volume is created, it can be connected to any AFS path name with the file services command, fs. It may seem odd that the fs command suite rather than vos is used to make volume connections into the AFS namespace but no real volume management is taking place. The operation just inserts some data into the specified directory structure much as the creation of a symbolic link doesn't make a new file but just makes a pointer to a file. The command is:

```
$ fs mkm /afs/example example.vol
$ ls /afs
example
$ fs lsmount /afs/example
'/afs/example' is a mount point for volume '#example.vol'
```

Again, you can see that no location information is needed to connect a path in the file namespace with a given AFS volume. The entire purpose of the AFS system is to make sure that every client desktop sees the same file data. AFS fulfills this goal by querying the volume location server to find the current home for the volume and reading or writing file data to that server. Though the subcommand is mkm, which stands for make mount, in this chapter we use the term *connection* to distinguish the common, lightweight, lazily evaluated AFS

lookup mechanism from the per-client, heavyweight, and relatively static
UNIX mount command.

The exact path name used as the connection is up to you: here the volume
name is example.vol, but the connection point is example. There's no
restriction on the name of the connection point: the linkage to the underlying
volume is hidden inside the visible directory name. And there's no restriction
on the location of the volume's data; the parent volume root.afs may be
stored on one disk while other volumes may be on any other server.

Also, note that the path name, /afs/example, did not exist prior to the
fs mkm command being run. In UNIX, when a disk partition is mounted into
the file namespace, a directory must be created before the mount is made. In
AFS, making a connection between a path name and a volume creates the path
name as a byproduct.

(Long-time AFS administrators will worry that these initial examples do
not follow the namespace conventions of the AFS community. Later in this
chapter we'll discuss how to create a normal-looking cell; these conventions are
important when making connections to other cells around the world. But the
internals of AFS know nothing of the conventions. Right now, let's concentrate
on the functionality of volumes and connections.)

The command fs lsmount lists the volume name connected to a path
with a somewhat verbose English sentence. This is typical of Transarc's command output; it requires some clever script writing to parse the sentence and
extract the relevant information from the command output.

As the connection information is stored in the file system itself, clients contact the appropriate servers as a matter of course when navigating in AFS. And
this means that all client workstations see and retrieve data from the new volume when they access the new directory, /afs/example.

```
$ ls -ld /afs/example
drwxr-xr-x   2 afsadmin staff         2048 Mar 29 09:15 /afs/example
$ ls /afs/example
$
```

This unexciting demonstration actually shows off the power of AFS. Any
AFS client that wishes to examine the data inside this directory must retrieve the
data from some remote server. AFS doesn't store the location information in the
connection point but rather stores the volume name; when crossing into a new
volume, each client will ask the volume location database about the volume,
find out which file server stores that volume's data, and then query that

machine to get the data. Though there happens to be no data in that directory—
it was created just a few minutes ago—everything that makes AFS an enterprisewide distributed file system had to occur to get access to this new directory.

Note that there are no maps that must be pushed out, nor do any administrative commands need to be run on remote desktops. AFS clients get to volume data by finding out, on the fly, which volumes constitute the namespace.
Once the connection is made, all AFS clients will see the new directory name
because AFS servers guarantee to tell a client when new data is available.
Because all clients get connected to the local cell through the well-known path,
/afs, and all changes to the namespace are seen by all clients, therefore only a
single file namespace is visible to clients.

This single namespace can be a drawback for some. But it is relatively easy
to use local client operations (e.g., symbolic links) to generate per-client views
of parts of the namespace. The great benefit is that whatever special purpose
paths may be constructed for a particular client, there will still be access to the
same cellwide namespace visible to all clients. In the new world of distributed
computing, it is no small blessing to have at least one namespace that can be
guaranteed available to all clients.

Additionally, this single namespace scales well because it is trivial to
extend it as broadly or deeply as desired. Volumes can be created on any file
server that has disk space available, and that volume can then be attached to
any point in the file tree. This can certainly be managed with NFS automounter
or NetWare's client maps, but note the efficiency of AFS: the single fs mkm
operation is all that is needed to let all clients in the cell (or, actually, the Internet) know about and get to the file data.

After you have created a volume, you can run several basic administrative
commands.

```
$ vos rename example.vol example.one
Renamed volume example.vol to example.one
$ vos remove fs-one a example.one
Volume 536870937 on partition /vicepa server fs-one deleted
```

Again, note which commands require location (server and partition
names) information and which do not. The rename subcommand simply
changes the name associated with the internally managed volume identification number. No change is made to the actual volume on the disk, only to the
data in the volume location database.

But note, because volume connections are made between an AFS path name and a volume name, renaming a volume can cause clients to not find file data. A client trying to traverse into /afs/example will look up the home location for the volume named example.vol—that was the volume name which was connected to the path name; the volume location databases will now correctly claim to know nothing about that volume. This may be exactly what you desire to happen; otherwise, you've just made an administrative mistake.

This example demonstrates an important management principle of AFS. Regarding volumes and files, there are three places data is stored to provide distributed file services: the VLDB—replicated on multiple servers; the physical volume data—stored on file servers in vice partitions; the files, directories, and connections to other volumes—real data stored within the volumes themselves.

Different commands operate on different pieces of this system: Volume creation makes a real volume on a server and adds that information to the location database; the fs mkm command adds a connection point to a volume in an existing directory. Renaming a volume just changes one piece of data in the location database without changing any connection information or modifying volume headers on disk at all.

The final command in this small example is the deletion of a volume with the remove subcommand. This command will make changes to all of the management databases: the location database will be altered by removing the specified volume's name and information and the volume, and, therefore, the volume's files and directories, will be deleted from a server and partition.

Upon successful completion of the vos remove command, all of the AFS database information will be synchronized, no location information will point from a volume to a specific server, nor will the server still hold that volume's file data. But one piece of information remains—the connection between the name /afs/example and the now-nonexistent volume example.vol. If you try to list the directory now, you'll be quickly told that no place in AFS stores the data.

```
$ ls /afs/example
/afs/example: No such device
```

To help guard against connecting to nonexistent volumes, the creation of such a connection results in a warning being displayed, though the connecting directory is still created.

```
$ fs mkm /afs/demo demo.vol
fs: warning, volume demo.vol does not exist in cell hq.firm
$ ls /afs/demo
/afs/demo: No such device
```

Many commands can be used to query AFS and each may access a different piece of the system to display administrative information derived from internal databases, server disks, or volume data. Here, three commands query file servers.

```
$ vos listpart fs-one
The partitions on the server are:
     /vicepa      /vicepb
Total: 3
$ vos partinfo fs-one
Free space on partition /vicepa: 1029576 K blocks out of total 1031042
Free space on partition /vicepb: 1029576 K blocks out of total 1031042
$ vos listvol fs-one
Total number of volumes on server fs-one partition /vicepa: 1
root.afs                              536870912 RW            5 K On-line

Total volumes onLine 1 ; Total volumes offLine 0 ; Total busy 0

Total number of volumes on server fs-one partition /vicepb: 0

Total volumes onLine 0 ; Total volumes offLine 0 ; Total busy 0
```

Three commands, listpart, partinfo, and listvol extract information about a specific server, partition, and volume on disk. They do not query the volume location database but get their data from a specific file server.

The listpart subcommand prints out a brief line of volume information for each named partition or (if no partition is named) all partitions on a server.

The partinfo subcommand prints out an even more succinct summary of a server's partition usage. This information is most convenient when you are trying to decide which server's partitions have the most free space before creating a volume expected to contain a certain number of files.

The listvol subcommand prints out data gleaned from the volume headers stored on a file server. The volserver process on each file server machine keeps track of data concerning all the volumes stored on disk. The complete volume header includes the volume name, with full .readonly or .backup extension, the type of the volume, the numeric identification number, any identifiers for related volumes, such as read-only, the current size of the volume in kilobytes, the size quota of the volume, the volume creation date, the date that the volume data was last updated, and the number of times that the volume has been accessed recently.

AN EXAMPLE VOLUME

Let's look at a straightforward example of volume administration and see more precisely how files and directories are handled by AFS. The following commands will create a new volume, connect it to the file tree, and populate it with some data.

```
$ mkdir /afs/tmp
$ vos create fs-one a sample.vol
Volume 536870943 created on partition /vicepa of fs-one
$ fs mkm /afs/tmp/sample sample.vol
$ ls /afs/tmp
sample
```

We start by making a directory underneath /afs. Although we're in the AFS file namespace, there's absolutely no reason for every directory to be connected to a new volume. As you create your own file tree, you'll find that the topmost levels are often related to new volumes, but there's only social conventions to enforce this layout.

A new volume is then created and connected to the namespace at the directory /afs/tmp/sample. You can enter the directory and create new files and subdirectories as desired.

```
$ cd /afs/tmp/sample
$ date > foo
$ date > bar
$ mkdir d
$ date > d/baz
$ ls -1R
.:
total 4
-rw-r--r--   1 afsadmin staff          29 Mar 29 13:00 bar
drwxr-xr-x   2 afsadmin staff        2048 Mar 29 13:00 d
-rw-r--r--   1 afsadmin staff          29 Mar 29 13:00 foo

./d:
total 0
-rw-r--r--   1 afsadmin staff          29 Mar 29 13:00 baz
```

Once the volume `sample.vol` is connected to the file namespace, navigation in the `/afs` tree is performed just as any other NFS or local directories are traversed, and files are created by using whatever tools fit your purposes. In this case, command-line tools are used, but AFS works equally well with any graphical browsers or file managers.

(The files created in this example are owned by the user `afsadmin`, because that is the creator's current authentication. This identity is used by the AFS `fileserver` process as the owner of any file data created by the user. Chapter 7 discusses file ownership and permissions in more detail.)

All file and directory data—everything visible through normal user-level operations—winds up being stored in a volume. During the installation of the first file server, you created the first volume, `root.afs`, which is normally assumed to be connected to the AFS namespace at `/afs`. Where and how you create and attach other volumes to the namespace is entirely at your discretion. To a certain point, you don't have to make any other volumes; all the files and directories under `/afs` will simply live in `root.afs`. But by creating more volumes, you break a large set of data into manageable pieces and allow the use of other AFS tools, such as per-volume replication.

The only size limit to an AFS volume is the size of the underlying disk partition. For many years, most UNIX operating systems limited the size of a partition to two gigabytes. Now, many mechanisms can be used to manipulate disks with much larger partitions and partitions can even be built on top of striped, concatenated, or mirrored disks. A `vice` partition used for AFS volume storage can use these mechanisms or other hardware-based backends for increased reliability or performance; Chapter 9 looks into some of the issues involved. But for now, all we are concerned about is the standard UNIX file system in which the volumes exist.

Whatever the effective limit on volume sizes, most volumes in an average cell will be fairly small, on the order of 10 to 100 megabytes. This is simply a convenience. It is natural in AFS to have a single volume per user's home directory, per project development area, per software package, and per operating system module. Most cells will contain several hundred, if not thousands of, volumes. Several users or projects can certainly share a volume, which would lead to a much smaller volume population, but because a volume has a storage quota, it is fairer to subdivide shared areas into individual volumes. And with finer-grained subdivisions of the entire organization file namespace, it becomes easier to perform certain management tasks. For example, if users each have their own home volume, moving volumes to appropriate servers as users move from department to department becomes a simple operation. And having more, smaller volumes makes it possible to redistribute the used file space among all file servers, a task that can even be automated.

In practice, the added flexibility gained through thoughtful divisions of the file namespace gives AFS much of its power. On the other hand, with hundreds of volumes, there may be times when a volume is incorrectly administered. The only cure is to adhere to strict naming conventions; although there may be thousands of volumes in a large organization, there may only be five to ten types of volumes, each having a very regular pattern to its name and a well-defined path name to which it is connected.

In the simple example above, two AFS volumes are of concern to us, `root.afs` and `sample.vol`. Underneath the `/afs` directory, which is stored in the `root.afs` volume, we create a directory `tmp`. Because new data is being added to a volume, any other clients that had accessed `/afs` and had cached that directory's data will be contacted and told that new data is available. Beneath the `/afs/tmp` directory, more data is added to the file system, in this case, a connection to the volume `sample.vol`. In the `/afs/tmp/sample` directory, some small files and subdirectories are created. These will be stored inside the `sample.vol` volume on whichever file server happens to be hosting that volume.

Because disk space is cheap but not free, AFS allows an administrator to impose a quota on the number of kilobytes allowable in any given volume. Because all data stores are allocated to a specific volume in AFS, the system is able to track total disk space usage on a per-volume basis. When created, each volume has a default quota of 5 megabytes. This quota can be changed by an administrator as needed.

```
$ fs listquota /afs/tmp/sample
Volume Name              Quota    Used    % Used    Partition
sample.vol               5000      7        0%         0%
$ fs setquota /afs/tmp/sample 100000
$ mkfile 20M /afs/tmp/sample/bigFile
$ ls -l /afs/tmp/sample/bigFile
-rw-r--r--   1 afsadmin staff     20971520 Mar 29 13:06 /afs/tmp/sample/bigFile
$ fs listquota /afs/tmp/sample
Volume Name              Quota    Used    % Used    Partition
sample.vol               100000   20487     20%         8%
```

Here, the `sample.vol` volume has the default quota of 5,000 kilobytes or almost 5 megabytes. The `setquota` subcommand increases the allowable quota to 100,000 kilobytes or almost 100 megabytes. (To be precise, you'd have to set the quota to 102,400 kilobytes to equal 100 megabytes.) If desired, you can use a quota of 0 kilobytes to turn off quota limits on the volume, which means, in practice, that the amount of storage permitted is limited only by the available space on the `vice` partition. Next, a standard UNIX utility `mkfile` creates a file with a fixed size, 20 megabytes. You can see that the volume quota now shows 20 percent usage while the partition, at only 8 percent usage, has much more space left.

Quotas are an effective management tool to delegate responsibility for data ownership to the users. In many companies, the impression is that disk space is an unlimited resource and effectively free. When disk space inevitably runs out, an uproar reaches the administration staff which must hunt down the largest sets of files, identify their owners, and persuade those owners to delete any egregious offenders. In AFS, the use of quotas permits administrators to proactively manage disk space: by putting a set of users' volumes on a particular partition and assigning each a quota, administrators can know that no individual user can use up disk space that belongs to another user. Although one user will eventually fill up his home volume with his own data, that problem will not stop others from continuing with their work. An administrator can help the user delete some data, or increase the quota, or—as we'll see later in this chapter—can even move the volume, in toto, to another, more spacious, partition.

The `quota` subcommand illustrates another odd feature of the AFS command set. Certain commands, especially in the `fs` command suite, perform operations on volumes, and yet the options to the command take a path name as their argument. This makes no difference to AFS because only a single volume provides storage for any given path name. This implies that the policies you create for naming volumes and path names are very important. There are usually fewer than a dozen kinds of volume names and places where those volume types get connected; limiting the number of volume policies makes it easy for administrators to remember which volumes are connected to what paths, and vice versa.

With the built-in quotas and accounting for disk space enabled by AFS, it is even possible to charge-back users of the file system for services rendered. Though such a scheme is heavily dependent on the politics and internal economics of an institution, at least the data is easily collectible. Of course, for certain uses or certain users, no predefined quota limit is preferable: setting a quota to zero allows the volume to grow as large as possible according to the underlying partition device drivers.

And just as airlines often book more passengers on a plane flight than there are seats available, AFS administrators often allocate larger quotas for all the volumes on a given partition than the partition could possibly hold if all volumes were filled to capacity. For example, you might create a dozen user volumes, each with a quota of 100 megabytes and all residing on a single 1 gigabyte partition, an overbooking of 200 megabytes. As long as other disk monitoring tools check for space shortages, this overbooking can allow some of these users to reach their quota limit without bothering the other users and without causing you to recalculate quotas for each set of partitions' volumes.

Figure 4-1 illustrates the result of these commands on the server disks. The view is of the internals of the partition in which the volumes were created and of the internal links between the volume and its files. If you print a directory listing of the `vice` partitions, only small (76-byte) files will be seen, one for each volume stored in the partition and each named after its numerical identification number.

```
$ cd /vicepa
$ ls
V0536870934.vol   V0536870943.vol   lost+found
$ ls -l
total 20
-rw-------   1 root      other        76 Mar 29 08:41 V0536870934.vol
-rw-------   1 root      other        76 Mar 29 09:53 V0536870943.vol
drwx------   2 root      root       8192 Mar 28 17:40 lost+found
```

The actual files and directories that are stored in an AFS cell cannot be seen from a user's view of the partition. Internal to the partition, all of the data is stored in the file server's native disk file system format, with inodes pointing to directory and file data and additional inodes pointing to access control list information. (The `lost+found` directory is a normal UNIX file system artifact and is not related to AFS.)

Figure 4-1 shows both volumes as named files on the disk partition. In each are directories, files, and subdirectories. Not shown are the pointers between the file names and the disk blocks storing the file data. Notice how the volumes are linked together: the `root.afs` volume, with volume identification number `536870934` has stored inside it a directory entry `sample` that

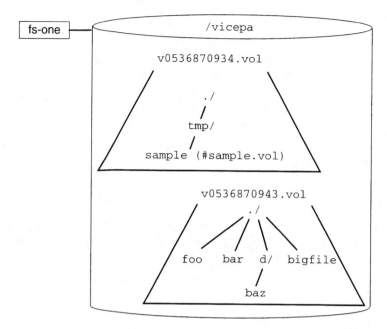

Figure 4-1 Internal View of AFS `vice` Partition

points to a volume name, `sample.vol`. This volume, number `536870943`, doesn't know what its name is in the file system, nor does any database in AFS know. The only connection between the two is that made by the namespace entry `sample`.

Returning to the disk partition, except for the oddly named directories and the fact that the volume's file names are not visible in the standard UNIX directory structure, this is a fairly ordinary UNIX file system. As most of these details are hidden from users and even administrators, there is little that can be done to manipulate AFS files from the outside. Don't forget that the vendor's file system check program, `fsck`, needs to be changed (normally during the installation of an AFS server) so that it doesn't corrupt the file system by imagining that the invisible files should be given temporary names and relinked into the `lost+found` directory.

Otherwise, ordinary UNIX administration commands can be used as needed to examine the `vice` partitions, although there is little to be done that is not handled by the AFS command suite. For example, the `vos partinfo` command is almost the same as the standard UNIX `df` administration command.

```
$ rsh fs-one df -k /vicepa
Filesystem                 kbytes    used    avail capacity  Mounted on
/dev/dsk/c0t1d0s4          1145592   1466 1029576     1%     /vicepa
$ vos partinfo fs-one a
Free space on partition /vicepa: 1029576 K blocks out of total 1031042
```

Note that the total size reported by the partinfo command is equivalent to the used plus the avail kilobytes reported by the df command. The total kbytes which df reports includes some extra spare space kept internally by the server operating system.

BACKUP VOLUMES

The illustration of a volume's internal structure helps to explain what AFS means by a *backup volume*. The adjective backup is a misnomer. While it is tangentially related to the archival process, a *backup volume* is really a read-only snapshot of a volume's contents. Let's run a few more commands and then look at the results.

```
$ vos backup sample.vol
Created backup volume for sample.vol
$ fs mkm /afs/tmp/sample.bak sample.vol.backup
$ ls /afs/tmp/sample /afs/tmp/sample.bak
/afs/tmp/sample:
bar       bigFile  d           foo

/afs/tmp/sample.bak:
bar       bigFile  d           foo
```

The vos backup command performs several operations: First, it finds the location of the named volume and creates a new volume with the same name and a suffix of .backup on the same server and the same partition as the original. Rather than copy all of the original volume's file data, the servers copy only pointers to the data. For experienced UNIX administrators, the effect is similar to making a new directory containing hard links to the file data.

This new backup volume, sample.vol.backup, is a first-class volume to AFS. In other words, it has a name, a volume identification number, and a physical existence on disk. Most commands that accept a volume name can be given a backup volume name, and the expected operation will be performed. For example, the next command in the above scenario, fs mkm mounts the backup volume in the namespace, giving its contents a path name of its own. Just as access to the path name /afs/tmp/sample will access files in the volume `sample.vol`, so `/afs/tmp/sample.bak` will access files in `sample.vol.backup`.

Right now, the backup volume points to the original volume data, so listing both paths shows the same data. Now, see what happens when we access the original volume and make some changes to its files.

```
$ rm /afs/tmp/sample/bar
$ date > /afs/tmp/sample/newFile
$ ls /afs/tmp/sample
bigFile   d           foo    newFile
$ ls /afs/tmp/sample.bak
bar       bigFile   d        foo
```

The first list directory command shows us that the original volume's files have been changed as expected. The second list directory command shows that the backup volume still has pointers to the original data—the deleted file still exists. Figure 4-2 shows what the internal pointers now look like.

Because the backup command just copies the pointers to the file data and does not copy the file data itself, a backup volume is quite cheap; it takes up very little disk space (just enough to hold the copies of the pointers) and it takes very little time to make. Also, while the pointers are being copied, the original volume is locked against any changes by users, so the backup volume consists of a frozen snapshot of a volume, a completely consistent and static view of the volume's contents for a particular moment in time.

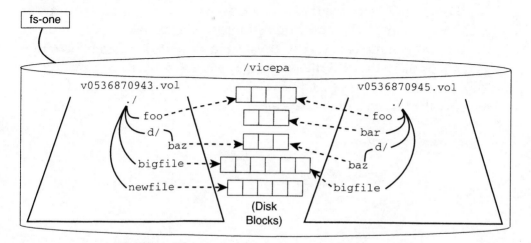

Figure 4-2   Internal View of `vice` Partition with Backup Volume

This ability to snapshot a volume is why the `/afs/tmp/sample.bak` directory still contains the file bar, which was deleted from the read-write master after the backup volume was snapped.

Not quite every AFS command can operate on backup volumes as simply as with the original. For example, you can use the `vos create` command to make a volume with a name like `tmp.backup` but doing so doesn't make the volume a backup volume. And because real backup volumes point to the same data as the original volume, the backup volumes must exist on the same server and partition as the original. Again, this is not unlike a UNIX hard link to a file, which can only exist on the same partition as the original file. (Note that the volume backup command does not have any options to specify a different partition or server.) And, finally, you can see here that the backup volume is read-only:

```
$ date > /afs/tmp/sample.bak/anotherFile
/afs/tmp/sample.bak/anotherFile: cannot create
$ rm /afs/tmp/sample.bak/bigFile
rm: /afs/tmp/sample.bak/bigFile not removed: Read-only file system
```

These backup volumes are an important feature of AFS and are used regularly to provide users with on-line access to a snapshot of their home directory files. Users backup volumes can be mounted once in some well-known area, either one set aside for all backups or perhaps inside the home directory itself. Every night an administrative script can snapshot the volumes which store the home directories. Then, during the day, user's can easily retrieve files which they have accidentally deleted by simply copying the file from the backup directory. Having user's restore this data themselves can drastically reduce the need for administrator intervention after simple typing mistakes.

The backup volume is normally considered as part of an administrative package with its master read-write volume. The `vos examine` command displays some information on both. Otherwise, the `listvol` subcommand can be used to verify the existence of the backup volume.

```
$ vos examine sample.vol
sample.vol                           536870943 RW        20487 K  On-line
    fs-one /vicepa
    RWrite   536870943 ROnly          0 Backup  536870945
    MaxQuota      100000 K
    Creation     Sat Mar 29 09:53:50 1997
    Last Update Sat Mar 29 10:29:38 1997
    1017 accesses in the past day (i.e., vnode references)
```

```
        RWrite: 536870943      Backup: 536870945
        number of sites -> 1
            server fs-one partition /vicepa RW Site
$ vos listvol fs-one vicepa
Total number of volumes on server fs-one partition /vicepa: 3
root.afs                        536870934 RW          6 K On-line
sample.vol                      536870943 RW      20487 K On-line
sample.vol.backup               536870945 BK      20487 K On-line

Total volumes onLine 2 ; Total volumes offLine 0 ; Total busy 0
```

In the examine subcommand output, you can see that the backup volume identification number, in line three, has been filled in. (As a matter of fact, the backup and read-only volume identification numbers are preallocated so that every newly created read-write volume is assigned a number three more than the last.) In the listvol view of the volume headers on the file server's partition, you can see that the read-write volume sample.vol holds 20 megabytes of data, and it appears as though the backup volume sample.vol.backup holds another 20 megabytes. Actually, the backup volume points to the same 20 megabytes as the read-write master.

In AFS, the term *clone volume* is often used interchangeably with backup volume. More properly, a clone volume is the internal name used for a volume composed of pointers to another volume's data. As we'll see when we examine how to move a volume from server to server, these internal clone volumes are used occasionally by AFS when it needs to make a snapshot of a volume for its own use.

Backup volumes can be used to provide users with access to a snapshot of their home directory files and also to create a stable image from which to perform archiving for other group or development volumes. In both of these cases, administrators often need to make backup volumes for a large set of volumes. The vos backupsys command can be used with an argument that is a regular expression used to match one or more volumes in the system. For example, if we had ten users with their own home directory contained in their own volume and named, as is customary, with a prefix of user, then backup volumes for all users can be created with:

```
$ vos backupsys user
done
Total volumes backed up: 10; failed to backup: 0
```

This one command will search the volume database to find all read-write volumes having names with the given prefix and will then proceed to make backup volumes for all of them. Even with a large number of matching volumes, making backups for the volumes will take a very short time and consume very little disk space. Many sites make backup volumes of all volumes in the system; even if all backup volumes are not made available in the file system all the time, it is somewhat easier to create all of them than worry about the exact regular expression needed for a particular subset.

The `backupsys` subcommand is often added as a `bos cron` job or even a UNIX `cron` job so that backup volumes are made every midnight. There is only one backup volume for each read-write, so every time this command runs, only a snapshot of the current files in a volume is saved. If you delete a file on Monday, the backup volume made on Sunday night will still be holding onto that file data. But on Monday night, the new version of the backup volume will be a snapshot of the current contents of the volume files; because the file in question has been deleted, the new backup volume skips over it, and the deleted file is finally, truly, deleted.

The drawback to backup volumes is that while they do not take up much space (they are just copies of pointers to file data), they do make it more difficult to delete space. For instance, given the above example, backup volumes of all user volumes are made every midnight. If for some reason a large file, perhaps a process core file, in someone's home directory needs to be deleted to free up disk space on the volume's partition, you might try simply deleting the core file. Yet the backup volume would still retain a pointer to the file, and therefore the operating system (which is still managing the partition's file system) would not release the file's space. Because the backup volume is read-only, you cannot remove the file there. How then to remove the file? The solution is simple: make a new backup volume. This solution works because the previous backup volume's pointers to data will now be zeroed out, causing the last link to our hypothetical core file to be dropped and the data to be cleaned out.

Data kept in a backup volume is not counted against a user's quota. If during the day, a user creates a lot of data and fills up her volume, all of that data will be caught in the nightly backup snapshot. On the next day, if much of the home directory data is deleted, the user can proceed to create a whole volume's worth of new data. Effectively, the user has access to the backup volume's quota of (read-only) data and the master volume's quota. This feature can be exploited by savvy users, but given a realistic scenario with regular volume snapshots taking place every night, can cause little damage.

Backup volumes are yet another instance where AFS provides functionality that simultaneously makes administrators' lives easier and more complicated. Backup volumes can reduce requests for archive file restoration, but explicit management policies must be implemented and advertised to make the feature useful.

MOVING VOLUMES

There is one AFS volume operation that, all by itself, makes the entire system worthwhile. When shown how to move a volume from one server's disk to another server on-line and transparently to active users of the volume, administrators are overjoyed. With such an effect, this operation deserves to be described in some detail. The command line is simple enough.

```
$ vos move sample.vol fs-one a fs-two a
WARNING : Deleting the backup volume 536870945 on the source ... done
Volume 536870943 moved from fs-one /vicepa to fs-two /vicepa
```

Naturally, a command that is going to move a volume needs location information; in this case, it needs arguments describing exactly where the named volume exists now and the server and partition to which it will be moved. But that's it: the volume and all of its contained files and directories have been moved from one AFS file server to another. Because AFS clients get access to files by querying the databases for volume locations and then querying the appropriate server, all clients will still be able to find the new location of this volume's data as a matter of course.

Note that because backup volumes are really only containers of pointers to the read-write volume data, when we moved the read-write volume data, the backup volume would have pointed to invalid areas of the partition. In this situation, the vos move operation deletes the old backup volume. If necessary, you should create a new backup volume at the read-write volume's new home.

As mentioned, clients have no trouble finding AFS files no matter which server the files are stored on. But even better, clients can access this volume even while it is being moved. To make this example interesting, let's initiate, on another AFS client, some processes that access the volume while we run the vos move command.

```
$ cd /afs/tmp/sample
$ while true
> do
> date > foo
> cat foo
> done
```

This trivial shell command will loop forever as fast as the date can be written to the AFS file system and then read and printed on the terminal display. Now that something is accessing the system, let's imagine that the file server needs to be rebooted because a disk is added, or that the user will be moving to a different building, or that the current disk is getting a little too full. Whatever the reason, the volume must be moved to a different server while a user is accessing the volume's file data. During the move, the shell command will print something like the following on the display:

```
. . .
Sat Mar 29 10:50:42 EST 1997
Sat Mar 29 10:50:42 EST 1997
Sat Mar 29 10:50:43 EST 1997
afs: Waiting for busy volume 536870943 (sample.vol) in cell hq.firm

Sat Mar 29 10:50:58 EST 1997
Sat Mar 29 10:50:58 EST 1997
. . .
```

Although there is a service delay during a few moments of volume transfer, the delay is actually quite small, irrespective of the volume's size. More importantly, note that the read and write operations returned successfully—no errors were reported by the commands. Though one of the write requests hung for a moment, all file services continued to function correctly throughout the volume movement.

The internal machinery to make all of this happen is not too difficult to understand. It simply makes use of all the volume techniques we've seen up to now:

1. The volume is locked during the creation of a clone volume. This clone is distinct from any backup volume and because it takes but a fraction of a second to create, the cloning causes hardly any interruption.
2. A volume is created at the destination site and a check is made to make sure that enough space exists for the move.
3. The clone of the original volume is then dumped and restored into the destination site.

The reason for dumping the clone rather than the original is that the original volume might be somewhat large. Without the clone, we would have to lock the original volume during the entire data move operation. By making a clone and copying it over, we can copy over the bulk of the volume's data in the background while a user continues to access the volume.

4. Once copied over, the clone volume has served its purpose and is deleted.

5. Because the copy operation will take a certain amount of time, the system must now copy over any new data which may have been written to the original volume. It locks the original volume and copies over any incremental changes to the destination site.

Although the copy of the clone might take a certain amount of time, it is expected that few changes will be made to the original volume during the copy and therefore copying the incremental changes will take a small amount of time. It is during this final stage of the move operation that the volume will become busy for a brief period and so a small delay might be seen by the user.

6. Once all changes have been made to the destination site, the new volume is brought on-line, the original volume is put off-line, the volume location database is updated, and the volume state is unlocked.

From now on, any future access to the volume will be sent to the new destination site. In our example, the write operation finishes successfully by writing to file server `fs-two`, and the shell command loop continues.

7. Finally, the AFS system deletes the original volume along with any original backup that may have existed.

In our example, an AFS client happens to be writing and reading file data from the volume as it is being moved. At the beginning, the `vos move` operation is performing some administrative set up and copying over a clone of the volume. During this time, the client sees no change to the volume's availability. However, when the incremental changes are being copied over, one store operation will hang because the volume server on the source file server has set the volume state to busy.

The client sees that the volume is busy and will retry the store request every twenty seconds. Eventually, when the move operation finishes, the client's store request to the source file server will fail because the volume is no longer stored there. The client will immediately query the volume location

database for the new location of the volume and will send the storage request
to the destination file server. Although the user sees the write operation hang
for a brief moment, the key is that the operation succeeds—the shell command
that is writing some data to a file returns without error.

There is one step in the process that occurs before any movement of data
takes place; that step ensures that sufficient space is available on the destination
server for the volume move to succeed. In earlier versions of AFS, this check was
not performed, and the move operation would fail and would have to back out
of its transactions. Now, the check is done first and takes care of the problem in
most situations; however, during the move operation, a user could be creating
large files on the destination site and thereby still cause an out-of-space error.

Though the vos move command is robust and powerful, it does have to
perform a complex series of operations to complete its job. You might want to
use the -verbose option to watch the move operation; if any problems crop
up, you will have a better idea of what state the file server is left in.

```
$ vos move tmp.bar fs-one b fs-two a   -verbose
Starting transaction  on source volume 536870964 ... done
Cloning source volume 536870964 ... done
Ending the transaction on the source volume 536870964 ... done
Starting transaction on the cloned volume 536871006 ... done
Creating the destination volume 536870964 ... done
Dumping from clone 536871006 on source to volume 536870964 on destination ... done
Doing the incremental dump from source to destination for volume 536870964 ...  done
Deleting old volume 536870964 on source ... done
Starting transaction on the cloned volume 536871006 ... done
Deleting the clone 536871006 ... done
Volume 536870964 moved from fs-one /vicepb to fs-two /vicepa
```

The vos move command vividly demonstrates the specific design goal of
AFS: a distributed file system that can be efficiently managed. Although AFS
was engineered at a university, it is no academic exercise. The vos move command is a crucial tool needed by administrators as they manage disk farms and
servers. Without it, operators are forced to wait for off-hours before performing
necessary work, and users must put up with constant service outages. With this
command, centralized control of large-scale computing populations becomes
almost pleasurable.

THE VOLUME LOCATION DATABASE

The volume location database is clearly the heart of AFS. The vlserver process on the database servers manages a file holding the names, locations, and

miscellaneous statistics about all the volumes in the system. As we've seen, there are a few kinds of volumes used in AFS, but all types of volumes are based on an original volume, the read-write master. From that read-write volume there may be a backup volume or even multiple read-only replicas.

A few vos commands are available to read information out of the volume location database directly. The listvldb subcommand prints out all location data stored by the system.

```
$ vos listvldb

root.afs
    RWrite: 536870912
    number of sites -> 1
       server fs-one partition /vicepa RW Site

sample.vol
    RWrite: 536870943
    number of sites -> 1
       server fs-two partition /vicepa RW Site

Total entries: 2
```

Each entry is based on the read-write master volume. Only the name of the read-write is stored; the read-only and backup volumes have well-known suffixes (.readonly and .backup) automatically appended. Along with the volume name, each volume has its own numeric identifier. These identifiers are used internally to tag a particular volume, but most AFS commands also permit their use as arguments in place of the more memorable volume name. Note that each type of volume has its own number, which is usually assigned consecutively; if the read-write is volume N, the read-only is N+1, and the backup volume is N+2. As we'll see shortly, multiple read-only volumes share the same numeric identifier just as they share the same name.

The database also holds a counter of how many total sites are storing this volume's data; for each site, the exact file server name, vice partition, type of volume, and volume status are recorded. (If you're wondering where the backup volume for sample.vol went, it was deleted as a consequence of the volume move operation.)

Finally, a lock is available for each volume and maintained by the VLDB server. As various operations are taking place, the volume is locked so that other commands cannot intervene and corrupt the database.

The listvldb command does not query the file server system that is actually storing the data. You can see that this command shows no information about the size of the volume or its quota. The only data in the database is the name of the servers for the read-write and any read-only versions of the volume. You can append arguments to list volume location database information about a single volume, all volumes on a server, or all volumes on a server's partitions.

Whereas a listvldb command queries only the volume location database, the vos examine command queries both that database and the volume server, volserver, on the file server machine that is storing the read-write master. These queries are one reason that an examine command takes slightly longer to run than other informational commands.

Because the AFS volume location database is distinct from the physical volumes residing on disks in the vice partitions, the two can get out of synchronization. If certain vos operations are interrupted (perhaps due to a crash or network failure), it may be that the location database thinks that volumes exist in certain places but that the disks themselves contain different sets of volumes.

Most of the time, the volume location database will point to the correct set of file servers and partitions. Sometimes, the database may have incorrect entries, suggesting that a volume is on a particular server when it is not, or missing entries, when a volume is available from a server but is not listed in the database.

There are two mechanisms to manually fix either problem: you can use vos delentry to delete a single entry from the database, and vos zap to delete a volume from a disk. Neither command will change the other's data as it performs its deletion: delentry will not delete a volume and zap will not delete a database entry. When performing this direct surgery on AFS, don't forget that changes to the location database are simple modifications to some pointers, whereas using zap to delete a volume from disk will remove real data from the disk. The former can be corrected, the latter not without restoring data from an archive tape, if any.

Here is an example of a mismatch between a disk partition and the location database.

```
$ vos listvldb -server fs-two
VLDB entries for server fs-two

sample.vol
    RWrite: 536870943
    number of sites -> 1
        server fs-two partition /vicepa RW Site

another.vol
    RWrite: 536871001
    number of sites -> 1
        server fs-two partition /vicepa RW Site

Total entries: 2

$ vos listvol fs-two a
Total number of volumes on server fs-two partition /vicepa: 1
sample.vol                            536870943 RW        20487 K On-line

Total volumes onLine 2 ; Total volumes offLine 0 ; Total busy 0
```

You can see that, according to the location database, the read-write volume
another.vol in partition /vicepa on server fs-two is not actually stored
on the disk itself. Before fixing this problem, it would be wise to check into how
this happened; it's possible a volume move operation was interrupted or a disk
partition was restored abnormally. AFS does not have any mechanism for regularly auditing the system to determine if such an out-of-synchronization situation exists. You'll want to write a few scripts to check the listvol output
against the listvldb report. However the circumstance is discovered, it must
be fixed. One solution will be to simply delete the location data.

```
$ vos delentry fs-two a another.vol
$ vos listvldb
VLDB entries for server fs-two

sample.vol
    RWrite: 536870943
    number of sites -> 1
        server fs-two partition /vicepa RW Site

Total entries: 1
```

The vos suite includes two general purpose synchronization commands,
syncserv and syncvldb, that automatically perform certain fixes of mis-

matches. Take a moment to memorize which command does what because their purposes are easily confused:

- `vos syncvldb`—Scans the server `vice` partitions and adds to the location database any volumes that are found on disk but not in the database.
- `vos syncserv`—Reads the location database and checks the disk partitions for the existence of the volume. If the volume is not found on the indicated server, the entry will be deleted from the database.

These two operations are relatively safe in that neither will delete any irreplaceable file data from the disks themselves—they will only add or delete entries from the location database. In the worst case, only data in backup volumes may be deleted. If `syncvldb` finds two backup volumes for a single read-write volume, it deletes one of the backup volumes. Similarly, if `syncserv` finds that a backup volume is not on the same server and partition as the read-write, it deletes the orphan backup volume. But if two copies of a read-write volume are found, `syncvldb` does not choose one for deletion but simply prints out an error message; you'll have to manually choose which one to `zap`.

During most of these volume server operations, an entry in the database will be locked. If one of these commands is interrupted, this lock may remain. Subsequent commands that attempt to operate on the same volume will return with an error. When this situation happens, you can unlock the volume with `vos unlock`; all volume entries in the database can be unlocked en masse with `vos unlockvldb`.

Unfortunately, there's no way to tell the difference between a volume that is locked because of a problem with a `vos` operation and one locked because another administrator is running a valid though lengthy `vos` operation. With fewer active AFS administrators needed for a given site, it may be easier to distinguish between these possibilities. Otherwise, if the volume is small, you can be assured that no volume operation would take a long time; if the volume is still locked after half an hour, you might assume the lock has been orphaned. If the volume is particularly large, you might want to wait longer.

On the other hand, you can use `vos lock` to deliberately lock a volume to prevent volume operations from occurring. You can list information on all locked volumes with the `vos listvldb -locked` option.

The most common reason for the appearance of locked volumes is that a `vos` operation was interrupted during execution. This interruption can result in volumes remaining locked in the database, clones made during move operations left lying around on server partitions, or the location database getting out of synchronization with volumes on the partition. Depending on the scenario, you may have to synchronize the databases or zap some volumes to restore order to AFS.

REPLICATION

An AFS client spends its days asking the location database where a volume lives and then getting file data from the specified server. To provide automatic fail over from inaccessible servers, AFS enables you to create read-only copies of entire volumes. When a client reads data from a replicated volume, the location information returned to the client includes the names of all file servers storing read-only copies. If a client receives no response from one of the replica's servers, it will simply ask the next server in its list until it finds an available system.

Read-only replicas are not a substitute for disk mirroring or RAID systems. Instead, replicas provide alternate physical locations for copies of a given read-write volume so that the volume's data can continue to be available despite server or network outages. Normally, only those read-write volumes with infrequently changing data, such as system binaries, vendor packages, applications, development products, or just the top-level directories of volume connections, will be placed in volumes that are replicated.

All replicas of a read-write volume are read-only snapshots in much the same manner that backup volumes are snapshots. One difference is that backup volumes can exist only on the same disk partition as their master; replicas, on the other hand, can be stored on file servers anywhere in the cell.

One administrative advantage to these read-only replicas is that they are all guaranteed to be the same. When an administrator has finished polishing the contents of a read-write, the read-only copies can be explicitly updated. From then on, any changes to the master are written only to the master; it requires an explicit administrative command to re-release the changes to the replicas. And because the replicas are read-only, it is impossible to make changes to any one replica. Thus, AFS file replication integrates administration of client fail over with the task of making the fail over copies available.

To replicate a volume, you must first register the locations with the location database, then explicitly generate the copies. As an example, let's make sure that the topmost volume in our cell, root.afs, is maximally replicated.

```
$ vos addsite fs-one a root.afs
Added replication site fs-one /vicepa for volume root.afs
$ vos addsite fs-two a root.afs
Added replication site fs-two /vicepa for volume root.afs
$ vos listvldb root.afs
root.afs
    RWrite: 536870912
    number of sites -> 3
        server fs-one partition /vicepa RW Site
        server fs-one partition /vicepa RO Site
        server fs-two partition /vicepa RO Site
```

The vos addsite commands register the locations for the read-only replicas of the volume root.afs. As with the volume creation command, its
arguments are a fileserver name, a vice partition, and a volume name. This
registration need be done only once, whenever a new replication sites is added.
The listvldb command lists the contents of the location database for the
root.afs volume; it shows that the replica sites have been registered. Note
that there is no indication of the read-only volume identification number
because the data has not been copied over yet.

Once you've administered where a volume's data should be replicated,
you can update all of the replica sites with current copies of the volume date
with the release subcommand. This command performs the actual data copy
from the read-write master volume to all the registered read-only copies. The
release command accesses the VLDB to find out which file servers have been
assigned copies of the volume, contacts each file server machine, and checks
the volume's directories and files to bring the replicas up to date.

```
$ vos release root.afs
$ vos listvldb root.afs
root.afs
    RWrite: 536870912      ROnly: 536870913
    number of sites -> 3
        server fs-one partition /vicepa RW Site
        server fs-one partition /vicepa RO Site
        server fs-two partition /vicepa RO Site
$ vos listvol fs-one a
Total number of volumes on server fs-one partition /vicepa: 2
root.afs                          536870912 RW          9 K On-line
root.afs.readonly                 536870913 RO          9 K On-line

Total volumes onLine 2 ; Total volumes offLine 0 ; Total busy 0
$ vos listvol fs-two a
Total number of volumes on server fs-two partition /vicepa: 2
```

```
root.afs.readonly               536870913 RO            9 K On-line
sample.vol                      536870943 RW        20487 K On-line

Total volumes onLine 2 ; Total volumes offLine 0 ; Total busy 0
```

Now, the location database shows that the read-only volumes have been populated, and the `vos listvol` command, displaying volumes that physically exist on disk, lists the two new read-only volumes.

Note: For efficiency, the entire volume is not transmitted during each release; only changed files and directories are transmitted. Since version 3.4a, release operations are performed in parallel, so that incremental changes in up to five read-only copies can be updated simultaneously.

Now, when accessing the path `/afs`, a client workstation will access the volume location database, discover that the directory contents are stored in the volume `root.afs`, and realize that `root.afs` can be accessed through its replica volumes on either file server `fs-one` or `fs-two`. Knowing that all read-only copies of a single read-write master are the same, the client is free to retrieve a volume's file or directory data from any accessible replica.

In fact, broadly reliable access has been available only with AFS version 3.4a: prior to this version, if the read-write version was unavailable, read-only versions were unavailable. Now, clients will search for any read-only volumes no matter what the condition is of the read-write master.

If a client workstation reads data from one file server which is storing a read-only volume and fails to get a reply, it falls back to the next site on its list. Only when this list of read-only volumes is exhausted will the client report an error.

It may seem odd that the client will not make one last attempt to get the data from the read-write. To understand why, let's assume we have a volume full of an application's binary programs and that volume is replicated on two sites. If those two sites are unavailable, it seems reasonable to want the client to try to get the program data from the read-write. But recall that the replicas were created via an explicit release operation executed at an arbitrary time, e.g., when an administrator had decided that the master volume's data was ready for replication. After release, the read-write volume may very well have been edited with new versions of programs. AFS guarantees that all replica volumes are file-for-file and byte-for-byte duplicates of each other so clients can successfully fail over at any time during the reading of any information from one read-only to another. As the read-write is not guaranteed to be a duplicate, no fail over from read-only to read-write is permitted.

It's easy to force a failure and watch clients fail over. On a client, listing the
/afs directory requires reading data from one of the read-only versions of the
root.afs volume:

```
$ ls /afs
tmp
$ vos listvldb root.afs

root.afs
    RWrite: 536870912      ROnly: 536870913
    number of sites -> 3
        server fs-one partition /vicepa RW Site
        server fs-one partition /vicepa RO Site
        server fs-two partition /vicepa RO Site
```

As long as either fs-one or fs-two is available, access to data in the volume will succeed. We can use a bos command to shut down the servers on fs-
one (the command is described in more detail in Chapter 9). Once fs-one is
not running any AFS server processes, reading from the directory might produce a fail over event.

```
$ ls /afs
tmp
```

Of course, since we just read and cached the directory data in the previous
example, it is still available. Using cached data may not seem like a fail over
scenario, but it is a valuable mechanism by which a client is able to continue
working without worrying about servers, disks, and networks.

If some other user were to change the contents of this directory, our client
would be called back and told that the cached data was out of date. But we can
also force the data to be flushed from our cache with an fs subcommand. The
next listing of the directory will then have to be directed to an available server.

```
$ fs flush /afs
$ ls /afs
afs: Lost contact with file server 192.168.3.21 in cell hq.firm (all multi-homed
   ip addresses down for the server)
tmp
```

Once the cache is flushed, the next read request takes some time to return.
During this time, the client's kernel was waiting for a response from fs-one;
after about one minute, the request timed out, and the client then checked to see
if the volume's data was available from any other server. As the volume is

known to have read-only copies on fs-one and fs-two, the client requested the same data from fs-two. Though a somewhat forbidding message is printed on the terminal note that the list directory command has returned successfully. (As you can see, the client actually tried to access any other network interfaces available on the server; multihomed servers are described in Chapter 9).

Now that the client knows that fs-one is unavailable, it does not request any other read-only volumes' data from that server but sends further requests to other sites. Later, when contact with fs-one is reestablished, the client records this fact and uses fs-one as needed.

This fail over works well for replicated data. Nonreplicated data, such as a user's home directory, is subject to the availability of the single server in which the data is stored. Here, the /afs/tmp/sample directory is based on a non-replicated volume, sample.vol. With the sole server down, there's no way at this point to retrieve the data.

```
$ ls /afs/tmp/sample
afs: Lost contact with file server 192.168.5.22 in cell hq.firm (all multi-homed
    ip addresses down for the server)
/afs/tmp: Connection timed out
```

The "Connection timed out" message indicates a serious error with the client reading or writing data to AFS.

In general, the best practice is to replicate a volume as much as possible. Unfortunately, replication is limited to 11 copies for any read-write master. This is not a terrible inconvenience because a single read-only copy should be able to support several hundred clients (thanks to aggressive client caching). So, 11 replicas should support many thousand clients without even beginning to burden a cell with overloaded servers. If, however, because of network topologies or other concerns, particularly large cells need more than 11 read-only volumes, you can use a simple administrative hack of manually copying the master read-write data into multiple slave read-writes; each of the slave read-writes could then have its own 11 replicas.

To save storage space, an important optimization is performed for a read-only replica registered for the same server and partition as the read-write master. In this case, the co-located replica will be implemented via a clone volume, similar to a backup volume. This particular replica will therefore take up practically no space. This is the conventional practice for read-only volumes: the first registered replica is at the same site as the master; the others, full copies of the read-write volume data, are scattered around other file servers as dictated by the client workstation access patterns.

Volume replication also provides some measure of transaction control. When a volume is released to several replication sites, each site will either wind up with completely consistent data for the new volume or it will have the previous version of the volume. (Unfortunately, there's no transactional guarantee that all of the replicas will be updated or rolled back to the previous version.)

When replication begins, the volume location database marks each read-only version of the volume as being the "Old Release"; the read-write version is set to "New Release," because it holds the version of the volume data which will be copied to all the read-only volumes.

A temporary clone of the read-write volume is then made (similar to the temporary clone used during the vos move operation) and this release clone is then distributed to all read-only volume sites. As each read-only is updated successfully, it is marked as having the "New Release."

When all of the read-only sites have successfully completed the release and all have the "New Release" flag set, then all flags are cleared. Therefore, no release flags are normally seen when the volume location database is examined. But if errors occur during the volume release operation, you should check on the success of the release with vos examine.

```
$ vos release root.afs
Failed to start a transaction on the RO volume 3
Possible communication failure
The volume 536870912 could not be released to the following 1 sites:
                        fs-two /vicepa
VOLSER: release could not be completed
Error in vos release command. VOLSER: release could not be completed
$ vos listvldb root.afs
root.afs
    RWrite: 536870912     ROnly: 536870913     RClone: 536870913
    number of sites -> 3
        server fs-one partition /vicepa RW Site  -- New release
        server fs-one partition /vicepa RO Site  -- New release
        server fs-two partition /vicepa RO Site  -- Old release
```

In this example, the fileserver process on fs-two was temporarily stopped during the replication to simulate a crash. Note the results in the site definition block, the line-by-line detail for each version of the volume in the cell. Following some of the lines, the words "New release" or "Old release" indicate that the release operation failed at some point and that certain servers have the new version of the volume and other servers the previous version.

The usual reasons for partially completed replication are server failure, network failure, corrupt disk partitions, or AFS server process failures. You must use other techniques to determine which problem caused the failure: bos status to see if the servers are available, ping to check the network connectivity, etc. Once fixed, a subsequent vos release will update the replica sites that failed previously. When no "New release" or "Old release" flags are set in the volume location database, you can be assured that all read-only volumes contain the exact same set of files.

Note that AFS replication does not solve all replication needs. Read-write volumes, whether they're masters for read-only copies or just users' home volumes, have no built-in data mirroring of their own. It might be wise to store read-write volumes on RAID or other highly reliable storage for increased availability.

CLIENT PATH PREFERENCES

In a conventional AFS namespace, clients will exhibit a built-in prejudice to retrieve file data from any available read-only volumes. When given the option of fetching a file from the read-write master or any one of several read-only replicas, clients will generally choose to read from a replica.

This built-in bias makes sense because when reading data, a client would like to hedge its bets, so that if the current volume becomes inaccessible, it will have no problem asking any other available replica for data. Servers, too, understand that files in read-only volumes change less frequently than other files and, rather than establish callback guarantees on a file-by-file basis, the server establishes a callback for the read-only volume as a whole. Then, when the read-write master is released to the replicas, any client that has cached a file from a replica will get a short message from the server saying that the cached copy is invalid. This technique dramatically shortens the list of files that a server needs to track.

This read-only path preference depends on the exact layout of your AFS namespace. For the moment, let's assume that the prejudice for retrieving file data from read-only volumes is attempted every time a client encounters a new volume in the AFS namespace. After reaching a volume connection at some directory name, a client requests the locations for the read-write and any read-only volumes. If any read-only volumes are listed, the client will read the file data from one of them.

By convention, every AFS cell has a volume named `root.afs` connected to /afs; ours was created during the set up of our cell. Invariably, administrators will want to replicate this volume. Right from the start, a client will be reading data from one of the read-only volumes of `root.afs`. In our simple file tree described previously, the next connection point encountered, /afs/tmp/sample, pointed to a volume with no read-only replicas, so files had to be read from the read-write. Because this is a read-write volume, we have been able to write data into the directory.

A subtle but important aspect of the namespace has been glossed over here. Because of the bias toward getting data from read-only volumes, an AFS client when changing directory to /afs/tmp, will be in a read-only portion of the namespace. How then was the connection to the volume `sample.vol` made at /afs/tmp/sample? Any writes, including making volume connections, should have returned a permission-denied error.

The answer is obviously that the volume connection had to be created in the read-write version of the `root.afs` volume. During the initial set up of the cell, there were no read-only volumes, so the connection could have been done at that time. And, in fact, this scenario describes how the original cell's volumes are connected during installation. The `root.afs` volume is replicated only after the first few volumes are set up.

But once a volume is replicated, a client will get data from the read-only. The question is now, how are subsequent changes made to the topmost volume? One answer is to simply make a new volume connection in some writeable directory and to specify the -rw option to force clients to read and write data from the read-write volume.

```
$ cd /afs/tmp/sample
$ fs mkm root-afs   root.afs   -rw
$ fs lsmount root-afs
'root-afs' is a mount point for '%root.afs'
```

Here, we've made an explicit read-write volume connection in a writeable directory by using the -rw option to the fs mkm command. The lsmount command output isn't too verbose about this fact: read-write connections are denoted by the prefix % in the output, whereas general mount points, as default connections are formally called, have the prefix #. This is a simple idiom to read but tedious to automate. Someday, Transarc may supply more informative output or, even better, appropriate command return codes. For now, though, we're stuck with parsing the character string of the command output. After the connection is verified, we can change into this new directory and write a new file into the read-write master volume.

```
$ cd root-afs
$ date > newFile
$ ls
newFile  tmp
$ ls /afs
tmp
```

As the two directory listings show, while the read-write volume contains the new file data, the read-only copies of root.afs don't yet have the new data—read-only volumes are physically separate copies of read-write. This behavior allows an administrator to test changes to the read-write master before releasing the new version of the volume to the world.

```
$ vos release root.afs
Released volume root.afs successfully
$ ls /afs
newFile  tmp
```

When the volume is released, the changes are copied over to each read-only replica; clients that have previously retrieved data from the volume are called back and told that their data is out of date. The next time they go to read that data, as in the final directory listing in the example above, the latest version of the volume's data is retrieved.

Now we have two techniques for making changes to data in read-only, replicated volumes. The first technique works only before a volume is ever replicated. The second technique always works, but takes some additional administrative steps to do right. To finish the example, the explicit read-write connection would be removed after the administrative operation is complete. Alternatively, you could simply follow every general volume connection command with an explicit read-write connection somewhere else in the namespace and leave it there for long-term administration.

In day-to-day usage, most administrators will use a third technique to make changes to replicated volumes: manipulating the built-in bias an AFS client has for getting data from either the read-write or a read-only volume. As any AFS client traverses a given path name, each directory element is examined; at each level, the client must choose whether to retrieve underlying data from one of the multiple read-only volumes or from the single read-write volume. Whenever a client is faced with a choice, the client will retrieve data from either of these types of volumes depending on the current bias.

The rules are simple and sensible: clients begin by desiring to retrieve all data from read-only volumes, if available, because these volumes are known to be replicated and therefore highly available.

This read-only bias remains valid until the examination of the path turns up a volume that is not replicated. Once a directory level that has no read-only volume supporting it is crossed, the client bias is switched. If any further directories are entered, the data is retrieved from the read-write master no matter how much the volume is replicated.

In the normal course of events, the `root.afs` volume attached to `/afs` will be replicated, as will several of the subdirectories. Therefore, as any new volume connection is traversed, as long as the volume is replicated, data is retrieved from one of the available read-only volumes.

In the example above, therefore there was no need to add the option `-rw` to the volume connection command; it could simply have been:

```
$ fs mkm /afs/tmp/sample/root-afs   root.afs
$ fs lsmount root-afs
'root-afs' is a mount point for '#root.afs'
$ rm /afs/tmp/sample/root-afs/newFile
```

In Figure 4-3, the path name `/afs/tmp/sample/root-afs` is analyzed element by element, and the bias at each level is described. At the top, a client begins by looking for read-only replicas, and the volume under `/afs`, `root.afs`, has replicas available. So, when fetching the directory contents, the data is directed to any of the available replicas, with a fail over if necessary.

The `/afs/tmp` path is not a mount point but a simple directory still in the `root.afs` volume; its contents are fetched from one of the replicas as well. Because this directory level is fetched from a read-only volume, no new files or directories can be created under this path name.

The next path element, `/afs/tmp/sample`, is supported by an unreplicated volume, `sample.vol`. Because no read-only versions are available, the client must fetch the data from the read-write. This data is cached just as all data fetched from AFS is cached. But now, the client knows, so to speak, that it is reading data from a more vulnerable area of the file system, an area not backed up by multiple replicas. So, for the remainder of the path, all data fetches will go to each volume's read-write master. This is called a *read-write path*: any path names

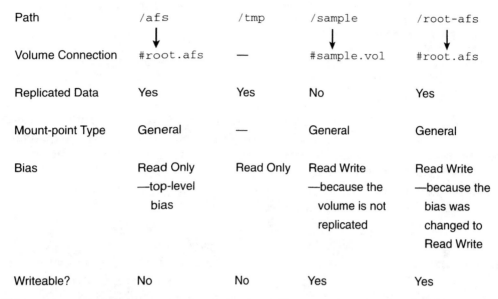

Path	/afs	/tmp	/sample	/root-afs
Volume Connection	#root.afs	—	#sample.vol	#root.afs
Replicated Data	Yes	Yes	No	Yes
Mount-point Type	General	—	General	General
Bias	Read Only —top-level bias	Read Only	Read Write —because the volume is not replicated	Read Write —because the bias was changed to Read Write
Writeable?	No	No	Yes	Yes

Figure 4-3   Path Preferences: /afs/tmp/sample/root-afs

names under this will implicitly refer to data in read-write volumes. Underneath /afs/tmp/sample, the /afs/tmp/sample/root-afs directory points to the replicated root.afs volume but because we are now on a read-write path, we will fetch its contents from the read-write version of the volume.

We can use the fs examine command to find out which volume is being accessed at any AFS path. The command allows us to easily demonstrate which elements of the path shown above are in read-only versus read-write paths.

```
$ fs examine /afs
Volume status for vid = 536870913 named root.afs.readonly
$ fs examine /afs/tmp
Volume status for vid = 536870913 named root.afs.readonly
$ fs examine /afs/tmp/sample
Volume status for vid = 536870943 named sample.vol
$ fs examine /afs/tmp/sample/root-afs
Volume status for vid = 536870912 named root.afs
```

Administrators must be aware of which files are on read-write paths and which will access the read-only replicas. While maintaining this mapping appears to be a burden, it is easy to layout top-level directories to help out. The simplest mechanism is to create the following volume connection.

```
$ fs mkm /afs/.rw root.afs   -rw
$ vos release root.afs
$ ls /afs
tmp/
$ ls /afs/.rw
tmp/
```

Both /afs and /afs/.rw are connections to the same volume,
root.afs. The former is a general connection, which means it will use a read-only volume if available, whereas the latter is a hardcoded read-write path.
This scheme ensures that a read-write path will always be available to any volume anywhere in the tree. Access to /afs/.rw will permit reading or writing data to the root.afs master volume.

In Figure 4-4, the path /afs/.rw/tmp/sample is analyzed.

Here, the /afs directory entries are retrieved from a read-only as before.
But the next element, /afs/.rw, is an explicit mount point to the read-write version of a volume. As such, even though this volume is replicated, the contents of the directory are fetched from the read-write master. And from now on, we're on a read-write path: each path element will be fetched from the read-write master volume that is storing its data.

When we reach /afs/.rw/tmp, the directory contents will be fetched from the read-write version of its volume, root.afs. In the previous figure, the /afs/tmp directory was still located on a read-only path; with the use of the explicit read-write mount point at /afs/.rw, we're able to switch a client over from read-only to read-write bias. Since /afs/.rw/tmp is on a read-write path, files or directories may be created here (as long as other file permissions permit).

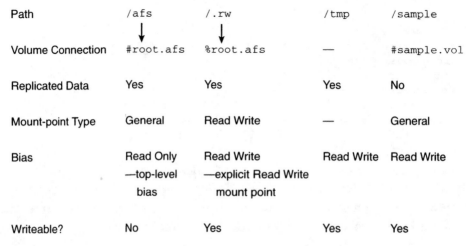

Path	/afs	/.rw	/tmp	/sample
	↓	↓		
Volume Connection	#root.afs	%root.afs	—	#sample.vol
Replicated Data	Yes	Yes	Yes	No
Mount-point Type	General	Read Write	—	General
Bias	Read Only —top-level bias	Read Write —explicit Read Write mount point	Read Write	Read Write
Writeable?	No	Yes	Yes	Yes

Figure 4-4   Path Preferences: /afs/.rw/tmp/sample

Again, the fs examine command confirms this bias.

```
$ fs examine /afs
Volume status for vid = 536870913 named root.afs.readonly
$ fs examine /afs/.rw
Volume status for vid = 536870912 named root.afs
$ fs examine /afs/.rw/tmp
Volume status for vid = 536870912 named root.afs
```

No more examples are needed because path preferences do not keep switching back and forth. The only rule is that clients start off preferring to fetch data from read-only volumes. Once the client encounters either an explicit read-write volume connection or a volume that has only a read-write existence, then the client will prefer to fetch data from the read-write volume no matter how many replicas may be available. Once a client switches to a read-write preference, there's no way to switch back to a read-only preference—there's no such thing as an explicit read-only mount point.

To check your understanding, think about what would happen if the root.afs volume were not replicated. In that case, /afs would have to be resolved by the read-write version because no read-only volumes are available. But this puts us on a read-write path immediately. This bias means that every AFS path name will cause data to be fetched from its read-write volume even if all other volumes are replicated. Once you are on a read-write path, it is difficult to get off. When designing your cell's path names and supporting volumes, make sure that any connection made to a replicated volume will be accessible via a path composed of general mount points, each of which points to a replicated volume. And this includes the topmost volume, root.afs.

Don't forget: the description of a path or volume as read-only or read-write refers only to the volume access itself. Final permissions depend on the user's authentication credentials and the access control list associated with a given directory. Through a reasonable use of access controls, only administration staff will be able to actually write or remove files from the topmost areas of the AFS namespace.

You may be wondering if there's a potential problem with two connections to the same volume: both /afs and /afs/.rw are pointing to root.afs. Multiple mount points don't present a problem for AFS. Each path in the AFS namespace is supported by a single volume. Additional paths to the same volume simply provide multiple names for the same data. No matter which path is given, the client will use the same file identification number to access a file or directory. The only problem is in keeping straight a mental picture of the file namespace. The more paths with different names that lead to the same set of data, the more confusing will access become. This is even more of a problem when circularities exist in the path names, that is, when child directories contain connections to volumes higher up in their path. Again, AFS is being asked for file data only one directory element at a time, so it will never be confused. Humans, on the other hand, can quickly grow dizzy with such connections.

The /afs/.rw connection is just such a circularity, but owing to its top-level location and well-known purpose—providing a clearly read-write path to the entire AFS namespace—it is sufficiently self-explanatory. A few conventions such as this will make administration easier by reducing other arbitrary and poorly communicated practices.

Once some simple conventions are in place for naming paths and volumes, using the file system quickly becomes second nature. Until then, if you encounter a permission-denied error when writing to a seemingly accessible directory or, conversely, when permitted to write to what should be a read-only area, consider examining the full path name of the given directory. Only when each path name element is supported with a replicated volume will the last directory refer to read-only storage.

The proliferation of volumes can lead to several simple errors. After adding a new volume connection to a replicated area of your cell, you might replicate and release the new volume but forget to re-release the parent volume, that is, re-release the volume that is storing the new volume connection. AFS has no built-in understanding of which volumes contain connections or mounts to a given volume. We may refer to a parent volume but only you will know which volumes need to be released when connections to new volumes are added.

Other times, when several new third-party software packages have been added, many volumes will need to be released. When you're in a hurry, it's easy to forget to release all the changes. When you don't see what you expect to see in any given volume, take a step back and make an explicit check with the data in the master volumes, by carefully examining the read-write path. In AFS, you can depend on the fact that all clients see the exact same file data and path names all the time; but all the data and paths in the read-write area will always be completely consistent, whereas certain replicated volumes may be released while others may not be. If you are confused by apparent discrepancies, make sure all the master read-write volumes have the correct data and then release all of the associated read-only volumes.

A common question is whether it is possible to replicate a user's home directory volume. Given that any volume can be replicated, the fundamental answer is yes. But because a user's files are usually being written quite often (e.g., when reading and writing mail), vos release operations would have to be performed often just to keep the replica volume up to date. And with the built-in client prejudice for getting data from the read-only version of a volume, a user's home volume would have to be connected to its path name with the read-write flag. With a large number of users operating in a cell, all of this specialized administration may be too great a burden.

However, when certain volumes are especially important, there is no reason not to replicate them. Imagine a volume to which critical data is being written. There is no facility in AFS for mirroring writes to remote disks. Read-only volumes placed at a few locations around an enterprise with releases happening once an hour, for example, could provide a useful safety net. It might be wise, for instance, to provide such on-line archives for home directories of senior managers and other friends. During certain outages, you could restore the data from the read-only much more quickly than recovering it from tape.

CONVENTIONAL NAMESPACES

Figure 4-5 illustrates a typical cell of the AFS namespace and shows how the volumes that store the data are conventionally connected. In this section, we'll perform administration on our example cell to bring it in line with these practices. (The rest of the cell, volume, and directory examples in this book will use this conventional namespace rather than the somewhat contrived paths we've seen so far.)

The root of the AFS namespace is at the directory /afs which is connected to the volume root.afs. When we look at client administration in more detail, we'll see that there is no explicit fs mkm command which makes this connection; rather, it is the AFS client daemon itself which has this linkage hardcoded. And this root volume connection is predefined to be a general mount point, which means that the current client prejudices for read-only or read-write access apply. Because there are root.afs.readonly replicas available and we've not yet encountered a read-write mount point, read-only access is the bias.

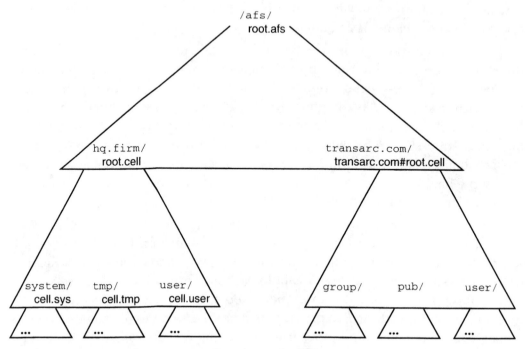

Figure 4-5   Top-Level Namespace Showing Volume Connections

The next directory level of a typical namespace consists of connections to the local cell, other cells in the enterprise, and cells at other organizations. Perhaps because of the file system's origins in the academic world and the generally free information flow in the Internet community, it is common to connect to many other sites and to publicize your own site to others. But this is only suggested practice; many sites connect only to their local cell or cells. In this cell, our hypothetical organization, HQ, Inc., will store its file data underneath the directory /afs/hq.firm which is a mount point to the local volume root.cell; the directory /afs/transarc.com will connect to the volume root.cell at Transarc's cell.

Indeed, the directories under /afs will invariably be connections only to volumes named root.cell, one of which will belong to the local cell, with the others belonging to remote cells. The existence of a volume named root.cell at all cells, under which the rest of a site's files and directories are located, is an important convention of the AFS namespace. (Indeed, the Transarc documentation claims that this name is required.)

We'll clean up our top level by creating our own cell's standard root.cell volume and connecting it underneath /afs. To make the connection, we'll of course need to use a read-write path to ensure that we can write into the `root.afs` volume.

```
$ cd /afs/.rw
$ vos create fs-one a root.cell
Volume 536870918 created on partition /vicepa of fs-one
$ fs mkm hq.firm root.cell
$ ls
hq.firm      tmp
```

We'll also get rid of the subdirectories in `tmp` by using the `fs rmmount` command to remove the connection between the directory names and their volumes. Then we'll check that all we can see is the single connection to our local cell and release these changes to the `root.afs` replicas.

```
$ fs rmmount tmp/sample
$ fs rmmount tmp/sample.bak
$ rmdir tmp
$ vos release root.afs
$ ls /afs
hq.firm
```

While performing this administration, notice how easy it is to effect changes to the enterprisewide distributed file system. By using the read-write path, administrators can clean up, restructure, or fix other problems in the read-write volume, examine the changes, and then release them to all users in one operation. And these administrative operations can be performed on any client of our cell because all clients see the same namespace including any read-write paths.

Up to now, we've used the directory `/afs/.rw` as the well-known entry-point to an obviously read-write path. But the usual AFS convention is to create a read-write path named after the local cell with a `.` prefix. We can easily change our namespace to follow this practice, check the new paths, and then release the improvements.

```
$ cd /afs/.rw
$ fs mkm .hq.firm root.cell -rw
$ fs rmm .rw
$ ls -a
.hq.firm     hq.firm
$ fs lsmount .hq.firm
'.hq.firm' is a mount point for '%root.cell'
$ fs lsmount hq.firm
'hq.firm' is a mount point for '#root.cell'
```

```
$ vos release root.afs
$ ls -a /afs
.hq.firm     hq.firm
```

We're now left with just two connections to our local cell: a regular mount point /afs/hq.firm offering reliable access to replicated data (once we have created replicas for root.cell) and a strictly read-write mount point /afs/.hq.firm to provide a consistent path to all master volumes.

In our tidied-up namespace, underneath /afs/hq.firm we will install three main subtrees, system, tmp, and user, which are connected to the volumes cell.sys, cell.tmp, and cell.user, respectively. These three volumes will undoubtedly be replicated as much as are root.afs and root.cell, to ensure the most reliable access to a cell's namespace. The system subtree is a place to store binaries for hardware vendor's operating system releases. The tmp directory will be used for random administration and user will be used to collect our organization's home directories.

While so far each directory level in our conventional namespace has its own volume connection, this is not necessary at all: these three path names could be simple directories in the root.cell volume. One reason against making these directories is that changes to the topmost levels of the namespace are somewhat rare, whereas changes to the tmp and user (and lower) levels will occur frequently. As making changes requires editing a volume's contents and releasing the changes, most administrators would rather work in smaller and more discrete volumes to limit the time needed to propagate the changes and to reduce any potential problems. Thus, the upper levels of the /afs namespace usually represent small and individual volumes, and the lower levels, such as user homes or application development areas, are leaf volumes containing several dozen megabytes or more of files and directories.

First, we'll create the necessary second-level volumes.

```
$ vos create fs-one a cell.user
Volume 536870954 created on partition /vicepa of fs-one
$ vos create fs-one a cell.tmp
Volume 536870957 created on partition /vicepa of fs-one
$ vos create fs-one a cell.sys
Volume 536870960 created on partition /vicepa of fs-one
```

Then, we'll add volume connections to them underneath our local cell. As you see, we use the /afs/.hq.firm path to make sure we are writing into the read-write version of the root.cell volume.

```
$ fs mkm /afs/.hq.firm/user cell.user
$ fs mkm /afs/.hq.firm/tmp cell.tmp
$ fs mkm /afs/.hq.firm/system cell.sys
```

Finally, we'll add replication sites for our local cell's top volume and release to the world the changes just made. Client machines are guaranteed to be called back when changes are released to read-only volumes, so we can immediately see the new version of /afs/hq.firm on every client in the cell:

```
$ vos addsite fs-one a root.cell
Added replication site fs-one /vicepa for volume root.cell
$ vos addsite fs-two a root.cell
Added replication site fs-two /vicepa for volume root.cell
$ vos release root.cell
Released volume root.cell successfully
$ ls /afs/hq.firm
tmp  sys    user
```

As soon as any significant data is added to the system, tmp, or user directories, those volumes should be replicated and released just like the root.cell volume. Usually, your cell's most important top-level volumes will be replicated across the same set of servers. It's easy to pick one file server, perhaps the first one installed, as the master server, on which the read-write copies of volumes are stored, and then replicate the volumes to all of the other file servers in the cell. While we don't show the individual steps here, you can assume that the cell.sys, cell.tmp, and cell.user volumes are similarly replicated.

When individual user volumes need to be constructed, similar operations are required, except that replication of home directories is usually not performed. Many more details, such as authentication and ownership, are also important, but as far as the volume management goes, the steps are:

```
$ vos create fs-one b user.zed
Volume 536870964 created on partition /vicepb of fs-one
$ fs mkm /afs/.hq.firm/user/zed user.zed
$ vos release cell.user
Released volume cell.user successfully
$ ls /afs/hq.firm/user
zed
```

See Figure 4-6 for a visual depiction of this cell layout.

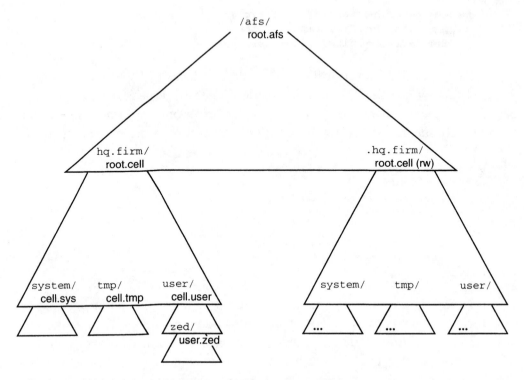

Figure 4-6 The Local Namespace and Volume Connections

This arrangement of names, volumes, and replication allows us to have a highly available and efficient file storage system with relatively inexpensive hardware. Given several AFS file servers, we can easily replicate the read-only volumes onto all of the servers for the highest reliability. Individuals' home volumes can be added anywhere space is available and moved around as needs dictate without burdensome administration or interruption to users.

Additionally, some of the servers could be arranged so that only read-only volumes are stored there. If a server contains only data that is replicated elsewhere, there is no need for it to be built with expensive RAID disk subsystems or clustered hardware technology. The requirement for reliable data availability is handled transparently by the AFS client; each client knows where all of a replica's available read-only volumes are stored and will fail over on their own from non-answering servers to other servers. The capital overhead and administrative costs of hardware-based solutions can be concentrated on the servers that house the read-write volumes.

Now that our local cell looks correct, we'll add in a connection to a remote cell. Making intercell connections is very simple. First, make sure that a client

has the foreign cell's database servers listed in its file /usr/vice/etc/
CellServDB. All access to AFS file data must first be resolved by discovering
a volume's location through a query to a cell's database server; the
CellServDB file lists the database servers for each cell to which you desire to
communicate. The connections to the remote cell are conventionally made just
underneath /afs and right next to our own local cell all within the root.afs
volume.

You may notice that we no longer have read-write access to this volume in
our cell, but we can easily make a temporary mount to perform the administration. Note that here, we're using a read-write path to place us in a guaranteed
writeable area of the root.afs volume. Once there, we create our intercell
mount point.

```
$ fs mkm /afs/.hq.firm/tmp/root-afs root.afs
$ cd /afs/.hq.firm/tmp/root-afs
$ fs mkm transarc.com root.cell -cell transarc.com
$ fs lsmount transarc.com
'transarc.com' is a mount point for 'transarc.com#root.cell'
```

All that is added to the regular fs mkm command is the cell name. Again,
the lsmount output must be visually parsed to determine that we have an
intercell general mount point: a # character delimits the volume and cell name.
The temporary read-write mount is removed, changes are then released to all
read-only copies, and access to Transarc's cell is available. Our cell's namespace
now looks like that in Figure 4-5.

```
$ cd /afs
$ fm rmm /afs/hq.firm/tmp/root-afs-rw
$ vos release root.afs
$ ls /afs
hq.firm      transarc.com
```

You might note that no one asked Transarc for permission to access their
file tree. No permission is needed because Transarc's AFS files are completely
protected by the Kerberos mutual authentication protocol. It is understood that
Transarc can reject access to any user, at any directory level of their tree, and
they may well have done that at the top of the root.cell volume. The connection point does not guarantee that any data requests will be authorized,
only that a local AFS client will be able to look up the relevant servers (via the
CellServDB database) and ask for data.

With the connection to Transarc, accesses to /afs/transarc.com will request data from the volume location servers at that site and from there request file data from the file servers. Because Transarc permits a certain amount of public access, we're then able to see some directories and files from across the Internet. We don't need to perform any additional connections to Transarc's volume data; their administrators have already stored those connections in their root.cell volume. When our desktop machine reads that remote directory data, it will see the volume mount points and show them to us as subdirectories.

```
$ ls /afs/transarc.com
group  home  public  sys
```

This seemingly open access to other people's cells is remarkable for two reasons. First, the internal transport protocol used by AFS has been specifically designed to work well on wide-area networks to the point that accessing files on the Internet from across the country or even around the world becomes a commonplace activity. Granted, file retrieval times depends on just how well connected a site is, but the protocol is efficient and (mostly) successful. The list of organizations, companies, universities, and government institutions which participate in this namespace is quite long.

The second point to be made about this open availability is that it is subject to the strict access controls obeyed by AFS. With the strong authentication guarantees of the Kerberos system, file access can be permitted or denied with complete confidence. In fact, if a site purchases a source license to the AFS system, once the source is installed, symbolic links point from the purchaser's copy back into Transarc's home cell and namespace, enabling the purchaser to obtain source updates via the wide-area file system itself. And the only access control is that provided by Transarc's own AFS Kerberos implementation, an amazing example of having faith in your product.

Of course, your cell's root.afs and the connections to other cells which it contains are under your complete control. No two cells are likely to have exactly the same connections underneath /afs. You may choose to include connections to as many or few remote cells as you see fit. Once your cell is stable, you can mail the appropriate stanza of your CellServDB file to the info-afs mailing list. From there, many sites will see the data and connect your cell's root.cell volume into their tree. At the same time, Transarc will collect and make available the cumulative set of CellServDB entries.

If you've made your cell visible to the outside world, it is difficult to make it invisible. Although AFS access controls are an effective and extremely strong mechanism to thwart unauthorized access to data, once a cell's database servers are known to others, they will at least be able to access public areas of your cell. Moving the servers to new IP addresses or denying access to the AFS IP ports with a firewall is the only effective way to be sure of cutting off all outsiders.

If you have multiple cells in your own organization, you must follow a similar publishing practice and add connections to the `root.cell` volumes of the other cells to each cell's `root.afs` volume. Each client will need to have complete entries for all cells in their `CellServDB` file for the lookups to these intercell mount points to succeed. The use of the static `CellServDB` file makes client administration cumbersome when adding remote cell access, but until recently there has been no generally recognized solution to global directory services. At the least, all that must be updated are the few database servers in a cell, and these rarely change.

Let's take a closer look at how the intercell and local cell connections are resolved. Note that our local cell's entry point, `/afs/hq.firm`, was not created with a `-cell` argument. Just as a UNIX workstation has well-known disk mount points under which all files are internally known only by their inode number, so too in AFS, a volume connection point is dereferenced with respect to the current cell. The topmost volume, `root.afs`, is searched for in the local cell as determined by the value contained in the file `/usr/afs/etc/ThisCell`. All non-intercell connections under `/afs` will be assumed to reside in this local cell. When the path name `/afs/transarc.com` is traversed, it is easily identified as belonging to a remote cell, so that `root.cell` volume will be searched for in Transarc's cell; any further volumes encountered in that subtree will then be assumed to be in that cell until another intercell connection is crossed.

One last point: traversing intercell connections can reset client preferences back to read-only paths. Normally, a client's preference for read-only data starts from the (usually replicated) `/afs` path; this can switch to a read-write bias when a read-write mount or a non-replicated volume is encountered and from then on the client will alway prefer to read or write any more data on the path to the master volumes. But when crossing over from one cell to another, a client will check the mount point for replicated volumes and if any are available, as

there would be for Transarc's `root.cell` volume, the client will return to its
read-only bias.

DELETING VOLUMES

Now that we've considered how to create an AFS file system by connecting volumes, let's consider how to delete data and volumes. The connection point is as easy to tear down as it is to put up.

```
$ ls /afs/hq.firm/user
zed
$ fs lsmount /afs/hq.firm/user/zed
'/afs/hq.firm/user/zed' is a mount point for '#user.zed'
$ fs rmmount /afs/.hq.firm/user/zed
$ vos release cell.user
$ ls /afs/hq.firm/user
$
```

The `rmmount` subcommand takes a path name; if the path name is a volume connection, the name is deleted. In this example, the change takes place in the `/afs/hq.firm/user` directory, which is backed by the `cell.user` volume. Because this volume is replicated, we use the `/afs/.hq.firm` path to ensure that we're following a path which uses read-write volumes so that the deletion will be permitted. Once the changes are made to the read-write master, we must release the changes to the replicas so that all clients will see that Zed's home directory has been disconnected.

The `rmmount` subcommand does not destroy any real data; it deletes only the user-visible connection to the files and directories stored in the volume. In some respects, this effect is similar to a UNIX-style `unmount` command. As long as no other connections to the volume exist, no one will be able to access the home directory's files.

To truly delete the data, run `vos remove`.

```
$ vos listvldb user.zed
user.zed
    RWrite: 536870964
    number of sites -> 1
              server fs-one partition /vicepb RW Site
$ vos remove fs-one b user.zed
Volume 536870964 on partition /vicepb server fs-one deleted
$ vos listvldb user.zed
VLDB: no such entry
```

The operation to delete a volume requires that the specific file server and vice partition be named as well. This is not much of an issue when dealing with a read-write volume because it exists in only one place in the cell; but the same command can be used to delete read-only volumes, in which case the specific server and partition must be listed to differentiate which one of the replicas is to be deleted.

As is to be expected from UNIX, this delete operation really deletes the data. There is no built-in trash-can available from which the data can be retrieved. To ensure against premature deletion, you may want to stage volumes to be deleted. You do this staging by removing the volume connection points and then renaming the volume by adding a suffix, say, user.bob.X. (The suffix can't be too long because the volume name length is restricted). At the end of the week, you could retrieve all the volume names in the system, select those that match the suffix, perhaps archive them up to tape, and then delete them.

Note that the remove operation performs two deletions: the first deletion removes all the file data contained in the volume on the specified disk partition. The second deletion removes the volume's location information from the VLDB. As always, when dealing with volume operations, you should always have in mind the changes that are being made to real volumes on disk and the changes that must sometimes be made to the volume location database. Naturally, the volume remove operation must be reflected in both places.

Deleting a backup or read-only volume requires a little more explanation. Because backup volumes are implemented as clones that simply point to the same data as the master read-write, when a read-write is removed, the backup (if it exists) is automatically deleted.

It is possible to delete only the backup volume from the disk and the VLDB by specifying the exact name and location. We can quickly create and delete a backup volume and use the listvldb subcommand to see the appearance and disappearance of the backup.

```
$ vos backup user.rob
Created backup volume for user.rob
$ vos listvldb user.rob
user.rob
    RWrite: 536870967     Backup: 536870969
    number of sites -> 1
       server fs-one partition /vicepa RW Site
$ vos remove fs-one a user.rob.backup
```

```
Volume 536870969 on partition /vicepa server fs-one deleted
$ vos listvldb user.rob
user.rob
    RWrite: 536870967
    number of sites -> 1
        server fs-one partition /vicepa RW Site
```

Deleting a read-only volume is a similar operation. You'll recall, though, that creation of a read-only involves two steps, adding the bookkeeping information to the VLDB followed by releasing the read-write to the replicas. When given a read-only volume name and site as arguments, vos remove will delete both a read-only volume and the site information in the database. For example:

```
$ vos listvldb cell.sys
cell.sys
    RWrite: 536870960      ROnly: 536870961
    number of sites -> 3
        server fs-one partition /vicepa RW Site
        server fs-one partition /vicepa RO Site
        server fs-two partition /vicepa RO Site
$ vos remove fs-two a cell.sys.readonly
Volume 536870961 on partition /vicepa server fs-two deleted
$ vos listvldb cell.sys
cell.sys
    RWrite: 536870960      ROnly: 536870961
    number of sites -> 2
        server fs-one partition /vicepa RW Site
        server fs-one partition /vicepa RO Site
```

To change only the site information kept by the VLDB, use the remsite subcommand.

```
$ vos examine cell.sys
cell.sys
    RWrite: 536870960      ROnly: 536870961
    number of sites -> 2
        server fs-one partition /vicepa RW Site
        server fs-one partition /vicepa RO Site
$ vos remsite fs-one a cell.sys
Deleting the replication site for volume 536870960 ...Removed rep-
lication site fs-one /vicepa for volume cell.sys
$ vos listvldb cell.sys
cell.sys
    RWrite: 536870960
    number of sites -> 1
        server fs-one partition /vicepa RW Site
```

Just as addsite, remsite modifies only the information in the volume location database and does not affect the data on disk. The listvldb operation we've been using for many command examples shows just the information in the VLDB. When you run a listvol command to see which volumes are really on disk, you can see that the cell.sys.readonly volume still exists, so we'll have to use the zap subcommand to reclaim the disk space. Note that zap can be used to delete any volume, read-write, read-only, or backup, but in the last two cases, the complete volume name must be given.

```
$ vos listvol fs-one a
Total number of volumes on server fs-one partition /vicepa: 11
cell.sys                         536870960 RW          2 K On-line
cell.sys.readonly                536870961 RO          2 K On-line
...
$ vos zap fs-one a cell.sys.readonly
Warning: Entry for volume number 536870961 exists in VLDB (but
we're zapping it anyway!)
Volume 536870961 deleted
$ vos listvol fs-one a
Total number of volumes on server fs-one partition /vicepa: 10
cell.sys                         536870960 RW          2 K On-line
...
```

Rather than use remsite and zap, use the remove subcommand, giving it the read-write volume name and the read-only location, and all the right work is done. Using remsite without keeping track of the on-disk read-only volumes is one way that the disks can get out of synchronization with the VLDB.

QUERYING THE DATABASES

The vos status command returns information about the volserver process on a file server machine. Most of the time, the volserver is simply waiting for something to do and so it will respond with "No active transactions." If it is performing an operation or is stuck on some job, it responds with:

```
$ vos status fs-one
Total transactions: 1
----------------------------------------
transaction: 146  created: Sat Mar 29 14:18:16 1997
volume: 536870970  partition: /vicepa  procedure: SetFlags
----------------------------------------
```

The `volserver` process responds with, for each active transaction, the time it started, the volume number, partition, and procedure that it was performing. During volume dumps and restores, a line may be displayed showing the number of bytes written or read.

There are a number of ways to determine which volume is the container for a particular file; many commands in the `fs` command suite will return with this information. While many of these commands are available for users to get information, the `fs examine` command is designed for administrative use.

```
$ fs examine /afs/hq.firm
Volume status for vid = 536870919 named root.cell.readonly
Current disk quota is 5000
Current blocks used are 5
The partition has 977059 blocks available out of 1031042
```

This command queries the volume server to get information from the volume's header in the `vice` partition.

Each volume's header on disk includes a status flag that is maintained by the `volserver` process on the file server machine. It can be one of:

- On-line—The volume is accessible.
- Off-line—The volume is not accessible, possibly due to other problems discovered by the `volserver`.
- Needs salvage—The `volserver` has detected internal corruption of this volume. (Salvaging is discussed in Chapter 9.)

To see this flag and other information about the volume, use the `-extended` option to the `vos examine` command. The status flag is displayed at the end of the first line of output followed by a large amount of additional information.

```
$ vos examine root.afs -extended
root.afs                          536870912 RW            7 K used 3
files On-line
    fs-one /vicepa
    RWrite  536870912 ROnly  536870913 Backup  536870914
    MaxQuota       5000 K
    Creation    Tue Aug 13 12:01:09 1996
    Last Update Sat Mar 29 12:32:32 1997
    77 accesses in the past day (i.e., vnode references)
```

```
                        Raw Read/Write Stats
        |--------------------------------------------------|
        |      Same Network       |      Diff Network       |
        |-----------|-------------|-----------|-------------|
        |   Total   |    Auth     |   Total   |    Auth     |
        |-----------|-------------|-----------|-------------|
Reads   |       8   |        8    |       0   |        0    |
Writes  |      33   |       33    |       0   |        0    |
        |--------------------------------------------------|

                    Writes Affecting Authorship
        |--------------------------------------------------|
        |    File Authorship      |   Directory Authorship  |
        |-----------|-------------|-----------|-------------|
        |   Same    |    Diff     |   Same    |    Diff     |
        |-----------|-------------|-----------|-------------|
0-60 sec|       3   |        0    |       7   |        0    |
1-10 min|       0   |        0    |       7   |        0    |
10min-1hr|      0   |        0    |       3   |        0    |
1hr-1day|       0   |        0    |       2   |        0    |
1day-1wk|       0   |        0    |       0   |        0    |
> 1wk   |       0   |        0    |       1   |        0    |
        |--------------------------------------------------|

    RWrite: 536870912      ROnly: 536870913
    number of sites -> 3
        server fs-one partition /vicepa RW Site
        server fs-one partition /vicepa RO Site
        server fs-two partition /vicepa RO Site
```

The number of accesses in the past day reflects the number of times that a client has retrieved data from the volume since midnight. Of course, these are accesses that are not satisfied by the client cache. When a volume is moved, this number is reset to zero.

The next two sections of the -extended output attempt to categorize today's data access further. The raw read and write statistics are simply the number of data fetches and stores against files located in this volume. The number of reads and writes are further broken down into the number of requests that came from the same network as the server and those that came from a different network. (The server uses the class of its network interface to determine whether a request comes from a different network.) The final breakdown is the number of protocol requests that were sent by authenticated users versus the total number, which includes requests sent by unauthenticated users.

The section entitled "Writes Affecting Authorship" tracks the number of actual changes to data stored in the volume. These statistics are broken down by the relative time at which the changes were stored, by changes to file data versus directory entries, and finally, by changes made by the owner of the data (the Same person) or by users who are not the owner (a "Diff" or different person).

With this information, you can make some potentially interesting observations about the users and desktops accessing your volume data. If you're trying to speed up file access and decrease network contention by placing certain volumes on servers attached to the same network as a set of clients, the raw statistics will tell you whether your effort is successful. You could also audit volumes regularly and move those that have not been accessed in the last week to different servers, keeping front-line servers more focused on a smaller set of rapidly changing volumes.

SUGGESTED PRACTICES

Volumes lie architecturally somewhere between client-visible path names and server disk partitions. This layer of indirection is where most administration takes place and where standard conventions are best followed. As volumes can be seen only through the AFS command-line interface, it is critical that their existence be organized. Don't allow volumes to be created arbitrarily, with seemingly random names and connection points. Because organizations need to store only a few kinds of data—home directories, applications, development areas, operating system binaries—only a few naming conventions are needed. Given that only 22 characters are available for the entire name, such conventions are even more strongly suggested.

The easiest convention to remember is based on standard prefixes. We've seen user. as a prefix to a login name for the name of a home volume. Others might include sys. for system binaries, dev. for development areas, group. for organizational units, etc. Each of the generated volume names will also have an implicit place in the file system namespace: e.g., user.name would be connected to /afs/hq.firm/user/name.

Some sites use additional prefixes or suffixes to indicate backup policies or other administrative behavior. In general, this is a simple way to make AFS administration systematic. But with the 22-character limit on volume names, additional special naming practices have a high price.

The general answer to this problem is to construct a database of volume control information outside of the standard AFS command suite. In the database, you can store a variety of information without the need to abuse the limited resource of volume names. The database can keep track of backup schedules, replication policies, volume ownership, among other information. In particular, you can use a database field to mark volumes that are to be deleted.

Other policies could include storing certain subsets of volumes on certain file servers. The home directories of a particular department might best be kept on a set of servers that are housed near (in a network topology sense) their users. The names of users in a department and the location of file servers is the kind of data which can be stored only outside of the AFS databases in a system of your own devising.

The inherent flaw with this type of database is that it is not maintained by the AFS system itself. Just as the volume location database may become unsynchronized with respect to the volumes on `vice` partitions, an external volume database may not accurately reflect the existing state of affairs. Only regular auditing of both systems will ensure their usefulness.

When establishing replication policies, make sure that all necessary volumes are replicated. Because replication is used to make file data highly available, you'll have to use your volume and path name conventions to guarantee that the file's volume and all of its parent volumes are replicated. If the parent volume isn't replicated (and its parents, etc., all the way back to `root.afs`) then small outages of the file server may prevent access to that file's volume no matter how many replicas exist for it.

Also, remember that volume connections are stored only in the file system itself. Neither the volume nor the volume location database tracks where the connection to the volume is made. A corollary of this is that multiple connections can be made to a volume. For instance, a home volume could be connected to `/afs/hq.firm/home/alice` as well as `/afs/hq.firm/sales/personnel/alice`. Generally, multiple connections are deprecated by administrators because they want to know that they can stop all accesses to a volume's data by removing a single connection point. But multiple connections can be useful; for example, when performing a quick inspection of a volume's contents, you can connect to it in your home directory. Or, better, when writing automatic administration scripts, you can use a temporary directory to perform additional connections to volumes.

Again, note that the only permission needed to make a volume connection is the permission to write into the specified path name. Any AFS volume can be mounted in your home directory, for instance, even the CEO's home directory. But getting to the data in that volume means passing through the access control list at the root of the volume; if that ACL locks out all navigation, no one can get in. But if it allows reading and writing, so be it.

Because no database contains the list of volume connections (except the data in the file system itself), there's no way of guaranteeing that multiple paths to a volume don't exist. One way to audit this situation is to run `sal-vager` regularly in verbose mode; the output in the `salvager` log file displays discovered paths to volumes.

One last suggested practice is not to slavishly follow convention but to experiment, preferably in a small test cell, and use the tools of AFS to develop policies that make your organization work better. For example, the volume names `root.afs` and `root.cell` are purely conventional. You should feel free to construct an AFS namespace that suits your requirements. There's nothing wrong with not having other cell's namespaces visible directly under `/afs` nor does there have to be a `/afs` at all.

As we'll see when we examine client configuration in the next chapter, the client cache manager must be told which top-level volume should be assumed to be mounted at which UNIX directory. While `/afs` and `root.afs` are well-known defaults, you may prefer another entry point. With a little bit of hacking, you can usually provide the best of both worlds. Though AFS encourages the use of single, global namespaces, certain organizations, such as financial institutions, require that different desktops not be able to access certain directory areas. Normally, that means either using group entries on ACLs or multiple AFS cells. But per-desktop root volumes are another possibility.

SUMMARY

How many volumes will you wind up with? Some sites use AFS only for production binary delivery and can get by with a few dozen. Others have volumes for all users, all development projects, and each version of software packages, easily leading to several thousand volumes. AFS can manage this scale with just a few servers; the database processes certainly have no problem with this number.

These volume management operations are the bread-and-butter of AFS administration. Rather than perform tasks on servers and manually push around location maps, AFS uses volume operations. The collection of operations—creation, making connections to the namespace, movement, and backups—provides enterprises with precisely the set of tools needed to manage file data.

As should be clear by now, AFS's designers were not interested in providing the atomic elements of distributed file services. Rather than developing commands that manipulate fundamental units of file service, they were trying to solve their own real-world problems of controlling a centralized storage system. Contrast the CMU designers with, for example, the designers of the X Window System™, who provided only the most fundamental items of a graphical library. Their motto was "mechanism, not policy," and it took years until elements such as scrollbars were standardized with the Motif® library.

In the case of CMU and Transarc, this philosophy is practically reversed: the tools provided give us policies first, such as only a single namespace or a single backup volume. There is no way to access items like clone volumes for arbitrary commands; we are given only the commands that implement policies such as moving a volume or creating a single backup.

In this chapter, the term connection was used when describing the process of stitching together volumes and directory names to create a file namespace. This terminology was chosen because some people have been confused by the traditional use of "mount" to mean an operation that a client performs. It should be clear by now that volume connections are not mounted by clients nor is the information stored in a separate database. The connections are in the file system itself and are, therefore, subject to the same caching and guaranteed consistency semantics of all other AFS file data, that is, all clients see all files, and all connections, all the time.

Now that we've studied the process of volume connections, we'll revert, for the rest of the book, to the normal AFS usage and refer to volume mounts, read-write or general mount points, and the like.

CHAPTER 5

Client Administration

At times, server management may seem like keeping a dozen plates spinning on sticks. Happily, that's not quite accurate. Even so, client administration is much simpler, though there are still several details that can be managed to optimize performance and reliability. The following sections describe the management needed to keep AFS clients well connected to their local and other cells.

In the previous chapters, the administration process managed pieces of the entire AFS cell directly; however, in much of the following, AFS commands manipulate the state of a single desktop machine. As such, the authentication process is less demanding: cell management needs a Kerberos-authenticated AFS administration credential, but client administration requires only the local superuser (UNIX root) access. There's no danger of breaking the AFS security model because all that can be accomplished with UNIX root is local process and file manipulation. Commands that require root privilege are noted in the text: the examples indicate root usage with a # prompt rather than the regular prompt $ used for nonprivileged users.

CONFIGURATION

Running an AFS client consists mainly of setting up a few small configuration files, setting aside a cache area, installing the dynamically loaded kernel module supplied by Transarc, and then starting up the client AFS daemon, afsd. The configuration files and cache area are one-time administration issues; loading the kernel module and starting afsd must be done during every reboot. These two steps can be done almost whenever desired during booting. However, because many sites like to store as much data as possible in the file system, including many administration tasks, it is most common to run afsd as soon as possible during booting. For most UNIX-based systems, this means right after the configuration of the network interfaces, after the first few lines of the system rc files have run.

The configuration files include /usr/vice/etc/CellServDB, /usr/vice/etc/ThisCell, and /usr/vice/cacheinfo. (Remember that all the client configuration files are located under /usr/vice, and those of the server are located in /usr/afs.)

The client's CellServDB file is similar to that of the servers, with this exception: rather than just requiring the names and addresses of the local cell's database machines, any other cells the client will need to talk to must also be listed. This list includes any other of your organization's cells and any external sites, such as Transarc. The format of the file is the same as on the server:

```
>hq.firm         # our example cell
192.168.3.11     #   db-one
192.168.3.12     #   db-two
192.168.5.13     #   db-three
>transarc.com    # Transarc Corporation
158.98.14.3      #   oscar.transarc.com
158.98.3.2       #   ernie.transarc.com
158.98.3.3       #   bigbird.transarc.com
```

This file's contents must be laid out correctly with no blank lines permitted. The line's beginning with the ">" character signal a new stanza of information for a cell; that sentinel is followed by the cell name, some blank spaces, and finally a "#" character followed by a comment, typically a readable version of the cell name.

Each of the following lines of cell information specify one of the database servers. The Internet address of the server in dotted-quad format is listed, followed by a "#" character and the DNS host name of the server. *The DNS host name is not a comment—it is a required field.*

Other than the formatting of the specification lines, the order of the database servers in a cell and the order of the cells in the file are irrelevant.

The ThisCell file contains just a single word, the name of the local cell. This file is examined by most user-level commands to define the local cell. In our example it would contain:

```
hq.firm
```

To make the cache area, first decide whether to have a memory- or a disk-based cache. Putting the cache into the kernel memory may be the easiest option, but it is unlikely that this solution will result in the best performance of the system. Though the in-memory cached data can be stored and read quickly, the small size of the cache will likely cause many more cache misses, and therefore more frequent requests to the server, which in turn leads to greater server load.

Even so, memory caches work well enough that they can certainly be useful in certain circumstances, and certainly if the desktop machine has no disk. When a memory cache is used, all of the cache configuration information is passed to the kernel on the command line of the client daemon process. On a Sun workstation running Solaris, the command lines would look like this:

```
# modload /kernel/fs/afs
# afsd -memory
afsd: All AFS daemons started
```

Here, the `modload` command installs the new AFS kernel module, which includes the AFS client file system operational code and the new system calls used to initiate client services. During the installation of the client, the kernel module is usually copied from `/usr/vice/modload/libafs.o` into the correct location, depending on the type of the operating system.

UNIX vendors will provide one or more ways to do this: by statically building a new kernel with the desired functions, by dynamically loading a module into a running kernel, or by loading all kernel modules at boot time. Under SunOS™ you can either build a new kernel or dynamically load the module; Under IBM's AIX, you must dynamically load the module; under Digital UNIX, you must build a new static kernel. For dynamic loading, Transarc provides a program, `dkload`, for several platforms. Read the installation manual and the latest release notes for information on correctly updating the kernel.

There's not too much difference in the administration overhead for building a new kernel versus dynamically loading the module during the booting process. For the kernel internals, the result is almost exactly the same: the AFS procedures are link-edited into the kernel address space, and certain system tables are adjusted to include the new file system type. If your site distributes customized or bug-fixed kernels as a matter of course to desktops, then compiling a static kernel with AFS extensions may be straightforward; otherwise, performing the dynamic module load during every reboot is a fairly quick and reliable process.

In any case, the effect is to add new functionality into the operating system. When the `afsd` command executes, it forks itself four times and in each runs one of the new system calls. When you examine the system process table, you'll see four `afsd` processes running, one for each of the kernel-based execution threads necessary for AFS.

Besides their generally larger sizes, disk-based caches have one important advantage over memory caches: the file data cached on disk survives a machine reboot. A user who has run a large program stored in AFS will have it transferred to the local disk and will execute it from cache no matter how many times the user logs off or shuts off the machine. Since the file will be recached whenever it is updated, the automatic file caching process immediately solves many software distribution problems.

Disk-based caches usually place their cache files in the directory `/usr/vice/cache`. In general, bigger is better, though larger caches take longer to initialize the first time around. Some studies have reported that most of the benefits of a cache are reached at around 70 megabytes. It seems reasonable, given the larger internal disks now routinely installed by vendors, to make client caches anywhere from 100-300 megabytes large. You configure the location and size of the cache by entering the data into a one-line file, `/usr/vice/etc/cacheinfo`. The file stores three pieces of information: the initial entry point into the AFS file name space (normally `/afs`), the location of the cache directory (normally `/usr/vice/cache`), and the size of the cache in kilobytes (100000 would equal almost 100 megabytes). The `cacheinfo` file would therefore look like this:

```
/afs:/usr/vice/cache:100000
```

The daemon startup commands would look like this:

```
# modload /kernel/fs/afs
# afsd
All afsd daemons started.
```

During the very first startup of the daemon, the kernel will initialize the cache area by making file entries in the cache directory. If you list the contents of the cache directory, you'll see several hundred files named V1 through perhaps V1000 or more, depending on the specified size of the cache. These empty files are created and their internal disk positions stored in memory so that the AFS client code can access the cache's disk blocks as efficiently as possible. Initial afsd startup is somewhat proportional to the number of V-files which need to be created.

On initial startup, don't use the daemon's -verbose option as a separate console message will be printed for each V-file created in the client cache. You may want to run this option if you suspect that the afsd program or kernel module is completely corrupted. Otherwise, for any decently sized cache, this option will only serve to substantially delay the initial startup configuration of the client. One way around the long startup time is to create the cache V-files on one machine. Then, use a UNIX disk dump/restore mechanism to copy over the information directly onto a new client's local partitions rather than having afsd formally create each file one at a time.

Once the cache files are created, the client daemon attaches to the cache area quickly enough. The main job of the afsd daemon is to mount the AFS file system onto the local machine. As with other UNIX mount commands, the top-level directory, /afs, must exist before the mount executes. Because afsd may take a second or two to begin (especially during the first initialization), it will help to add a dummy file underneath the UNIX directory.

```
# mkdir /afs
# touch /afs/AFS_NOT_RUNNING
# ls /afs
AFS_NOT_RUNNING
```

When afsd is started as a background process, you can check for the existence of the dummy file and, when it is no longer visible, you can assume that AFS is up and running. Here's an example, using the shell command language.

```
# afsd &
# while [ -f /afs/AFS_NOT_RUNNING ]
> do
>     sleep 5                  # loop while the local file is visible
> done
# ls /afs                      # AFS is now available
hq.firm    transarc.com
```

Once the afsd daemon has finished mounting the AFS file system on the /afs mount point, examining /afs will retrieve the AFS file and not the UNIX sentinel file. In normal use, this mount will happen right away, but if a machine has been misconfigured or the AFS kernel module is corrupted, then no mount will occur and /afs/AFS_NOT_RUNNING will continue to be visible.

CACHE MANAGER

On subsequent startups of the disk-based cache manager, you'll see slightly different output.

```
# afsd
Starting AFS cache scan...
Found 1690 non-empty cache files (29%)
All afsd daemons started.
```

After the first use of AFS on a client, there will be some number of remote files cached locally. As the afsd process starts, it reads through these files, notes that this cached data could be reused, and prints a message showing how many files it discovered.

These are files and directories that have valid FIDs and data blocks and are potentially up to date and usable. But because the client may have missed a callback from the server saying the file is out of date, each file will need to have its version number checked via a quick, small RPC call to the server. This check is done as the files are accessed; if the server agrees that the local file is up to date, the client reestablishes a callback promise with the server and returns the data to the calling application.

Besides having files under /afs available, there is little evidence that AFS is running on a client. If you examine the standard UNIX process status output, you can find the cache manager daemon, seen here on a Solaris machine:

```
$ ps -ef
UID    PID  PPID  C    STIME TTY      TIME CMD
root   237     1  0 17:16:37 ?        0:00 /usr/vice/etc/afsd
root   238     1  0 17:16:37 ?        0:00 /usr/vice/etc/afsd
root   239     1  0 17:16:37 ?        0:03 /usr/vice/etc/afsd
root   240     1  0 17:16:37 ?        0:00 /usr/vice/etc/afsd
. . .
```

The afsd program is actually quite small and does little more than copy some configuration information into the kernel and then run some newly installed system calls, each of which usually just schedules some threads of execution inside the kernel. It is these nonreturning threads that you see as the multiple afsd processes in the output of the ps command.

These kernel operations are collectively known as the *cache manager*. The job of the manager includes:

- Requesting data from the servers on behalf of user applications and storing it locally
- Answering callbacks from the server to identify out-of-date data and to respond to periodic probes from file servers
- Probing the file servers regularly, flushing the volume mappings once every hour, and freeing up kernel memory as needed for data structures used to maintain the system
- Some background processing to pre-fetch file data and perform delayed writes

Because the threads continue forever once started, `afsd` never exits; it is impossible to kill the process. Certain pieces of information transferred into the kernel, such as the name of the local cell, cannot be changed once the cache manager is running. As the process cannot be restarted, a client machine must be rebooted if the local cell name is to change.

As mentioned, disk-based caches appear to be many, many files in the cache directory. The cache directory is normally readable only by the superuser, although there's nothing that can be done to the cache except through AFS administration tasks. If you insist on looking in the cache, you'll see it looks something like this:

```
# ls -l
-rw-------   1 root     other          0 Aug 13   1996 AFSLog
-rw-------   1 root     other     462816 Apr  5 13:44 CacheItems
-rw-------   1 root     other          0 Aug 13   1996 VolumeItems
-rw-------   1 root     other          0 Aug 13   1996 V0
-rw-------   1 root     other          0 Aug 13   1996 V1
-rw-------   1 root     other          0 Aug 13   1996 V2
-rw-------   1 root     other          0 Aug 13   1996 V3
-rw-------   1 root     other          0 Aug 13   1996 V4
...
-rw-------   1 root     root          10 Mar 30 17:11 V8993
-rw-------   1 root     root          29 Mar 30 17:01 V8994
-rw-------   1 root     root          29 Mar 30 17:00 V8995
-rw-------   1 root     root          29 Mar 30 16:36 V8996
-rw-------   1 root     root          11 Mar 30 16:35 V8997
-rw-------   1 root     root        2048 Mar 29 16:55 V8998
-rw-------   1 root     root        2048 Mar 29 16:55 V8999
```

The `CacheItems` file holds the mappings between the V-files and the AFS files stored by the V-files; it is flushed from kernel memory to disk once a minute. The `VolumeItems` file holds mappings between the volume names the manager has traversed, their identification numbers, and any file server sites that store the volumes' files.

The files in this directory are, of course, owned by the cache manager. Any careless administration here, such as deleting data or using space which has been reserved by the client cache, can result in a kernel panic. This area must also be restricted to any access by nonprivileged users. The file data is stored on the local disk in the V-files; anyone who can read the files can reconstruct the file data (though identifying which files hold what data can be difficult).

Each V-file stored one file or one piece of one file. By default, the size for a V-file is 64 kilobytes; this value can be set to a power-of-2-sized number of kilobytes on the `afsd` command line. The size of the V-file is referred to as the *chunk size* of the cache. This size is the same as the amount of data retrieved from the server with one request. Figure 5-1 shows how the V-files and chunk sizes are used by the cache manager.

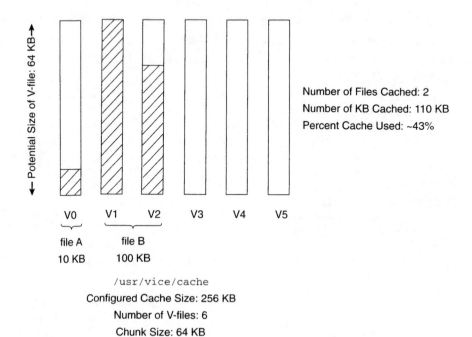

Number of Files Cached: 2
Number of KB Cached: 110 KB
Percent Cache Used: ~43%

Figure 5-1   How the Client Cache Stores Data

In the example, the chunk size has been left at the default of 64 kilobytes. You can see two files are cached, `fileA` is 100 kilobytes and `fileB` is 10 kilobytes. The smaller file was retrieved in a single client request and stored into a single V-file; the larger file took two requests and is stored into two V-files. Though it may look like the empty space in the first and third V-file is wasted, be assured it is not. The example has artificially set the cache size to just 256 kilobytes, 6 V-files, and a 64 kilobyte chunk size. The two stored files are using 110 kilobytes of the total cache size; therefore, there are three more V-files in which to store another 146 kilobytes of available cache space.

The `-chunksize` argument to `afsd` changes the maximum size of each V-file and the amount of data retrieved from file servers on each request. The argument to this option is not the actual size in kilobytes. To force the chunk size to be a perfect power of 2, the argument expresses the size as the log to the base 2 of the chunk size: 10 indicates a chunk size of 1024 bytes or 1 kilobyte, 11 indicates 2 kilobytes, 16 is the default size of 64 kilobytes, and 20 would create a large chunk size of 1024 kilobytes or 1 megabyte.

Larger chunk sizes make sense when clients will be fetching data from file servers close to them on the network or when attached by fast links, such as 100 megabit Ethernet or FDDI. Smaller chunk sizes might be appropriate for slower network's connectivity, such as 56 kilobit serial links. Unfortunately, this chunk size is set for the entire cache and cannot be tuned on a per-cell or per-volume basis. Inasmuch as directory listings tend to be much smaller on average than files but are cached in V-files too, the chunk size will always be a compromise.

Once the chunk size is specified on the command line and the cache size is defined in the `cacheinfo` file, the manager can compute the number of V-files that will be created. The algorithm is constructed to create many more V-files than you might expect. The number created will be the larger of:

- 1.5 times the cache size divided by the chunk size
- The cache size divided by 10,240
- The value of the `-files` option
- Or 100, as a minimum

For a 100-megabyte cache and the default, 64-kilobyte chunk size, there will be 10,240 V-files created according to the second rule listed. (The AFS System Administration Guide wrongly reports that the divisor is 10,000.) The equation is really the cache size in kilobytes divided by 10; this value is equal to the cache size in bytes divided by 10 * 1024, or 10,240. The algorithm is derived from file system studies that show that the average file size is around 10 kilobytes.

The purpose is to build a cache that can hold as many average-sized files as will fit into the total cache size. If the average size of your files is small, then you will underuse your cache. Looking back at Figure 5-1: if your files averaged 1 kilobyte each, then, after the sixth file, your cache would start to invalidate previously cached files, even though only 6 kilobytes out of 256 kilobytes are stored.

While AFS clients try to store as many average-sized files as possible, the client also tries to take care of large files by retrieving them in large chunks and storing each chunk in a single V-file for easy access. This is an attempt to have the best of both worlds, and only experimentation with your environment and your file usage patterns will show whether the cache is being effectively used. Because a single folder or directory is considered a file and takes up a single V-file, clients that constantly traverse hundreds of directories might see lower than expected performance.

The first option to adjust is the total size of the cache: raise it generously and see how that helps your local performance. Next, try increasing the chunk size; some sites with small cells and good networks find that 1-megabyte chunks work well. If you recognize that the cache is woefully underutilized, increase the number of V-files by supplying a larger number as argument to the -files option of afsd.

Normally, a UNIX administrator would be wary of extremely large numbers of files in a directory as looking up any individual file would be a time-consuming operation. When the AFS cache area is allocated upon initial startup, pointers to each V-file are stored in an internal hash, thereby bypassing normal UNIX directory searches and making individual cache file lookup extremely fast.

The CacheItems file holds information about each V-file, such as the AFS file identification number and the chunk's position in the file. There are exactly as many entries in this file as there are V-files. A portion of this information is cached in kernel memory for efficient lookups. Normally, the kernel will cache half the number of entries up to a total of 2,000. Use the option -dcache to set this value exactly. If desired, you can configure more than 2000 entries but this practice is not recommended. AFS version 3.4 had a bug which required the number of dcache items to be set on the command line; as of 3.4a, the cache manager will be able to calculate a best value on its own.

One other set of data stored inside kernel memory is a cache of status information about the locally cached AFS files. Use the -stat option to set this number exactly; by default, the number of entries cached is 300.

As you can see, it's possible to set values for different cache parameters, some of which can contradict each other. The most important item to administer is the total size of the cache because most of the other values can be automatically determined. Table 5-1 shows how the cache size and other optional values will result in a working cache.

Table 5-1   Possible Cache Configuration Options

Disk-based Caches							
Configured			Resulting				
cache size	chunk size		cache size	chunk size	number V-files	memory dcache	file stat	volume cache
64 MB	default		64 MB	64 KB	6,554	2,000	300	50
100 MB	256 KB		100 MB	256 KB	10,240	2,000	300	50
200 MB	1 MB		200 MB	1 MB	20,480	2,000	300	50

Memory-based Caches							
Configured			Resulting				
cache size	chunk size		cache size	chunk size	number V-files	memory dcache	file stat	volume cache
16 MB	default		16 MB	8 KB	2,048	2,048	300	50
24 MB	default		24 MB	8 KB	3,072	3,072	300	50

The number of background daemons dedicated to pre-fetching file data and delayed writing is by default 2. Machines that will be heavily used by many processes or many users may benefit from an increased number of background daemons (to a maximum of 6). Use the -daemons option.

Two other options to afsd allow you change some of the client cache manager's assumptions about the initial connection to AFS. You can use the -mount-dir option to mount the AFS file system at a different directory than /afs, and the -rootvol option to specify that that directory is to be connected to a different root volume than the default, root.afs. Having AFS mounted at a different directory is a small convenience, though you could just create a symbolic link from anywhere on the client to /afs.

In-kernel memory caches work exactly the same as do disk-based caches, except that certain parameters are interpreted differently because of the normally reduced size of the cache. For example, no cache directory is created, even though it is still specified in the cacheinfo file, and rather than storing data into V-files, cached data is stored in contiguous chunks of kernel memory with the default size of 8 kilobytes for each chunk. There is also no CacheItems file nor a VolumeItems file as all entries are in memory.

As users proceed with their day-to-day work, files, directories, groups, and various other data will be cached by the client. You can quickly check how large the cache is and how much is being used with the command

```
$ fs getcacheparms
AFS using 81487 of the cache's available 100000 1K byte blocks.
```

The cache size can be adjusted on the fly if desired.

```
# fs setcachesize 120000
New cache size set.
# fs getcacheparms
AFS using 81487 of the cache's available 120000 1K byte blocks.
```

When you configure the cache, be aware that it will help in the long run for the cache to reside in its own disk partition. The AFS kernel module makes many assumptions about its cache, not the least of which is that the cache is solely under its control. Giving the cache its own partition helps to ensure that no other processes can inadvertently use up cache disk space.

The size of the cache indicated in the cacheinfo file or on the command line should be about 95 percent of the actual size of the partition. As mentioned, the cache area holds many large data structures that manage the AFS client protocol and also holds the space for the file cache itself. The cache size parameter describes only the area of the file chunks, so some leeway must be made for other data. If you set aside a 100-megabyte partition, you should only configure 95 megabytes of file cache.

Memory caches need to be large, but because the space is needed for running programs and other non-AFS kernel structures, you will have to experiment to find a good balance between cache and application performance. Memory caches of less than 1 megabyte will not be functional; at least 5 megabytes should be available. Chapter 10 describes some tools you can use to determine the cache hit ratio.

Note that even disk-based AFS caches use the kernel's memory buffer pool when reading and writing data to disk. For example, during an application write request, the written data is really stored in the operating system's buffer cache or memory-mapped file segment. Regularly, this data will be swept out of the cache by the kernel and stored on disk, but this is only an optimization used by the kernel to speed up disk writes. As far as the cache manager is concerned, when it re-reads newly cached file chunks the manager reads the data off the disk. If the client is lucky, the data will still be in a memory segment which will further speed up operations.

One final comment about the client cache: Multiple users on a single workstation will share their cache but authorization checks are performed separately for each user. If one user reads a publicly available file, the next user will find and use that data in the cache. If the file is not public but only permitted to the first user, the next user will find the item in the cache, the authorization check will be performed, and that read or write access will be denied.

FINDING AFS SERVERS

Managing the client's database of cells is usually a simple process. The CellServDB file must be a local file; it is read once by afsd which passes the data into the kernel as AFS is starting up. You can see the cells that the kernel knows about with this command:

```
$ fs listcells
Cell hq.firm on hosts db-one db-two db-three
Cell transarc.com on hosts oscar.transarc.com ernie.transarc.com
bigbird.transarc.com
```

To administer changes to a client CellServDB, simply edit or copy over a new version of the file. But because the cache manager reads the file's contents only at startup, you can't just edit the file and leave it at that. To make changes to a running client, you should make the changes first to the file and then run an fs command to install the new data into the kernel module.

```
# fs newcell transarc.com oscar.transarc.com ernie.transarc.com
# fs listcells
Cell hq.firm on hosts db-one db-two db-three
Cell transarc.com oscar.transarc.com ernie.transarc.com
```

One nice feature of the `newcell` subcommand is that you can give DNS names as arguments to the command rather than having to determine the absolute IP addresses and edit them into a file. Indeed, you could dynamically add the majority of the cell server database to a client's kernel rather than relying on the static `CellServDB` file. You'll still need to bootstrap the process with your own cell's entry in the file, though.

As a machine contacts file and database servers, it constructs a table of preferences which it uses when determining which servers to prefer. The value runs from 1 to 65,534; a lower value indicates a stronger preference. The values can be thought of as the cost or distance to a server—a lower value is cheaper or closer to a client.

File server machine preferences are calculated as the systems are discovered during volume lookups. Default values are assigned on the basis of implicit network address information:

- 40,000—If the server is on a different network than the client or the server's network data is unavailable
- 30,000—If the the server is on the same network as the client; also if the server is at the end of a point-to-point link from the client
- 20,000—If the server is on the same sub-net as the client
- 5,000—If the server is running on the client

As can be seen, these preferences will generally encourage a client to access the closest server according to the network topology. File servers which are seen to be closer, that is, on the same subnet as the client, get numerical values higher than other file servers. During an outage, if a file server fails to respond to a file access request, its preference value will be made greater than any other server. If the request was for a file in a read-write volume, the client is out of luck; if the request was for a file in a read-only volume, the client will try to contact the next closest server that is storing a copy of the same read-only volume.

Administrators can manually adjust the preferences used by a client to predetermine which replica sites it chooses to use. The current preferences can be viewed with the `fs` command:

```
$ fs getserverprefs
fs-one        20014
fs-two        20008
```

To have a client prefer the server fs-two over all other servers, use the
setpreferences subcommand with a suitable value (from 0 to 65,534):

```
# fs setserverprefs fs-two 1000
# fs getserverprefs
fs-one          20014
fs-two          1004
```

From now on, if a read-only is available from multiple servers, the client
will prefer to retrieve file data from fs-two.

The preferential value for fs-two is not exactly 1000 because the client
kernel numerically ORs the desired value with a random 4-bit number. When
preferences are calculated automatically, this technique ensures that each client
sees slightly different preferences by default and therefore automatically distributes the load from a set of clients across all replica servers.

Similar preferences can be set for access to database servers. Rather than
having a client pick a volume location or protection database server at random,
you can adjust the preferences.

```
# fs getserverprefs -vlservers
db-one          20006
db-two          30012
db-three        30008
# fs setserverprefs -vlservers db-one 6000
```

Actually, clients are proactive in their search for inaccessible servers. Every
10 minutes a client will send a probe message to each database server in its list
and to all file servers which have established callbacks for it. If no response is
received, the client assumes the worst and marks the server as being down. The
next requests to be sent to that server will be redirected to either another database or file server, as needed, but the client will also assume that this failure
will be quickly corrected; it will probe the down servers every three minutes
waiting for their resurrection. Users may notice messages to this effect on the
system console.

Server preference rankings are the standard mechanism by which a central
administrator can begin to control the network traffic from a client. In a typical
wide-area network, there may be high-speed LANs at the departmental level,
with medium-speed links between separate buildings. A natural AFS architecture would position file servers with standard sets of replicas and a database
server in each building. This locality will benefit clients as long as they are

aware of the logical distances between themselves and the servers. The server preferences metric provides that measure but at the same time is only a hint to the client. If the cheapest or closest servers are unavailable, the cache manager will move on to the next available system, even if that system is located elsewhere on the WAN. In a working environment, AFS therefore provides optimizations to maximize the distributed file system; if that environment begins to fail, AFS will try to work around the faults.

As with the `CellServDB` file, there is no mechanism in AFS for the centralized control of this information. To extract the best values for a client, you might want to keep a file in a well-known location. A program could easily read the file and compute preferences on the basis of known network or geographic indexes. You should also note that numerical preferences for a cell are reset to default values when the `fs newcell` command is used.

Adventurous administrators could deliberately have different machine entries for the same cell in the `CellServDB` file on different clients. If client A's `CellServDB` file listed only the `db-one` machine for our cell, the effect would be similar to `db-two` and `db-three` having an infinitely large numerical preference and `db-two` and `db-three` would never be contacted by this client. The only benefit to this arrangement is that it guarantees that the client could never contact certain database servers; with a fully populated `CellServDB`, no matter what preferences were initially set, the client might eventually fail over to using `db-two`. This technique would effectively forbid a particular network path to a client. As long as the AFS servers' `CellServDB` contains the complete set of database servers, there's no danger of the server data becoming inconsistent: all clients will still see the same data. This client-side-only solution simply helps to direct traffic in a deterministic fashion.

Another way to manipulate the AFS namespace on a per-client basis is to have different clients mount AFS using different root volumes. The standard convention is to have all clients mount the well-known `root.afs` volume with multiple, second-level mounts of the local and various remote cells' `root.cell` volume. Some enterprises might want to have certain client populations—perhaps a set of production users—connect to a different root volume, maybe, `root.prod`. The benefit is that their namespace could be deliberately constrained so that access to certain volumes would be difficult. However, maintaining strict administrative control over two or more root level volumes may outweigh any perceived benefits; and anyway, restricting access can be performed more reliably with AFS access control lists.

Even with AFS replication and fail over, there is one failure mode that is not handled perfectly. Normally, when a file is requested and the request times out due to either a network failure or server crash, the client will try to perform the same read request from another server. When the file is not replicated, the client will have to report this failure as an error to the user. If the requested file is a running binary and the read request was intended to page-in a program text segment, the result will be a process crash. If the file is a replicated binary, this situation is highly unlikely because at least one of the read-only server will probably be available. Still, the problem could arise if, say, the client's network interface card failed.

An NFS client can specify the elasticity of the protocol connection with the -soft or -hard option to the NFS mount command. Soft connections return errors on failures; hard connections will hang, repeating the operation until, once the underlying failure has been corrected, the request succeeds.

In AFS, all access is essentially soft which means that an error will be returned if there is no server response. The problem is that in extraordinary circumstances when all all replicated read-only copies are temporarily unavailable, running processes may fail. This is contrary to the goal of a highly available file service. The lack of a hard-retry option for read-only volumes—which admittedly would only come into effect under very rare circumstances—is an oversight of the AFS design.

PROTOCOL OPTIMIZATIONS

Up to now, the AFS file access protocol has been discussed at a somewhat high level. For practical reasons, certain optimizations have been added to the system to improve its performance without changing the essential architecture. The simplest improvement is that when a client fetches a chunk of a file from a server, it will return with that data and then go ahead and get the next chunk from the file, prefetching it from the server in anticipation of a user's subsequent read request.

As previously described, when a client accesses a file in a read-write volume, the server keeps track of that access in order to send a callback to the client if the file is ever changed. The problem with this noble policy is that the server will have many thousands of files and clients and therefore, the server will potentially have to track a tremendous amount of information. To reduce the size of this table, each server timestamps the access and after 30 minutes deletes the client from the list of accessors for that file.

Naturally, clients are aware of this optimization. They know that if they haven't been called back about a file in 30 minutes, the server has deliberately forgotten about them. So, if a user needs access to a file later than 30 minutes after the previous access, the client cache manager knows that it can't rely on the absence of a callback to assume the file is unchanged. In this case, the client sends a brief query packet to the server to check on the file's version, using the uniquifier number. If the local copy is still the most current, the server and client reestablish another callback guarantee; if a new version is available, the client will quickly bring over the new file and set up the usual callback. This optimization keeps the spirit of the general callback architecture alive while saving considerable bookkeeping effort on the server.

When accessing a file in a read-only volume, servers do not do much bookkeeping at all, under the assumption that read-only volume data changes infrequently. So rather than keep a per-file list of client accesses to read-only data, servers track only per-volume accesses. When the read-write master is released over to all read-only versions, the server calls back just those clients that have read from the volume.

This optimization was introduced with AFS 3.4a, but its importance cannot be overstated. Previously, read-only data would unilaterally be invalidated by clients every two hours. Because read-only data is presumably some set of production binaries released from a read-write staging, it was assumed that the data would not change frequently and so a two-hour timeout would suffice to keep it fresh. If a user needed to see the latest data, a command was available to flush data.

This assumption sounds reasonable but in practice caused precisely the problem that AFS tried to guarantee would never happen: different files seen by different clients. Now that AFS servers send messages to clients when read-only data changes, all clients know that they will always see the latest data all the time.

You can still use the `flush` subcommands if you'd like. One version, `fs flush`, marks the named file's local copy as invalid, thus causing the client to retrieve the data from the server on the next access. With the aid of the `getcacheparms` subcommand, we can see precisely how flushing invalidates cached file data.

```
$ fs getcacheparms
AFS using 50467 of the cache's available 120000 1K byte blocks.
$ ls -l bar
```

```
-rw-r--r--   1 afsadmin staff     10485760 Mar 29 15:06 bar
$ fs flush bar
$ fs getcacheparms
AFS using 40227 of the cache's available 120000 1K byte blocks.
```

Another subcommand, flushvolume, causes all file data associated with a volume to be invalidated. However, there is no command available to flush the entire file cache. If an entire client flush is required, it can be simulated by resizing the cache to zero bytes momentarily.

```
# fs getcacheparms
AFS using 40227 of the cache's available 120000 1K byte blocks.
# fs setcachesize 0
New cache size set.
# fs setcachesize 120000
New cache size set.
# fs getcacheparms
AFS using 0 of the cache's available 120000 1K byte blocks.
```

As mentioned, the current release of AFS keeps clients informed of changes to both read-write and read-only file data. The only data that is not invalidated when it changes is information on volume locations and mappings between volume names and identifiers. But the lack of an explicit invalidation protocol for this data does not cause any problem. For example, the first time a client notices a volume connection, the volume identification number and location data is retrieved from the VLDB and cached for further use. If the volume is moved, a client will not be told of the new location or that the cached data is invalid. The reason is simply that volume moves are rare events, rarer even than changes released to read-only volumes. Clients only learn that a volume has moved when they try to access its old location; the volserver on that server will respond with an error and that will cause the client to turn to the VLDB server and retrieve the new location information. Hence, no user or application will see a location inconsistency.

Although there is a small delay as the correct data is fetched, it's really not much more of a delay than would be needed even with some sort of callback. And it is reasonable for the client to bear the burden of correcting the data rather than forcing the server to keep track of yet another set of callbacks. However, to reduce the number of wrong requests, cached volume data is marked invalid once an hour, forcing the client to retrieve the latest location and volume name to identifier mappings reasonably often.

One small inconsistency can still slip through, though it is mostly noticed by administrators. Let's create a volume and make a volume mount point; the mount point is only a directory and volume name stored in the file system, but the client cache manager will need to cache the mapping between the volume name and its identifier number.

```
$ vos create fs-one a vol.1
Volume 536871010 created on partition /vicepa of fs-one
$ fs mkm vol.1 vol.1
$ ls vol.1
$
```

All works as expected and the client has now cached the mapping between the name vol.1 and the volume number 536871010. Now, we cause that volume identifier to change by deleting the volume and creating a brand-new volume with the same name.

```
$ vos remove fs-one a vol.1
Volume 536871010 on partition /vicepa server fs-one deleted
$ vos create fs-one a vol.1
Volume 536871013 created on partition /vicepa of fs-one
$ ls vol.1
vol.1: No such device
```

As you can see, when accessing the mount point, the client tries to retrieve data from the file server but is told that the volume, by that number, no longer exists. When the client queries the VLDB by using the old identification number, the VLDB also responds that that volume doesn't exist. This result is returned to the directory listing program as a prominent error.

The problem is that the mapping between the volume name, vol.1, and its identification number was never invalidated. In the unlikely event that this situation occurs, you can use the checkvolumes subcommand to invalidate all data, such as volume-identifier mappings, which has no callback mechanism. After invalidating the mapping, the client will have to fetch the up-to-date data.

```
$ fs checkvolumes
All volumeID/name mappings checked.
$ ls vol.1
$
```

Again, this situation is rare as clients flush all such mappings from their cache once an hour.

Manually flushing the file cache is not needed at all because it is the client cache manager's job to occasionally flush files on its own in order to free up space in the disk area reserved for the cache. Inevitably, a client's cache may be filled with data: both cached chunks being read and chunks that have been written by some application but not yet shipped back to the server. When the cache is filled in this way and a user process wants to read some data not yet cached, the cache manager must choose which local chunks can be invalidated and overwritten with new chunked data.

When choosing data to free up, the client first flushes any files from read-only volumes. As this data is readily available, it is considered to be cheap and hence not much of a burden to retrieve. This read-only data is further prioritized by timestamp: file data with the oldest timestamp will be flushed first. After all the read-only data has been flushed, if the cache manager needs still more local space, files from read-write volumes will be flushed. In this case, while it is presumably more important than read-only data, it can still be retrieved as needed. Again, the oldest files are flushed first.

At the extreme, on machines with a very small cache, there may be a case where there are only write chunks in the cache—chunks which a process is perhaps still in the act of writing. Here, the cache manager will not be able to make room for read chunks, so it returns an I/O error to the requesting application. This behavior is quite rare, usually requiring pathological circumstances and memory caches less than 5 megabytes. Applications that are reading file data and observe I/O errors will have to either retry the requests internally or be rerun by the user.

One final cache optimization concerns writing large files. The protocol states that as an application is writing file data, the data is stored locally. When the file closes, all the data is shipped to the server, which can then store the whole file as a single transaction. But if the file is larger than the local client cache, the client is forced to send the file to the server in pieces. It would violate the protocol to overwrite the current version of the file with the new data before the close occurred, so the server writes the data to its `vice` partition under the new version number of the file. If other users need access to this file while the writing is still in progress, they will be accessing the correct, previous version. When the file is finally closed, the previous version is discarded, the new version put in place, and interested clients are called back. The effect is exactly the same as with the regular protocol, though it takes some additional work by the client and server.

As of AFS release 3.4a, some additional options have been added to the client side to help manage the timing of write requests. One problem is that because files are only normally written back to the server when they are closed, large files can cause an apparent performance bottleneck.

A new option permits files to have a different behavior: the file is written back to the server at close, but the `close` system call returns before the write operation is finished. This behavior allows the process to continue, although it introduces a potential point of error. But even though the `close` system call returns earlier than expected, the AFS protocol is maintained; this user process continues to hold a lock to the file during the write, and no other write-on-close operation on another machine will interfere with this version of the file. The primary drawback is that with the `close` system call immediately returning, the program will most likely not be notified of any failures during the write processing.

This *storebehind* behavior can be turned on for all files greater than a certain size or for a set of named files. The benefit with this option is that it can be used by any users for any file to which they have write permission; all other storebehind options require root privilege.

Alternatively, the exact behavior of the `close` system call can be set with the `-allfiles` option. Normally, any `close` system call returns only when all bytes have be sent to the server, in other words, when zero bytes remain on the client. The `-allfiles` option specifies the different number of kilobytes which could remain on the client still waiting to be sent to the server when the close system call returns: `-allfiles 100` would return control to the calling process when any file of any size had sent all but 100 kilobytes back to the server.

At some point, a client machine might crash due to either a hardware or an operating system fault. If the crash occurs with no open files, then, upon reboot, the cache manager will realize that server callback notices may have occurred while the client was unavailable. So, after a reboot, the client does not assume that any cached files are valid and therefore checks each file open request against the file's version number on the server.

If a client crash occurs when a file is open for writing and data has not been shipped back to the server, the newly rebooted client simply discards the locally written data; because the process that was writing the data is no longer available, there's no way to send a coherent copy of the file to the server. For this reason, application writers using AFS to store critical file data via a long-running process should regularly close or otherwise force recently written data to the server's disk.

If the crash occurs during a `close` request, all of the data may be stored correctly on the local disk and some will have been written to the server. On the server, this data will be stored in a new, partially completed file. After the write connection to the server is lost, the server will assume that the client has crashed and will delete the partial file. The client on reboot will not be able to recreate the state of the system, and the data will be lost.

During a client reboot, the local operating system's disk consistency check program runs to maintain the integrity of the internal file and directory data structures. Unlike AFS file servers, the `fsck` program on the client should remain the vendor's standard executable.

WINDOWS NT CLIENTS

PCs running Windows NT version 3.51 or greater are now able to use a native port of the AFS client to access a cell's files. This port makes available to the NT desktop all the benefits of the AFS caching protocol: highly reliable read-only data access, location transparency for data stored on any AFS server on the Internet, and the integrated security model. The only concession in this release is that only memory caches are supported so that the cache is not persistent across reboots.

The installation and configuration steps are similar to the ones described above for UNIX clients, with some PC-like flourishes. But Transarc does not support file or database servers on PCs, nor are any server or cell administration commands ported to the PC client. The Windows NT port is solely concerned with those items that will configure the client properly, connect the desktop to the AFS cell, and authenticate the user.

Once AFS is installed onto a PC, two additions are made to the standard NT administration toolset: an AFS Client Configuration tool in the Windows Control Panel and, in the Control Panel Services list, an AFS daemon entry. Additionally, a program group labelled Transarc AFS is added to the program manager or "Start" menu.

During initial set up, you'll be asked if you want to configure the client immediately. When the client configuration tool runs, a dialog box enables the NT client administrator to change certain parameters of the client. These parameters are similar to the ones managed by the UNIX `cacheinfo` file and `afsd` command line options. Figure 5-2 is a snapshot of this dialog.

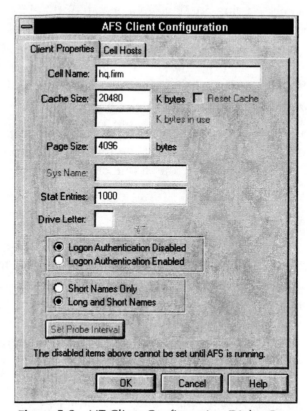

Figure 5-2 NT Client Configuration Dialog Box

The dialog box has two tabs to allow you to modify basic AFS client parameters and to set up a list of cells available to this client. The following parameters must be set:

Cell Name—Enter the name of the local cell into this field.

Cache Size—Enter the size of the cache you want the AFS client to use. The Windows port uses reserved areas of the NT virtual-memory page space to store the cached file data. Although the cache uses virtual-memory which uses the local disk as a backing store, this is not a disk cache—cached data is not persistent across machine reboots.

Because other NT programs use large amounts of virtual-memory space too, you may need to change your NT operating system configuration to allocate more virtual-memory space before resetting the AFS cache size. After installation, the default size is 20 megabytes, indicated as 20,480 one-kilobyte blocks. You can enter any size as long as it is not greater than the virtual-memory available on the machine. If you can, adjust your memory configuration to allow for 50–100 megabytes of cache. While AFS is running, you can increase, but not decrease, the cache size.

This field also displays the size of the cache currently being used.

Reset Cache—Pressing this dialog button sets the cache back to the installation default of 20 megabytes.

Page Size—Enter the page size used by the AFS client. The client cache manager keeps file data in chunks of the virtual-memory space. Each chunk, called a page, is by default 4 kilobytes large. You can set the page size to any power of 2, say, 2, 4, 8, 16, etc., kilobytes.

Unlike those of a UNIX AFS client, these page sizes are not the same as the chunk size used when retrieving data from an AFS server. NT clients use a fixed chunk size of 32 kilobytes.

Sys Name—Enter an alternate AFS system name. When navigating through path names that contain elements named `@sys`, the local client cache translates the `@sys` element name into this name. The default value is `i86_nt`. This value can only be reset once the client is running.

Stat Entries—Enter the number of files for which the client will cache status information. This information is cached in addition to the data cache size set above. By default, 1,000 files can have status records cached.

Short Names Only/Long and Short Names—This pair of radio buttons determines how this client will translate long names of files in AFS. With "Short Names Only" checked, any file name in AFS that does not conform to the 8.3 convention—8 characters followed by an optional three character extension—is displayed with some of the rightmost eight characters replaced with a tilde and some unique, randomly set characters: a file named `longFileName` could be displayed as `longF~x1`. Additionally, suffixes longer than three characters are simply truncated: an HTML file named `index.html` will be displayed as `index.htm`.

When "Long and Short Names" is checked, no translations are used. In most cases, this is the preferred option. Now that current versions of Windows can understand long file names, it makes sense to have PCs access the same files in AFS with the same names as other UNIX systems.

Figure 5-3   NT Cell Configuration Dialog Box

Set Probe Interval—Enter an alternate value for the client cache probe interval. In normal operation, a PC AFS client (just like a UNIX AFS client) will send off an RPC query to the file servers it has encountered during the client's running lifetime. When an RPC fails to return, the client can guess that the server (or the network) is down and will take steps to work around the problem if possible. The interval can be set, in seconds, from 10 minutes to 1 second.

The second tab in the configuration dialog box enables you to manage the list of available cells similar to the list in the `CellServDB` file on a UNIX system. This list is kept in the file `afsdcell.ini` and can be maintained and downloaded separately. The dialog box presents a graphical interface to edit the entries as illustrated in Figure 5-3.

The "Cells" button pops up a scrolling list of all the cells that have been entered into the cell/server mapping. This dialog box permits editing this list with an additional set of buttons.

- **Add**—This button activates a further dialog box in which you can enter the name of a new cell and the set of database servers associated with that cell.

- **Delete**—After a verification pop-up, the selected cell is deleted from the local mapping.

- **Edit**—This button displays a dialog by which you can change the name of a cell or make modifications to the list of database servers associated with a cell.

Most changes to these configuration parameters will require a reboot in order to take effect.

Once AFS is configured, you can run the Services tool in the Control Panel to enable the AFS cache manager. This tool can also set up the cache manager to start upon every reboot if you select the "Automatic" type from the startup button.

Once the cache manager is set to run, you can attach the AFS cell file namespace to any drive letter desired, either by issuing a command or by connecting to a network drive in the File Manager. Before connecting, you need to know the host name of the PC; run the `hostname` command if necessary. Also, even though user authentication is performed later (see Chapter 7), a user name must be presented at connect time. Given a PC desktop named `clientpc` that Alice is using, she can attach the AFS cell to her Z: drive by entering at a command prompt:

```
C:> net use z: \\clientpc-afs\alice
```

Internally, the NT AFS client cache accepts normal Windows Server Message Block requests from the NT kernel. These SMB requests are examined by the AFS client code with, as on a UNIX client, some requests satisfied locally and others requiring that further requests be sent to an available server by means of AFS's regular Rx protocol.

The only difference in the caching system is this: currently, directory caching is not supported because of the difference in UNIX versus NT style caching—NT wants to cache whole-path lookups, whereas UNIX wants to cache individual path element data.

Windows NT supports a universal name convention for file names, beginning with a double backslash. When the `net user` command is run, the NT client's operating system will check with the installed distributed file systems to see if they have encountered the universal name `clientpc-afs`. Even though AFS does not use a universal or domain-based naming scheme, the `-afs` suffix is recognized as the signal for AFS to start up and use the other configuration information to attach to the local AFS cell.

If you are more comfortable using the File Manager interface rather than the command line, simply open a File Manager and select "Connect Network Drive" from the Disk menu button. Using the same PC host name and user as above, in the resulting dialog box, enter `\\clientpc-afs\alice` in the Path field and press the OK button.

After you run either the command line or File Manager interface, you can gain access to the top of the local cell's file namespace by changing to the Z: drive.

```
C:> z:
z:> dir
 Volume in drive Z has no label.
 Volume Serial Number is 70AF-4815

 Directory of Z:\

05/14/97   09:20p         <DIR>         HQ.FIRM

05/14/97   10:01p         <DIR>         TRANSARC.COM
```

From here on, file navigation and access is straightforward. As you move between files and directories, you'll notice a slight time lag on the first reference to a file. Then, once the file is cached, the performance will be practically equivalent to local performance. The PC client behaves in this respect much like its UNIX counterpart: When files are accessed in read-write volumes, all data is read and cached; all saved file data is written to the server and other clients are informed of the changes. Read-only data is accessed by contacting any of the available servers.

If your local cell includes connections to other cells on the Internet, there's no extra configuration needed to get to that data; the connections will have been stored in the top-level directories of AFS itself. All files and directories your desktop UNIX box can see are visible all the time from this NT desktop (permissions permitting). Simply by accessing files with path names like z:\transarc.com\public, you can read public data stored at Transarc headquarters, just as you can from UNIX clients.

Though AFS provides access to files from either UNIX or NT clients, it doesn't know anything about the files or their contents, nor does it understand what the applications using the files are trying to do. Differences between UNIX and NT will continue to be a sore point; file and directory naming rules may be different, and text files will still use different conventions to signal end-of-line and end-of-file. As for file names, the NT client will perform translations as needed through its native SMB-based, name-lookup module.

The Windows port comes with several executables, libraries, and DLL files, which are all stored in the general support directory C:\Trans32. In this directory, some AFS commands are provided that are similar to their counter-parts on UNIX. Among the command-line executables ported to NT are: `fs.exe`, `klog.exe`, `tokens.exe`, and `unlog.exe`. Some functionality, such as server preferences, is not currently supported. Other AFS commands are available from a new menu option in the File Manager tool bar; some of these commands are discussed in Chapter 7.

PC-ENTERPRISE

Another software package is available to help connect PC clients to AFS. Plati-num Technology offers PC-Enterprise for the Windows 95, Windows 3.11, straight DOS platforms and even Macintosh System 7.0+. Previously known as PC-Interface™ from Locus, it provides authenticated access to the AFS file sys-tem as well as access to UNIX domain printers.

The PC-Enterprise server process runs on an AFS UNIX client. A down-stream client of this machine will contact the PC-Enterprise server process when reading or writing files. The actual data movement into or out of AFS is therefore mediated by the AFS UNIX client; this client acts as a sort of translator from the PC-Enterprise client's protocol into the AFS protocol. The AFS servers and data do not see or hear the PC-Enterprise client directly.

For authenticated access, software that permits local user authentication against the AFS cell's security system is installed on the downstream client. When run on this client, the procedure spawns a subprocess on the AFS client with the given authentication credential. This subprocess can then access any file permitted to the user on the AFS client, which can include the local UNIX file system, any NFS mounted systems, etc.

Note that because a PC-Enterprise client is not an AFS client, there are no `CellServDB` or cache size issues to manage. All access to the distributed file system takes place through requests sent to an intermediate workstation that is running the AFS client code.

Once PC-Enterprise is installed, the PC client side immediately attaches the translator machine's file namespace to an available drive letter:

```
C:> login
username: alice
password:

C:> d:

D:> cd \afs\hq.firm
```

```
D:> dir
 Volume in drive D has no label.
 Volume Serial Number is 419E-7320

 Directory of D:\

 05/15/97   11:21a            <DIR>            GROUP

 05/15/97   11:17a            <DIR>            SYS

 05/15/97   11:18a            <DIR>            TMP

 05/15/97   11:15a            <DIR>            USER
```

INSTALLING CLIENTS AND AFS PATHS

Although the AFS file system is an ideal repository for much file data used by users and processes, you may wish to store certain data on the client disk itself. Some sites may desire to prune this set of client-side files to the absolute minimum; others may want to have relatively disk-full clients. In either case, AFS can still be used as the ultimate storage area for these files. As needed, you would copy the appropriate set of client-side files from some standard location in AFS to the local disk.

Transarc provides a utility, called package, that automates this copying process. The system permits you to define the files, directories, links, and devices to be installed on a client. You can run the package command on each client, perhaps during the booting sequence, to check for new versions of the files stored in AFS and to install them if necessary on the local disk.

In the package definition files, you can use variables to define common paths and file permissions and to resolve file names, depending on the hardware architecture and operating system version a particular client is running. This prototype file is then processed by a Transarc-supplied utility, mpp, to produce a configuration file specific to a given client. See the AFS System Administration Guide for a full discussion of this system.

A public domain system, called depot, performs a similar function. Transarc's FTP site contains some information on where to find the latest version of depot.

Without automatic fail over to redundant file data and without the caching of frequently used files, most administrators of desktop computing sites try to put many important programs and libraries on a client's local disk. With

AFS's fail over and aggressive caching, manually copying files to a desktop is somewhat of a wasted effort. Because AFS has matured to the point that the performance of cached files approaches access to purely local files, it is an unnecessary administrative burden to decide which users on which client machines need which subsets of all available files. Better to let AFS automatically and silently keep the appropriate files cached locally, based on the current user's particular access patterns.

This caching strategy suggests that almost all normally local files be stored in AFS: the user's home directory, application files, software development environments, and even the majority of system files. It is a fairly straightforward exercise to pare down to a few dozen the number of files that absolutely must be installed onto a computer. On UNIX systems, these are most likely the kernel, /etc/init, some /etc/rc files, and, of course, the AFS client daemon and configuration files. The system boots in much the usual way, but as soon as the network is configured, the AFS client starts up. Strategically placed links from the local disk into a suitable area of the AFS namespace then give the illusion that all the other startup files are available. And since these files are most likely cached, the overhead to get to the data is negligible. Also, because these files will be replicated, the booting client is guaranteed that the files will always be available.

With the advent of the World Wide Web, there is a lot of talk of "thin clients" getting their data from the network. AFS provides this functionality now. An aggressive administrator can streamline the installation of an AFS client to just the few minutes that it takes to copy the right kernel and related files onto local disk. Not only are all other system files stored in AFS so that updating system software is trivial, but a desktop's specific configuration data is also stored primarily in the centrally managed file system where it can be coordinated, backed up, and managed easily.

Typically, the @sys path name element is used to link from a standard path name to a platform-specific one. When the AFS kernel module is loaded at system boot time, it includes a hardcoded value that is substituted every time the path name component @sys is seen. This procedure enables users on different machine types to use the same path—any file or directory path name that includes an @sys element—to access suitable binaries for their architectures.

For example, Transarc suggests installing a set of their software tools in a standard directory in AFS. Because each machine type Transarc supports requires its own set of binaries, a path which includes @sys allows all clients to use the same path to retrieve the appropriate set of binaries.

When installing the Sun version of the software built for the Solaris 2.5 platform, you could copy the programs into a directory named /afs/ hq.firm/os/afsws/sparc_sunos55/bin; you would copy the IBM version into /afs/hq.firm/os/afsws/rs_aix41/bin. Note that the exact name of the architecture is embedded as a single element in the path name. These names are preset as the respective translations of the @sys element in the Sun and IBM cache managers.

To use this automatic translation, create a symbolic link from /afs/ hq.firm/os/afsws/bin to @sys/bin. Now, no matter if a user's system is a Sun or an IBM machine, the path /afs/hq.firm/os/afsws/bin will be automatically directed to the correct architectural subdirectory.

That path name is somewhat long and difficult to remember, so you could install one more symbolic link on each client from /usr/afsws to /afs/ hq.firm/os/afsws. Finally, a user can configure the PATH variable to include /usr/afsws/bin. On a Sun machine, this link will evaluate to /afs/ hq.firm/os/afsws/bin, and then to /afs/hq.firm/os/afsws/@sys/ bin/, and then, finally, to /afs/hq.firm/os/afsws/sparc_suno55/bin; on an IBM machine, the link will point to /afs/hq.firm/os/afsws/ rs_aix41/bin.

Transarc's default names for @sys paths are usually good enough for most organizations. As ports to new hardware and operating system levels are produced by the company, they add a new value only when their AFS software needs a nontrivial change. If their code (which uses many kernel and networking interfaces) doesn't need a new @sys value, your application program probably doesn't either. But if you do need your own values, use the fs sysname command. In normal use, you would run this command immediately after loading the AFS kernel module so that all accesses to files in AFS will be translated the same way.

The drawback to @sys paths is that they usually require a few symbolic links on the client and server side. The benefit is that executables for multiple architectures can be installed and managed in a single file namespace through the use of simple directory utilities, links, and path names.

Another common convention is to install a symbolic link at the top of the /afs tree so that a machine's local cell can be determined easily: for example, /afs/@cell is installed as a symbolic link pointing to hq.firm. The @cell name has nothing to do with per-client @sys lookup but is intended to remind users of the @sys convention.

CONVENIENT PATH NAMES

It's quite likely that even if you use AFS today, you'll be using another file system tomorrow, perhaps DFS or even NFS. This possibility makes it unwise to construct all of your administration procedures with embedded path names that include the /afs/ prefix. It may be better to use a neutral name as your own suffix. That way, you can point it to whatever system you choose and even construct more convenient top-level directory namespaces. For example, you could make /hq/ a symbolic link to /afs/hq.firm, thus making the global AFS namespace available and providing an easier-to-type day-to-day equivalent. That way, a user's home directory could be just /hq/home/alice. Different divisions of an organization might want a similarly abbreviated namespace, for example, /sales could point to /hq/sales or /afs/hq.firm/sales.

These abbreviations, however, will probably have to be maintained on the local disk of all client machines. Yet with a little creativity, file namespaces that are easy to remember and type can be constructed to fit almost any purpose. And sometimes, this convenience is important not just for typing but for the program's execution.

As an example, let's compare how NFS and AFS deal with home directories. With the NFS automount daemon, it is common enough to have everyone's home directory available from either /u or /home. But because of the architecture of automount, if you list the /home directory, for example, you'll see nothing. You must explicitly ask for an individual's home before it will be mounted. This makes it very difficult to browse for information; if you don't know a user's exact login name, you can't scan the directories because they are not yet mounted. You also can't expand a path name with wildcards, as in ls /home/*/.mail, for example, to see who's using a particular software package.

On the other hand, AFS presents a totally consistent image of the file system to all clients. Once an administrator has connected a user's volume to a name like /hq/home/alice, everyone can see it. So, browsing is made very easy. The price of this consistency is that for large organizations, putting all the users in one directory makes for a very long directory listing. Having a thousand users get their home via automount is no big deal because only one or two homes will be mounted on a given desktop at any time. But in AFS, /hq/home could be filled with a thousand names; while this is not a problem technically, many programs, including ls and graphical directory browsers, want to get file information for each and every entry in the directory so they can display appropriate information, such as a folder or file icon. This process can take a lot of time: each entry in such a directory must have its status information read and, possibly, some of the initial bytes of file data examined, just so some graphical navigator can display a pretty picture of the file. Of course, once cached locally, this access will be quick, but the initial access will be slow and will cause much network traffic.

To speed up access, you might divide the home directories among several subdirectories. Almost any such scheme will do. Many organizations have chosen to use completely arbitrary subdirectories: /hq/home/user1/alice, /hq/home/user2/bob, etc. Others set up directories that reflect the organization's internal structure: /hq/sales/home/alice and /hq/research/home/bob. The drawback here is that for every reorganization and personnel change, home directory path names have to change.

Another solution is to use a simple algorithm based on the user's name: use a subdirectory named after the first letter of the login name: /hq/home/a/alice, /hq/home/b/bob. This solution is similar to the arbitrary method in that the subdirectory has no intrinsic meaning but has the benefit of being completely predictable. This one-level of indirection reduces the size of each home directory area to a manageable number; from a random list of 1,000 common login names, a single directory containing all 1,000 entries is broken down to 26 subdirectories, the largest being /hq/home/s with 300 and /hq/home/m with 200 names. Some large sites, such as the University of Michigan, which supports over 60,000 home directories, have gone to the extreme of using the first two letters as keys to subdirectories, as in /hq/home/a/l/alice, /hq/home/b/o/bob. This plan may seem silly, but the largest subdirectories now turn out to be /hq/home/s/a with 30 entries and /hq/home/m/e with 20 entries; the paths are easy to use, and the small number of directory entries can speed up many applications.

A compromise is to offer more than one solution, perhaps having a primary path based on an algorithmic-style name, while making other directory structures available, such as an organization tree, implemented with either symbolic links to the home directory or additional mount points to the home volume.

SET-USER-IDENTIFIER PROGRAMS

Programs can be installed in the UNIX file system such that when executed, the user running the program will be able to obtain different user rights. This capability to set a new user identity is stored in an extra permission bit in the file system, the setuid bit. When any user runs a setuid program, the program will execute using the identity of the file's owner—often root. That way, for example, certain programs will be able to write into secure areas of the local file system no matter who runs the program.

Creating and permitting the execution of setuid programs is a serious security issue because a fundamental unit of control, a user's identity, is being automatically delegated. Only the owner of a file may set the setuid bit; thus, only the UNIX root user may create a program which will set its user identity to root.

As an example of such a program, the UNIX substitute user program, su, is installed as setuid-to-root so that, when run by a someone who knows a different user's password, the program can substitute the new user's privileges. Here, the su program has been copied into AFS so that we can examine how to grant or deny access to setuid programs. You can see its setuid status by examining the owner execute-bit.

```
$ ls -l /afs/hq.firm/sys/bin/su
-r-sr-xr-x   1 root staff       15820 Jul 25 21:07 su
```

AFS client's naturally see a global file namespace, so there is a security risk when running a remote call's setuid programs. Normal attacks on AFS are barred by the use of Kerberos to manage user credentials; you cannot read or write file AFS data from servers to which your identity has not been mutually authenticated, and neither can any other AFS user on the Internet read or write your cell's data without your specific access control.

However, when another cell's files are accessed, there is a danger that a remote executable was installed as a set-user-id to root, and you'll have no assurance that that binary won't damage your local UNIX system. The worst that such a program could do is delete local client files and crash the machine, it could not attack files in the AFS namespace. Crashing a desktop, though, is bad enough.

AFS manages this risk by permitting each client to selectively trust or not trust other cells (including your own) setuid files. The assumption is that because a cell is a single domain of administrative control, you must decide whether or not you trust a remote cell as a whole. Because this decision affects the local UNIX files and operating system of a single client, setuid trust for any remote cell is a per-client issue. If your organization consists of multiple cells, all of these cells will typically be trusted, and each client will have to turn on remote trust via a small script run soon after the AFS client code is loaded. You can see whether or not a cell is trusted with the getcellstatus command. To turn off a cell's setuid trust, the superuser uses the setcell subcommand.

```
$ fs getcellstatus hq.firm
Cell hq.firm status: setuid allowed
$ su root
Password:
# fs setcell hq.firm -nosuid
```

Now that this client no longer trusts the setuid nature of the local cell, you can see that the copy of the su program we installed into AFS appears to have changed its owner execute permission:

```
$ ls -l /afs/hq.firm/sys/bin/su
-r-xr-xr-x   1 root staff       15820 Jul 25 21:07 su
```

The status hasn't really changed; the bit is just masked by our distrust. To turn on the setuid bit of a program stored in AFS, you'll set the client to trust the cell, become root, and also obtain Kerberos credentials as an AFS system administrator. Only then will you be able to create a setuid-root program.

The default status for AFS is to trust the local cell, that is the cell as named by the desktop's /usr/vice/etc/ThisCell file, and to distrust all other cells. In regular use, this works well. Sites that have multiple AFS cells for a single enterprise should modify their startup scripts so that all of their managed cells become trusted.

TIME SERVICES

When we discussed the set up of the cell servers, we described the need for a precise enterprisewide time service. AFS database and file servers are normally set up to use NTP to maintain their clocks but clients are not. Rather, the cache manager assumes that one of the file servers contacted during regular operations will return the correct time; the client will therefore adjust the local clock to keep in time with the servers. Every five minutes, the cache manager will query that server's current time and adjust the local clock.

Some critics claim that the AFS client time service is not as well behaved as the NTP standard time service. Rather than slow down or speed up the local clock to smoothly synchronize with the server clocks, Transarc clients reset their time in one second jumps—backward or forward—if necessary. Not only might this practice disrupt certain critical applications, but setting the clock backward could easily lead to transient time-skew problems.

When afsd does reset the time, it prints a message to the console:

```
afs: setting clock back 2 seconds
```

There's no need to rely on Transarc's time services though. If your site is using a public domain NTP system on all clients, then you should run afsd with the -nosettime option to stop the client daemon from adjusting the time on its own.

MESSAGES

The cache manager occasionally needs to display messages to users and administrators. You can use the fs messages command to modify exactly how the messages are shown. By default, administration messages are printed to the system console, and user messages are printed to the user's terminal session. Given that today's users are often running graphical environments, the console messages may disrupt a user's display and the user may not be paying attention to any attached terminal. So, redirect messages to the log in /usr/vice/ cache/AFSLog by running:

```
# fs messages -show none
```

By supplying either the argument user or console to the show subcommand, you can reset the user messages to display on the user's terminal session or reset the administration messages to display on the console.

SUMMARY

AFS client administration is quite straightforward. The daemon that begins cache management is all that's required—aside from a few configuration files— for users to access the cell's files.

Unlike many other UNIX-based services, AFS clients do not use standard systems such as the network services map or the Sun RPC portmap. Instead, the configuration consists of knowing the location of the AFS cell's database server machines. Once that is known, all other communication is hardwired into each client's kernel module and administration commands.

As long as a sufficient cache is provided, users will quickly see the performance and reliability guarantees of AFS begin to work. When introducing AFS into an organization, it is important to show off the robustness of the system to new users; you can demonstrate this by simply unplugging file servers from the network. When users see that their client is able to work around such problems, they'll be much more forgiving of other AFS issues such as understanding access control lists.

But while AFS provides the image of an ever-present file system to clients, there's no reason for clients to be bound only to a single storage system. Each client can still be an NFS client, server, or almost any other computing or database platform in your organization. Certainly nothing in the AFS kernel module takes away the ability of a UNIX workstation to run multiple file system protocols or any other tasks. A system that is simultaneously an active AFS and NFS client simultaneously can be a benefit during the transition period because different sets of files can be stored in either file system until the best location for the data has been found.

This chapter concludes a three-chapter introduction to AFS administration. In the previous two chapters, we've seen how to set up servers and how to construct an AFS namespace. Now that we've connected our desktop clients and users to our cell, we can introduce users to AFS so they can use the system in day-to-day work.

Managing Users

$\mathbf{S}$o far, we've seen how to build a volume and install it as a directory into the AFS namespace. While file management is certainly a large part of AFS administration, of equal importance is managing user identities and data security. This chapter addresses the tasks needed to set up and manage user identities. The AFS identification programs—logging in and confirming authentication—are described in Chapter 7. The next several sections discuss the tasks needed to integrate users into an AFS cell. Like all AFS cell administration, these tasks can be performed from any desktop in the cell but only by a properly authenticated administrator.

KERBEROS

Before you learn the administrative steps to control user identity and security, you should understand the basics of the Kerberos system. Kerberos was designed at the Massachusetts Institute of Technology in the mid-80s as a mechanism to authenticate, or securely demonstrate the identity of, users of their campus distributed computing environment. It is based on a private key distribution model devised by Needham and Schroeder in 1978; *private key* means that some part of the system, a trusted server, shares a secret (an encrypted key) with a single user.

The knowledge of this private key is sufficient for a Kerberos server to agree that users are who they say they are. This admission is encapsulated in a ticket of information which the user can offer to other services, as if to say, I claim to be a certain user; if you don't believe me take this ticket and ask the Kerberos server to check that that ticket confirms my identity. Several good papers (two are listed in the Bibliography) describe the exact protocol steps needed to establish this authentication, and the details are not difficult to understand. What makes the Kerberos wire protocol interesting for us is that no information is passed in the clear, and tickets can be judged authentic or not only by asking the Kerberos system about their validity.

A significant feature of Kerberos is that not only are users permitted to prove their identity, but server processes can do so as well. Thus, the system is most often referred to as providing mutual authentication: not only does my ticket prove I am who I say I am, but seeing your ticket proves to me that you are who you say you are. For AFS, this means that the file server knows that you're you, and you know that you're talking to the one and true server storing your files.

Even though the local- or wide-area networks may be insecure and may even have somewhat untrustworthy client operating systems, the Kerberos protocol provides users and servers with trustworthy authentication. Previously, a user's identity had only to be demonstrated on a local desktop. Standard UNIX systems would then have little recourse but to accept that local identity as a given; Kerberos permits a user to offer a ticket containing authentication information that can be *proven* valid.

Some of the assumptions of the system are worth examining: First, the Kerberos server and database must be highly trustworthy. Large organizations should take any means necessary to ensure this.

- Put the server in a secure room.
- Use combination locks or smart-cards to restrict access.
- Eliminate almost all other processes, and certainly all unnecessary network connectivity to that server. For example, the Kerberos server should not also be the e-mail server.
- Load system software from the vendor's own media and check it to make sure that no changes have been made to critical executable files.
- Scrutinize any operating system or application security updates and prudently install them.

It is accepted that it is practically impossible to steal or subvert Kerberos security by examining the network protocol itself. But the client desktop is another story. Given that the operating system and Kerberos software has not been tampered with, there is little that needs to be trusted. However, on a public workstation with insufficient security, the Kerberos login program itself be replaced with software that snoops keystrokes or passwords in the clear. This possibility is one reason why the thin desktop model is important: it's easy to reboot and reinstall all operating software that will effectively clean and resecure a desktop.

Here's an introduction to Kerberos terminology as used in the rest of this book.

Realm—A domain of control. A single Kerberos database of user and password information is a unique authentication domain and a single administrative unit. Users query that database to obtain authentication tickets; those tickets indicate that the user's identity had been validated against that Kerberos database—that realm—alone. Each realm is given a name, usually based on the organization's DNS name, much as is the AFS cell name.

Principal—A Kerberos identity, whether it is a user or a server process. Principals are simply strings similar to regular user identifiers. Often, they are composed of two parts separated by a " . " to specify different principals shared by a single user. As an example, user Alice could have a regular principal `alice` and also a special principal instance, `alice.admin`. A fully qualified principal name includes the realm name; in our hypothetical realm, Alice's principals would be `alice@hq.firm` and `alice.admin@hq.firm`.

Password—A string of characters used to prove an identity to the local system. Note that the Kerberos database (like the traditional UNIX password file) does not store passwords directly. Instead, only an encrypted form of the password is stored. This encryption is performed by cryptographically modifying the user's password with an internally generated string. The output of this modification is the user's key.

Ticket—A data packet that stores some information which can be used to validate a principal's authentication by a particular service. A user's ticket contains the user's principal, the service name, an expiration time, a randomly generated session key, and some miscellaneous bookkeeping data. Once a user and a service have agreed to accept each other's identity, the session key will be known to each and can therefore be used by either to encrypt significant data that must be transmitted between them.

Ticket-granting Ticket—A particular ticket granted by Kerberos as a bootstrap so that other service tickets, such as the file server or the AFS group database server, can be obtained without requiring additional entering of a user's password.

Authorization—Kerberos makes a distinction between authentication, the process of proving identities, and authorization, the act of deciding what objects or actions are permitted to a user or system. The Kerberos system is concerned only with authentication; it is up to application servers, which include most of the AFS servers, to implement policies and procedures for storing and manipulating permissions.

Kerberos—In Greek mythology the name for the three-headed dog that guards the gates of Hades.

AFS'S KERBEROS

During the development of AFS, the CMU engineers were interested in using a better authentication system than that traditionally provided by UNIX systems. Their networked campus of thousands of workstations required a security model far different from that of a single time-sharing system designed for only dozens of directly attached terminals. Luckily, at about the same time, MIT was exploring the use of the Needham-Schroeder algorithms as the basis of their distributed security system.

AFS's Kerberos is based on the work started at MIT but is a separate implementation with slight and significant differences and certain added administrative functions. While both MIT and Transarc's server use what is now referred to as the Kerberos version 4 protocol, there are a few problems when trying to use one set of clients with another's server.

One assumption made by AFS is that a standard AFS cell is equivalent to a Kerberos realm. For any sites not running Kerberos, this is a safe assumption: introducing AFS into an organization will by default create the first Kerberos realm. So, it makes sense that only those clients attaching to the file servers will be concerned with AFS security. As of version 3.3a, Transarc's clients and servers can use any realm name you specify.

Normally, an AFS client will use the cell name as part of the local password encryption stage. This usage is different from MIT Kerberos, which uses a different name as an encryption seed. The problem with mismatched seeds arises only if an organization wants to use or is already running MIT's Kerberos version 4 or 5.

If you're not already using MIT's version, there are a few reasons to adopt it. Many public-domain and commercial software applications have been adapted to use Kerberos authentication services based on this publicly available implementation, and consulting firms and independent software vendors provide other value-added services on top of the standard Kerberos.

Transarc's Kerberos makes the most sense when no other Kerberos implementation is running at a site. And, naturally, the administration of the Transarc system is optimized for their file services. In addition, AFS's Kerberos server offers some built-in features, such as automated database replication and other administrative commands, that are not available in the standard MIT version 4.

An interesting technical difference between the two systems is the choice of locations for storing user tickets. At MIT, the goal was a portable authentication system for all platforms. The only logical storage location for the user tickets was the local file system. CMU, on the other hand, had already made the choice to install pieces of their file system in the client's running kernel. Therefore, it was a simple matter to associate ticket information with the kernel's per-user data structure. Because of the special nature of these tickets, they are referred to as *tokens* in AFS.

Placing tokens in the kernel makes sense because the kernel is the only intrinsically protected domain on desktop. It is conceivable that tickets stored in files are less secure than those stored in the kernel. However, in reality, if a hacker has a mechanism to become root, steal a ticket, and somehow use that to gain privileges, it's not that much harder to get the necessary information out from the kernel versus a file. In both cases, however, the ticket will be valid only for requests originating from that particular workstation.

For full details of using MIT Kerberos version 4 or 5 with AFS, contact Transarc product support. Briefly, the suggested steps are:

1. Install an initial AFS cell on a machine as usual. The AFS Kerberos server, `kaserver`, can then be stopped and its job deleted by using `bos` commands.
2. Install a principal named `afs` in the MIT Kerberos database with an instance named after the AFS cell name. In our example cell, the principal would be named `afs.hq.firm@hq.firm`. Notice that the principal name is `afs` and the instance name is `hq.firm`; the additional dots in the instance name can confuse some standard Kerberos commands.
3. Use the standard Kerberos `ext_srvtab` program to extract the AFS service key. `ext_srvtab` is one of the commands that does not handle the

extra dot characters in an instance name, so you'll need to compile a new version of this command that doesn't erroneously check for such instances.

4. Use the Transarc `asetkey` command to install this extracted service key into AFS's key file `/usr/afs/etc/KeyFile` on each of your AFS servers. The `asetkey` command is a replacement for the `bos setkey` process. You can pick up the source for the command from Transarc's FTP site.
5. Put the MIT Kerberos realm name in the AFS configuration file `/usr/afs/etc/krb.conf`. If you wish, you can make a symbolic link from this file to the standard `/etc/krb.conf` file.

Now that the AFS servers have been converted to contact and use the MIT Kerberos servers, users will have to use MIT commands to authenticate with Kerberos: after running a normal MIT `kinit` program to obtain authentication credentials, they must run `aklog` to convert those file tickets into AFS kernel-based tokens. Since you'll be able to obtain the source code for all of these commands, you will probably want to try and integrate the `kinit` and `aklog` programs into a single command.

Similarly, users must use the MIT `kpasswd` command to change their passwords. And administrators must use the MIT `kadmin` administrative suite rather than AFS's `kas`. Transarc's user authentication system is described in more detail in Chapter 7; the `kas` suite is described below.

For compatibility, Transarc ships with AFS versions of certain commands that communicate with MIT Kerberos. These commands can be installed and used as substitutes for the standard versions that understand only the Transarc Kerberos implementation. The commands are: `klog.krb`, `tokens.krb`, `pagsh.krb`, and `login.krb`.

USER DATABASES

Whereas a standard UNIX user name is stored only in the password file or NIS map, an AFS identity must be included in the UNIX password map, the Kerberos authentication database, and the protection group database. Because the information is stored in three databases, there is the potential for the databases to disagree. Administrators must follow strict procedures to ensure that all users are represented in all three systems.

The simplest reason for insisting that all databases agree can be seen with a directory listing program like `ls` or a file browser. When displaying the owner of a file, each program extracts the numeric user identifier from the file system and, in UNIX, utilizes the password file or NIS map to convert that number to a user name. But in AFS, a user's Kerberos principal is used by the file system as the owner of newly created files. When a program tries to display the textual equivalent of the owner identity, if the identifier in the password map does not match the principal, the wrong user will be displayed as the file owner.

As an example, in the previous chapter, we obtained Kerberos authentication as `afsadmin`, the AFS administrator principal created during system installation. When we created files in AFS, we showed the file details by using the `ls` program.

```
$ ls -ld /afs/example
drwxr-xr-x   2 afsadmin staff        2048 Mar 29 09:15 /afs/example
```

The output of the `ls` program looks correct only because we had previously entered the name `afsadmin` into our password maps. When unauthenticated users create files in open areas of AFS, AFS will assign the numeric identifier 32766 as the file's owner. Unless you want to see that number displayed as the owner in directory listings, you should enter a name with that identification number in the password maps. Any name will do; most sites choose `anonymous` or `noauth`.

In a fully functioning AFS organization, the different pieces of information contained by the three databases are:

- Password file or NIS map—Contains the user login name as a lookup key, a numeric user identifier, a numeric group identifier, an encrypted UNIX password, the user's full name and home directory, and the choice of tty-based shell program to run. This database is maintained with the native tools, such as an NIS map, of the client operating systems.
- Kerberos database—Contains the name and password for each user. This database is maintained by AFS itself.
- Protection database—Contains the numeric identifiers of all users and groups and maintains the list of group membership used to calculate access control privileges. This database is also maintained by AFS.

This chapter deals primarily with Kerberos database administration. The Transarc version of this database stores the following information for each user:

- Principal—The login name of the user or the name of the server, such as `afs`.

- NOADMIN flag—grants permission to issue privileged `kas` commands. Default is NOADMIN; can be set to ADMIN.
- CPW flag—Permits user to change the password. Default is CPW; can be set to NOCPW.
- TGS flag—Allows the Kerberos ticket-granting server to grant tickets to the user. Default is TGS; can be set to NOTGS so that a request to obtain tickets for a user will fail.
- SEAL flag—Permits the ticket-granting service to use this entry's key field as an encryption key. When the flag is set to NOSEAL, the `kaserver` will not create service tickets for this principal. A service ticket is a ticket that enables processes rather than users to authenticate.
- Key and version number—The principal's encrypted password. Previous versions are available to the system. They can be used to ensure that passwords are not reused.
- Date of last change of password.
- Entry expiration date—After this date, no authentications will be permitted.
- Password's expiration date.
- Limit on number of consecutive failed authentication attempts.
- Lockout time—Specifies for how long no user is permitted to authenticate to this principal after the limit on the number of consecutive failed logins has been reached.
- Maximum ticket lifetime—The longest length of time for which this principal's credential will be good.
- Last modify time—Time of the last change to the principal's entry and person who made the change (except for password changes).

SETTING UP A USER ACCOUNT

Given a user with an existing UNIX identity, the following steps set up a user's authentication and protection identity in AFS. First, we can query our local services to find out basic information on the user.

```
$ ypmatch david passwd
david::1235:24:David::/afs/hq.firm/user/david:/bin/sh
```

In this case, we use the NIS map to confirm that the user's login name is david, his UNIX ID is 1235, his full name is David, and the home directory has been set ahead of time to the AFS path name /afs/hq.firm/user/david.

The empty password field in the entry indicates that the standard UNIX login programs will not be used with this login. In this case, we've replaced the system's login program, /bin/login, with one provided by Transarc for each client platform. This new login performs Kerberos authentication against the password stored in the AFS databases and automatically creates a credential token upon success. As an administrator, we'll now begin the installation of credential information into the databases:

```
$ pts createuser david 1235
User david has id 1235
```

First, use a pts command. This command initializes a user's name and identification number. We must do this first because AFS keeps only vital authentication information, such as the user name and password, in the Kerberos database. All other user data, such as a numeric identity, real user name, and other group information is stored in a separate system, the protection database. (The protection database and the pts suite are discussed in Chapter 7.) The createuser subcommand of pts stores the user's numeric identifier in the database; as discussed, we enter the same ID as that stored in the UNIX password file to force AFS and UNIX to show the same name for the same identifier in both file systems.

Problems sometimes surface when you try to merge different UNIX administrative domains into a single AFS cell. With multiple UNIX servers, your organization may have two users who happen to share the same numeric identifier. As long as they are not both using the same server, there's no problem. If both sets of users are to be entered into the same, single AFS Kerberos database, one of their identifiers will have to change. This may mean that you will have to search the existing file systems; any files owned by one user may have to have their numeric ownership changed to the new identifier.

If no number is entered via the createuser subcommand, the next available number is used. In the protection database, the system tracks the available numbers with an internal counter named UserMax. When no number is mandated on the command line, the value of UserMax is used and the counter is incremented. If a number is entered that is larger than any previously issued identification number, UserMax is automatically bumped up so that the next automatically generated number will be one more than the entered number. This method ensures that the system can always determine a valid new identification number without having to search through all of its entries. You can even manually set UserMax to a higher value if you want to set aside a portion of the numeric space for your own assignments.

Now that the user name is a user in the protection database, we can create a Kerberos principal with the same name and give it an initial password.

```
$ kas create david -admin afsadmin
Administrator's (afsadmin) Password:
initial_password:
Verifying, please re-enter initial_password:
```

You can see that the kas create command has an additional option, -admin, to specify an AFS administrator's name. The command immediately responds with a request for the administrator's password. If no name is given, the command prompts for the password of the user issuing the command; unless you're logged in as an administrator, you won't be able to run administration commands. AFS makes a strong guarantee that the user running the command is an administrator.

All communication between the kas command and the kaserver process is encrypted. One note on this administration command: when executed with no subcommand arguments, it runs a mini-shell with its own prompt. This feature is useful when you execute multiple kas commands as it limits the need to type in a system password for each command.

```
$ kas -admin afsadmin
Administrator's (afsadmin) Password:
kas> create david
initial_password:
Verifying, please re-enter initial_password:
kas> create harry
initial_password:
Verifying, please re-enter initial_password:
```

There are a few restrictions on user names stored in the database: the name can't be longer than eight characters, and the name can't contain certain punctuation characters. And, because the system uses the name afs for its own identity, if you have a user with a login name afs (perhaps a user with those initials), that user will have to have a different login to work with AFS.

The next few commands are simple volume manipulation commands, similar to those described in the previous chapter, used to create a suitable home directory volume.

```
$ vos create fs-one a user.david
Volume 536870976 created on partition /vicepa of fs-one
$ fs mkm /afs/.hq.firm/user/david user.david
$ vos release cell.user
Released volume cell.user successfully
$ ls /afs/hq.firm/user
david  zed
```

User volumes are not required for each and every Kerberos identity, however, depending on your site policies. Users may have their home directories on local disk or accessible through NFS or NetWare. Users with home directories not in AFS should still be given an appropriate Kerberos credential; this credential enables the user to access the AFS file system as permitted and to run other Kerberos-enhanced applications.

KERBEROS AND PASSWORDS

When David's user name was created, the Kerberos administration command kas was used. In practice, there is very little day-to-day administration of the Kerberos database. As long as each user has an identity in Kerberos, then that user can get an authenticated credential which can be used by various clients and servers to make guarantees about that identity. This is just like an employee identity card: it takes a minute to set up and the employee can use the card every day, but otherwise, no one fiddles with it.

Like all of the AFS databases, the information in all the entries is replicated to all running kaserver processes and stored on each database server's disk. One of these server processes is designated as the master copy, or sync site in the Ubik protocol parlance, and all writes are registered at that site before replication to other servers. Lookup requests are sent to any available server. Until there is a catastrophe with a server CPU, disk drive, or network, no manual administration is required to keep all of this running smoothly.

Permission to run many Kerberos administration commands is restricted to those logins that have been set up with special privileges. During installation, at least one login has exactly that privilege. Chapter 9 presents some more details on how to extend that privilege.

Once authenticated, users can change their own passwords.

```
$ kpasswd
Changing password for 'david' in cell 'hq.firm'
Old password:
New password (RETURN to abort):
Retype new password:
```

The `kas setpasswd` subcommand permits an authorized administrator to reset any user's password. When run, it first challenges the existing administrator to reauthenticate. Here, the administrator running the command is `afsadmin`.

```
$ kas setpasswd david -admin afsadmin
Administrator's (afsadmin) Password:
new_password:
Verifying, please re-enter new_password:
```

Note the difference between `kpasswd` and `kas setpasswd`: `kpasswd` challenges for the old password of the issuing user and will reset that user's password. `kas setpasswd` challenges for the issuing user's password only if the user is permitted as an AFS administrator; it can reset any user's password.

Most people will acknowledge that choosing a new password is not to be taken lightly, yet few go through much effort to create a good password. With the Kerberos system, it is more difficult to guess passwords than with conventional UNIX passwords, but guessing can be made even more unlikely if users could be forced to pick a good password. Transarc's implementation of Kerberos allows user passwords to be up to 1024 characters in length. If users consistently use long passwords, the ability to crack encrypted data on the network will practically vanish.

To help guard against poorly chosen passwords, the Kerberos administration system includes an external program which can check password guessability and reject proposed passwords that fail arbitrary criteria.

Transarc provides a simple version of a password-checking program with the AFS product; your site can engineer its own version to perform any checking desired. The only requirements are that the program be named `kpwvalid`, that it be stored in AFS in the same directory as the `kpasswd` program, and that the directory have no write permission for anyone. These restrictions deny anyone the opportunity to install a Trojan Horse. Password checking is turned off by simply removing or renaming the program, for example, to `kpwvalid.off`.

The program must accept as input two lines of data. The first is the old password, the second is the new password. Transarc's version of `kpwvalid` simply checks that the new password consists of at least eight characters. Whatever the algorithm for checking passwords is, the result must be printed onto the standard output; a single zero indicates the password is acceptable, any other numeric output indicates rejection. If you write your own program, make sure the program is thoroughly debugged before installation; it would also be somewhat more secure if the passwords, which are sent via interprocess communication from kpasswd to kpwvalid, are themselves encrypted in the password validation program's memory before any lengthy processing is performed.

Traditional password mechanisms are sometimes called *claim/knowledge systems* because they are based on two pieces of information the user provides: an identity that the user claims and knowledge of a secret (the password) that only the user is supposed to know. One drawback to this is that the identity claim is unsupported by any other piece of information such as a physical identity card or other external confirmation. This flaw permits an attack on a cell's security by someone claiming to be a legitimate user and then attempting to guess the secret password.

AFS provides a mechanism by which consecutive failures to log in will cause the account to be unavailable for further logins for a specified interval. Once locked out, the user will have to wait for the interval to elapse before any new login attempt will be allowed. Anyone trying to guess the user's password will be forced to spend an inordinate amount of time waiting for new chances to guess rather immediately trying another password.

```
$ kas setfields david -attempts 10 -locktime 30
```

Because the attack vector relies on an exhaustive search of the password namespace, an attacker will normally be trying thousands of passwords. This suggests that the number of failed attempts can be set fairly high and the lockout penalty can be rather severe. With the number of failed attempts set to 10, a legitimate user with a mental block will either remember the correct password or give up and call an administrator for help, whereas a programmatic attempt to guess the password will be stopped every 10 tries and, in this case, forced to wait 30 minutes. The number of failed attempts can be set anywhere from 1 to 254; a value of 0 turns off this defense completely.

The lockout time is specified in minutes or hours:minutes. Due to the mechanism by which the time is stored in the databases, the time is actually rounded up the next highest multiple of 8.5 minutes; the minimum lockout is 8.5 minutes, the maximum is 36 hours. A lockout time of 0 indicates an infinite lockout.

The implementation of the lockout process is interesting. Along with each Kerberos server's normal database files in /usr/afs/db is an auxiliary file, /usr/afs/local/kaserverauxdb, in which are stored the current number of failed login attempts. Given a cell with three Kerberos server instances, each instance is allocated one-third of the number attempts. When attempting to log in, if a user fails to enter the correct password more than the allotted number of tries for that server, that server will refuse to answer any more requests for the lockout-time interval. The next time the client login program tries to contact that server, it will react to that refusal by failing over to one of the other two Kerberos servers and attempting the login there. Eventually, if the password continues to be entered incorrectly, all the servers would have been contacted and all of them would have locked out the user.

If a user does get locked out, an administrator can unlock the account.

```
$ kas unlock david
```

For additional security, passwords can be given a time limit for their existence. Once the password lifetime is exceeded, the password will not be valid. Administrators can set this with:

```
$ kas setfields david -pwexpires 30
```

The argument is the number of days, from 1 to 254 days, that a new password is valid. An argument of 0 indicates that passwords never expire.

One last mechanism to secure AFS accounts is to forbid the repetition of previous passwords. The previous 20 passwords are stored and compared against new passwords. To prevent reuse:

```
$ kas setfields david -reuse no
```

On the other hand, a reuse value of yes permits the user to reuse passwords.

After the above three administrative polices are set, the Kerberos database entry for david now looks like this:

```
$ kas examine david
User data for david
    key (1) cksum is 1630388111, last cpw: Sat Mar 29 15:36:39 1997
    password will expire: Mon Apr 28 16:36:39 1997
    10 consecutive unsuccessful authentications are permitted.
    The lock time for this user is 34.1 minutes.
    User is not locked.
    entry never expires.  Max ticket lifetime 25.00 hours.
    last mod on Sat Mar 29 15:39:06 1997 by afsadmin
    don't permit password reuse
```

Only a checksum of the key is normally displayed. The checksum permits administrators to compare keys between `kaserver` instances to check for inconsistencies without providing information that could be used for a brute-force attack. To display a list of instances stored in the database:

```
$ kas list -admin afsadmin
Administrator's (afsadmin) Password:
AuthServer.Admin
krbtgt.HQ.FIRM
afsadmin
david
afs
carol
alice
```

There is also a command to report on the internal statistics collected by the Kerberos servers. You can use the `-server` option to direct the query against a particular server.

```
$ kas statistics -admin afsadmin -server db-two
Administrator's (afsadmin) Password:
6 allocs, 0 frees, 0 password changes
Hash table utilization = 0.150000%
From host c0a8030b started at Sat Mar 29 11:44:31 1997:
  of 16 requests for Authenticate, 9 were aborted.
  of 2 requests for CreateUser, 0 were aborted.
  of 1 requests for SetPassword, 0 were aborted.
  of 4 requests for SetFields, 0 were aborted.
  of 2 requests for GetEntry, 1 were aborted.
  of 14 requests for ListEntry, 2 were aborted.
  of 1 requests for GetStats, 0 were aborted.
Used 0.510 seconds of CPU time.
1 admin accounts
```

The output is somewhat arcane but lets you know that the server is up, responding to requests, and shows how many of which requests it has performed. The last line shows one interesting tidbit of information: only one account has the ADMIN administration flag turned on.

TICKET LIFETIMES

When users authenticate themselves with the AFS Kerberos servers, credentials are returned, stored, and automatically presented to other servers when access checks must be made. Normally, these credentials, or tokens, have a valid lifetime of 25 hours. To determine the actual value, AFS checks the lifetimes of three different principals and uses the shortest lifetime; thus cellwide defaults can be easily maintained.

The three principals checked and their default ticket lifetimes are:

- The user's principal—25 hours
- The principal `afs`—100 hours
- `krbtgt.<CELLNAME>`—720 hours, which is 30 days

AFS administrators can reset the default lifetimes with the `kas set-fields` command. The `afs` principal permits a cellwide maximum lifetime to be set; the `krbtgt.<CELLNAME>` maximum is hardcoded as part of the AFS Kerberos system. A user's tickets are therefore by default 25 hours; administrators can extend this ticket lifetimes to 30 days. An option to the user authentication command permits users to request shorter, but not longer, ticket lifetimes. To change a user's ticket lifetime:

```
$ kas setfields david -lifetime 168:00
```

The value assigned is in seconds; if the value includes a `:`, then the value is the number of hours and minutes: 100 is one hundred seconds, 100:30 is one hundred and a half hours. Here, David's tickets have been assigned a lifetime of 168 hours, equivalent to one calendar week. For David to actually receive tickets with this lifetime, the `afs` principal's ticket lifetime will have to be increased as well, in keeping with the system's minimal lifetime policy outlined above.

Longer ticket lifetimes have the potential to be misused. On the other hand, shorter lifetimes require users to run the login authentication process more often. Hence, users can request shorter ticket lifetimes than the security policy set up by the administrator allows, but not longer lifetimes. In general, user tickets are configured with either one-day or one-week lifetimes; administrator tickets are often reduced to only one or two hours to lessen the chance that an unlocked workstation will be left with powerful tickets lying around.

THE USS UTILITY

For each user at your site, you'll usually have to add a home volume, create credentials and group info, and install some standard login profile files. Transarc provides the `uss` utility for automating the process of adding users. The utility is based on an optimized and very terse language with which to describe a

standard set of AFS commands to run when a user is to be given an AFS identity, home directory, etc. This utility allows you to set up a template for new
user initialization; once set up, this template can be used to create and install all
of the above listed information for one or a hundred users in a single action.

As we've seen, a normal user in a simple cell will be given a Kerberos principal, a protection service name, a volume, and often a set of common login
profiles. For each of these items, you can write a single line in a template file
and then feed the complete template file to the uss command. For example:

```
V user.$USER $SERVER.hq.firm /vicep$PART 5000 /afs/.hq.firm/user/$USER $UID $USER
all system:anyuser rl
D $MTPT/Mail 0700 $UID $USER all system:anyuser none
F $MTPT/.cshrc 0755 $UID /afs/hq.firm/sys/setup/cshrc
F $MTPT/.mwmrc 0755 $UID /afs/hq.firm/sys/setup/mwmrc
A $USER 90 noreuse 5 10
X vos backup user.$USER
X fs mkm $MTPT/.oldFiles user.$USER.backup
```

Let's assume that this template is in the file uss.template. When you
run the following command, each line causes one or more AFS administration
tasks to be run.

```
# uss add -user carol -realname Carol -uid 2347 -server fs-one -part a -pass
carol
```

The arguments to uss set variables that are used in the template to specify
the exact value of various options to each command line. The first line of the
template, which begins with the letter V, creates a volume named user.carol
on the server fs-one and partition /vicepa. The quota of the volume is 5
megabytes, and the volume will be mounted at /afs/.hq.firm/user/
carol. After being mounted, it is given an access control list, which permits
Carol to read and write in the directory but permits any other user only to read.
(See Chapter 7 for more information on access control lists.)

The next three lines install various standard directories and files into
Carol's new home directory. The D line creates a directory, /afs/.hq.firm/
user/carol/Mail, with UNIX permissions and AFS access controls that permit only Carol to read and write into the directory. The two F lines copy files
from a standard set up directory to Carol's home directory.

The A template line sets up Carol's authentication information in the Kerberos database. The name of her Kerberos login will be carol, and the password will be set to the one mentioned on the uss command line. In addition,

each password will have a lifetime of 90 days, cannot be reused, and if someone tries to log in to Carol's account but fails to get the password right five times in a row, the login will be locked out for 10 minutes.

The final two lines run commands that are appropriate for our example site. An AFS backup volume is immediately made of Carol's home volume and is mounted in her home directory under the subdirectory `.oldFiles`.

A typical V line, as shown previously, performs all the volume manipulation commands needed to connect a user's home directory to the namespace. For AFS sites with a large number of users, it is inconvenient to put all users (potentially thousands) into a single directory. In the template file, you can specify several parent directories that will be used to spread out users: `uss` automatically chooses the directory with the fewest existing entries as the destination of the volume connection.

As you can see, this system is highly optimized for user account creation in an AFS cell. This system can be used for other standard, well-known volumes but isn't quite powerful enough for all circumstances. For other volumes, you'll have to decide whether `uss` is sufficiently flexible or simply write a shell script that runs the various AFS administration commands one by one. The AFS System Administration Guide has many more details on additional template definition lines and usage notes.

Even within the standard use of `uss`, some steps still must be performed externally to the system. After you run `uss`, you must install the user's name, identity number, and home directory path name into the UNIX password file or map. You must also release the parent volume to the user's home mount point, `vos release cell.user`.

Besides adding users, you can also use `uss` to delete a user. Doing so will delete the user entry in the Kerberos identity database, the protection database, the user's home directory volume, and volume mount-point. Rather than use a configuration file, this command simply uses command-line options to specify the volume and mount point.

To run many additions or deletions at once, you can create a file containing all of the options to the `uss` commands you want to run, and `uss` will perform the add or delete user operations. Using the file method is slightly better than simply running these commands in a simple shell script because, if an error occurs, the commands are automatically retried up to three times and if the problem persists, the error conditions are correctly flagged and reported.

SUMMARY

Kerberos administration may be the most arcane aspect of AFS administration. This is a shame because plenty of available information describes the protocol in bit-by-bit detail. As the system has been around for almost a decade, many improvements have been integrated, and the security issues raised by the protocol are well understood.

If Kerberos is new to your organization with AFS, you would do well to discuss the system with an outside vendor or consultant. The authentication credentials can be used for many more purposes other than providing secure access to files. Either the Transarc or the MIT Kerberos database can be the foundation for a new security infrastructure.

As for administration, the new tasks outlined here are likely to be used fairly often as users join and leave an organization. One of the more important aspects of the system is making sure that the Kerberos database, the protection database, and the UNIX password maps are all kept in synchronization.

In typical fashion, Transarc supplies a tool, uss, that can help you add users to your AFS cell. Whether this particular tool fits your purposes is up to you. If not, the AFS administration commands are not difficult to run manually or in your own scripts and procedures.

Now that we have got a functioning cell and users, we can take a look at how users can actually make use of the distributed file system.

## CHAPTER 7

Using AFS

Until now, we've examined straightforward administration of AFS. Thankfully, the majority of these tasks, such as setting up a client cache, must be managed only once. After all of the servers have been installed, desktop computers initialized, and the basic file namespace constructed, it's the users who will actually manipulate the files and directories. And though this chapter is devoted to the special features and limitations of the file system, the majority of the time a user will never notice anything odd—or even interesting—about AFS.

The one striking feature of the system is that all the files managed by AFS, which usually means everything below /afs in the file tree, are guaranteed to be visible to everyone at your site. This simple fact quickly becomes a touchstone on which everyone depends. Navigation though the file tree, whether with the command-line cd command or clicking on a folder icon in a browser, works just as if the files were on a local disk.

Even so, there are several details about which users and developers should know. Some of these details are commands that could work differently in AFS than in UFS; some few are file behaviors that are somewhat different and unexpected; and others are new functionality that should be mastered.

The biggest difference between UNIX and the AFS system is the notion of authentication and permissions. This is one area with which users must become comfortable.

AFS permissions are managed by a list of access controls attached to each AFS directory level, and the identities on each list are restricted to AFS identities. This last requirement results in one powerful security aspect of the system: UNIX root identity does not have any equivalent Kerberos identity or credential. Whereas UNIX superusers have broad authority to manage the desktop computer and read and write all files in the local file system, UNIX root has no special privileges in the AFS file system. Thus, while certain poorly written UNIX system services have security holes that can allow hackers to gain superuser access to the desktop, that identity will confer no special privileges to any directory or file in AFS. Such privileges are restricted to those identities that have received Kerberos-blessed credentials.

In regular use, UNIX root is reserved for administration, such as installation of client services, of the desktop machine. When performing AFS management, administrators will keep their personal non-root UNIX identity and, additionally, authenticate as AFS system administrators.

This chapter discusses the implications of these authentication issues and how access controls lists work. More general user questions follow, including how to check for possible AFS client problems and how AFS affects the use of standard UNIX commands and programming idioms.

AUTHENTICATION

So far we've glossed over how one becomes authenticated. User identity, however, is one of the more intricate and visible aspects of life in AFS. Simply put, users in an AFS environment have two identities that must be managed: the original, conventional UNIX identity and an AFS identity controlled by the Kerberos authentication protocol.

A standard AFS client installation will replace the vendor's login program with one written specially by Transarc (described in detail in the system software section below). Once integrated, this login checks a user's name and password against the Kerberos database maintained by AFS and, if successfully matched, then spawns a login shell with the user's UNIX identity and AFS credential set to the correct values.

These values are normally set to the same number so that when new files are created and assigned the owner's AFS identity, UNIX processes looking up the printable string associated with the number in the password file or NIS map will display the correct user name. This equivalence must be managed by AFS and system administrators.

To see your AFS credentials, use the `tokens` command.

```
$ id
uid=1235(david) gid=10(staff)
$ tokens

Tokens held by the Cache Manager:

User's (AFS ID 1235) tokens for afs@hq.firm [Expires Apr  3 00:13]
--End of list--
```

Here, the UNIX `id` command prints out the user's identity according to the local operating system. The second command, `tokens`, displays the Kerberos authentication data. In AFS, a *token* is a data object which correlates a user's UNIX process with an AFS identity. Because of the Kerberos protocol used, the token represents not only an extremely trustworthy identity to the AFS servers but also allows the user to know that the correct AFS cell has been contacted—this is the result of the mutual authentication process.

Note that the command `tokens` is plural; there's room in the credential list for additional identities that would be authenticated to additional cells. Each identity lists the user's AFS identity number, as stored in the protection server database. Recall that David was set up with identity number 1235; for no good reason, the `tokens` command prints out only the numeric form of the user's identity and not the more useful character string.

Each credential request is authenticated against a specific cell and each token has an expiration time. In this case, the cell is `hq.firm`, and the expiration time is April 3rd at 00:13.

If new credentials are needed or the vendor's login program has not been replaced with an AFS-ready version, you can use the `klog` command.

```
$ klog david
Password:
$ tokens

Tokens held by the Cache Manager:

User's (AFS ID 1235) tokens for afs@hq.firm [Expires Apr 3 00:15]
--End of list--
```

These token credentials are stored in the running operating system alongside the user's traditional UNIX identity. The fact that AFS credentials are stored separately from the user's UNIX identity means that a user could have

AFS credentials for a principal that has a name different from the user's UNIX identity. Having different credentials than one's UNIX identity can be confusing and is generally discouraged; because AFS has a flexible group identity mechanism, there's little reason to have shared accounts, so users will almost always obtain their credentials corresponding to their own login.

One important effect of the klog program is that it obtains credentials that are associated with the current process and will be inherited by all child processes. Thus, all subprocesses run by the user will have the same AFS credentials. But because the credentials are shared among the parent and children, any change to credentials in a child process will cause a change to all related processes. If you are logged in and running a window manager with many separate terminal sessions, any credential obtained during the login procedure will be shared; if you change tokens via klog in one terminal session window, the tokens in the other sibling windows will reflect the new credential. Often this is exactly the desired effect.

Sometimes, however, a user wants to have different credentials on the same machine: if a user needs to invoke administrative privileges in one window, there's no need for all the user's windows to become privileged as well. In this case, the user can use the pagsh command to create a new process authentication group with its own set of credentials.

A *process authentication group* is a unique number the operating system uses to identify the token that is associated with a user. The number is unique rather than based on a user's UNIX ID so that the same user can get different tokens in different PAGs, if desired. The kernel copies a PAG number from parent to child processes, so all the processes spawned in a login session will have the same PAG and therefore the same token. The klog command generates new or different tokens to be used with the current set of processes that share a PAG number.

```
$ tokens

Tokens held by the Cache Manager:

User's (AFS ID 1235) tokens for afs@hq.firm [Expires Apr  3 00:15]
--End of list--
$
$ pagsh
$ tokens

Tokens held by the Cache Manager:

--End of list--
```

The first `tokens` command displays the normal credentials David received when he logged in to his desktop. His AFS credentials match his UNIX ID. After he runs the `pagsh` program, he created a new subshell process, just as if he had started a new interactive shell. This command is managed by the client's AFS kernel module and not only creates a new subshell but places that process in a new process authentication group. As the second `tokens` command shows, this new subshell has no AFS credentials

Now that a new process group has been created, David is free to run another `klog` program to obtain any credentials for which he knows the password. New programs initiated at this point will run under the new, different AFS credentials.

```
$ klog carol
Password:
$ tokens

Tokens held by the Cache Manager:

User's (AFS ID 2347) tokens for afs@hq.firm [Expires Apr  3 00:15]
--End of list--
```

Any other programs started by David prior to the `pagsh` command will still be running under David's AFS credentials. As the parent shell is still running, David can `exit` the new process group's subshell, return to the parent, and confirm that it's token is unchanged.

```
$ exit
$
$ tokens

Tokens held by the Cache Manager:

User's (AFS ID 1235) tokens for afs@hq.firm [Expires Apr  3 00:15]
--End of list--
```

Regular users need to understand that their true AFS identity is separate from their UNIX identity and that they must use the `tokens` command to make sure that they are authenticated correctly. All processes that are run after getting an authenticated identity will execute with that identity's privileges. Even UNIX `setuid` programs will execute with the same AFS authentication, though with a different UNIX identity.

Users should also know about the pagsh command as a way to create a new set of processes that can obtain different authentication credentials without changing the credentials of any other process. The need to create new authentication groups will be somewhat rare for users but fairly common for administrators.

As seen in the output of the tokens command, an AFS credential has an expiration date. The time limit attached to a new credential is controlled by the AFS administrator. If a user is suddenly unable to read or write files in directories that were previously available, one reason may be an expired token. Check for expiration with the tokens command, but make sure that the tokens command prints out a meaningful result—if a pagsh has been executed at some point by the user, the tokens listed in one window may not be the same as the tokens in a different window.

Users can request shorter ticket lifetimes if desired. Note that only certain values for lifetimes are allowed; other values are silently rounded up. For example, lifetimes less than 10 hours and 40 minutes are granted at the next highest 5-minute interval; a lifetime request of 6 minutes would be answered by a ticket good for the next 10 minutes. Lifetimes greater than 10 hours 40 minutes are granted in ever-increasing intervals. See the AFS command reference for details. In the next example, you can see that the expiration time is 10 minutes after the current time, even though a lifetime of 6 minutes was requested.

```
$ date
Sat Mar 29 16:51:43 EST 1997
$ klog david -lifetime 0:06
Password:
$ tokens

Tokens held by the Cache Manager:

User's (AFS ID 1235) tokens for afs@hq.firm [Expires Mar 29 17:01]
--End of list--
```

Kerberos authentication credentials present a few problems with some conventions of UNIX computing. First, tokens obtained on one client are not automatically available on other clients. If you use the UNIX rsh command to open up a shell on a remote system, that shell will not have tokens. To solve this deficiency, Transarc's AFS product comes with an improved rsh server that can perform additional mutual authentication with the Kerberos system to obtain tokens on the remote system. This system is discussed later in this chapter.

Second, authentication is not integrated with UNIX `cron` jobs. A *cron job* is a command that is configured to run at a certain time, such as every night at midnight. These jobs are managed by a root process, `cron`, on the local client and are automatically invoked under the user's UNIX identity. There is no mechanism for obtaining Kerberos credentials for these jobs; whereas a solution for the remote shell problem can at least be based on a user's authenticated token on one machine, a `cron` job has no token at all. Additionally, manually initiated, long-lived application servers will usually need to retain their tokens for longer than the maximum ticket lifetime.

"Power users" are often unhappy with this situation. Remote or timed execution has been part of their development toolbox for a long time. AFS administrators and managers should be quite sensitive to this meed and consider these users' concerns when designing a new computing environment.

On the other hand, `cron` was invented before distributed file systems were commonplace and the remote versions of commands were written with a virtuous trust model in mind. In a modern enterprise, general standards have yet to be developed for dealing with untrusted hosts. Nevertheless, important applications that need to write files without a strong authentication guarantee can certainly coexist with AFS: the files can either be explicitly made world-writeable or the files can simply reside in a standard UNIX local file system.

To improve security, you can set up an ACL to include a computer's IP address as a group member. That way, all applications or `cron` jobs running on a specific machine will be able to read or write into a given subdirectory of the file system.

If more limited ACLs are needed, then a Kerberos credential will have to be obtained for the job. The issue that needs to be addressed is how to refresh the credential over the course of several days or weeks, a time period during which normal tokens will expire.

Transarc provides an unsupported tool, `reauth`, to help with this scenario. When run from the command line, the `reauth` command takes as argument a Kerberos principal name and password and uses that password to get the user's credentials. The process then forks a copy of itself, and the parent process continues to run in the background, sleeping for a specified interval. When the parent process wakes up, it refreshes its token by using the password (which now exists only in the process memory). This cycle then continues.

These tokens are automatically available to all jobs in the process authentication group, so child processes will find that they always have a fresh, usable token with which to prove their identity. In typical use, the `reauth` command looks like:

```
$ reauth 43200 david davespassword
$ tokens

Tokens held by the Cache Manager:

User's (AFS ID 1235) tokens for afs@hq.firm [Expires Apr  8 08:24]
--End of list--
```

Here, the tokens obtained by `reauth` are available in the subshell. Any subsequent jobs initiated from that command line will discover that their tokens are automatically refreshed by their parent. The refresh interval in this example is 43200 seconds or 12 hours, which is well before the default 25-hour token expiration. The `reauth` command is simply a wrapper for legacy jobs. The only bulletproof solution is to identify the critical applications that depend on a strong security system and upgrade those to utilize the Kerberos authentication protocols. Meanwhile, some of the commercial Kerberos vendors might be able to provide some support.

Finally, the `unlog` command discards all tokens held by the current user. This step is important because leftover tokens could be used by a malicious root user on the same client.

PROTECTION DATA

While the Kerberos database stores a mapping between names and passwords and is used as the controlling protocol for authenticating users and servers, most of the data associated with a user's identity is stored in the protection database, managed by the `ptserver` process on the database servers.

You can query the protection database with the `pts` command.

```
$ pts examine alice
Name: alice, id: 17001, owner: system:administrators, creator: afsadmin,
  membership: 0, flags: S----, group quota: 20.
```

The database contains all the system data about the named user or also, as we'll see later, groups or machines. Note the identification number assigned to the database entry. While, normally, AFS uses this number only internally, it is most important to synchronize the user AFS identification numbers with the UNIX identiers. When files are created in AFS, the creator's AFS identification number is stored as the owner of the file. Later, when common UNIX programs such as `ls` retrieve that number, they convert the number into a name by looking at the `/etc/passwd` file or NIS map and not the AFS protection database. (We discussed the creation of the Kerberos and protection database entries in Chapter 6.)

Also stored in the protection database are the entry's owner and creator. The creator field holds the name of the AFS identity that created the entry, mainly for auditing purposes; the owner is the person who currently has the power of administration. For user entries, the owner is always `system:administrators`.

The membership field displays a count of the number of groups to which this identity belongs. For newly created users, this number will be 0. The last field, the group quota, is a simple numeric quota on how many groups the user is permitted to create. The default group quota is 20, but this number can be adjusted by a system administrator.

The second-to-last field, flags, stores several pieces of information in a 5-character word. Each position holds a value for a single privacy flag, which can be a hyphen, a lowercase letter, or an uppercase letter, though not all values have meanings for both user and group entries. The default set of privacy flags permits all users to examine the protection database entry. For user entries, the complete list of valid values and their meanings are as follows:

STATUS flag, first character:

S   All users can examine the status of the user.

s   Only the user and members of the `system:administrators` group can examine the entry.

OWNERSHIP flag, second character:

O   All users can list the groups that this user owns.

–   Only the user and members of the `system:administrators` group can list the owned groups.

MEMBERSHIP flag, third character:

M   All users can list the groups to which this user belongs.

–   Only the user and members of the `system:administrators` group can list the groups to which this user belongs.

ADD flag, fourth character:

There is no meaning for this privacy flag for a user entry.

REMOVE flag, fifth character:

There is no meaning for this privacy flag for a user entry.

As you can see, many of these privacy flags have meanings only when applied to group entries, as explained later in this chapter. In practice, the defaults, which permit everyone to see this data but allow only the user (or administrator) to list the groups owned by the user or of which the user is a member, are acceptable.

ACCESS CONTROL LISTS

Having talked about access control lists for so long, we'll finally look at their precise definition. ACLs control permissions on directory and file access. Whereas a normal UNIX permission is a string of read-write-execute permissions for three classes of users—the owner, a group, and everyone else—an AFS ACL allows more permissions to be set for a variety of users or groups.

An AFS ACL is a list of rights and is defined on a per-directory basis. All of the entries in a single directory share the same base ACL; you can't set different AFS access controls on different files except by moving the file to a different directory. Each ACL on a directory consists of a list of at most 20 entries; each entry consists of an identity—either a user or group—and the combinations of rights granted to that identity.

Seven rights are predefined by AFS: four control access to the directory and three provide permissions for all files in that directory.

The four directory rights and their abbreviated character code (in parentheses) are:

- lookup (l)—Permits a user or group to list the contents of the directory. Members of the `system:administrators` group always have permission to list directory contents, whether this right is explicitly listed or not.
- insert (i)—Permits a user or group to add files or subdirectories to a given directory.
- delete (d)—Permits a user or group to delete entries from a directory.
- administer (a)—Permits a user or group to manipulate the ACL for a directory. Members of the `system:administrators` group always have permission to manipulate ACLs, whether explicitly listed or not. And users are always permitted to modify their AFS home directory ACLs.

The three rights that affect all of the files in a directory equally are:

- read (r)—Permission to read file content and to query file status.
- write (w)—Permission to write file content and to change UNIX permission modes of files.
- lock (k)—Permission to use full-file advisory locks.

Some AFSers use the mnemonic "wildkar" to remember these seven rights.

To examine an ACL, use the `fs` command. Here's a typical ACL for a user's home directory.

```
$ cd /afs/hq.firm/user/alice
$ fs listacl .
Access list for . is
Normal rights:
  system:anyuser rl
  alice rlidwka
```

The ACL has two entries: the first entry displays the rights of the group `system:anyuser`; members can read the file contents and list the directory's files. The second entry shows the rights for the user `alice`. She can perform all actions, read files, list the directory, insert files, delete files, write file data, lock files, and administer the directory ACL.

Inside the directory are four files:

```
$ ls -l
total 6
-rw-rw-rw-   1 alice     staff          29 Mar 29 16:57 file1
-rw-------   1 alice     staff          29 Mar 29 16:57 file2
-r-xr-xr-x   1 alice     staff          29 Mar 29 16:57 script1
-rwxr-x---   1 alice     staff          29 Mar 29 16:57 script2
```

Let's look at the each file in the directory. Though each still appears to have rights defined by the nine UNIX permission bits, in AFS the group and world permissions (the top six bits) are completely ignored. If stored in a UNIX file system, `file1` would be readable and writeable to Alice, as well as to members of the group staff and the world. Because it is stored in AFS, the fact that the top six bits are `rw-rw-` and that the file has a group owner of staff is completely irrelevant.

All that is relevant are the bottom three bits. For file1, the file is nominally rw-, that is, readable and writeable but not executable. User Alice, since she has full rights in her entry in the ACL, can read and write the file. Looking at the UNIX group and world permissions, you'd think that others could write to the file as well, but for anyone other than Alice the only matching ACL entry is for system:anyuser and the permissions listed permit only file reading.

Again, for file2, the fact that the top six bits of the UNIX permissions are empty is irrelevant. The bottom three bits permit reading and writing; this is the same as the permissions for file1. Alice's ACL entry endorses those permissions, while any other user can still read the file, despite the attempt to block reading by changing the UNIX group and world permissions.

For script1, the bottom three bits permit reading and execution but not writing. Here, even Alice is not permitted to write the file; although the ACL on the directory includes file writing permission, the bottom three bits take precedence. Alice is therefore permitted to read and execute but not to write to the script. Other users are permitted to read the script because of the r permission and the rl system:anyuser ACL entry. They can also execute the script because of the UNIX x permission; execution is permitted for any file with the x permission bit on as long as an ACL entry permits reading by the user.

Finally, it may appear to a UNIX user as though script2 can be edited and executed only by Alice and just executed by anyone in the group staff. They would be wrong: AFS users know that, as with file2, the permissions for script2 are based on the ACL stored in the directory. Because this ACL permits anyone to read the files in the directory, any file (such as script2) with the user read bit set will be readable by anyone. And because the user execute bit is set, anyone may run this script.

The appearance of the user write bit for script2 also suggests that anyone with access to the file may edit it. According to the directory ACL, the only authenticated user permitted to edit the file is alice; everyone else has only read permissions.

The rules are quite simple, though very different from standard UNIX:

- A single ACL on a directory controls directory access and access to all files in the directory.
- The group and world permission bits are completely ignored.
- The user permission bits are the final modifiers of access to the file for any user who is permitted access by the ACL.

The result is that the UNIX user r bit gives anyone listed in an ACL entry with read and lookup the right to read the file. Without that r bit, no one may read the file, no matter what the ACL says.

The UNIX user w bit gives anyone listed in an ACL entry with write and lookup the right to write to the file. Without that w bit no one may write to the file.

The UNIX user x bit is still used by the operating system to permit the file to be executed by anyone with read and lookup rights on an ACL entry. Without the user x bit, the file will not be executable for any user.

As for directories, all nine UNIX permission bits as well as the owner and group name are completely ignored. Only the four AFS ACL rights (list, insert, delete, and administer) for any listed identities are used.

Although so many bits are ignored by AFS, they are still stored in the system and can be set with the usual tools of chmod and chown. Anyone with ACL write permissions can change the mode bits of files, and anyone with ACL insert, lookup, and delete permissions can change the mode bits of directories.

Once again, AFS appears to provide a daunting interface to file system activity. The reality, though, for manipulating AFS files, is that permissions on directories are completely described by the ACL, while file permissions begin with the leftmost three rwx permission bits and are finally constrained by any matching ACL entry.

Conveniently, AFS copies the ACL on a parent directory over to a new subdirectory at the time of creation. In the above example, the new subdirectory newDir gets a copy of the ACL on /afs/hq.firm/user/alice, which was shown in the previous example. This is a real copy; if Alice's home directory ACL is later changed, newDir will retain the original copy.

```
$ mkdir newDir
$ fs listacl newDir
Access list for newDir is
Normal rights:
  system:anyuser rl
  alice rlidwka
```

Setting ACLs is straightforward. To add or modify the access controls for the new directory, you use the setacl subcommand. The subcommand requires a directory name and then a set of pairs of arguments; each pair is an AFS identity (either a user or group name) and a corresponding set of ACL rights.

The ACL rights can be specified with the single character abbreviations, or one of the following simple words can be used:

- `read`—Gives `rl` permissions: read and list rights.
- `write`—Gives `rlidwk` permissions: read, list, insert, delete, write, and lock rights; all rights but administer.
- `all`—Gives `rlidwka` permissions.
- `none`—Erases the identities ACL entry, if it existed at all.

Here, the `newDir` directory created above has two additional entries added to its ACL.

```
$ fs setacl newDir bob rlidwk
$ fs setacl newDir carol rl system:anyuser none
$ fs listacl newDir
Access list for newDir is
Normal rights:
  carol rl
  bob rlidwk
  alice rlidwka
```

The `listacl` subcommand lists each entry's rights using the single character abbreviations and always in the order `rlidwka`. You can clear out an ACL and install a whole new list of entries with:

```
$ fs setacl newDir alice read -clear
$ fs listacl newDir
Access list for newDir is
Normal rights:
  alice rl
```

The combination of automatic copying of ACLs to new subdirectories and the use of the shorthand ACL rights words makes ACL management a relatively simple task. Because all files in a given directory share an ACL, each directory becomes a container in which similarly permissioned files are stored. Remember that to give a file a different access control characteristic, move the file to a directory that has a different ACL. Also note that moving a file to a new directory may give the file dramatically different access rights.

One final detail helps users manage ACLs: The owner of a directory—as seen with `ls -ld` command—always has administer rights on the directory ACL no matter what the ACL says. This convention makes it hard to lock yourself out of your own home directory even after you make a mistake with your `setacl` command.

One other subcommand copies an entire ACL from one directory to another. This feature is especially useful for complicated ACLs. To aid new users with ACL management, it may be beneficial to introduce one or two standard directories into their new AFS home directory. They can then use the `copyacl` command immediately to ensure proper access to their personal directory structure. In Carol's home directory, there are two predefined directories:

```
$ cd /afs/hq.firm/user/carol
$ ls -l
total 8
drwxr-xr-x   2 carol    staff        2048 Mar 29 17:06 Private
drwxr-xr-x   2 carol    staff        2048 Mar 29 17:06 Public
$
$ fs listacl Public Private
Access list for Public is
Normal rights:
  system:authuser rl
  carol rlidwka

Access list for Private is
Normal rights:
  carol rlidwka
```

She can now easily create a new directory with permissions similar to the `Private` subdirectory.

```
$ mkdir personal
$ fs copyacl Private personal -clear
$
$ fs listacl personal
Access list for personal is
Normal rights:
  carol rlidwka
```

Note that the `-clear` option to `copyacl` is needed to clear any entries on the destination directory that are not in the source directory. The default is to copy entries over from source to destination, setting permissions as needed, but not to remove any extra entries that preexisted in the destination.

It is common practice not to put a `system:administrators` entry into each ACL in AFS. Thus, anyone authenticated as a member of that group cannot automatically read and write files. If administrators do need to edit some files, they can always modify the ACL—that right is theirs no matter what the ACL says. This extra step ensures that administrators take an explicit action to read or write otherwise private files, a step that respects the rights of users without unduly hindering administration.

NEGATIVE RIGHTS

When listed, an ACL displays the title "Normal rights" because AFS also allows you to specify negative access rights. Negative rights can be a powerful tool for permission management, but to understand them you should read the Transarc manual diligently.

One small problem with group identities on ACL entries is that someone else will likely be administering the group membership. For example, suppose Bob should not have read access to a directory's files. You can easily restrict the directory's reading rights to some group to which Bob doesn't belong, but if Bob convinces the group's owner to add him to the group, your ACL restriction will be subverted. Negative rights can help.

```
$ mkdir secrets
$ fs setacl -negative secrets bob all
$ fs listacl secrets
Access list for secrets is
Normal rights:
   system:anyuser rl
   carol rlidwka
Negative rights:
   bob rlidwka
```

The final determination of rights on a file involves checking what is allowed by the bottom three UNIX permission bits, rwx, comparing that with a matching user or group entry listed under Normal rights and rejecting any listed rights for matching users or groups under Negative rights. Above, the directory secrets is completely unavailable to bob because all the AFS rights are removed by the negative ACL entry.

GROUPS AND ACLS

AFS groups are completely distinct from traditional UNIX groups usually stored in the file /etc/group or the NIS group map. A UNIX group can be assigned to a UNIX file system file or directory as the group owner that controls the read-write-execute permissions for a collection of users. An AFS group is used only for the assignment of permissions as an entry in an access control list on an AFS directory. Just as a UNIX group name cannot be entered into an AFS ACL, neither can an AFS group be used as a group owner of a UNIX file.

Note that an AFS file still has a UNIX group name attached to it; this group name can be maintained for appearance's sake but is otherwise ignored. Some UNIX tools or public utilities may use group identification numbers and permissions for their own access control, and commands such as `tar` or `cp` will want to copy the UNIX group owner. Otherwise, the use of UNIX groups in an AFS site will probably be relegated to legacy software.

AFS groups can be created by any AFS user. Once the group is created, only the owner can administer the group. Because AFS user identities are given positive identification numbers from 0 to 32767, AFS groups are given negative identification numbers from -1 to -32768. When a group is created, it is given either the next available slot or the number specified on the command line.

Group names themselves are either a single word or two words separated by a colon, such as `managers`, `alice:friends`, or `system:administrators`. For colon-separated group names, the word to the left is the user name of the assigned owner of the group. To create their own groups, users must follow this convention; AFS will only allow Alice to create groups that begin with `alice:` such as `alice:friends`. This example finally explains what `system:administrators` means: it is a group named `administrators` owned by the AFS system itself. Aside from their built-in existence, it and the other system groups are regular AFS groups and can be used on directory ACLs like any other user or group name.

There are three predefined system groups.

- `system:anyuser`—All users who use an AFS computer are members of this group regardless of any or no AFS Kerberos credentials. This group therefore has no explicit members, so you can't list the membership of the group as you can with other groups, nor is the group mentioned when you list all the groups to which a user belongs. This group provides a simple way to allow or restrict read or write access to an area of the file system.
- `system:authuser`—The group name is a short form of "authorized users" and includes all users who have successfully obtained Kerberos identity credentials in the local cell. For a given ACL, the local cell refers to the AFS cell in which the directory is stored. As with `system:anyuser`, you cannot list the members of `system:authuser`, nor is the

group listed in a user's group membership list. With this group, you can conveniently permit or deny access to parts of the AFS file system intended just for users on your network who have received legitimate user credentials.

For example, system software, such as /usr/bin programs or /usr/man documentation that points to files stored in AFS rather than on the desktop's local disk, is often given system:anyuser read and list permissions so that anyone can access this basic information. But the entry point to a company's production binaries or home directories could be given system:authuser so that only employees of the company (according to Kerberos) could access this more sensitive data.

- system:administrators—This group's members must be explicitly defined. During installation of AFS, a well-known identity, usually afsadmin, is created as the sole member of the group. Later on, you may want to add certain individuals to the membership list. Because this group is defined explicitly through administration commands, the membership list can be printed out.

  Besides being available as an AFS group to put on directory ACLs, members of this group are given extra permissions to use various AFS utilities:

  - Members can run privileged pts commands, for example, to create single word group names.
  - Members can change the ownership of files.
  - Members normally have implicit rights to list the contents of any AFS directory.
  - Most importantly, members can always administer access rights on every directory ACL. Normally, ACL administration is permitted only to those users or groups with the a permission listed in an ACL. Because system:administrators can implicitly administer any ACL, it is usual to not explicitly add system:administrators rights to directories.

The system:anyuser and system:authuser can be used to both grant and deny access to parts of the file system. In fact, sometimes system:authuser should be used if an ACL also has negative access rights. In the previous example, Bob was denied rights to read the secrets directory. But because the directory happened to be readable by system:anyuser, it is a simple matter for Bob to unlog, lose his AFS credentials, and have the system:anyuser access rights apply. This is a good time to use the system:authuser group, because only users with valid Kerberos credentials can pass through the security ACL.

```
$ fs setacl secrets system:authuser read system:anyuser none
$ fs listacl secrets
Access list for secrets is
Normal rights:
  system:authuser rl
  carol rlidwka
Negative rights:
  bob rlidwka
```

This example is actually a reasonable action to take if someone in a company is fired. Near the top of the company's AFS tree, a system:authuser entry coupled with the addition of negative rights for the ex-employee will be a strong impediment to any last-minute file accesses.

Though all groups are created and owned by a particular user, any user can add any group names to an ACL. So, once Alice creates her group, alice:friends, her co-worker Bob might use that group to deny its members access to one of his directories.

To manage administration and membership of groups, use the pts command. New group names can be up to 63 characters long but can consist only of any printable characters except uppercase letters and the colon. The membership of a group is limited to 5,000 members. In the following example, we'll see how Alice, authenticated as herself, manages her group.

```
$ pts creategroup alice:friends
group alice:friends has id -206
$ pts adduser -user carol alice -group alice:friends
$ pts membership alice:friends
Members of alice:friends (id: -206) are:
  carol
  alice
```

Alice is free to create groups and add members at her discretion, and she can examine the members of the group, find out what groups she owns and manages, and find out which groups have her as a member.

```
$ pts listowned alice
Groups owned by alice (id: 17001) are:
  alice:friends
$ pts membership alice
Groups alice (id: 17001) is a member of:
  alice:friends
```

Now that her group of friends has been created, she (or anyone) is free to add that group to an ACL on a directory.

```
$ cd /afs/hq.firm/user/alice
$ mkdir secrets
$ fs listacl secrets
Access list for secrets is
Normal rights:
  system:anyuser rl
  alice rlidwka
```

In Alice's home directory, you can see that the new subdirectory `secrets` has an ACL automatically inherited as a copy of its parent's ACL. In this cell, that ACL was set up so that any user, whether authenticated to AFS or not, could read and list entries in the home directory but not write or delete files. Alice, naturally, has complete rights to her home. As the owner of her home directory, she has implicit administration rights, no matter what the ACL says.

```
$ fs setacl secrets alice:friends read
$ fs setacl secrets system:anyuser none
$ fs listacl secrets
Access list for secrets is
Normal rights:
  alice:friends rl
  alice rlidwka
$ ls -ld secrets
drwxr-xr-x   2 alice     staff        2048 Mar 29 17:19 secrets
```

For the new subdirectory `secrets`, Alice adds an ACL entry and modifies another entry so that no one but she and her friends can read the files there and only she can write, delete, and administer those files. Note that these entries were added one at a time; without the `-clear` option, each additional `setacl` subcommand simply adds a new entry, such as `alice:friends`, or modifies an existing entry, such as `system:anyuser`.

The UNIX permissions on the `secrets` directory are somewhat misleading. The bits were set according to the UNIX `mkdir` command and Alice's user bit-mask setting (`umask`). The resulting bits, rwxr-xr-x, suggest that all UNIX users can at the least navigate into the directory. But AFS doesn't use the top six permission bits or the UNIX group identity at all. Here's what happens when AFS user Bob tries to access the directory.

```
$ tokens

Tokens held by the Cache Manager:

User's (AFS ID 5321) tokens for afs@hq.firm [Expires Mar 30 18:49]
--End of list--
$ cd /afs/hq.firm/user/alice
/afs/hq.firm/user/alice
$ cd secrets
/bin/ksh: secrets:   not found
```

It's instructive to understand exactly how this access permission is checked. When a user runs a command that causes an AFS file to be accessed, such as the change directory command above, the client kernel sends a message to the appropriate server asking its fileserver process to check the permissibility of the action. The process notes which AFS identity and machine are requesting the check and asks a protection database server to return the *Current Protection Subgroup* for the user. This CPS is a list of all the groups to which the user belongs, including, for completeness, the groups system:anyuser and, if the user is authenticated, system:authuser. The fileserver process can then check the CPS list against ACL entries and permissions.

A problem arises when a user tries to enter a directory and is denied access. Sometimes, after complaining to the appropriate administrator, the user might be made a member of an appropriate group. But if the user immediately tries to access the directory again, access will still be denied because the fileserver has already received a CPS list for the user's active connection and it has no way to know that the CPS has changed.

Since there is no notification process for group membership changes, the user must log in again; this process causes a new connection to the server to be made, and a new CPS list, which will include the new group membership, will be retrieved by the file server. (In some ways, this is similar to adding a UNIX user to a UNIX group; the user must log in again to cause the group list to be recalculated.)

Most of the time this re-login is not needed because connections between users and file servers are terminated periodically, which causes new CPS lists to be retrieved many times during the course of a day.

When a user is a member of more than one group, it's possible for different groups to be entered into an ACL with different permissions. In this case, the user will have the access rights of the union of the groups. For example, if Bob is in two groups, readers and writers, he will have whatever access rights are available to either group.

```
$ pts membership bob
Groups bob (id: 5321) is a member of:
  bob:writers
  bob:readers
$ cd /afs/hq.firm/user/bob
$ ls -l
total 4
drwxr-xr-x   2 bob      staff       2048 Mar 29 17:27 aclUnion
$ fs listacl aclUnion
Access list for aclUnion is
Normal rights:
  bob:writers lidwka
  bob:readers rl
$
$ date > aclUnion/foo
$ cat aclUnion
Sat Mar  29  17:30:22 EST 1997
```

Bob can create and write to the file aclUnion/foo because, as a member of writers, he has l, i, and w rights. He can then read the file because as a member of readers, he has the l, and r right.

An AFS group can have at most 5,000 members; this is an odd limit, apparently due to the implementation of the pts command itself. More importantly, you cannot have a group as a member of a group. It would be nice if alice:friends could be composed of alice:colleagues and alice:bestFriends. This arrangement would permit simpler management of hierarchies of users and groups, although it would also make ACLs harder for users to interpret. In any event, this functionality is not supported.

MORE GROUP MANAGEMENT

Let's examine some of the internal details of Alice's group.

```
$ pts examine alice:friends
Name: alice:friends, id: -206, owner: alice, creator: alice,
  membership: 2, flags: S-M--, group quota: 0.
```

You can see with the examine subcommand that Alice's group has a negative identification number, as do all AFS groups, that it was created by Alice, and that it is owned by her as well.

As groups are created, an internal counter is adjusted to keep track of the lowest group identification number. If, during creation, no identification number is offered on the command line, the counter, named GroupMax, is used and decremented. If a number offered is lower in value than `GroupMax`, `GroupMax` is set to a new value of one less than the offered number. That way, new groups can always be given new identification numbers automatically. Knowing this, administrators can artificially set the value of `GroupMax` (with the `setmax` subcommand) so that a range of numbers is set aside to be assigned as desired.

The flags are interpreted similarly to user entries as outlined earlier: The `S` flag means that anyone can examine the status of this group; the `M` flag means that anyone can list the members of the group. This is the default for groups. The three hyphen-valued flags indicate that only the owner or `system:administrators` can list the ownership, and add and remove members.

For groups, here is the list of valid flags and their meaning.

STATUS flag, first character:

S   All users can examine the status of the user.

s   Only the members of the group and `system:administrators` can examine the entry.

OWNERSHIP flag, second character:

O   All users can list the groups that this user owns.

–   Only members of the group and `system:administrators` can list the owned groups.

MEMBERSHIP flag, third character:

M   All users can list the groups to which this user belongs.

m   Only members of the group can list the complete group membership.

–   Only the owner and `system:administrators` can list the group membership.

ADD flag, fourth character:

A   Any user can add users to the group.

a   Only members of the group itself can add other users to the group.

–   Only the owner and `system:administrators` can add users to the group.

REMOVE flag, fifth character:

r   Only members of the group itself can remove users from the group.

–   Only the owner and `system:administrators` can remove users from the group.

Currently, the owner of `alice:friends` is Alice. It may well be that one day, Alice will leave the organization and her friends may want to keep using that group. In this situation, the group owner or a member of `system:admin-istrators` can transfer ownership to another user.

```
$ pts chown alice:friends bob
$ pts membership bob:friends
Members of bob:friends (id: -206) are:
  carol
  alice
$ pts examine bob:friends
Name: bob:friends, id: -206, owner: bob, creator: alice,
  membership: 2, flags: S-M--, group quota: 0.
```

As stated, the left-hand side of a group name is the owner of the group. After Alice uses the `chown` subcommand to transfer ownership, the protection system automatically renames the left-hand side to the new owner's name. Because AFS directory's ACL entries are stored using the identification number of the group, an ACL will be displayed with the correct group name.

```
$ fs listacl /afs/hq.firm/user/alice/secrets
Access list for secrets is
Normal rights:
  bob:friends rl
  alice rlidwka
```

Having users manage their own groups is a distinct advantage over regular UNIX functionality. But most organizations will require many standard groups, such as sales or staff, that are cumbersome for individual users to manage and really shouldn't have an ordinary user's name as a prefix. For these situations, AFS permits the creation of groups that have single words as names.

Only members of `system:administrators` can create a group name consisting of a single word. Other than the restriction on who can create the group, a single-word group acts just like a two-word, colon-separated group. The advantage to single-word groups is simply the implication that there is no static owner for the group. This appearance is a convenience for certain groups in an organization: It might be better to have a group named `sales` with no owner explicitly named, rather than have a group named `alice:sales`, which would have to be renamed if Alice left the company.

And yet, though an administrator may create a group named `sales`, the administrator will probably want to transfer ownership of the group to a regular user. Changing the ownership of a group transfers management responsibility of the group, so an administrator may delegate responsibility in a controlled way. Here, an administrator creates and changes ownership of the sales group.

```
$ pts creategroup sales
group sales has id -209
$ pts chown sales carol
$ pts examine sales
Name: sales, id: -209, owner: carol, creator: afsadmin,
  membership: 0, flags: S-M--, group quota: 0.
```

Despite the fact that Carol did not create the group, a fact recorded in the pts database, she will now have as much control of the sales group as if it had been created by her. The choice of whether a prefix-less group is owned (and managed) by an administrator or delegated to another user depends on the usage policies of your organization.

There are two interesting variations of this delegation. Rather than change ownership to a user, an administrator can assign ownership of a group to a group. This delegation implies that any members of the owning group can manage the group. A regular use of this feature is to create a set of users that can control a group of other users, such as when the leaders of a software project are given control of a group consisting of all developers on the project.

The second use of group ownership is to create a self-owned group, that is, a group that can be managed by any of its members. This implies that any member of the group can add other members as desired, which may be exactly the right policy. But this also means that any member can remove any other member from the group; self-owned groups therefore demand a certain amount of trust from their members.

The current owner of a group (or any member of a group owner) is permitted to transfer ownership to another user or group. As colon-separated groups reflect the user ownership by the leftmost word in the group name, so changing the individual owner of a group may result in a change to the group name. Consider Alice's group alice:friends: If Alice were to change ownership to Bob, the group would be automatically renamed to bob:friends, and such a name change would be visible on any ACL entries.

A problem exists when transferring ownership of group-owned groups created by users. Alice can change the ownership of alice:colleagues to the group alice:friends. But when alice:friends has its ownership transferred to Bob, though its name is now bob:friends, the name of the group `alice:colleagues` does not change. AFS simply doesn't go through all the mechanics to make this change happen. For consistency, group owners can make name changes themselves with the `pts rename` command.

As people join organizations, their identification numbers must be assigned systematically. In general, it's a bad idea to reuse the UNIX numeric identity of a person who has left an organization. If the user identifier is simply reassigned, there will usually be a large number of files in various places in the file system that will now be owned by the new user, with no particular indication that they were created by the earlier user.

Similarly, it's a bad idea to reuse AFS numeric identities. If the AFS number is reassigned, then the name listed on an access control list will change to that of the new user; this access control will probably not be what was intended. It's better to just remove the previous user identity from the system. When displaying an ACL that has an entry containing a deleted user name, the numeric identity is printed instead. This makes it clear that the ACL should be edited to take explicitly into account new employees. Use the `fs cleanacl` command to automatically remove such entries.

That people tend to join and leave companies regularly, argues for putting users into AFS groups and entering the groups onto ACLs instead. Then, when a person leaves the firm, only the group membership would need to be edited and the ACL will not need to be modified or cleaned at all.

MACHINE GROUPS

One small problem with ubiquitous file visibility is that some software vendors license their products to a certain set of machines and not to users. For software that must be licensed only to a set of users, it is straightforward to create a protection group containing those users, perhaps give ownership of the group to the individual in charge of licensing, and then to apply that group to the access control list where the software is stored. To solve licensing on a per-machine basis, AFS permits the creation of machine groups.

A *machine group* is just a protection group that has as members the network addresses for a set of machines. Just as a human must first be listed as a regular user in the protection database before being added as a member of a group, so too must a machine be set up as a user. Use the regular user `pts create` command to set up a machine as a user.

```
$ pts createuser 192.168.3.94
User 192.168.3.94 has id 17002
```

To help reduce the number of entries that must be added to the protection database, it's possible to use a wildcard value, 0, in certain positions of the IP address:

- A.B.C.0 would match all machines whose IP address ranges from A.B.C.0 to A.B.C.255.
- A.B.0.0 would match all IP addresses on all subnets from the A.B.0 subnet to the A.B.255 subnet.
- A.0.0.0 would match all addresses on all subnets from A.0 to A.255.

These wildcards work only as specified above; there is no way to specify matches such as A.0.C.0 or to specify 0.0.0.0. Also, note that the client subnet mask is not used for calculating wildcards; if your subnets are laid out with nonstandard masks, using these wildcards may result in more or fewer matches than desired.

For most purposes, this IP-address user is a normal entry in the protection database. Because of the layout of the database, certain data fields must be filled as best they can:

```
$ pts examine 192.168.3.94
Name: 192.168.3.94 id: 17002, owner: system:administrators, creator: afsadmin,
  membership: 0, flags: S----, group quota: 20.
```

The user-id field, normally set equal to a user's UNIX identification number, is here set to the next number available above the UserMax high-water mark; The owner is set to system:administrators, and the identity of the person adding the entry is stored as the creator. The number of groups to which this entry is a member is set to 0; the privacy flags are set to S to indicate that anyone can examine this entry; and the group creation quota for this machine entry is set to 20 (though no groups can be created by this identity because no one can authenticate as a machine).

Although this procedure has created a pseudo-user entry in the database, you cannot add this entry as-is to an ACL. You must first add the machine entry to a group; that group can then be added to an access control list on a directory in AFS with any desired permissions. Adding a machine entry to a group is the same process as adding a user to a group.

```
$ pts adduser 192.168.3.94 bob:friends
$ pts membership bob:friends
Members of bob:friends (id: -206) are:
```

```
carol
alice
192.168.3.94
```

Once a machine is added to a group, listing the groups to which a machine belongs works as expected.

```
$ pts membership 192.168.3.94
Groups 192.168.3.94 (id: 17002) is a member of:
  bob:friends
```

Remember that the purpose of machine groups is to permit access to software from a certain set of desktops. By adding a machine entry to a group and adding that group to an ACL, any user on that machine, whether authenticated to any AFS identity or not, will have the permissions granted to the group. In normal usage, this suggests that a group will have only user entries or only machine entries.

Now that the group has been set up, you can add it as an entry on an ACL with whatever permissions you desire.

There is one final quirk to the implementation: it's common for several top-level directories of the AFS namespace to be permitted only to sys-tem:authuser, that is, any user can access the rest of the namespace, but only if the user has been authenticated as a user, any user, of the current cell. Machine groups are intended to be useful for any person logged in to a workstation so that software licenses can be honestly followed. Therefore, when an unauthenticated user is using a machine that is a member of a group entry on an ACL, the user's implicit credential is elevated to system:authuser, but only if the machine entry in the group is an exact match, not a wildcard.

This rule permits any user of a given desktop to effectively have sys-tem:authuser credentials for a directory. As long as that directory has an ACL that includes the specific machine's IP address as a member of a group entry, any user of the desktop, and only that desktop, would have access to the directory.

In retrospect, using IP addresses does not seem like a well-thought-out solution to setting up machine identities; IP addresses are not inherently meaningful or memorable, and for clients with multiple network connections, each of its network addresses will need to be added to a group membership. According to the AFS client/server protocol, the packets on the wire are identified by IP address only, so something or someone must go to the trouble of translating names into addresses. It would be helpful if the AFS server processes themselves could manage to translate names into IP addresses through the use of the Domain Name System or Network Information System. But the AFS system is not designed to rely on any other external protocols, and in the mid-80s, systems like DNS were not particularly stable or widely used. Now that time has passed, it would be useful for Transarc to revisit this issue; Version 3.5 promises better support for multi-homed systems.

Machine entries and groups are a significant feature of the AFS system. The Open Group's DCE system generalizes machine identities somewhat to permit more flexible (and easier to understand) machines, groups, and ACLs.

VOLUMES REVISITED

Because the details of access controls and groups are somewhat involved, we only hinted at many of the permissions surrounding volume management in the preceding two chapters. Most importantly, when a volume is created, it has a default ACL consisting of a single entry that gives `system:administrators` all rights. Whichever directory name is connected to the volume will reflect this initial ACL.

```
$ vos create fs-one b tmp.foo
Volume 536870988 created on partition /vicepb of fs-one
$ fs mkm /afs/.hq.firm/tmp/foo tmp.foo
$ fs listacl /afs/.hq.firm/tmp/foo
Access list for /afs/.hq.firm/tmp/foo is
Normal rights:
  system:administrators rlidwka
```

To maintain consistent and appropriate access controls in your AFS cell, immediately after creating and connecting a new volume reset the ACL to an appropriate value. The reason for fixing the ACL quickly is that ACLs for any new subdirectories in the volume are copied over from the parent's ACL; if you set the top directory ACL correctly right after creation of the volume, the odds are good that most subdirectories will have reasonably correct ACL.

Members of `system:administrators` do not have to be put on an ACL. By default, these members have l (list) and a (administer) rights, so even if not mentioned explicitly on any directories in a cell, an authenticated administrator will be able to read the file namespace and reset any ACL to perform any needed operation. Many sites use this ethic to good effect; others add `system:administrators` rights to ACLs as they see fit. It probably makes most sense to pick one convention and try to keep all directories in the cell consistent. If the `system:administrators` group is listed in some ACLs but not others, some users may get the impression that removing the entry from a directory will actually make the data impenetrable, which is not, strictly speaking, true.

BACKUP VOLUMES

Besides a user's home volume, a snapshot of the user's directory is usually made every night. Thanks to the design of AFS, this snapshot is a volume that can also be mounted in the file namespace to allow easy retrieval of files mistakenly deleted. It is common for backup volumes to be created for all volumes in the system so that the archive process can use this stable and consistent image when writing the data to tape. But, while all backup volumes could be added somewhere to the namespace for easy access, only backups of user volumes are typically connected to well-known paths. Many site administrators add a user's backup volume to a hidden directory in the user's home directory with the administration commands:

```
$ vos backup user.zed
Created backup volume for user.zed
$ fs mkm /afs/hq.firm/user/zed/.oldFiles user.zed.backup
```

Now, it is a simple matter of education to permit users to access last night's snapshot of their data. The connection to the backup version of the volume is made once. Because it is a change to the AFS namespace, it is visible to all clients. The snapshot command can then be run as often as desired to provide users with access to a read-only copy of their files. Once administrators have set up a job to recreate the backup volumes every night at, say, midnight, it becomes trivial for users themselves to correct careless file deletions with no system intervention.

Some sites have found, however, that a subdirectory in a user's home directory which mirrors the home directory is a little confusing for some users. Even though the backup volume is read-only, it can bewilder some. One cure is to put the volumes in other locations, `/afs/hq.firm/users/.alice`, or `/afs/hq.firm/.user/alice`, or even not to preinstall the volume at all, but to wait for the inevitable cry for help and then to miraculously create the connection, explain the solution, and save the day.

The latter strategy, in fact, is what is often done with most other volumes. With a multilevel set of development directories, sources, source control, groups of programmers, and test, beta, and production binaries, each with its own volume of files, it becomes a little difficult to have well-known or obvious locations for the backup volumes. In these cases, it is easier to simply run an `fs mkm` command on the volume in question when the need arises.

CHECKING FOR ERRORS

Once users are somewhat capable of dealing with ACLs and authentication questions, there may still be occasional problems with basic network connectivity or server responses. Sometime, users may wonder if odd behavior is due to a server and/or network outage. A convenient command is `checkservers`.

```
$ fs checkservers
All servers are running.
```

This command attempts to contact each file server that the client has previously contacted. If your client has been retrieving files only from server `fs-one`, this command will check only with that server to see if it is still available.

Note that this command is more useful when run in the background. If any servers are down, the command takes some extra time to run in order to make sure that the server isn't simply slow. Since it may take some time to run, you probably don't want to run the command in the foreground because it may be hard to interrupt. When services are down, the response is:

```
$ fs checkservers &
$ These servers are still down:
        fs-one.hq.firm
```

You may see other error messages displayed either in your current terminal session or on the desktop's system console. If you've tried to write a file that would put you over your quota, you'll see the following error:

```
$ mkfile 1M large-file
large-file: No space left on device
```

The device in question is the underlying volume or partition. As described in Chapter 4, the user should use the `fs listquota` command to see where the space shortage is located.

Other error messages may indicate a more serious problem with connectivity.

```
$ touch newfile
afs: failed to store file
```

As the `touch` command creates a zero-length file, there can't possibly be a space problem. If the condition is repeatable, it indicates a severe failure of the network connection or server processes. If a volume happens to be in the middle of moving from one disk to another at the same time that you're trying to access it, you'll see:

```
$ cd /afs/hq.firm/user/david
Waiting for busy volume 536870976 in cell hq.firm
$
```

As long as the move operation being performed behind the scenes succeeds, your command will eventually succeed. If the volume is truly missing, you'll see a more direct error message.

```
$ cd /afs/hq.firm/user/zed
/afs/hq.firm/user/zed: No such device
```

This problem may be due to an out-of-date mapping of volume name to identification number in your desktop cache manager, as described in Chapter 5. You can update all such mappings with the `fs checkvolumes` command. If the volume access still returns an error, notify your administration staff of the problem.

```
$ fs checkvolumes
All volumeID/name mappings checked
$ cd /afs/hq.firm/user/zed
/afs/hq.firm/user/zed: No such device
```

The most common problem with users accessing AFS is that their Kerberos authentication credential has expired. Although unauthenticated access to AFS normally results in a permission-denied error, sometimes the results are confusing. At the first sign of trouble, always run a `tokens` command to see exactly what AFS understands your credentials to be.

If you can't remember your password and your administrators have set up Kerberos to lock accounts after a certain number of failed attempts, you may see the following message:

```
Unable to authenticate to AFS because ID is locked—see your system admin
```

At this point, only an administrator can unlock the account. Of course, if you haven't forgotten your password, this message may indicate that someone else tried to guess his way in to your account.

AFS VERSUS UNIX

Several differences between AFS and UNIX affect commonly run commands. Most of these differences are subtle and may only be noticed by administrators or developers; casual use of AFS by UNIX applications or users is not likely to run into any unforseen problems. Below, we compare some aspects of AFS and UNIX.

File Ownership: A user's AFS token is distinct from a UNIX identity. As long as administrators have installed AFS normally, users will obtain tokens that have exactly the same identification number as in UNIX. This fact is important because when files are created in AFS, the assigned ownership is based on the token identification number, not the UNIX identifier. This practice ensures that each file is given an owner's identity that has passed Kerberos authentication guarantees. If a user is not authenticated and creates a file in a publicly writeable area of AFS, the file will be assigned an owner identification number of 32766.

When UNIX applications, like /bin/ls, or file browsers are reading file information in AFS, they usually use the /etc/passwd file or NIS map to translate between identification numbers and user names. To ensure that such translations make sense, keep the maps up to date. Don't forget to add a user named anonymous mapped to number 32766.

Change Mode: The UNIX change mode command, chmod, used to change permissions on files and directories, is also used in AFS for a similar purpose. Yet AFS provides a richer set of group membership tools and a more general-purpose list of access controls for multiple identities. When manipulating the traditional UNIX permissions, remember that these nine bits are stored and listed correctly, but only the bottom three bits are used when determining final access. General users can use chmod as always, but users must examine the file's directory ACL for complete permission information.

Note that the setuid bits on an executable (used to change the effective user identity for a running process) work but only affect the UNIX identity of a process. Because AFS identities are managed by Kerberos-authenticated credentials, a program with the setuid bit set will cause the effective UNIX user to change but not the Kerberos credential. In particular, because the root identity has no meaning to AFS—UNIX superuser status does not confer any special AFS administrative rights—setuid root programs can be run to administer a desktop's processes and files but not to manage AFS.

Chapter 5 discussed how files and cells could be set up to run setuid programs. Use fs getcell to check if a setuid program is actually available with the setuid-bit set.

```
$ fs getcell hq.firm
Cell hq.firm status: setuid allowed
$ ls -l /afs/hq.firm/sys/bin/su
-r-sr-xr-x   1   afsadmin   staff          15280  Apr 10 11:39  su
```

The other overloaded UNIX permission bits, such as the sticky-bit and the setgid-bit, are stored correctly in AFS and are used correctly by the UNIX operating system.

Change Owner or Group: Normally, chown and chgrp, the commands used to change the ownership or group of a file can be run only by the root superuser identity in UNIX. Because root on a workstation is not trusted in AFS and because that workstation can see the entire globally visible AFS namespace, root alone cannot change owner or group of AFS files or directories. To run these programs, you must in addition be authenticated as a member of system:administrators.

Groups: UNIX group information is not used in AFS at all, so you may decide to delete many groups from the /etc/group file or map. But there is still the need for certain system groups such as wheel, kmem, or bin used by several UNIX-based administration commands. The AFS kernel module does nothing to impede the use of UNIX groups for UNIX services. You can enter group names and membership in /etc/groups or the NIS maps, and that information will be reflected in a process's internal group identity which can be listed with the groups command.

AFS happens to use two entries in the per-process group table to store the Process Authentication Group information. When running the groups command to list UNIX group membership, you will therefore see two large numbers printed alongside the regular group names. This is an unfortunate side-effect of needing to store PAG data in the kernel somewhere where the data will be correctly propagated to child processes. The group table serves this purpose but the output is a left-over indication that AFS is third-party software not quite perfectly integrated into a vendor's operating system.

Make Devices: Besides regular files and directories, UNIX file names can refer to block or character special devices to allow easy naming of hardware or system services. Such special devices are not supported in AFS. Any special devices such as sockets, pipes, or tape drives cannot be stored with an AFS path name.

Links: Symbolic links are aliases from one file to another. AFS provides full support for these links with one small exception concerning the characters permitted in the symbolic link name. On UNIX systems, volume connection information is stored in the same place as the symbolic link data. In fact, a connection point acts a little like a symbolic link to a name that begins with # or %. These two characters are the ones that the fs lsmount command uses when it prints out the connection point for a given path. Because of this, if you manually create a symbolic link to a file that begins with either of those two characters, the AFS kernel module will try to interpret the rest of the name as a volume name. (Volume connections require a few more pieces of data to be set, so you can't really make a volume connection with symbolic links alone.)

Hard links create another problem. Within a single directory, hard links are permitted between any two files. But as ACLs are stored on a per-directory basis and not per-file, a link from one file to a file in another directory is not permitted because it would not be possible to determine which ACL should control the file. Because hard link semantics require that the two names refer to the same file, one file name in one directory would be controlled by that directory's ACL, while the file name in the other directory could have a different ACL. The first ACL might permit writing while the other ACL would not.

AFS's solution is to not permit hard links between files in different directories. This may cause more problems than it solves: many third-party installation procedures create hard links of just this kind. When a new software package is running its installation process, for example, an AFS administrator is often faced with errors caused by bad AFS hard links. Unless the error message is particularly verbose, it can take some investigation to determine which files should have been linked. The correction is usually simple enough—just change the hard link to a soft link.

Copying Files: In AFS, copying files and subdirectories from one directory to another can produce a subtle problem with profound effects. Because all standard UNIX commands know nothing about the access control lists attached to each AFS directory, a previously private file in one directory may become public when copied to another directory. Typically, an unintentional change in permissions happens after a user runs a `tar` or `cp -R` command. Often enough, the ACL inheritance property on newly created subdirectories causes the correct ACL to be installed. Other times, a post-copy ACL cleanup is the required fix.

Transarc provides a tool, the `up` program, which copies a directory and its contents recursively to a destination directory. As the file data is copied, the ACLs will be copied correctly as well. When the `up` program is run as root under `system:administrators` privileges, the ownerships of the copied-to hierarchy are set to those of the source hierarchy; otherwise, the destination files are assigned the ownership of the user running the program.

One particularly interesting feature is that `up` checks timestamps to see what needs to be copied. If the `up` job is cancelled in the middle of copying a large subtree of files, then reissuing the command later will not cause the already copied-over data to be recopied.

Renaming Files: As in UNIX, files can be renamed or moved from one file name to another, even when renaming a volume mount point. The only considerations with AFS are those that concern UNIX: If the file is being renamed within the same disk partition, no significant data movement is needed; only the pointers in the directory entries themselves must be updated. But if the file is to be renamed to a location on another disk, the entire file must be read and then written to the new location and then the old data must be deleted. This is exactly what must happen in AFS whenever a file is being moved from one volume to another, even when the destination volume resides on the same disk partition as the source.

Disk Space Usage: Many users are quite familiar with the concept of distributed file systems. Most of the time, these file systems are explicitly connected to a particular server's location on the network. During day-to-day use of the system, it is common to ask the system to display the amount of room left on the current server's disk with the UNIX command `df`. This command does not return any useful information when applied to a directory in AFS.

```
$ cd /afs/hq.firm/user/alice
$ df -k .
Filesystem              kbytes      used    avail capacity  Mounted on
AFS                    9000000         0  9000000       0%   /afs
```

The df command's unuseful output can cause problems with certain shell scripts, particularly scripts attempting to install third-party software onto a disk.

Users who run df must understand that there are other ways of getting the same information. When concerned about how much disk space is left, a user should know that not only is there a hard-limit on disk space—the total size of the disk partition—but there is also a soft limit, a usage quota, set by local administrative practice. To find out how much of the physical disk has been used, you can run an fs subcommand.

```
$ fs diskfree
Volume Name           kbytes      used      avail      %used
user.alice            1031042     1478    1029564        0%
```

The listquota subcommand tells you how much room is left in the current volume and also how much room is left on the disk.

```
$ fs listquota
Volume Name           Quota      Used    % Used   Partition
user.alice            100000        9        0%          0%
```

The quota is simply an administrative limit placed on the amount of data that a volume can hold. As such, it is relatively easy for an administrator to increase that quota. In practice, you might find a volume that has several dozen megabytes of quota available, but the volume is stored on a disk partition that is completely full. In this case, to provide the full quota's worth of storage, you will have to move the volume onto another, less full disk surface.

This last discussion raises one other issue that initially bothers some users. Over many years of use, users have come to understand that the physical location of their data was never likely to change except under extreme circumstances. AFS, however, provides administrators with several tools to move replicated or read-write data around the system without having to reboot clients or laboriously push out maps of information. When a user wants to know where exactly in the AFS cell their data is located, the rejoinder is "Why do you want to know?" The point is that AFS does a very good job managing the location information itself. Whereas it was almost necessary for users to keep track of file locations themselves so that they could contact their data from random clients, this is precisely the functionality that has been deeply integrated into AFS itself.

There are commands to display location information, but users should be warned that it is far more subject to change than before. And this is ultimately beneficial. For example, when there are disk space problems, users home directories can be moved around until the needed storage has been made available—and this movement occurs on-line, transparently to users. In the morning, a home directory may be stored on one server, and in the afternoon, it may be on another. As long as access to data is uninterrupted and has good overall performance (because of caching), users should not care too much about where that data is stored.

The simplest way to find out which AFS server is managing a particular file is with another fs subcommand.

```
$ fs whereis /afs/hq.firm/user/alice
File /afs/hq.firm/user/alice is on hosts fs-one
```

For data stored in a read-write volume, this command produces a straight-forward answer. When asked of a read-only version, the response is a bit more verbose:

```
$ fs whereis /afs
File /afs is on hosts fs-two fs-one
```

In this case, the client doesn't respond with a single server name but with the complete list of servers that are currently known to have the file in question stored. Again, because AFS guarantees that all of the listed servers have exact copies of the replicas, it doesn't matter too much which server is providing the data. To find out exactly which server is delivering the files, use the getpref-erences subcommand and find which server is the closest (the lowest numerical) preference.

```
$ fs getserverprefs
fs-two                                                                   1007
fs-one                                                                   5003
```

Knowing that the file /afs is available from either server, you can see that fs-two is the preferred server, at least according to this client.

Finding Files: One interesting fact about the hierarchical namespace of most computer file systems is that they are optimized for lookup only by discrete path name elements. A general index is almost never maintained for complete names or file metadata, and certainly not for content. To search for files, the UNIX `find` utility is used to laboriously descend through a file system looking for files matching certain criteria such as name, age, or permissions.

One standard option to `find` is `-mount` or `-xdev` which, according to the on-line documentation, will not cross mount points. Be careful when reading UNIX documentation like this; the mount points referred to by the `find` command are UNIX mounts. This option will blithely crisscross AFS volume connections without problems; as far as most UNIX commands are concerned, the totality of the AFS namespace, including any connections to remote file servers or multiple cells, is regarded as a single mount point, a single file system.

The GNU project's version of `find` has been enhanced for AFS: when compiled with the appropriate options, it supports the `-fstype afs` predicate, which is `true` if the file is stored in the AFS namespace. This enhancement can be used to prohibit a `find` request from descending into `/afs`.

File Timestamps: A standard UNIX file system tracks three different timestamps for each file: the last time the file was accessed, the last time the file data was changed, and the last time file metainformation (such as the permissions) was changed. In the internal data structures, these timestamps are named the `atime`, `ctime`, and `mtime`. Because AFS file servers aren't involved in most file accesses—they're satisfied by client cache—the servers can't store a last access time. Instead, when timestamp information is requested by the `stat` system call, the server looks up the last time of file data change and uses that for the other two timestamps.

A short program to display these three timestamps shows that they are kept in sync.

```
$ date > foo
$ show_timestamps foo
last access:          Sat May 29   17:34 EST 1997
last status change: Sat May 29   17:34 EST 1997
last modify:          Sat May 29   17:34 EST 1997
```

After waiting a few seconds, we run a command to change the status of the file.

```
$ chmod 444 foo
$ show_timestamps foo
last access:          Sat May 29   17:34 EST 1997
last status change: Sat May 29   17:34 EST 1997
last modify:          Sat May 29   17:34 EST 1997
```

In a UNIX file system, the chmod command would have caused the status-change timestamp to change. As you can see, no AFS timestamps changed at all. On the other hand, if we append some data to the file, the times will all be updated.

```
$ date >> foo
$ show_timestamps foo
last access:          Sat May 29  17:36 EST 1997
last status change: Sat May 29  17:36 EST 1997
last modify:          Sat May 29  17:36 EST 1997
```

It's hard to construct a real-world scenario that requires each of these timestamps to be accurately kept. One place this could cause confusion is with the find utility: the command can search for files with particular atime, mtime, or ctime modification times. Such commands could produce unexpected results in AFS.

lsof Utility: This popular UNIX administration command prints out the open files in use by any process on a machine. It's very handy for finding out who is using what files or programs. Unfortunately, this program has not been ported to fully understand AFS file names. The latest versions of the tool can at best report that a particular file opened by a process is one stored in AFS.

Temporary Files: AFS is a distributed file system whose performance can approach that of a local disk over a relatively long series of transactions. But, it will still send file data over the network to a server which is probably busy with other users as well. To increase application efficiency, you should try to use temporary space on local disk for files that will probably be discarded quickly. Developers, especially, might want to redirect their compiler output from the distributed system to temporary space. Also, user's downloading data from the Web can place the files on their local disk. This suggestion, of course, applies to any other distributed file system, from NFS to Novell.

PROGRAMMING ISSUES

Developers should be aware of all of the issues presented so far in this chapter: credentials, access controls, and differences with certain UNIX commands. Additionally, developers should be aware of a few operating system idiosyncrasies and how these interact with the standard programming interfaces. Even so, the overwhelming majority of programs will work correctly in an AFS environment; you may find that hard to believe after making it this far through the book, but if AFS were not successful at providing near-UNIX semantics, it simply wouldn't be as popular as it is.

The most obvious change from UNIX is in the behavior of the `write` and `close` system calls. As a process writes data, that data will be stored locally. When the process closes the file, the writes will be shipped to the server. The only detail that must be mastered to make a process AFS-friendly is to always check the error code from the `close` operation.

If the `close` operation shows an error, all is not lost, for the client cache will still have the original copy of the written file data. In essence, all that must be done is try the `close` again. Whether the retry succeeds depends on why the `close` failed the first time.

As an example of how failure to catch close errors causes problems, we can take a look at a real-world situation. Soon after AFS was becoming popular, many sites found a problem with the `gzip` and `compress` programs. Both of these programs read a file and write out a compressed version of the same data. Internally, the program would open the input file for reading and an output file for writing. When the input was read and compressed successfully, the input file would be deleted. This program runs correctly in AFS, but it did not check the close system call for error conditions.

The problem arose when the program tried to compress files in volumes that were approaching their storage quota limit. When the compression program ran, the output file was written (locally) correctly, but the `close` operation failed because storing the compressed file would have forced the volume to go over quota. As the program did not check the return code from the `close` operation, it did not know that the compressed version of the file had not been saved on the file server. So, since all seemed fine, the program finished by deleting the original, uncompressed file. The result was that running the `compress` program on a file in a full volume caused the original file to be deleted.

On a standard UNIX system, this scenario doesn't cause a failure because one of the write operations will fail before ever getting to the final close. And the code diligently checks all write return codes.

For AFS, the fix was trivial and has been integrated into the `compress` and `gzip` programs: When closing the compressed file, check the return code and delete the original file only if the `close` operation returned successfully. If the `close` failed for whatever reason, there is no need to try to rewrite the data; simply report the error to the user. The user would then have to make some more room available.

Developers should learn from this example and take simple steps to work around it. One technique to save a file while writing is to occasionally issue `fsync` operations. This system call causes the client cache manager to send the data immediately to the server, which will (as of Version 3.4a) write the data to its disk. Sometimes, this is exactly the behavior required, but programmers should not get in the habit of sending `fsync` after every write because this practice will result in very poor performance; the server must accept the written data, write it to its own disk, and reply to the client for every write.

One good use of `fsync` is when writing log files. Applications often open a file for writing and periodically write a line of information to it indicating their progress on some task. Each line written to AFS would have to be followed by a `close` or `fsync` for other clients to be able to read the data. Alternatively, you may decide that log files should not be written to AFS at all but rather should be written to local disk or use a true distributed system log facility, such as `syslog`.

There is, however, a simple workaround for any long-running or legacy job that writes to a file regularly without closing it. Any other process authorized to access the file can perform the `fsync` on the file and cause the intermediate writes to be flushed back to the server. A simple utility can be written to manage any such long-lived log file by executing `fsync` system calls on the file every thirty seconds or so.

Before writing to a file, of course, you must have authorization to do so. The most accurate way to see if you have permission is to simply open the file and ask for write access. No matter what file system the file resides on, this method will tell you definitively if access has been approved. Some software would rather just test for the permission; on a UNIX machine, such software will often check the permission bits and compare them with the current user identification. As we've seen in this chapter, checking permission bits will often lead to an incorrect conclusion because most of the access controls are in the directory ACL, not in the file's permission bits.

Checking permission bits directly is, in general, a bad idea because such software is much less portable. But programmers must also be careful when using libraries that provide an `access` procedure to check for authorization. Some of these procedures are system calls that check the bits; others are intermediate libraries that perform other checking. And some programming languages, such as Perl, provide their own implementation. There is no absolute solution to this problem, since library writers or programming language developers are free to provide any services they see fit. With the advent of POSIX-endorsed access controls, there should be an ACL-ready mechanism for determining authorization. For now, the best method is to simply open the file with the desired permission—read or write—and manage any errors that are returned.

Developers use a number of programming clichés to solve obscure problems. One trick is to create an invisible file for temporary storage: After a file is opened for writing, the unlink operation is called on the file, which effectively deletes the file name from its directory. The process still has a handle with which to write to the file, but no one else in the system can see or open the file. When the file is finally closed, the operating system will realize that the file has no entries in the file system and will instantly delete it.

The problem with this scenario for AFS is that if the file is flushed from the client cache for some reason (for example, the process may write more data to the file than can fit in the cache, or the cache needs space for some other files), then the client is unable to recache the data from the server because the file has no name.

In this situation, the cache manager has no choice but to rename the file. When the client realizes that an unlink system call is being performed on an open file (and the client has more than enough information in the operating system to determine this), then the file is renamed to .__afsXXX, where the final characters of the name are chosen to not conflict with any other unlinked temporary file in this directory. When the final close operation runs, this oddly named file is deleted. You may therefore see files with this type of name when processes that have opened unlinked temporary files are running somewhere in the cell. Or, you may see such files if those processes crashed or were killed and did not have a chance to close the file. This behavior is very similar to the operation of such files in NFS.

Full-file advisory locks as provided by the flock system call are supported. However, AFS does not support byte-range locking of files, as provided by lockf or certain options to fcntl. These system calls will always return without error but in fact do no byte-range locking at all. Instead, when an application tries to grab a lock on a range of bytes, the program will continue successfully and the kernel will write a message in the terminal window from which the program was initiated.

```
afs: byte-range locking not implemented; make sure no one else is
running this program
```

This message is intended only to serve notice that the program does not own a lock to a section of the file. Since very few UNIX programs use byte-range locks, this situation does not often happen.

Programs that use whole-file locks are slightly more common. For these programs, AFS supports the `flock` primitive for processes on the same client. Processes on separate clients using `flock` on the same file will not block, as they would normally. Instead, the `flock` returns with an EAGAIN or EWOUL-DBLOCK error that should be checked by the program code. Because advisory locks depend on cooperating processes anyway, this is not too unreasonable.

In summary, programmers should use whole file locks only and when acquiring such a lock, use the blocking form of the system call. If either advisory or mandatory distributed file locking is required by your applications, you should look into using DFS because it correctly supports full POSIX file semantics.

Memory-mapped files present similar problems and similar solutions. The first question is how well memory-mapped files are supported by the underlying operating system itself. If they are supported, then most memory-based operations on files will work, but with the usual AFS caveats. That is, multiple processes on the same or different hosts can read a memory-mapped file correctly. When data is being written to a memory-mapped file, multiple processes on the same client will be able to see the changes, but other clients will not see the new data until the file is closed. Again, DFS provides a more complete implementation of single-site semantics for memory-mapped files.

Sparse files are files to which data is written noncontiguously. When the concrete data is separated by more than a page-size of empty space, most file systems will not create a physical page for these holes. A sparse file could be created by opening a file for writing, moving to position 1,000,000, and then writing a single byte of data. This file will usually require only a single page of disk for storage. To most processes reading this file, the file will seem to be one million bytes long because during reading, the operating system will notice the holes and return zero-filled pages, as required, until the 1,000,000th byte is reached; at that point, the byte of data will be returned, and the end-of-file will be reached.

Such files are partially supported by AFS to the extent that processes can create a sparse file. However, whenever that file is moved or copied via AFS procedures such as moving the volume, backing up or restoring the file, or most commonly, by creating a read-only replica, the copy of the file will be expanded to fill out all of the holes. The example file above will cost only one-page of storage on the server housing the read-write master volume, but any other servers storing read-only copies will need a megabyte of storage. While all user-level data accesses will see the correct data in the correct locations, the disk overhead of the file may not be optimal.

SYSTEM SOFTWARE

Along with the AFS executables and utilities, Transarc also supplies versions of several conventional UNIX programs: `ftpd`, `login`, `inetd`, `rcp`, `rlogind`, and `rsh`. Most of these behave exactly like their UNIX versions, except that during the authentication phase, in addition to performing regular UNIX checking, they also perform AFS's Kerberos authentication steps.

The simplest example is `ftpd`. This daemon program is normally configured to run on a server to permit remote clients to access local files via FTP (File Transfer Protocol). A user running a generic `ftp` client anywhere on the net can contact the server to request file transfers to or from the server. The protocol includes a query and response message to check the client user's name and password so that access to files on the server can be properly authorized. In the AFS version of `ftpd`, the name and password are presented to Kerberos for authentication. If Kerberos confirms the user's identity, the daemon is granted the user's AFS credentials, which can then be used to read or write files in the AFS file namespace anywhere the user has been permitted.

This enhancement will be useful if your organization needs to transfer file to clients that are not running AFS or are outside of your administrative domain. The machine which is designated the FTP server can be any AFS client in your cell, since all files in the namespace will be visible to any of your clients. Configuring the daemon is a simple matter of updating the Internet daemon set up file, `inetd.conf`, with the new name of the program file.

Similarly, the `login` program has been enhanced. The new version performs all the usual tasks of logging a user into the system and also obtains Kerberos authenticated credentials. These credentials are associated with a new process authentication group, similar to the effect of running the `pagsh` program, outlined above.

Since the AFS Kerberos implementation includes some extra functionality, such as password aging, the `login` program needs a way to pass along some of this information automatically. When Transarc's `login` is run, a new environment variable, named `PASSWORD_EXPIRES`, is set in the user's login shell; its value is the number of days left for which this user's password will be valid. It is intended to be used by system administrators to signal an impending expiration date to users. Other than its informational value, it has no functional bearing on the authentication process.

Transarc supplies three versions of login based on the BSD 4.3 UNIX version; the appropriate binary as needed should be installed as /bin/login.

- login—For stock AFS sites. This version checks the local /etc/passwd file and will refuse logins to users with no entry or with a "*" in the password field. AFS authentication is then attempted; if successful, the user is logged in with UNIX and AFS credentials. If the authentication failed, the password is checked, using the local UNIX verification procedure; if successful, no AFS credentials are issued, but a local UNIX login is permitted.
- login.krb—For sites using MIT Kerberos version 4. This version does all the stock AFS login procedures checks with a standard MIT Kerberos server, and then stores the Kerberos ticket in a file, /tmp/tktNNNN, named after the number of the user's process authentication group. Many applications based on the MIT Kerberos implementation expect this file to exist.
- login.noafs—For AIX 3.2 clients only. This version performs no AFS Kerberos authentication at all.

Using this replacement should make the introduction of AFS much less stressful for users and administrators because it will automatically get Kerberos tokens for users whether or not they know about AFS. The only remaining issue for users will be checking on expired tokens.

Now that AFS credentials have been obtained, it would be useful for other UNIX remote access programs to use them. The Berkeley r-commands allow users to run commands or copy files between trusted systems. They do this by having each system keep a list of which other systems it will trust; this trust takes the form of accepting the UNIX-level authentication information from a remote host as being valid. In AFS, the vendor's r-commands will work exactly the same, but of course, the UNIX-level authentication is not used by the AFS ACL authorization scheme.

A system is needed that will permit tokens on one machine to be usable on other machines in the cell. Transarc supplies versions of rsh, rcp, rlogind, and inetd to make this plan work.

The inetd daemon is a process that coordinates communication among remote programs. It is normally started at boot time and listens for connections on a variety of ports; when a request comes in, it initiates a predefined process as the peer for the incoming connection. Transarc's `inetd` performs similarly, but is usually configured to handle only the AFS versions of the remote access commands as well as to automatically manage the transfer of authentication information so that the peers can be executed under the correct Kerberos authentication credentials.

To implement these AFS remote access commands, first comment out the vendor's `inetd` configuration, in `/etc/inetd.conf`, for the shell and login services, then create an auxiliary configuration file, `/etc/inetd.conf.afs`.

```
# AFS configuration for inetd.conf.afs
#service type    prot wait   uid    program               argv
ta-rauth stream tcp  nowait  root   internal              ta-rauth
shell    stream tcp  nowait  root   /usr/etc/rshd         rshd
login    stream tcp  nowait  root   /usr/etc/rlogind.afs  rlogind.afs
```

Check with your vendor's manuals for the exact specification of this file; Sun systems would use `/usr/etc/in.rshd` for the shell program. Note that the login configuration line is needed only if the AFS `login` program is being used.

During the reboot sequence of this AFS system, start the `/etc/inetd.afs` daemon and set it up to read this configuration file. Meanwhile, the vendor's `inetd` daemon can start and take care of all of the other remote access protocols.

Modify the `/etc/services` file or map to include the remote authentication service. The exact operations differ by vendor, but usually you add the following lines to `/etc/services`:

```
auth            113/tcp         authentication
ta-rauth        601/tcp         rauth
```

Finally, install the AFS versions of `rsh` and `rcp`. When users use these programs, they will connect to a remote computer, the Transarc version of the server peer program will be connected to it, and the local program will pass along authentication information to the remote site so that the `rsh` or `rcp` process will have the same credentials remotely as the user does locally.

USING AFS ON WINDOWS NT

The authentication and access control issues raised previously apply equally to users on Windows NT platforms. Transarc's port provides both command-line and graphical interfaces to perform most user tasks. Foremost is the need for users to control their authentication. The latest implementation of AFS on NT integrates the NT login with the AFS Kerberos login, but checking on expired tokens is as important with NT as it is with UNIX.

If a user's password has been manually set the same in the NT domain manager as it is in the AFS Kerberos server, then the integrated login authenticates the user in both the NT and AFS worlds. Note that there is no integrated password change application nor even an NT version of the AFS Kerberos password-change program.

From the program manager, you can run the Authentication program in the Transarc AFS program group; or, from the File Manager, you can pick the Authentication item from the AFS pull-down menu. Either way, a dialog box pops up into which you can enter your name, password, and the cell to which you wish to authenticate. After you click on the OK button, the client contacts the AFS Kerberos authentication server, checks the information entered, and returns a token to the PC to be used when determining access to the cell.

To check the status of your AFS tokens, you can run the same Authentication program. When you have a valid token, this program displays the user names, cells, and expiration times of the tokens held. From this dialog box, you can also choose to discard any current token.

Command-line programs are provided for authenticating (klog.exe) listing credentials (tokens.exe) and discarding tokens (unlog.exe). These programs are used in almost exactly the same as their UNIX counterparts, already described.

One difference between these tokens and the UNIX implementation is that NT tokens are user-based only; there is no process authentication group that would permit one user to have different tokens in multiple windows. If you run two MS-DOS command-line interpreters, any klog operation in one will change the tokens used by the other interpreter and even those used by all the user's Windows-based applications.

The File Manager navigates the AFS file system as normal. However, there are a few differences between NT and AFS file semantics.

Any symbolic links stored in the AFS file system will not be seen by NT users. Instead, the AFS client code on the NT desktop will follow any links until a file is found. If the final link is a directory, the name shows up as a directory entry; if the link points to a file, the File Manager shows a file icon. Be careful of deletion—since the NT client does not know about symbolic links, the File

Manager delete operation (and the MS-DOS `erase` or `rmdir` commands) will not work. But a recursive deletion will follow the symbolic link and continue to delete the pointed-to data unlike the process on UNIX systems, where only the symbolic link is deleted.

The File Manager's AFS pull-down menu has many graphical interfaces to AFS functionality:

- Authentication—Displays dialogs to obtain, list, or delete AFS tokens.
- Access Control Lists—Display dialog boxes to list the ACL on a folder, add or delete entries, or clean an ACL of outdated entries. In the display of the access control list for a directory, each entry shows the user or group name and their rights, using the letters r, l, d, i, w, k, and a to indicate the standard AFS permissions.
- Volume/Partition—Displays information about the underlying volume associated with the file or folder currently selected in the File Manager. Besides the name of the volume, the dialog box shows the volume identification number, the volume quota, the total amount of space used in the volume, and the percentage of the quota represented by that space.

Three additional buttons on this dialog box pop up further dialogs: New Quota (if you are authenticated as a `system:administrators`) changes the quota size on the current volume. Partition Info displays information about the server's disk partition that houses the current volume, including its total size, the number of kilobytes remaining free for storage, and the percentage of the disk partition used for storage. Refresh Name/ID Mappings forces the client cache manager to delete its set of volume name and location information, which, in turn, forces the NT client to query the AFS servers for the latest information. (In normal operation, the client queries and stores this information as it navigates the file system.) This program provides a way to reset the client if troubles are suspected with access to certain file servers; it is similar to the `fs checkvolumes` command.

- Mount Point—This dialog permits you to display or manipulate AFS mount points in the current folder. The Show suboption displays information about the current folder's connection to the AFS cell. If the folder is an AFS volume mount point, the dialog displays the volume, cell name, and type of mount, either regular or read-write. The Remove suboption deletes the current folder if the folder is a mount point to an AFS

volume and you have permissions to delete entries in the current folder.
The Make suboption pops up a dialog which helps you create mount
points to AFS volumes: you enter the name of a new folder in the current
or other designated folder, the volume name, the cell name if not in the
current cell, and the type of volume connection (regular or read-write). If
you have permission to insert into the current folder, the mount will be
created as a new folder.

- Flush File/Dir—This menu item flushes the currently selected file or
  folder data from the client cache. Because AFS is constructed to perform
  the needed cache flushes automatically when any data changes, users do
  not ordinarily need to use this item.

- Flush Volume—Like the Flush File/Dir item, this service causes the client
  to flush all data in the volume containing the currently selected file or
  folder. Again, this action is not needed ordinarily. Note that flushing does
  not require any data to be actually deleted; the operation is practically
  instantaneous.

- Show File Servers—Clicking on this item displays a list of the server locations of the currently selected files or folders. Data that is not replicated,
  such as files in your home directory, will be shown as residing on a single
  server; data that is replicated, such as application programs that need to
  be highly available, will be shown as residing on several servers. In either
  case, this information is purely informational.

- Show Cell—Similar to the Show File Servers item, this service displays
  information about which cell is making the selected files or folders
  available.

- Show Server Status—Displays a dialog box showing a list of all the cells
  contacted since the last reboot, along with their servers. This list provides
  a glimpse into the internals of the client cache manager as it maintains
  information on the cells and servers it has discovered in the course of
  delivering file data to users. Because one job of the cache manager is to
  automatically fail over between servers when it has to deliver a file that
  has been stored on multiple machines, the cache manager keeps track of
  all the machines it has seen in the past and periodically queries them to
  see if they are still available. This dialog shows you that list of machines
  and their current status as understood by the local client.

You can direct the cache manager to report on the servers in the local cell, a
specific cell, or all cells it has encountered. There is also a check-box to make the

cache manager report on this information without querying the servers again; if you allow the client to query all the servers, there may be quite some delay as the client waits for a unresponsive server.

All of the above displays and services can be run from the command line. Included in the Transarc port to NT is the `fs` command, which can perform most of the above functions.

Missing from the NT port are other user commands such as the `pts` suite for manipulating group memberships. Also unavailable are the administration commands, such as the `kas`, `vos`, and `bos` suites. Presumably, the `pts` suite and perhaps other tools will be ported to NT in the future.

SUMMARY

It would be nice to report that users of AFS file services experienced no differences from local UNIX files. This expectation is bound to fail: distributed file systems are based on different assumptions of scale, performance, and security. Some of AFS's differences are debatable—choosing to implement close-on-write semantics is an architectural choice not everyone agrees with—but others such as access control lists are certainly improvements however complex they may seem to make things.

Users may complain about the need to obtain Kerberos credentials to access the file system. And they are right to demand improved services which mitigate the difficult use of these credentials, but returning to the overly trusting world of the Berkeley-style `rsh` and `rcp` commands is not the answer.

Access control lists and user credentials are two items which must be taught to all users of AFS. For most users, these two concepts will be all that needs to be known; most users do not need to know about volumes, servers, or Ubik. Their applications and file system navigation will work in AFS just as they did in NFS, NetWare, or locally.

The user population with the greatest need to understand any and all subtleties of the AFS implementation are application developers. Experienced developers should realize that AFS implements certain choices for file services that are neither inherently better nor worse than local UNIX semantics. Applications developed according to peculiarities of a local file system or a particular operating system interface may require some work to perform correctly on files in AFS. Yet such an application is inherently nonportable, anyway.

After reading through the list of differences in user commands, such as `chmod` and `df`, and programming procedures, such as `close` and `lockf` system calls, you might suppose that transitioning to AFS will be quite a chore, that every application will need to be checked individually, and that many programs and services will not work. Remember, though, that, over the years, the number of real problems with AFS and traditional UNIX applications has been found to be quite small.

The larger problem is not with computers and applications but with users. Where once they may have typed df to see how much disk space was available under a directory, users will have to remember to type fs listquota (or, abbreviated, fs lq). Users of Windows NT should have it a bit easier because these modifications can be integrated more easily into the graphical interfaces than they can into the command-line tools of UNIX.

This chapter is the only one that should be read by users or developers. In the next chapter, we'll return to the world of administration and learn how to archive the AFS volume data that has been created by others.

Archiving Data

An AFS cell's files present some unique problems to choosing an appropriate archival strategy. Not only must the file data itself be archived, but additional AFS data structures such as access control lists, users and groups, volumes, and the AFS databases must all migrate one way or another onto tapes. And regarding files and volumes, remember that volumes can easily move from one server to another—any mechanism to archive volumes must be prepared to get that data from the right server though that server may change from day to day.

Naturally, these constraints were realized early on in the development of AFS. True to form, the AFS answer includes another Ubik distributed database and a client/server system that can manage these specific issues. This management adds one more layer of complexity to an already large system. Many organizations have chosen to use only pieces of this system or even to use their own tools exclusively.

To add to the complexity, the terminology gets a little confusing. Up to now, the word *backup* has been used to denote the backup volume, the cheap, small clone used to snapshot a set of files in a volume. Here, of course, the subject is saving data by making copies onto a storage device whether the device is a tape, writeable CD, or whatever. In this book, the phrase *archiving* or *dumping* will refer to this copying process. Unfortunately, the command used to control volume archiving is also called `backup` and the various statistics about volume archives are stored in the backup database. So, we will use the phrase *archived* or *dumped volume* to denote a volume that has been copied safely to tape or some other media; that way, we can make sense of such concepts as using the `backup` command to archive a backup volume.

Besides the primary archive system, there are also simple volume-based dump commands that can perform piecemeal saving of volumes. These commands can help with small-scale archiving projects but are most useful for other administrative tasks such as duplicating parts of the file tree.

THE ARCHIVE SYSTEM

There are three sides to the AFS archive system: the command-line archive jobs and queries, the processes that actually control the tape drive or other media, and the configuration database that tracks and remembers what gets archived. Figure 8-1 shows these three pieces and illustrates how the archive commands connect the archive processes to the AFS file system. Administration of the process therefore consists of instructing, based on configuration data stored in the backup database, the tape controller job to perform operations.

The database holds several different tables of information: a set of dump schedules, a set of lists of volume names, and information about when each volume was dumped. The dump schedules and lists of volume names are defined as needed by the AFS administrators. The database also holds the names of the host machines to which the tape (or other media) devices are attached and assigns them an AFS port number with which to identify them. Once all these pieces are defined, the command-line interface can be used to store full or incremental volume archives to any of available storage devices.

AFS CELL DATABASES

Backup Database	Volume Location Database	File Servers and Volume Servers

| Backup Commands | ←→ | Backup Tape Coordinators | ←→ | Media |

Figure 8-1   Overview of the Archive Scheme

As with other archiving schemes, the configuration and care of this system is as important as actually performing the dumps. Briefly, configuration consists of the following:

- Setting up the backup database processes themselves
- Defining dump levels as an abstract hierarchy of names for full and partial dumps
- Defining names for sets of volumes, partitions, and file servers
- Configuring machines and ports to control the media

Once this information is configured, you can command the system to dump a particular volume set at a specified dump level to a particular named archive port. This command causes all the files, directories, and ACLs which constitute the set of applicable volumes to be dumped on to the specified archive device. At the same time a label identifying the dump is written to the tape and the information associated with that dump—its dump schedule, actual dump time, and list of volumes, is stored in the backup database. This tape label includes an expiration date to prevent inadvertent overwriting of valuable data. The label can be over written only by relabelling the tape; this relabelling not only changes the header data on the tape but also removes the associated information in the backup database.

You perform all of this configuration data and job control through the backup command, which has a multitude of subcommands. In addition to specifying the subcommands on the command line, you can enter an interactive mode by simply running the backup command with no options. In interactive mode, the command acts like a shell program: it prints out a prompt, backup>, and waits for the entry of a subcommand, which is then executed. The advantages to running interactively are that when you enter regular expressions that specify servers, partitions, or volume names, you do not have to quote the expressions to stop a UNIX shell from interpreting the expressions as file name wildcard characters. Additionally, you can list on-going dump jobs and kill them. In several examples below, we use interactive mode.

The backup database is managed by a server process usually running on the AFS database machines, just like the volume location, protection, or authentication database processes. In Chapter 3, during the initial cell set up, we created buserver processes on our three database servers. All of the archive configuration data is stored in this replicated database; because the data is replicated, the backup system can retrieve information as needed as long as at least one `buserver` process is running.

Recall that AFS databases are in their own right a distributed storage system. The protocol that ties them together, Ubik, tries to ensure that a single master database is available at all times to which all configuration storage requests (such as the addition of a volume set name) can be written. In our example cell, these processes run on their own machines so that administration of the file servers doesn't interfere with clients accessing the database information.

As with the other AFS databases, once the backup database is set up, very little administration is needed. The most important detail for the correct functioning of the servers is that their clocks are synchronized.

VOLUME SETS

Once the backup database is available, we can begin to configure our cell to perform the necessary archiving. The first step is to define which volumes are to be archived by grouping them together into named sets. Rather than specify each volume one-by-one on a dump command line, you can use these volume set names to archive multiple volumes in a single job.

A volume set consists of a 31-character name (using any characters except '.') that has one or more entries associated with it. When a volume set is used, the system scans all available volumes, matches each against all the entries in the set, and dumps all successfully matched volumes to tape. Note that each time a volume set is used, the set of volumes it refers to may change; the volume set is resolved into a complete list of volumes each time it is used in an archive command.

Each entry in a volume set consists of a regular expression for a volume name, a partition name, and a server name. A single entry may resolve itself into zero, one, or more volumes. While simplified regular expressions are used to define the volume names in an entry, partitions and hosts are defined only by a single name or a global match to any partition or host. There is no built-in limit to the number of entries associated with a single volume set, nor is there a limit on the number of volume sets themselves. The result is that, given this flexible description language, a series of volume sets can be defined, which can then be used in archive commands to store all AFS file data to a series of tapes.

We can easily set up some examples. As before, most of these commands require `system:administrators` credentials; refer to the command summary in Appendix A or the AFS System Administration Guide for more infor-

mation. When manipulating volume sets, you must create the volume set name
before you can edit the entries.

```
$ backup
backup> addvolset users
backup> addvolset fsOne
backup> listvolsets
Volume set users:

Volume set fsOne:
```

Using the subcommand `addvolset`, we first create two volume sets,
named `users` and `fsOne`, and then list all volume sets and their entries. Of
course, at this point, no entries have been added to the new sets. You can add
entries for a given volume set with `addvolentry`.

```
$ backup
backup> addvolentry users fs-one vicepa user.alice
backup> listvolsets users
Volume set users:
        Entry   1: server fs-one, partition vicepa, volumes: user.alice
backup>
```

Each entry in a volume set is listed with a corresponding position number.
As entries are added and deleted, a particular entry's position might change, so it
is important to use the `listvolsets` subcommand to identify entries precisely.

There are four mandatory arguments to `addvolentry`, the volume set
name to which the entry should be added and three arguments specifying the
entry: a server name, a partition name, and a volume name. In the first entry
added to the volume set `users`, we specified exactly which volume should be
matched. Only a single volume, `user.alice` if it exists on the server `fs-one`
and on partition `/vicepa`, will match the entry. In later commands which
dump a volume set to tape, the system will find and dump only those volumes
that match any of the entries in the volume set.

There's nothing wrong with this first entry, but in practice, it wouldn't be
too useful. First, there's no guarantee that the volume won't be moved from
one server or partition to another at any time. So, when the cell's machines or
disks are reorganized, this type of specific volume set entry would have to be
adjusted. The simple fix is to state that the entry should match the named volume when found on any server. The archive system does not permit entering
arbitrary regular expressions for server names; we must use either a single,

exact server name or an expression that will match any server name, .*. Similarly, for partition names, either a single, exact partition name must be entered or the .* regular expression to match any valid partition on the server.

The second problem with the entry is that the named volume is a user home directory and, as such, is not guaranteed to be in a consistent state at any single moment in time. Whether a given volume can be guaranteed to be consistent depends on the particular use of that volume; certainly, home directories or project development areas are subject to changes at almost any time of the day. Conveniently, AFS provides us with the tools to create consistent snapshots of a volume, the confusingly named backup volume. As long as we have set up our system to create backup volumes for areas like home directories, it makes much more sense to generate our archive tapes based on that stable snapshot rather than on the living directory area.

Therefore, to continue the above example, we've added another entry; this one says to match any server (.*) and any partition (.*) as it looks for user backup volumes (user..*.backup). This is a better matching expression for all of the user volumes we wish to archive, and the example finishes by deleting the overly precise first entry:

```
backup> addvolentry users .* .* user..*.backup
backup> listvolsets users
Volume set users
        Entry   1: server fs-one, partition vicepa, volumes: user.alice
        Entry   2: server .*, partition .*, volumes:  user..*.backup

backup> delvolentry users 1
backup> listvolsets users
Volume set users
        Entry   1: server .*, partition .*, volumes:  user..*.backup

backup> quit
```

The regular expressions permitted by the system are a subset of the expressions you may be familiar with in the sed or Perl programs. Regular characters, such as alphabetic or numeric characters in the volume name expression, must match exactly. Do the following to match other combinations of characters:

- Use a period, ., to match any single character.
- Use a set of characters surrounded by square brackets to match any single character from that set. For example, [xyz] would match only a sin-

gle "x" or "y" or "z". If the first character inside the square brackets is a caret, ^, the meaning of the match is reversed; [^xyz] would match any single character except for "x" or "y" or "z".

- Use any of the above (an alphanumeric character, a period, or a square-bracketed set of characters) followed by an asterisk to match the expression against any number of occurrences of the expression. For example, a* would match zero, one, or more "a" characters; xa*y would match either "xy", "xay", "xaay", etc.

- Use a backslash, \, to take away the special meaning of characters such as the period, square brackets, asterisk, or even the backslash. In the volume set entry above, user..*.backup, the intent is to match any volume name such as user.alice.backup or user.bob.backup. To force an exact match against the periods, construct the entry more precisely: user\..*\.backup.

Note that, as displayed by the last listvolsets subcommand, the previously numbered entry #2 is now the new #1; the numbers associated with volume set entries are purely for local volume set administration and are not long-lived identifications.

This volume set is now ready for use, but we will add another volume set to demonstrate other archiving policies. Rather than look for all the user backup volumes for archiving all at once, we may decide to archive all of a particular machine's partitions. This example adds a volume set with a single entry to match all the volumes on just a single server.

```
backup> addvolentry fsOne   fs-one .* .*.backup
backup> listvolsets fsOne
Volume set fsOne
        Entry   1: server fs-one, partition .*, volumes: .*.backup
backup> quit
```

Volume set entries can be created to fit practically any archiving scheme you want to implement. Through the use of regular expressions, you are guaranteed to archive any matching volumes on any server and partition pair as they exist at the moment that the archive command is run. No matter how many volumes are created or deleted during the day, or where those volumes may get moved to, when the archive command is finally run, the system will generate a list of matching volumes and begin the dump process.

When deciding on the structure of your volume sets, make sure that you have complete coverage for your cell's data. In particular, you should make sure that all read-write volumes are entered into a volume set by using their snapshot backup volume. But you need to also archive a copy of read-only volumes because they potentially contain a set of data different from that of the read-write volumes. When a tape coordinator process is getting data from volumes and writing it to tape, it uses the client's file server preferences to determine which servers' read-only volume it will read.

Previous to AFS version 3.4a, there was no simple way to determine which volumes a given volume set referred to. Now, you can use the `volsetrestore` subcommand; this subcommand is used to perform a complete restore of all volumes in a volume set. However, the `-n` option inhibits the actual restoration and will lists volumes which have been archived and which match a volume set's entries.

This output is especially useful because as volumes are manipulated by administrators during the normal course of events, it's important to make sure that each volume of file data in the cell is taken care of by at least one archival volume set.

DUMP LEVELS

It is not common practice in archive systems to archive all data to storage every evening. After all, most data in most file systems doesn't change from day to day or even week to week. A better solution is to follow a full dump on one day with a series of incremental dumps—which just copy to tape the data which has changed since the last full dump—to drastically reduce the amount of data that must be stored each evening.

Many archive programs use various options to determine the difference between a full and partial dump. AFS uses an abstract hierarchy of dump levels defined by the cell administrators. This approach permits an arbitrary set of full and partial dumps to be scheduled as needed, not only multiple partial dumps in between full dumps, but also partials within partials. Once defined, this abstract tree of dump levels is used to create timestamped archives. The system stores these timestamps and dump levels in the backup database.

While sounding abstract, the creation of the dump hierarchy is much like the creation of file system directories. Each level name in the hierarchy can contain up to 28 characters (except the period), and the levels are separated with slashes; the total length of the entire fully qualified dump level must be less than 256 characters.

A simplistic dump level could be created like this:

```
backup> adddump /new
backup: Created new dump schedule /new
backup> adddump /new/first
backup: Created new dump schedule /new/first
backup> adddump /new/second
backup: Created new dump schedule /new/second
```

You create the dump levels by simply adding each additional sublevel or sibling level on a separate line, much like the UNIX mkdir command makes subdirectories. Once you create the levels, you can display a somewhat graphical representation of the levels with listdumps.

```
backup> listdumps
/new
     /first
     /second
```

This hierarchy of dump levels is used during the dump command itself only to point out which file system changes are to be written to tape. The dump level names themselves are meaningless to the system. The only importance to the system is the position of the name in the slash-separated hierarchy. Again, this hierarchy is arbitrary; you can see that no dates or timestamps are stored with these names. When you use a dump-level name to create a particular archive on media, the system stores the current time and date with the dump level name of that volume set in the backup database.

A request for a /new dump specifies a full dump because it is at the top level of the dump hierarchy. All of the files, directories, and ACLs stored in a particular volume set will be written to tape. Dumping that volume set at the /new/ first level specifies an incremental dump relative to its parent, the /new dump. The system checks the timestamp of the /new dump for that volume set and any changes to the files, directories, or ACLs after that timestamp will be written to the tape.

A subsequent dump of that same volume set at the /new/second level will again compare timestamps of files versus the dump level's parent, /new. This process implies that a dump created at the /new/second level will contain all of the files changed and dumped at the /new/first level as well. Each entry at a particular level will cause an incremental dump to be performed relative to the last dump at the next higher level.

To dump only those changes relative to the /new/first level dump, you create a new level underneath it, perhaps /new/first/other. Dumps made at the /new/first/other level will write out only file changes between it and its parent, /new/first.

You can construct and use multiple dump-level hierarchies. Just remember that when asked to restore file data for a given day and time, you'll have to read the tape for the closest full dump prior to that date and then all of the incrementals available up to that date. If your archive schedule consists of incrementals based on incrementals—such as /new/first/other, which is based on /new/first, which is based on the full dump /new—you might have to read each of those three dump tapes to get back exactly the right set of files.

On the other hand, if your incrementals are cumulative—such as /new/first and /new/second, both of which are based on /new—then you'll just have to read two tapes. Which is better depends to some extent on how much data will be written to the tapes; and that depends on how fast the data changes and how many volumes are included in the volume set.

For this reason, construct as many dump hierarchy levels as needed to suit your administrative needs. Often, this means one hierarchy consisting of cumulative incremental dumps (/new/first, /new/second, /new/third, etc.) and another to facilitate incrementals based on incrementals (/new/first, /new/first/other, /new/first/other/more). One common hierarchy uses days of the week as reminders.

```
backup> listdumps
/sunday
        /monday
        /tuesday
        /wednesday
        /thursday
        /friday
        /saturday
```

Don't be fooled by these names, though; the dump-level names mean nothing to the system—you can perform any archive at any dump level on any day you like. In fact, there is not much help at all in AFS for managing regular execution of the archive process. We'll see that dumps can be arranged to occur at a future time, but this is not the same as setting up a job scheduling system to perform certain dumps every Monday, Tuesday, etc. Thus, as you use other scheduling systems (such as UNIX cron) to initiate dump activities, you'll need to specify which dump level you'll want to use at any given time or day.

Even with a dump hierarchy named after days of the week, you'll still have to specify yourself which dump level is needed for a given archive job.

As well as defining full and incremental dump levels, you can also configure an expiration time for dumps. When a dump of a volume set is made to tape, an expiration timestamp will be calculated and stored; the expiration timestamp permits the system to determine when it is valid to overwrite a previously written dump tape without operator intervention.

You can set expiration dates to either absolute or relative times. In the dump levels created above, the default expiration time is such that they are considered to be expired immediately. You set relative expiration times during dump-level creation like this:

```
backup> adddump /daily -expires in 7d
Created new dump schedule /daily
backup> listdumps
/daily  expires in   7d
...
```

The keyword in after the -expires option signifies a relative expiration date. The value is the number of days, weeks, and years in the future specified by a combination of digits and the letters d, w, and y, respectively. After a dump is made at the /daily level, it will be recorded as having an expiration date 7 days after the time the dump was started.

You set absolute expirations with the at keyword.

```
backup> adddump /offsite -expires at 12/31/97
backup: Created new dump schedule /offsite
backup> listdumps
/offsite expires at Wed Dec 31 00:00:00 1997
...
```

Here, a dump made at the /offsite full dump level will be set to expire on December 31, 1997. If you want a dump level never to expire, use the value NEVER.

Each time a dump is made at a certain level, this expiration information is used to calculate the new expiration date for the tape. So, every dump made at the /offsite level will expire at the end of 1997 whether the dump was created in January or December. Relative expiration dates will make each dump tape expire at a different date: A tape dumped at the /daily level on January 1 will expire on January 8; if dumped on July 4, it will expire on July 11. These expiration dates for tapes are stored in the tape label during dumping.

THE TAPE COORDINATOR

Besides setting up the volume and dump level configuration, you must manage the physical archive media by designating one or more machines in the AFS cell as tape coordinators. To set up a tape coordinator necessitates:

- A storage device attached to the machine.
- An AFS dump description on the device.
- A tape control process to perform the dump.
- An entry in the backup database that points to this process.

You can use almost any machine in the cell as a tape coordinator and, thanks to an improved description file in AFS version 3.4a, the actual tape drive can be almost any tape device, robotic jukebox, or even a plain file. The machine need not be one of the AFS servers, but because the tape coordinator process must have authenticated access to the volumes themselves, the machine must be, at least, a client of the cell.

Once you have identified the machine and attached the hardware, configure the device and then initiate a coordinator process. The process is named butc, which stands for backup tape coordinator; there needs to be one butc per archive device on the system. All configuration, logs, and error log files are stored in a standard directory on this machine, /usr/afs/backup. The file /usr/afs/backup/tapeconfig contains a line for each archive device describing the UNIX device name, information on the available size of the device, and a tape coordinator port number.

The first two items in the specification line are straightforward. The device name is simply the normal UNIX path name for the device, perhaps /dev/rst1. The size states how much room is available on the device and how much room is taken up by intervolume gaps. AFS includes a command, fms, to determine the standard capacity of the tape. For a tape drive attached to the UNIX device named /dev/rst1:

```
$ fms /dev/rst1
wrote block: 130408
Finished data capacity test—rewinding
wrote 1109 blocks, 1109 file marks
Finished file mark test
Tape capacity is 2136604672 bytes
File marks are 1910205 bytes
```

Depending on the size of the media, this command can take quite some time to complete. Transarc recommends that when you edit the size item in the `tapeconfig` file, you reduce the tape size 10-15 percent to allow for variations in differing tapes. If you use a compression tape system, you'll want to configure the tape drive to a much larger figure. Note that two sizes are reported: the total tape capacity and the size of the file marks. The latter is the apparent size of the space written to the device to separate each volume.

The last item in a `tapeconfig` device entry is the device's port number. The port number is a somewhat arbitrary number that enables the `butc` process to find out which device it controls. The port numbers and machine names are also entered into the backup database so that the `dump` command can locate the correct `butc` process.

The network connection between the `dump` and `butc` processes are implemented with ordinary IP sockets; the port numbers indicate which UDP port number the `butc` process will listen to on a particular machine. AFS dump port numbers can run from 0 to 58,511; AFS assigns a socket for each port offset from a starting port number of 7025 (7025 plus 58511 equals 65536, the maximum port number allowed on most UNIX systems).

Of course, although you can use any number from 0 to 58,511 for a port offset, this doesn't mean you can add 58,512 dump devices to your cell. Besides the fact that the system can only simultaneously manage 64 dumps or restores, a particular UDP port may be in use by some other network process.

As an example of setting up the device configuration file, create the `/usr/afs/backup` directory and make it writeable only by the UNIX superuser. Edit the file `/usr/afs/backup/tapeconfig` and add a separate line for each tape drive. The line consists of whitespace-separated entries for the size of the tape, the file mark size, the UNIX device name, and the port offset number. The example above would result in a line in the `tapeconfig` file like this:

```
2G 1M /dev/rst1 0
```

The size entries are in bytes but can be abbreviated by appending (no spaces) the letter "K", "M", or "G", which mean the usual kilobytes, megabytes, or gigabytes, respectively.

The port numbers can be assigned as desired. For sites with just a single tape drive, note that port number 0 is the default argument for most dump commands.

Once you complete the `tapeconfig` file, you must manually add to the backup database the association between the port number and the tape coordinator machine. In our example cell, the tape drive (and `butc` process) are attached to our second file server.

```
backup> addhost fs-two 0
Adding host fs-two offset 0 to tape list...done
backup> listhost
Tape hosts:
    Host fs-two, port offset 0
```

An administrator must initiate the `butc` tape coordinator program, often manually, on the machine that is indicated in the backup database. During startup, this process reads the `tapeconfig` file to determine the archive device from which it will be writing and reading. Once running, it waits for commands to be relayed to it by the `backup` command-line program, instructing it to dump or restore AFS volumes.

Obviously, being able to read volume data from AFS and copy it to some device is an operation that requires administration privileges. Before running `butc`, you must ensure that you have adequate credentials. If not, `butc` will complain that access to the backup database is denied.

```
$ butc 0
butc: no such entry ; Can't get tokens—running unauthenticated
Can't access backup database
    budb: access to database denied
```

You obtain credentials either from the administrator running the backup or, as of version 3.4a, with the `-localauth` option which uses the machine's local `KeyFile`. Since only file servers and database servers have a `KeyFile`, this option is applicable only when the tape drive is attached to one of these AFS servers. Also, because the `/usr/afs/backup` directory and files contain critical administrative data (though not AFS file or user data), they should be write-restricted to UNIX root. In our example, the tape drive we're using for archives is on our second file server, so we'll use the `-localauth` option while logged in as root:

```
# butc 0 -localauth
Starting Tape Coordinator: Port offset 0    Debug level 0    Aix Scsi flag: 0
Token expires: NEVER
```

Before data is written to the tape, there remains the question of how to ensure that a physical tape has been inserted into the tape drive. When run in interactive mode, butc queries an attentive operator to enter a tape cartridge and waits for the Return key to be pressed before proceeding. But butc can be run in an automated, batch mode where it will assume that tapes are pre-loaded or are loaded according to some predefined script which it can run itself. Batch mode is useful when the entire process can be automated and no operator will be present. Either the noninteractive batch mode entered by running butc with the option -noautoquery and then, normally, putting the job into the background.

```
# butc 0 -localauth -noautoquery &
1483
# Starting Tape Coordinator: Port offset 0   Debug level 0   Aix Scsi flag: 0
Token expires: NEVER
```

Here, the process number, 1483, and prologue are printed to the terminal screen interspersed with the terminal's next command prompt. We talk more about automating this process later in the chapter.

Now that a coordinator is running on fs-two and controlling a tape drive device, you can check that the system can interoperate with the coordinator by issuing a status request to a specific dump port. Note that this command (like most AFS administration commands) will normally be run from the administrator's own desktop machine or any other computer in the local cell.

```
backup> status 0
Tape Coordinator is idle.
```

The command interrogates the cell's backup database to find out which machine is controlling a device on port 0; in our example, the machine is fs-two. The command then sends a message to that machine on the indicated port offset port where the butc tape controller process has already been started. The tape controller responds that all is well and that it is waiting for instructions. If no coordinator was set up, the result would look like this:

```
backup> status 5
backup: No such host/port entry ; Can't connect to tape coordinator at port 5
```

During the run of a butc process, two files in the /usr/afs/backup directory keep a log of dumps and errors. The files are named after the devices listed in the machine's tapeconfig file. For our example, the device /dev/

rst1 will result in two files, each with the suffix rst1. The file containing a running log of information concerning the dump process has a prefix of TL_, so our log file will be named TL_rst1. The error log has a prefix of TE_, so the file in our case is TE_rst1.

For our current example, the tape coordinator has started successfully, so there is no output in the TE_rst1 file, and the TL_rst1 file contains the time-stamped startup messages.

```
# cd /usr/afs/backup
# ls -l
total 4
-rw-r--r--   1 root     other           0 Mar 30 11:30 TE_rst1
-rw-r--r--   1 root     other         160 Mar 30 11:30 TL_rst1
-rw-r--r--   1 root     other          18 Mar 30 11:30 tapeconfig
# cat TL_rst1
Sun Mar 30 11:30:55 1997
11:30:55 Starting Tape Coordinator: Port offset 0   Debug level 0   Aix Scsi flag: 0
11:30:55 Token expires: NEVER
```

TAPE LABELS

AFS is almost ready for us to dump volume data to a tape. But before we examine how the total dump process works, let's look at how tapes are labelled for use by the archive system. *Labelling* is the process by which identification information is written to the tape and also stored in the backup database. Labelling permits the system to answer queries regarding what times a volume was backed up and onto what tape.

When the system identifies a blank tape during a dump, it automatically writes a label to the tape. If a labelled and unexpired tape is found in the device when a new dump is about to be written to the tape, the dump is aborted. If you know what you're doing and want to reuse an archive tape, you should first relabel the tape. This operation causes the current tape label to be read so that the backup database can be adjusted to account for the effective erasure of this dump tape. After reading the tape and adjusting the database, the system writes a new default name of null to the tape label.

```
backup> labeltape -port 0
```

The labeltape command uses the port number argument to retrieve the archive device host name from the backup database, contacts the waiting coordinator, causes the label to be written to the tape, and also stores the label information in the database.

Of course, the tape coordinator needs to have a tape ready for this to happen. In batch mode, `butc` can be told to assume that a tape is ready. In interactive mode, `butc` will display on standard output:

```
Labeltape
******* OPERATOR ATTENTION *******
Device :  /dev/rst1
Please put in tape to be labelled as <NULL> and hit return when done
```

After inserting a tape, an operator must press the Return key:

```
Thanks, now proceeding with tape labelling operation.
* * * * * * * * * * * * * * * * * * * * * * * * * * * * * * * * * *
Tape blocks read in 10240 Byte chunks.
Labelled tape <NULL> size 2097152 Kbytes
```

The TL_rst1 file will record this information:

```
11:40:10 Task 1: Labeltape
11:40:10 Task 1: Prompt for tape <NULL>
11:40:13 Task 1: Proceeding with tape operation
11:41:36 Task 1: Labelled tape <NULL> size 2097152 Kbytes
```

And in the interactive administration window, the finished job will be indicated by a message written to standard output:

```
backup> Job 1: Labeltape (<NULL>) finished
```

As you can see, because the design of the system separates the administration process from the operational support of the tape drive, two commands—backup and `butc`—must be run and monitored. In normal use, administrators would manage the backup database and would schedule dumps to be made at particular times. The resulting tape operations would then be displayed on a display screen situated near the actual archive media. Of course, at small sites, the administration staff is the same as the operations staff; in these cases, it is common to view all commands on the same workstation display in adjacent terminal windows. In addition, two more terminal windows might be opened to continually show the latest lines in the tape log and error files.

After writing a tape label, it is good practice to read back the label.

```
backup> readlabel 0
Tape read was labeled: <NULL> size 2097152 KBytes
```

In operator interactive mode, `butc` does not assume that any current tape is the tape you want to read, so after the `readlabel` command is entered, `butc` again prompts for the tape to be inserted.

```
Readlabel
******* OPERATOR ATTENTION *******
Device :  /dev/rst1
Please put in tape whose label is to be read and hit return when done

Thanks, now proceeding with tape label reading operation.
*********************************
Tape label
----------
AFS tape name = <NULL>
creationTime = Sun Mar 30 11:40:10 1997
cell = hq.firm
size = 2097152 Kbytes
dump path =
dump id = 0
useCount = 0
-- End of tape label --

ReadLabel: Finished
```

The tape label appears to be empty but indicates that the label structure has correctly been written to the tape. The name stored in the label is a default name of null. When a dump is run, the name of the tape is changed to a string representing the volume set name, the dump level name, and a tape number index.

This tape name is used by the system to track which tapes hold which dumped sets of volumes. After dumping, say, the user volume set, to this tape, the name field will be rewritten and the information about which level of dump along with a timestamp will all be stored in the database. Later, when an operator asks to restore, say, Alice's home directory volume, the system will scan the database to find out which dump request caused that volume to be dumped; the appropriate tape can then be identified by the labelled name and timestamp.

The `butc` output (and the `TL_rst1` log file) shows more of the records that make up an actual tape label. In this example, most of the entries are default null entries that will be filled in when this tape is used to store an actual archive.

It is prudent to write this dump name and other identifying information on a printed label that can be physically affixed to the tape housing. When requested to restore a particular volume from a certain date, the system will prompt for a specifically labelled tape to be inserted in the tape drive; it'll be a lot easier to find the tape if it is correctly labelled than if you try to find it by trial and error. Robotic stackers often have bar-code readers and labels; in this case, you can associate the dump name with a bar-code number in some handy external database so that restoring files can also be automated.

RUNNING THE DUMPS

Now that you have completely configured the archive system, you can finally dump any volume set at any level. The command to create a complete dump of all of our users volumes to the tape device on fs-two is:

```
backup> dump users /full 0
```

Note the interrelationship of the configuration data and the archiving processes as shown in Figure 8-2. The butc process has its port number assigned on its command line, so it can read its configuration data in the /usr/afs/ backup/tapeconfig file on its local machine to obtain the device name and sizes of a particular tape drive. butc then opens up a socket connection at the specified port offset.

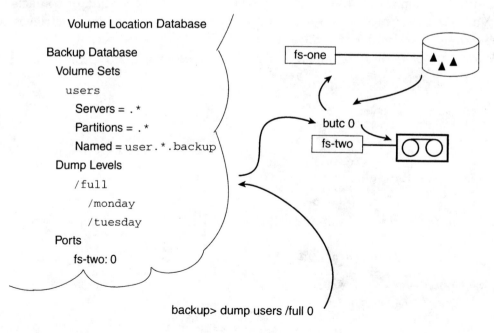

Figure 8-2   Interactions of the Backup System

The archive command, above, is told to dump a set of volumes at a given dump level to a given port offset. The command queries the backup database to find out the volume set entries—the servers, partitions, and volume expressions—for the named volume set. Then, by checking all the volumes in the volume location database, it determines which set of volumes currently matches the volume set specifications.

Next, it checks with the backup database again to find out what level of dump is requested. Complete dumps, that is, any top-level dump name, will cause all files in all the volumes of the set to be dumped in full. When given a two-(or more) level dump name, the system retrieves the time of the parent-level dump and passes it to the tape coordinator process so that only the incremental changes to files in a volume (on a whole file basis) are dumped.

The dump command then checks the database's list of hosts and ports to find out which machine is associated with the port. Now the dump process can connect to the butc tape coordinator on that machine to begin archiving volumes. The coordinator first reads the tape label; If the tape in the drive has a null label or if the tape label indicates it has expired, all is well. If the tape label has not expired, the operator is prompted for a new tape.

The names of the volumes, their locations, and the incremental time (if any) Are then transferred to the tape coordinator. The coordinator contacts the volume server process on the appropriate file server machines, retrieves the volume's data, and writes the appropriate files to the tape device.

After the dump command is started, the tape coordinator prompts an operator to insert a tape.

```
Dump users.full (DumpID 859740951)
******* OPERATOR ATTENTION *******
Device :  /dev/rst1
Please put in tape users.full.1 (859740951) for writing and hit return when done

Thanks, now proceeding with tape writing operation.
***********************************
```

In the interactive administration window:

```
backup> dump users /full 0
Starting dump of volume set 'users' (dump level '/full')
Total number of volumes : 6
Preparing to dump the following volumes:
        user.zed.backup (536870966)
        user.carol.backup (536870984)
        user.bob.backup (536870987)
```

```
          user.rob.backup (536870969)
          user.david.backup (536870978)
          user.alice.backup (536870923)
Starting dump
backup: Task 3: Dump (users.full)
```

This dump operation initiates an archive job and a coordinator task. The term *job* refers to an operation performed by the backup command, in this case, a particular dump to port 0. A single command session might spawn several jobs to several different ports. The term *task* refers to an operation run by a single tape-coordinator process. Normally, a butc process can perform only one task at a time. In this example, the backup command is running one job.

```
backup> jobs
Job 1: Dump (users.full)
```

And the coordinator at port 0 is running one task:

```
backup> status 0
Task 3: Dump: 4336 Kbytes transferred, volume user.rob.backup
```

When done, the backup job writes a message to its standard output.

```
backup> Job 1: Dump (users.full) finished. 6 volumes dumped
```

And the coordinator writes a message to the operator.

```
users.full (DumpId 859740951): Finished. 6 volumes dumped
```

A simple dump command, as above, creates a new *dump set*. Just before the volume data is written out, the tape label is adjusted so that the contents of the tape can be automatically verified. The label is based on the volume set name, the dump level path, and an index number of the tape. The backup command above would result in a label named users.full.1. For incremental dumps, the second word of this tape label is based on the final dump-level path element, for example, this volume set dumped at /sunday/tuesday would be labelled, users.tuesday.1.

When a dump causes more data to be written than can fit on a single tape, the operator is prompted to remove the old tape and insert a new one. In this case, the final word of the label, the tape index number, is used to identify multiple tapes if they are needed to hold the complete dump set. If a full dump of the user volumes takes three tapes, they would be named, users.full.1, `users.full.2`, and `users.full.3`. When each tape is written to, if the end-of-tape marker is seen, the second half of the volume is correctly written at the start of the next tape in the dump set.

You can add additional dumps to a dump set by running successive dumps requests with the `-append` flag. Doing so can help save tapes by putting many smaller dump sets onto the same set of tapes. Watch out for the terminology used here: a *dump* is a single volume set archive, either full or incremental. A *dump set* can be one or more dumps; the example dump just performed creates a dump set with the single dump of the `users` volume set.

While being dumped to tape, a volume will be taken off-line. Hence, it makes sense to create volume sets composed of backup volumes. Recall that making a backup volume takes very little time and space—these snapshots are ideal for dumping to tape. If you specify a read-write volume to be dumped, that volume will be inaccessible during the dump process, which could take a significant amount of time; if you specify a read-only volume, one of the read-only volumes will be off-line during the dump, but any clients accessing that busy read-only would automatically fail over to another read-only. Generally, the preferred mechanism is to dump a backup volume.

If a volume is otherwise unavailable during dumping (perhaps because it is being moved from one server to another), it will be ignored until the dump process has finished with all other volumes in the current set. The coordinator will then query the operator (if not in `noautoquery` mode) to see if it is okay to try again. The operator could then perform any additional maintenance and then finish the dump of the affected volume.

Other failures or interruptions to the dump process cause only a small problem. The volumes that were successfully written to tape will be recognized as such by the system; the volume being written at the time of the interruption and any subsequent volumes will not be recorded. Future queries and restoration requests will therefore retrieve only successfully dumped volume data.

The tape coordinator writes to its log file TL_rst1.

```
11:55:50 Task 3: Dump users.full
11:55:51 Task 3: Dump users.full (DumpID 859740951)
11:55:51 Task 3: Prompt for tape users.full.1 (859740951)
11:57:04 Task 3: Proceeding with tape operation
11:58:38 Task 3: Starting pass 1
11:58:51 Task 3: Volume user.zed.backup (536870966) successfully dumped
11:59:03 Task 3: Volume user.carol.backup (536870984) successfully dumped
11:59:16 Task 3: Volume user.bob.backup (536870987) successfully dumped
11:59:28 Task 3: Volume user.rob.backup (536870969) successfully dumped
11:59:44 Task 3: Volume user.david.backup (536870978) successfully dumped
```

```
11:59:56 Task 3: Volume user.alice.backup (536870923) successfully dumped
11:59:56 Task 3: End of pass 1: Volumes remaining = 0
12:00:09 Task 3: users.full (DumpId 859740951): Finished. 6 volumes dumped
```

An administrator can use the `backup` command's job numbers to abort an operation. Only jobs initiated in the current interactive session can be monitored and killed. During the example dump above, the running jobs were:

```
backup> jobs
Job 1: Dump (users.full)
```

This message is customized for each operation underway. The information listed includes:

- Job number
- Operation type: one of `Dump`, `Restore`, `Labeltape`, `Scantape`, `SaveDb`, or `RestoreDb`
- For dumps still being executed, the number of kilobytes written out and the name of the current volume being dumped
- For restores, the number of kilobytes read in

And optionally, a warning of pending activity or a possible error:

- `[abort requested]`, signalling that a job was requested to be killed but that the command was still queued for delivery to the busy `butc` process.
- `[abort sent]`, signalling that the `kill` request has been delivered to the `butc` process. Once killed, the job will not be listed at all.
- `[butc contact lost]`, indicating that the `backup` command cannot contact the associated `butc` process. The process has either failed or the network connection to the remote machine is unavailable. Occasionally, this message may appear simply if the `butc` process is inordinately busy with its operations.
- `[drive wait]`, notifying you that the `butc` process for this job is engaged; the job is waiting for the storage device to become available.
- `[operator wait]`, indicating that the `butc` process has issued a directive requiring operator intervention.

Finally, the lifetime value of the current authentication token is printed, as are any dumps scheduled to run at a specific time. Note that any currently running dumps that will run longer than the available token's lifetime or any dumps scheduled to start after the token's expiration will fail. The only recourse is to manually renew the token lifetime before the lifetime has been reached.

An administrator can abort any running job with the `kill` command.

```
backup> labeltape 0
backup> jobs
Job 1: Labeltape (0) [operator wait]
backup> kill 1
backup> jobs
Job 1: Labeltape (0) [abort request] [operator wait]
backup> jobs
Job 1: Labeltape (0) [abort sent]
backup> Job 1: Labeltape (0) Aborted
```

While active backup jobs can be listed (or killed) only for the currently invoked interactive session, any `butc` process in the cell can be queried about its tasks. Here, several status requests are sent during a single dump.

```
backup> status
Task 5: Dump:  [operator wait]
backup> status
Task 5: Dump: 4336 Kbytes transferred, volume user.carol.backup
backup> status
Task 5: Dump: 12874 Kbytes transferred, volume user.david.backup
backup> status
Task 5: Dump: 45873 Kbytes transferred, volume user.rob.backup
backup> Job 1: Dump (users.full) finished. 6 volumes dumped
backup> status
Tape coordinator is idle
```

The response to the status command is one of the following:

- `Tape coordinator is idle`.
- `Unable to connect to tape coordinator at port N`. Indicates either that the `butc` process is not running or hung for some reason or that the network connection between the two systems is down.
- Current task number. If a task is in progress, the response also displays the name of the operation, the number of kilobytes that have been transferred, either a specific volume name indicating the current volume being dumped or the more generic `restore.volume` for restore operations, and possibly additional status information.

When `backup` is running in interactive mode, you cannot exit your session if jobs are active. You must either leave the session running or kill the job before quitting.

```
backup> dump users /full 0
. . .
Job 1: Dump (users.full)
backup> quit
backup: Job 1 still running (and not aborted)
backup: You must at least 'kill' all running jobs before quitting
```

QUERYING THE DATABASES

Often, of course, a volume will have archived versions available on many tapes. There will likely be 7 to 14 tapes kept on-site representing one or two weeks of full and incremental dumps. Other full dumps could be kept off-site, perhaps one full dump for each of the last 12 months. All of this information will be stored in the database and can be queried either by asking which dumps contain a given volume or by asking about what volumes are stored in a given dump.

For information on where to find a volume's archives, use the `volinfo` subcommand.

```
backup> volinfo user.alice
DumpID    lvl parentID creation date   clone date      tape name
859743005 0   0            03/30/97 12:30  03/30/97 11:55 users.full.1 (859743005)
```

Each item of information is of critical importance when the need arises to restore volume data. Every line begins with a dump identification number that uniquely defines the tape. Because a dump may be an incremental dump, that is, it consists only of files changed since a previous dump was made, you need the dump identifier to find the physical tapes.

The `lvl` item indicates at what level in the dump hierarchy a dump was made. Full dumps, such as the level `/sunday`, are at level 0. The level `/sunday/monday` is at level 1, indicating an incremental dump. A volume archived at this level would need only the corresponding full dump restored first; archives made to higher dump levels, such as `/first/second/third`, will need more ancestor dumps restored. The `parentID` item identifies the needed parent dump.

The `creation date` listed is the timestamp when the archive operation was started. This item is not quite as accurate as you might need; if read-write volumes are being dumped and the dump operation involved many volumes which took several hours to run, the exact time a particular volume was written to tape could be hours later. Of course, if backup volumes or read-only volumes are being archived, you have much more assurance that a correct snapshot of the volume was written to tape. In fact, the clone date column records the time at which the backup or read-only volume snapshot was created. For read-write volume archives, the clone date is the same as the creation date, even though read-write volumes are not clones and the actual dump time for the volume is unknown.

The tape name item identifies the tape according to the rules outlined above for tape labelling: the name consists of the volume set name, the dump-level name, and the tape index number. Here, the name is followed by the dump identification number of the initial dump in the dump set.

For basic information about the latest dumps made, use the dumpinfo command.

```
backup> dumpinfo
     dumpid    parentid lv created           nt nvols dump name
  859743005           0 0  03/30/97 12:30  1      6 users.full
```

Use the table primarily to check up on the most recently produced archives. When you give a numeric argument, the command displays information about the N most recent dumps. On each line, you see the dump identification number, the parent dump identification number (if this dump was not a full dump), the dump level, the time that the dump was started, the number of tapes in the complete dump set, the number of volumes that were completely dumped, and the canonical name of the dump in the tape label. If the number of tapes of volumes is 0, then the dump request was killed or failed. Note that for the number of volumes stored in the dump nvols, a volume that spans tapes is counted twice.

For detailed information about the dump and all of the volumes stored therein, specify the dump identification number.

```
backup> dumpinfo -id 859743005
Dump: id 859743005, level 0, volumes 6, created: Sun Mar 30 12:30:05 1997
Tape: name users.full.1 (859743005)
nVolumes 6, created 03/30/97 12:30

Pos      Clone time      Nbytes Volume
  2 03/30/97 11:55         2558 user.zed.backup
  3 03/30/97 11:55        13983 user.carol.backup
  4 03/30/97 11:55         4787 user.bob.backup
  5 03/30/97 11:55         2489 user.rob.backup
  6 03/30/97 11:55      1051126 user.david.backup
  7 03/30/97 11:55        12010 user.alice.backup
```

Two lines of general information are displayed. The first line shows dump information, including the dump identification number, the numeric depth of the dump level (0 for full, 1 for an incremental, etc.), the number of volumes archived in this particular dump, and the date the dump was created. The next line shows the dump's tape name followed by, in parenthesis, the dump identification number of the initial dump in the set. The next line redisplays the number of volumes in the dump and the creation date of the dump.

The rest of the display is a table showing information about each volume as it is stored on the tape. The `Pos` column lists the volume's numeric position on the tape (with position 1 being used for the tape label itself); the `Clone time` column lists, for a read-only or backup volume, the time at which the clone was created, and for a read-write volume, the time at which the dump was made; the `Nbytes` column lists the size of the volume in bytes; and lastly, the `Volume` column displays the name of the volume.

This table provides enough information to manually manipulate the tape by administrators familiar with their operating system tools. For example, by using the UNIX `mt` tape command to move forward over a number of files, you can recover a particular volume dump from the tape with the `dd` (data dump) command and then restore it with the AFS individual volume restore command, `vos restore`. This technique is, in effect how a single volume restoration is performed by the archive system.

You can print even more detail by adding the verbose option, `-v`. Here, only the details for a single volume are shown.

```
backup> dumpinfo -id 859743005 -v
...
Volume
------
name = user.zed.backup
flags = 0x18: First fragment: Last fragment
id = 536870966
server =
partition = 0
tapeSeq = 1
position = 2
clone = Sun Mar 30 11:55:22 1997
startByte = 0
nBytes = 2558
seq = 0
dump = 859743005
tape = users.full.1
...
```

These queries help you to investigate the database, to understand the state of your available archives, and to check on the integrity of completed dump operations. For the most part, you will not need to run any queries such as these when you need to restore a tape; the restoration process itself will query the database and simply prompt you for the appropriate tapes, as we shall see.

One final query permits reading the current tape in the drive and displays the tape label and all volume headers found there. This is a good method for ensuring that you've retrieved the correct tape from your library or to check on a just-completed dump, though it may take some time to complete.

```
backup> scantape 0
backup> jobs
Job 1: Scantape [operator wait]
backup> status 0
Task 10: Scantape:
backup> Job 1: Scantape finished
```

The information about the tape is available in the butc operator window. It's similar to the verbose dumpinfo command.

```
Scantape
****** OPERATOR ATTENTION *******
Device :  /dev/rst1
Please put in tape to be scanned and hit return when done

Thanks, now proceeding with tape scanning operation.
*********************************
Dump label
----------
tape name = users.full.1 (859743005)
creationTime = Sun Mar 30 12:30:50 1997
cell = hq.firm
size = 2097152 Kbytes
dump path = /full
dump id = 859743005
useCount = 5
-- End of dump label --

-- volume --
volume name: user.zed.backup
volume ID 536870966
dumpSetName: users.full
dumpID 859743005
level 0
parentID 0
endTime 0
clonedate Sun Mar 30 11:55:22 1997
. . .
```

GETTING THE DATA BACK

As complicated as the process of configuring the archive system and coordinating the dumps might appear, getting the data back is much simpler. The only practical problem is making sure you can find the right tape; for that reason, when dumps are made, you are well advised to physically label or otherwise track the just-written media.

Restoring data can be done in any number of ways. The system can restore either a single volume, an entire file server's vice partition, or a volume set. It can be directed to bring a volume back on-line either as it was at its latest dump time or as it was at any time in the past. The restored data can overwrite the existing volume or can be written to a new volume. And when restoring an entire partition, the restoration can put all the volumes onto the original partition or to a new partition.

The simplest restore operation is a request to recreate a volume from the latest version available on tape, using the volrestore subcommand. To find which tapes must be read to perform a restoration, use the -n flag. Here's a simple volume restoration:

```
backup> volrestore fs-one a user.alice -n
Restore volume user.alice.backup (ID 536870923) from tape users.full.1
(859743005), position 7 as user.alice.
```

The volrestore subcommand takes several arguments, including a mandatory file server and vice partition name. When a volume is restored, the archived version of the volume is recreated and stored at the file server and vice partition named on the command line. By default, all restore operations recreate full volumes from the previous full archive and any intermediate incrementals. If the volume still exists in AFS but on a different server or partition, that version is deleted both on disk and in the VLDB in favor of the newly restored version. The result is that the VLDB and the server's disk partitions are kept in strict synchronization.

To run the command, add a port offset to indicate which tape coordinator should expect to read the dump tape.

```
backup> volrestore fs-one a user.alice 0
Starting restore
Full restore being processed on port 0
```

As the `volrestore` operation runs, the backup tape coordinator process prints out a request for a particular tape to be loaded into the tape drive; once the tape is loaded, the operator is prompted to press Enter.

```
Restore
******* OPERATOR ATTENTION *******
Device :  /dev/rst1
Please put in tape users.full.1 (859743005) for reading and hit return when done

Thanks, now proceeding with tape reading operation.
**********************************
Restoring volume user.alice Id 536870921 on server fs-one partition /vicepa .. done
Restore: Finished
```

If necessary, you will be prompted for further tapes of a multitape set to be inserted. These tape operations can be automated, depending on the hardware tape device available with a tape configuration file and some device-specific scripts, as described later in this chapter.

When given a read-write volume name, for example, `user.alice`, the system automatically determines if the backup volume or the read-write version was dumped to tape most recently and restores that version instead.

To restore the volume to a new volume name, use the `-extension` option; `-extension foo` will restore Alice's home directory to `user.alice.foo`. This option prevents the deletion or overwriting of an existing volume. After restoration, you can connect the new volume to any convenient path name for further administration.

If you want to get back an earlier version, rather than the latest version of this volume, specify the date with the `-date` option. Also, you can list more than one volume. Here, we're restoring two user volumes as archived awhile ago and putting the data onto a new server and partition; the new volumes will each have a suffix of `.restore` so that the users can peruse their old data without it overwriting their current home directories.

```
backup> volrestore fs-one b -volume user.alice user.bob -extension
.restore -date 03/30/97 -port 0
Starting restore
Full restore being processed on port 0
backup> jobs
Job 1: Full Restore, volume user.bob.restore
backup> status
Task 12: Restore: volume user.bob.restore
backup> Job 1: Full Restore finished
```

The `butc` window looks similar to previous examples.

```
Restore
******* OPERATOR ATTENTION *******
Device :  /dev/rst1
Please put in tape users.full.1 (859743005) for reading and hit return when done

Thanks, now proceeding with tape reading operation.
**********************************
Restoring volume user.bob.restore Id 536870991 on server fs-one partition /vicepb .. done
Restoring volume user.alice.restore Id 536870992 on server fs-one partition /vicepb .. done
Restore: Finished
```

Once the volumes are restored, you can see that they appear in the volume location database and on disk.

```
$ vos listvldb
...
user.alice
RWrite: 536870921      Backup: 536870923
number of sites -> 1
    server fs-one partition /vicepa RW Site

user.alice.restore
RWrite: 536870992
number of sites -> 1
    server fs-one partition /vicepb RW Site
...
```

In the last example, where the restoration was to a volume name with a new extension, an administrator must make an explicit mount point for the volume somewhere in the AFS file namespace.

```
$ fs mkm /afs/.hq.firm/tmp/alice.restore user.alice.restore
$ ls /afs/.hq.firm/tmp/alice.restore
file1    file2    newDir    script1   secrets
```

In addition to restoring old user data, a frequent use of the system is to restore a disk partition to recreate the state of a failed disk.

```
backup> diskrestore fs-one a
Total number of volumes : 29
Starting restore
Full restore being processed on port 0
```

This subcommand queries the file server to find out which volumes currently exist on a given partition. The system looks up those volumes in the backup database, displays a request to load the relevant tapes, and restores the volumes, overwriting any of the same volumes on that partition. You can restore the volumes to a new server and partition with the `-newserver` and `-newpartition` options, respectively.

If the `diskrestore` command is being used to fix a disk crash or other disaster, make sure that no `vos syncserv` commands are run before the restoration; `diskrestore` uses information in the volume location database to determine which volumes are affected. A `syncserv` subcommand will try to update the database with the available on-disk information, which, being unavailable or damaged, will incorrectly edit the database. (A `volrestore` operation does not consult the VLDB.)

After the `diskrestore` is done, perform a `vos release` to make sure all read-only volumes on all servers are equivalent. If the `diskrestore` is to a different server or partition, check any read-only sites listed in the VLDB and run `remsite` to delete any remaining pointers to the read-write volume on the original disk.

As of AFS 3.4a, a new subcommand `volsetrestore` enables you to restore the entire contents of a volume set just by naming the volume set rather than laboriously naming the volumes one by one.

Note that both `diskrestore` and `volsetrestore` query the current databases to find out the list of volumes affected; if volumes have been added or deleted since the dump, you may have unexpected results, such as a missing volume error or a volume missed during the restore.

(This problem might be avoided if the Volume Location Database were a repository of historical information regarding each volume, but it contains only a current view of the AFS file servers and disks.)

Since the backup database contains dump information based on individual volumes and their associated archive times and tape labels, you can create ad hoc volume sets to be used exclusively for `volsetrestore` operations.

Alternatively, the `volsetrestore` subcommand can take an option, `-file`, to name a file containing an arbitrary list of volumes to restore as well as restoration sites (server and partition name). The file must list one volume per line, with each line consisting of the server and partition name where the volume should be restored and the volume name itself. In this case, the backup database is searched to find the tapes where a given volume was last dumped (including the full dump and any necessary incrementals). Once read off of the tapes, the volume is restored onto the named server and partition, being deleted from any other server and partition, if needed.

One problem with the `diskrestore` and `volsetrestore` subcommands is that the restoration must operate against a single `butc` process; that is, all of the full and incremental dump tapes must be created on the same tape device. If different devices were used to archive incremental dumps, then the volumes can only be restored with the single volume `volrestore` command, which can use multiple port offsets.

AUTOMATING DUMPS

Normally, the backup tape coordinator prompts an operator to remove and insert tapes and perform other administration. This may be a good model if you have a dedicated operations staff that can attend to requests displayed on a console. If you don't have a staff and don't want to spend your evenings sitting around waiting for the dumps to begin, a few options are available to automate the process. And if the archive device is more sophisticated than a simple tape drive, you can customize the actions taken by the tape coordinator process when certain conditions are encountered, such as the need to unmount and mount tapes.

The simplest automation is set up by running the `butc` process with the `-noautoquery` flag. This flag causes the tape coordinator to assume that the right tape is in the drive. In this case, the coordinator does not need an interactive window because it will not ask an operator to insert a tape. But if multiple tapes are needed for large volume sets or for appending dumps to the dump set, an operator will still be needed to insert the additional tapes. Also, if an error occurs with the tape drive, such as no tape being found in the drive, an unexpired tape being used accidentally, or a write-protected tape being used, an error message will be displayed and a request will be made to change tapes.

Once you set up some automation, you can schedule dumps to occur at a future date. These scheduled dumps, called "timed dumps" in the AFS documentation, can either be a single dump command instructed to run at a given date or a file of multiple dump commands to run at a given date. Timed dumps are given a job number, which can be queried with the `jobs` subcommand, and can be killed prior to their start time. In interactive mode, the job is scheduled and a new prompt displayed:

```
backup> dump users /full 0 -at "03/30/97 17:00"
Add scheduled dump as job 1
backup> jobs
backup> jobs
Job 1: 03/30/97 17:00: dump users /full 0
       03/30/97 18:04: TOKEN EXPIRATION
```

Notice that the backup command keeps track of the Kerberos credential under which it runs and can determine that its administrative privileges expire at 18:04. If the dump had been scheduled for later than 18:04, backup would have warned that the token will expire before the dump proceeds. If no action were taken to reauthenticate, the archive process would fail because the command would have no authorization to read AFS volume and file data.

Note that in interactive mode backup immediately displays a new prompt permitting other work to proceed. In command-line batch mode, backup waits until the job has executed. As another option, multiple dump requests can be written into a file and then processed by backup with the -file option.

An alternate method of automating the process is to set up a configuration file that can specify an arbitrary set of programs or scripts to run, which could enable certain hardware actions to reset the archive device.

To configure such actions, create a file in the /usr/afs/backup directory with a prefix of CFG_ and a suffix based on the media device name, just like the tape log and error files, TL_ and TE_. Recall that upon startup, a butc process knows its port number only from its command-line argument. It uses that port number to find out which hardware device name it controls by reading the /usr/afs/backup/tapeconfig file. Now that butc knows its device name, if a file exists with a prefix of CFG_ and a suffix based on the device, it will read that file to turn on or off certain advanced coordinator features or enable extra actions to be performed during tape insertion or extraction.

The file consists of keyword-value pairs, one pair to a line. The allowed keywords:

- ASK and AUTOQUERY—Suppress querying an operator during dump or restore operations
- NAME_CHECK—Eliminates the coordinator's check for tape labels
- BUFFERSIZE—Increases a coordinator's memory cache to improve performance
- FILE—Directs the coordinator to read and write from a standard UNIX file rather than from a tape device

- MOUNT and UNMOUNT—Specify arbitrary executable programs to perform the actual tape insertion and extraction

With no CFG_ file present, the tape coordinator will prompt for many operations as described above. The following example configuration files modify those actions.

```
# cat /usr/afs/backup/tapeconfig
2G 1M /dev/rmt10 0
# cat /usr/afs/backup/CFG_rmt10
MOUNT /usr/local/bin/juke
UNMOUNT /usr/local/bin/juke
AUTOQUERY NO
ASK YES
NAME_CHECK NO
# butc 0
```

The tape coordinator started in the above listing will read the tapeconfig file and see that, because it is assigned to port 0, it will have to manage the device /dev/rmt10. For this case, it will also see that a configuration file exists named after the final path name element of the device, /usr/afs/backup/ CFG_rmt10. The coordinator will read the configuration file, the values of the keywords will modify the coordinator's actions.

For the MOUNT and UNMOUNT keywords, the values specify an executable program that will be run whenever the coordinator specifies that a file should be loaded or unloaded from the tape drive. This example names the file /usr/ local/bin/juke as the program to run during mount operations. This program—either a shell script or binary program—must be written to use any hardware media utilities to insert the correct tape into the tape reader. Because the program is spawned by the tape coordinator, it will have the coordinator's identity: root or the UNIX login under which the coordinator runs. The program will also have whatever AFS authentication credential is available, either a specific token indicating a member of system:administrators, an implicit administrator via localauth, or none. (The localauth option is new to AFS 3.4a).

For a MOUNT request, the specified program runs with five command-line arguments supplied automatically.

- The hardware device. For this example, /dev/rmt10.
- The particular tape operation the tape coordinator will be running. This operation is one of dump, labeltape, readlabel, restore, append-

dump, savedb, restoredb, or scantape. The purposes behind these named operations are described below.

- An integer describing how many times this operation has been requested. After an error of the current operation, the integer will be incremented and the operation retried. Use this argument wisely and don't fall into an infinite loop of retries.
- The tape name as defined by the archive system.
- The tape identifier, again, as defined by the system.

For the UNMOUNT operation, only two arguments are passed to the executable:

- The hardware device name.
- The tape operation. For UNMOUNT, the only operation is unmount.

Once control passes to the mount or unmount program, the actions executed are completely up to your needs and the media device's capabilities. When finished, the return code of the process will indicate whether the device was able to mount (or unmount) the tape: an exit code of 0 indicates success and the dump will continue; an exit code of 1 indicates failure and the dump will abort; any other exit code will cause a default action to take place or the operator to be queried, depending on the value of the ASK keyword.

The AUTOQUERY and ASK keywords control the amount of prompting the coordinator will perform. Both keywords can have values of YES or NO. A value of YES for AUTOQUERY permits the coordinator to query an operator for the initial load of a tape; NO implies that a tape will be in the drive. NO has the same effect as the -noautoquery option to the coordinator process.

The ASK keyword controls which prompts are to be asked when errors are encountered during butc operations. A value of YES for ASK will cause butc to prompt the operator to press Enter after tape loading requests; this is the default. NO means that butc will take a default action depending on which backup command was in effect:

- For errors during dump, the volume being dumped will be ignored.
- For errors during restore, the volume being restored is to be ignored.
- If backup cannot be determined whether more tapes are available in a dump set, NO implies that there are more tapes.
- If labeltape is writing to an unexpired tape, NO causes the tape not to be relabelled.

NAME_CHECK is a keyword that controls the behavior of the coordinator when it encounters previously labelled tapes. A value of NO permits the system to overwrite any tape label as long as the current date is later than the tape expiration date. YES indicates that the tape name in the label must be null or the same name as that for the current dump; this is the default behavior.

In summary, the above example file causes the tape coordinator to assume that a tape is properly loaded into the hardware device when starting operations (AUTOQUERY set to NO). When tapes must be loaded or ejected during multitape operations, the coordinator will use the executable program /usr/local/bin/juke (MOUNT and UNMOUNT set to /usr/local/bin/juke). This script will be executed with various arguments, depending on which backup command is to be run. During archive operations, the coordinator will write data to any expired tape in the tape drive (NAME_CHECK set to NO). Finally, the coordinator will prompt for operator intervention if errors are encountered.

Two extra keywords can be used to further customize the tape coordinator: BUFFERSIZE and FILE.

During dump and restore operations, data is temporarily stored in the coordinator's memory space in between reading from the volume server and writing to tape or reading from tape and writing to the volume server. Normally this memory space is limited to 1 tape block (16 kilobytes) for dumps and 2 tape blocks (32 kilobytes) for reads. You can set this space size to any value you deem appropriate for the archive device by specifying a value to the BUFFERSIZE keyword. The value should be in bytes, for example, 16384 or 16k for 16 kilobytes or 1m for 1 megabyte.

So far, the tape coordinator has assumed that it is dealing with a tape drive and will use certain operating system procedures and assumptions when reading and writing the volume data. You can set the keyword FILE to YES to indicate that the path name mentioned in the tapeconfig file is actually a regular file rather than a hardware device. The default value for FILE is NO, signifying a tape drive.

When dumping to files, the backup database stores positions in the archive medium in terms of fixed 16 kilobyte chunks as opposed to filemarks for other media.

Here's an example of dumping to file:

```
$ cat /usr/afs/backup/tapeconfig
1G 0K /var/backup/afs/fdump 1
$ cat /usr/afs/backup/CFG_fdump
```

```
MOUNT /usr/afs/backup/fileDump
FILE YES
ASK NO
$ butc 1
```

Here, the tapeconfig file specifies a size of 1 gigabyte for the archive media, in this case, just a file, /var/backup/afs/fdump, associated with port 1. The tape coordinator, which is attached to port 1, read the tapeconfig file and then read the configuration data in the file /usr/afs/backup/CFG_fdump. The configuration specifies that the archive media is a file (FILE is YES) and that, to load a tape—in this case, to initialize the dump file—the executable /usr/afs/backup/fileDump is to be run. Upon encountering errors, a default action (as listed above) will be taken.

The /usr/afs/backup/fileDump script can take care of certain issues peculiar to dumping to files. One difference between files and tapes is that new tapes can be inserted as needed, whereas a file named in /usr/afs/backup/tapeconfig is static. Another difference concerns the action to take if the file grows to fill the entire local file system. In regular operation, when the coordinator gets to the end of a tape, it prompts the operator for a new tape. But if the dump is to a file and the file system becomes full, what should be done? In this case, the tape coordinator process quickly closes the file, thereby saving whatever it has managed to write. An attentive operator could move the file to another disk partition, thereby allowing butc to continue the dump by writing to a new, empty version of the same named file. It is this type of administration that can more properly be accomplished by a shell script as specified by the MOUNT keyword argument. The Transarc documentation has several examples of scripts for situations such as these.

Automating the dump process presents a final problem regarding authentication. The backup commands can be executed only by authorized persons. To check the authority, AFS uses its own credential information and not the UNIX identity of the user. While members of system:administrators are normally permitted to run these commands, in fact, any AFS user or group listed in the /usr/afs/etc/UserList file is also permitted to run them as described in Chapter 9.

The same permissions apply to running a butc process: it must be run under an administrator's credentials. But watch out for the token expiration time. If you intend to start up the backup tape coordinator process once, be aware that whatever credentials you obtained before the process began will expire in a few days at best. It is extremely aggravating to find out that an overnight dump failed because of a token expiration in the wee small hours of the morning.

One way around this authentication problem is to run the `backup` or `butc` commands on an AFS server machine itself. When run under UNIX root identity and with the `-localauth` flag, the processes can use the `/usr/afs/local/KeyFile` to create a service ticket and therefore can always retrieve and store privileged data to the backup databases and file servers. This capability is most useful when you are automating an archive system. See Chapter 9 for more information on this flag.

SAVING THE BACKUP DATABASE

Practically all of the information about archives—dump sets, volume sets, tape hosts and offsets—is stored in a Ubik database maintained on the database server machines by the `buserver` processes. This database is therefore as precious as any other data held by the system. Because of this, a special subcommand, `dbverify`, performs internal integrity checks on the database and reports any errors. It's wise to perform this check regularly, especially at the beginning of any automated scripts.

```
backup> dbverify
Database OK
```

If the response is "not OK," there's a problem with the database. Such problems can be cured only by recreating the database from archived copies, as described below.

You can give an option, `-detail`, to the `dbverify` command to display additional information about the database. If any nonexistent tape coordinator hosts are stored, they will be shown. Also, if any internal disk blocks used by the database could potentially be reclaimed, they are listed as well. Large cells with sophisticated archive needs may find that the backup database has grown quite large. The database will contain an entry for each volume set, dump level, and for each dump created, a complete list of the volumes which the dump contained. The problem with a large database is not only the size required but the time needed to archive it and the time needed for the `buserver` processes to handle data insertions and queries. If the size does become a problem, you can reclaim the space by deleting obsolete dumps. Before doing so, it will be prudent to save the entire database, just in case certain information needs to be restored.

To write out the backup database to an archive device, use the `savedb` subcommand:

```
backup> savedb 0
backup> jobs
Job 1: SaveDb
```

As usual, the tape coordinator operator may have to insert a tape. The `savedb` operation will write the contents of the database to the desired port. The tape will be labelled `Ubik_db_dump.1`. Note that there is no dump level because all database archives are full. And note that if in an extreme instance the database does not fit on one tape, the tape index number will be incremented for each tape needed.

If the backup database is corrupted, you can use this tape to restore the database. This is a cumbersome process made worse by the fact that you'll have to individually add any information about each dump made since the last full archive of the database itself.

To start, you must delete the existing (presumably corrupt) backup database and allow the saved database to be written over it. First, shut down the backup database processes.

```
$ bos shutdown db-one buserver -wait
$ bos shutdown db-two buserver -wait
$ bos shutdown db-three buserver -wait
```

Second, manually log in to each database server and delete the backup database files.

```
$ rlogin db-one root
Password:
# rm /usr/afs/db/bdb.D*
# exit
$ rlogin db-two root
...
```

Next, restart the backup databases on each server.

```
$ bos startup db-one buserver
$ bos startup db-two buserver
$ bos startup db-three buserver
```

You should wait a minute for the `buserver`'s distributed database logic to settle down. Then, so that the `backup` command can find the tape coordinator, you must bootstrap the database by adding the tape machine and port offset back into the new, and empty, database. Only then can the backup database be restored.

```
$ backup
backup> addhost fs-two 0
Adding host fs-two offset 0 to tape list...done
backup> restoredb 0
backup> jobs
Job 1: RestoreDb
backup> Job 1: RestoreDb finished
```

Again, as usual, the `butc` operator will be prompted for the insertion of the appropriate tape.

```
RestoreDb
******* OPERATOR ATTENTION *******
Device : /dev/rst1
Please insert a tape Ubik_db_dump.1 for the database restore and hit return when done

Thanks, now proceeding with tape reading operation.
**********************************
RestoreDb: Finished
```

These steps restore the database as it was at the moment the `savedb` operation was performed.

```
backup> dumpinfo
dumpid    parentid lv created         nt nvols dump name
859746941          0 0  03/30/97 13:35 1     0 Ubik_db_dump
backup> dumpinfo -id 859746941
Dump: id 859746941, created: Sun Mar 30 13:35:41 1997

Tape: name Ubik_db_dump.1 (859746941)
nVolumes 0, created 03/30/97 13:36
```

Any volume sets that were archived after the time the database was saved will not be reflected in the database. This additional data can be restored only by reading all of the intervening tape labels and adding that data to the database. One by one, insert the dump tapes into an available tape controller device and run:

```
backup> scantape -dbadd -port 0
```

This command is similar to the scantape query shown previously, except that the tape label information and volume data are also stored back into the database.

Once you have saved a copy of the backup database, you can choose to delete old dump set data from the database. Delete old data only when you truly want to never again access the archive media. Deleting old data can help maintain a clean and small backup database. Deleting a dump set is easy:

```
backup> dumpinfo
     dumpid    parentid lv created        nt nvols dump name
  859743005           0 0  03/30/97 12:30  1     6 users.full
backup> deletedump 859743005
The following dumps were deleted:
        859743005
```

To delete multiple dumps, you can specify a start and end date; all dumps created between those times will be deleted.

COMMON STRATEGIES

The AFS archiving utilities can be used in a variety of ways to save data and restore it in the event of misadventure. Many sites simply use the tools as suggested in the manuals for archiving volume data, but others have implemented highly customized strategies.

First, don't forget that all AFS volumes can have a cheap snapshot, the backup volume, available and mounted in the file system. Colleagues can trivially recover accidentally deleted data in their home or project development directories from yesterday's snapshots. This not only makes life easier for users but reduces the administrative burden of maintaining a large distributed file system.

Unfortunately, only one backup volume per read-write volume is permitted. To archive successive sets of a cell's file data requires saving volumes to tape. A typical problem for administrators is deciding which volume sets to dump at what schedule. The use of regular expressions to define sets of volumes is a reasonable system for very well managed cells but in a less-organized organization, the proliferation of volume names and dump preferences can present difficulties for the dump scheduler.

A way around this dilemma is to construct an external database of volume names. You can regularly check this database against the contents of the volume location database to make sure that all volumes are accounted for; each volume can have a field specifies which dump schedule it needs. You can then scan this database and run commands to generate a new and accurate list of volume sets. Then, you can link the policies to automatically start up dump jobs to complete the dump process.

One AFS site manages its dump schedules by using special characters at the beginning of the volume name to help schedule the dump process. For example, a volume set can easily be defined for all volumes that begin with the letter "D," and another set for volumes that begin with the letter "W." Batch scripts can then be written to dump the "D" volumes every day and the "W" volumes once a week. The advantage of this scheme is that changes to the dump schedule for a particular volume can be made just by using the volume rename command without having to change anything associated with the backup database. The disadvantage is that there are only 22 characters available for volume names and, also, as a volume name is changed, all mount points to that volume in the file system have to be changed.

Some organizations have found that the backup utilities are too concerned with individual volumes and tape media. In their estimation, the existence of the snapshot backup volumes provides a good on-line archive for most user mistakes. The only other situation that needs to be handled is that of disk disasters. Rather than use the AFS archive system, you can survive disk disasters by grouping read-write or read-only volumes together on well-known disk surfaces and then using the UNIX data dump command dd to save a complete copy of all the disk blocks to tape. This copy could then be quickly read off tape and written to a fresh disk, which would then be swapped into position; a simple file server restart will attach the volumes found there without any awareness that this is a retrieval of archived data.

Another way to increase the efficiency of the process is to create a higher-speed network connection between the file server and the client hosting the backup tape coordinator. Because AFS file servers can now have multiple network connections, it makes sense to use an improved network topology to optimize archiving. If the butc host has multiple network connections, you should use client file server preferences to make sure that the higher-speed link is used during archiving; if the host has only a single high-speed link, that will be correctly used without any further administration.

A continuing problem with Transarc's archive system is that it is designed to be used by administrators alone. Many sites want the administrators to manage the archive processes but the users themselves to run some sort of interface to search for dumped data and perform the restores. For this and other reasons, AFS sites are either using AFS's single volume dump tools or looking to third-party software to supply other solutions.

VOLUME DUMPS

The vos command suite includes commands for taking the contents of a single volume, flattening out the contained files, directories, and ACLs, and storing that data in a file. This mechanism can certainly be used as the basis of an archive system, but because there is no integration volume sets or dump levels, this per-volume dump is usually used only for quick administrative tasks.

The simplest form of the dump command writes the contents of a volume to a file.

```
$ vos dump user.alice 0 /tmp/dumpFile
Dumped volume user.alice in file /tmp/dumpFile
```

During the process, the volume being dumped is locked out to any read or write access. For this reason, while you can dump the contents of either a read-write, read-only, or backup volume, it is more common to dump a backup volume. If the backup volume is out of date or doesn't exist, it can be created just before the volume dump.

The argument after the volume name tells the dump command whether to make a full or incremental dump of the volume. In this example, 0 specifies a complete dump. You can also dump only those files and directories that have been modified since a certain date. These incremental dumps are specified with either a date, in the format mm/dd/yy, or a date and time, in the format mm/dd/yy hh:mm. The hours in the time format should be in 24-hour notation; without a time format, the time of the incremental dump is assumed to be 00:00, the beginning of the day for that date. The final argument is the name of the dump file. When no file is specified, the dump goes to standard output.

The dump file's contents contain an ASCII representation of the volume, including all directories, files, ACLs, and volume mount points. If you are curious, you can examine the file with an editor, though there is little editing that you can do that would be useful. The next example demonstrates an incremental dump saved to standard output.

```
$ vos dump user.alice.backup "3/29/97 14:00" > /tmp/dump2
Dumped volume user.alice in stdout
```

Dumping a read-only volume is done similarly and normally doesn't require any extra effort. However, if you're in the middle of a disk disaster and you suspect that some read-only volumes are not equal to all others, be aware that vos dump will pick the read-only server from the list of available servers as stored in the volume location database. Read-write and backup volumes are stored only on a single server, so you can be sure that the data comes from that server. For a read-only volume, the only way to demand that a specific server be used as the source of the dump is by either deleting information from the VLDB or, more simply, by changing the file server preferences on the local desktop.

While any of the three volume types can be dumped, the vos restore command can restore only to a read-write volume, either an existing read-write volume or a brand-new one. Using the first dump file we've made, we can recreate Alice's home directory.

```
$ vos restore fs-one a user.alice /tmp/dumpFile
The volume user.alice 536870921 already exists in the VLDB
Do you want to do a full/incremental restore or abort? [fia](a): f
Volume exists; Will delete and perform full restore
Restoring volume user.alice Id 536870921 on server fs-one partition /vicepa .. done
Restored volume user.alice on fs-one /vicepa
```

Note that just as with the volume create or the backup restore commands, you must specify a physical location—a server and partition name—for the restored volume. If you specify a different server and partition for a read-write volume that already exists in the cell, the existing volume will be deleted in favor of the newly restored volume. As a side effect of the vos restore operation, the new volume is given a new volume identification number; the only way to retain the old number is with the -id option. Once this volume is restored, you may want to create a new backup volume or release the volume to its read-only replicas.

Incremental dumps of a volume can be restored either to a new volume or as overlays to an existing volume. If the restore is to a new volume, only the intermediate data in the incremental dump can be installed into the new volume. But if the incremental restore is to a previously restored version of the volume, then the incremental changes between the first dump and the incremental dump are applied to the previously restored volume.

Only since AFS version 3.4a could you correctly restore an incremental dump. Such a restoration requires no extra options on the command line because the information labelling the dump as incremental is stored in the dump file itself. A dump taken on February 1st that was made incremental to

January 1st will contain all the files and directories changed in January: including the new files, and information on the deleted files. Given a volume fully restored from the January 1st dump file, restoring the February 1st incremental will correctly add and subtract the necessary data to fully recover the volume.

Of course, incremental restores work only when restoring an incremental dump to an existing volume; if the restore operation is to a partition that does not contain a version of the volume, then the incremental is, in effect, a full restore. The incremental changes will affect only a preexisting version of the volume; when the incremental dump is to be overlaid on such a volume, you'll be prompted as to whether you want to perform a full or incremental restore or just to abort the process. You can set this preference on the command line with the -overwrite full or -overwrite incremental option.

Clearly, managing these dumps and restores for each volume in a large cell is an enormous task. That's exactly the purpose of the backup database; a repository for information on groups of volumes and all the dump dates. Only occasionally will it be necessary to use the vos dump and restore subcommands.

One occasion to use these commands is when making changes to critical volumes such as root.afs. Because the root.afs.readonly replicas are distinct from the read-write master, it is simple enough to make changes safely to the read-write and ensure that it has exactly the right subdirectories and volume mounts. But the paranoid administrator might want to make a quick manual volume dump just before making changes, in case some link or byte gets lost in the process. Backing out of the change is as simple as restoring the volume from the (thankfully) saved dump file.

Note that interrupted volume restore commands can result in corrupt read-write masters that will be taken off-line by the AFS volserver and will need to be salvaged and reconnected to the file system as discussed in Chapter 9.

AFS DATABASE ARCHIVING

Now that you have archived the file data and the backup database, what about the other databases: the volume location, the protection, and the Kerberos database? Transarc provides no particular tool to checkpoint these files, but the operations are simple. Because all database operations are serialized against the sync site, any other site becomes a perfect candidate from which to take a snapshot. In our hypothetical cell, our sync site happens to be db-one, so we can turn to db-two or db-three to grab a copy of the data. The plan will be to shut down the database servers there and then to simply copy the files to a suitable location, and later, archiving them to tape.

```
# hostname
db-two
# bos shutdown db-two -localauth
# cd /usr/afs/db
# tar cf /tmp/savedb.tar *
# bos restart db-two -all -localauth
```

This sequence of commands takes only seconds to complete. When the read-only database server restarts, it checks with the sync site, and if any write operations have occurred, a database transfer will occur, bringing db-two up to date with the other servers. Note that the /usr/afs/db directory has permission such that only the UNIX root user can read the files.

With a coherent version of the databases now copied into a convenient package, you should store the data onto other media—certainly onto tape or some other device that can be kept local and also archived off-site. In the event of a disaster, these archives will be the only way to recreate the list of users and groups (the volume location information can be recreated more laboriously with vos synchronization subcommands). Just be especially careful of the Kerberos database: it contains encrypted information about every principal in your AFS cell and, while decryption is hard, you should presume that bad people could be able to read the database.

Restoring the databases is almost as easy as archiving them. This time, you must perform the operations on the sync site. Retrieve the databases from tape and store the files in a handy location. Stop the databases on the sync site, copy over the saved database files to the database directory, and then restart the database processes.

```
# hostname
db-one
# bos shutdown db-one -localauth
# cd /usr/afs/db
# tar xf /tmp/savedb.tar
# bos restart db-one -localauth
```

Now, the sync site will wake up, look for its peers, possibly engage in an election to regain the master read-write status, and then force its version of the database on the other read-only database sites. In a minute or two, the elections and propagations will have settled. If you use this technique to restore the backup database, you'll still have to use the backup scantape command with -dbadd option to add any information from dumps made after the backup database was saved.

Although no special-purpose tools perform these procedures, the above command examples should enable you to archive the AFS database with ease. Since the databases maintain their stability through a variety of outages, performing a restoration from tape should be required only after a catastrophe. Other techniques for managing this information are presented in the next chapter in the discussion of Ubik database mangement.

THIRD-PARTY SOFTWARE

Truthfully, Transarc's archive system is not beloved of AFS administrators. It certainly manages volume-based archiving. But for larger sites that need more customization, the flexibility of the system tends to result in more places where errors can creep in. By its very nature, such a system is unwieldy, taking several hours to laboriously write data to tape. As this activity inherently interferes with the file systems (at least by imposing a bandwidth and server load), it is most often done at night. Any errors in the process are therefore discovered many hours after the fact and often result in the need to start the entire process over again.

Being a software company, Transarc cannot mandate any particular hardware storage device. Hence the need for the `fms size` discovery command, the `tapeconfig` file, and the automated configuration file. Yet all these aids do is shift the burden of writing the interface between AFS and the storage device onto the cell administrator. And writing bulletproof scripts amid the tangle of interrelated backup processes more often results in subtle bugs discovered only when critical volumes need to be restored.

Smallish cells with relatively flat growth rates will often need only a few tape drives and a fairly unchanging backup configuration. For these sites, the Transarc solution works well. Other, larger sites, with more frequent changes in configuration and size, need a flexible system that is also more tolerant of faults. This generally means a system with a strongly integrated set of hardware and software, plus all the attendant reporting and configuration tools.

Over the years, the AFS community was chicken-and-egged to despair by commercial archive vendors. The vendors didn't see a large enough market to warrant adapting their software to deal with AFS data, and the absence of robust, large-scale, easy-to-administer archive software suggested to potential customers that AFS was not production-ready.

Now, happily, the situation has changed, with several commercial solutions becoming available, including `vosasm` provided by BoxHill Systems Corporation that works with Legato's Networker™ archive system, IBM's ADSM™, and PDC's BudTool™. The following information is not an endorsement of any or all of the products but is listed to demonstrate the available support of AFS by archive vendors.

LEGATO'S NETWORKER

Legato Systems' Networker software has been a major archival system for UNIX systems for many years and has support for a variety of storage devices. In 1994, BoxHill Systems, a leading supplier of disk drives, produced a software product that permitted Networker to correctly dump AFS volumes.

The mechanism consists of a program, vosasm, that uses the standard vos dump command to create the archival data stream. That stream is then connected to Networker's nsrfile program, which dumps the data to the correct media. The result is a volume-oriented archive system. When Networker is configured to dump files in an AFS file server's vice partitions, it recognizes these partitions and identifies the AFS volumes stored there. When these volumes are set to be dumped up, vosasm creates new backup volume snapshots and then dumps the volume contents through Networker, which catalogs the archive activity and stores the data on the preconfigured tape.

The drawback to this architecture is that while it is volume-centric, it is not based on any attributes of the volume, such as name or purpose, but rather just on the collection of volumes currently located on a given server. As far as Networker is concerned, it is just storing large, oddly named files; it has no knowledge of the structures or files stored in the volumes. This works well for organizations with enough servers that individual servers and vice partitions can be allocated to different volume types.

Recovery is also based solely on volume location. Given a file or directory which is to be recovered, you must determine which volume has stored that data and also which server that volume resides on. Once logged in to that server, you can use Networker recovery commands to read the archived data file off the correct media and convert it back into an AFS volume.

Although there is no user-level, graphical front end to the recovery process, this mechanism does integrate AFS archives with the already strong Networker support of a variety of media devices. This, in addition to Networker's strong market presence, makes the solution attractive and sufficient. Legato Systems can be reached at http://www.legato.com.

IBM'S ADSM

IBM (which, after all, owns Transarc) has added support for AFS and DFS to their archival system, the Adstar Distributed Storage Manager, or ADSM. This system can dump straightforward AFS file data as well as interface to the system backup and can dump AFS volumes.

The straightforward file archives are run, as they must be, from an AFS client. With the ADSM user interface, you can assign simple AFS path names to dump schedules. As we said at the beginning of the chapter, this would not be good enough were it not for two features added by IBM. When archiving file data located in AFS, ADSM will take care to dump ACL and volume mount point information correctly. Additionally, you can specify an option in the configuration so that the dump process does not cross AFS mount points. While not going as far as to keep track of some volume information, these two features do provide you with useful functionality.

More conventionally, you can install an ADSM-ready tape coordinator process, `buta`. This coordinator looks to AFS much like a normal `butc` process; once `buta` is running, you can query the status, dump, or restore volume sets to and from the coordinator. The advantage is that this coordinator uses ADSM as its complete media manager. The coordinator, rather than managing individual tape mount and unmount requests, can now rely on the built-in hierarchical storage system of the system. In fact, most of the volume dumps are made to an ADSM server disk farm. Once the volumes are buffered on disk, ADSM transparently migrates the data to archive media as needed. These servers can range in scale from an OS/2™ or Windows NT system to a large-scale Sun Solaris, IBM AIX, HP-UX™, or even an AS/400™ or mainframe MVS™ machine.

Configuring ADSM is a complex process but one that makes AFS volume archiving trivial. Additionally, you can use ADSM to dump UNIX file systems with similar automatic media management. IBM can be reached at http://www.ibm.com.

PDC'S BUDTOOL

One final archive product that supports AFS is BudTool, made by PDC, Inc. This tool is not designed to be a soup-to-nuts file archiving system but is rather targeted at administrators who need a flexible engine that can be integrated with any given file storage architecture. Besides providing an open framework into which many different data devices can be incorporated, the lightweight nature of the tool also enables operators to retrieve information from archive media, using regularly available utilities.

BudTool's primary role is to associate a dump scheduling system with a media management interface. The media supported include all of the major archive devices as well as the automatic or robotic media changers. To use BudTool, you define a request to archive a fixed set of volumes and, when the schedule called for it, BudTool dumps those volumes to media via the vos dump commands. Once the volumes are archived, the tool's backup history database stores information about the dump event; later, you can browse this database and retrieve the specific tape holding a given dump. BudTool would then issue the appropriate media commands to find the correct tape and restore the volume.

Because the volume data is stored in a standard format, you can use a regular vos restore command to retrieve the data. In extreme circumstances, this feature will make disaster recovery much easier.

When used to archive an ordinary disk, BudTool can run commands to discover the available partitions on the disk. Unfortunately, the earliest releases of the product do not perform a similar action for AFS volumes: you cannot register a set of volumes by prefix or regular expression that will be expanded at run time into the current set of volumes matching the expression. Instead, you must register volumes individually and schedule them collectively. For large sites, with, for example, user home volumes constantly being added and deleted, this requirement will quickly prove burdensome. There are, however, some contributed utilities that can help to simulate volume sets, and PDC may be persuaded to provide more support for this function in the future.

Sites wanting a lightweight archive system that performs automatic media management will probably find that BudTool is a step above Transarc's configuration-file-based system, without the additional overhead of a completely proprietary dump architecture. PDC can be reached at http://www.pdc.com.

SUMMARY

The AFS archiving system solves the fundamental problem facing cell administrators: storing consistent copies of file data onto tape. And it does this with care to keep track of the peculiarities of AFS, such as the containment of file data to volumes, volume mount points, and ACLs that would otherwise be lost.

As far as this system goes, it works. Indeed, most sites will find that this system is all that is needed. But there is a lack of fine-grained control and flexibility on restorations that is occasionally irksome. Luckily, some third-party products can help solve some of these problems, especially with respect to large-scale tape systems.

The AFS solution is client/server based, as is typical in their system. It takes some training to understand the relationship between the server providing resources, such as the backup database, and the clients, such as the backup command. In some cases, one process is both a service and a client: the tape coordinator serves requests from the backup command suite but also requests data as a client of the volume and file servers.

It is important to understand this model and to create an archival mechanism which will fit your needs. There are enough ways to set up volume sets, dump levels, and media ports to solve almost every backup problem.

At this point, we've learned almost everything there is to know about the basic management of an AFS cell from the administrative as well as the user perspective. The next few chapters will discuss some of the finer points of administration and debugging of AFS.

## CHAPTER 9

More AFS Administration

With most of the AFS architecture and basic use described, we can now turn our attention to details of the administrative process that have previously been treated sparingly. The AFS command suites include not just the programs needed to get the system running but also extensive requests to query the status of the servers and custom programs to investigate the various protocols used.

AFS supports a number of interesting processes to help manage the installation and running of the servers themselves. These are, strictly speaking, not completely necessary to make AFS work, but Transarc's documentation imagines that all of their products are being used in concert. So, it will be beneficial to understand Transarc's idea of how a cell functions.

Some processes need to run only occasionally, such as during a reboot of a server. Others are available for constant monitoring of the system. Like the previous description of cell set up, this chapter describes a somewhat overwhelming number of new commands and services. While none will be needed by some sites all the time, they will nevertheless come in handy to all sites at some time.

Of course, to exercise all these processes, commands, and services, we'll first need to obtain administrative credentials.

ADMINISTRATIVE CREDENTIALS

The previous chapters on cell set up, volume administration, and backup have assumed that you obtained proper system privileges before running many commands. The AFS manual set describes in detail exactly what authority must be granted for each of the many dozen possible options and subcommands. We have so far skipped over these security issues in the belief that the infrastructure and process interrelationships were more important to the discussion. But now, before we begin to focus on detailed administration questions, it's time to describe the various ways an operator can be authorized to run these procedures.

There are essentially three ways to gain authority to run AFS administration commands and one more to control Kerberos:

- Being a member of `system:administrators`
- Being a member of a server's administration list
- Using the local authority of a server itself
- Having Kerberos administration privilege

Each type of authority grants a slightly different privilege, so pieces of the administration pie can be doled out to different people, thus enhancing the overall security of the system.

The first kind of administrator privilege, membership in the `system:administrators` group, is discussed in Chapter 6. A user can be authenticated as a member of this group in a variety of ways. Most commonly, a single, well-known login, such as `afsadmin`, is made a member of the group. The drawback with this well-known login is that a single password also becomes well-known. Just as easily, several user logins can be added to the group. The benefit is that each user will have a unique password. But, rather than require certain users to always have root privileges, a better solution is to create new logins to be used by certain users. While David will normally use the login name `david` when authenticating to AFS, a new login, perhaps `david.admin`, could be created, added to `system:administrators`, and thereafter used by David when he administers the system.

The commands for adding or deleting users from `system:administrators` are exactly the same commands used for regular group management. If we create for David an additional AFS login name of `david.admin`, we can add that identity to the membership of `system:administrators`.

```
$ kas create david.admin -admin afsadmin
Administrator's (afsadmin) Password:
initial_password:
Verifying, please re-enter initial_password:
```

```
$ pts adduser david.admin system:administrators
$ pts membership system:administrators
Members of system:administrators (id: -204) are:
  afsadmin
  david.admin
```

The benefits of using an authenticated identity which is a member of system:administrators are the right to issue all pts commands, implicit Administer right on all AFS directory ACLs, and the right to set quotas on volumes.

The second kind of administration privilege is obtained via server administration lists, which are contained in a file on each server and which list who is permitted to issue all bos, vos, and backup commands. This is a very powerful privilege inasmuch bos controls the running of all the AFS server processes and configuration data, vos commands control all file data storage, and backup is used to bulk-copy all files from and to the system. The file that contains this administration list is /usr/afs/etc/UserList; during installation, the afsadmin login is added to the UserList file. The file is manipulated with bos commands.

```
$ bos listusers db-one
SUsers are: afsadmin cell hq.firm
$ bos adduser db-one david.admin
$ bos listusers db-one
SUsers are: afsadmin cell hq.firm david.admin
```

Here, the change to the UserList file is made on the system control machine. This machine propagates the architecture-independent AFS configuration files between all AFS servers; therefore, the changed UserList will soon be copied over to db-two, db-three, fs-one, fs-two, and fs-three.

User names can also be removed.

```
$ bos removeuser db-one afsadmin
```

The third kind of administrative privilege is a default mechanism for programs running directly on the AFS servers. Like Kerberos, AFS distrusts desktop clients; all communication from a client must be through an authenticated RPC connection. And like Kerberos servers, AFS servers are distinguished machines that store critical data. Ordinary users should not be permitted to gain access to the servers; the server machines should, in fact, be placed in a controlled environment under strict supervision. There's not much point in claiming high security if the server is in a public location where someone can, at worst, yank a disk drive off the desk and at leisure scan the partitions for interesting data.

These concerns explain why most AFS management is performed through commands run on an administrator's own desktop. The command uses the Kerberos protocol to mutually authenticate with an AFS service. The user's administrative ticket and the service's own credential are used by the Kerberos protocol so that the user is assured that the service belongs to the cell and the service knows that the user has administrative privilege.

But if an AFS administrative command is run on the server itself—a server controlled only by the local operating system's security—that program may well have privileged status even though it has no AFS credentials at all.

Actually, AFS doesn't give up control quite this easily: local authentication mode is permitted only for processes running as UNIX root on an AFS server. To signify that an AFS command is to use the local default administrative privilege, you specify the -localauth option. The command then operates with the server key stored in /usr/afs/local/KeyFile. (See Appendix A for a list of which commands and subcommands support this mode of operation.) With this technique, it is easy to construct certain privileged batch jobs and other operational routines, so long as they are initiated by a root process. Note that because client machines have no KeyFile, there is no -localauth of any sort for regular AFS clients.

The final kind of administrative privilege is used to control Kerberos. The Kerberos system is somewhat special in that a special flag kept by the authentication system itself controls who has administrative control of the database. (This is exactly the same as the public-domain Kerberos software.) When the software is installed, at least one AFS login is initialized with this administration flag, called ADMIN.

Only those logins with the ADMIN flag turned on are permitted to run most kas commands. Even using the examine subcommand to see a Kerberos database entry and what flags are set requires the issuer to be an ADMIN (authenticated users can examine their own entry only).

```
$ kas -admin afsadmin
Administrator's (afsadmin) Password:
kas> examine afsadmin

User data for afsadmin (ADMIN)
   key (0) cksum is 553810536, last cpw: Sat Mar 29 15:31:46 1997
```

```
     password will never expire.
     An unlimited number of unsuccessful authentications is permitted.
     entry never expires.  Max ticket lifetime 25.00 hours.
     last mod on Sat Mar 29 15:32:09 1997 by <none>
     permit password reuse
kas> examine david

User data for david
     key (2) cksum is 2100489361, last cpw: Sat Mar 29 16:08:12 1997
     password will expire: Mon Apr 28 17:08:12 1997
     10 consecutive unsuccessful authentications are permitted.
     The lock time for this user is 34.1 minutes.
     User is not locked.
     entry never expires.  Max ticket lifetime 100.50 hours.
     last mod on Sat Mar 29 16:08:12 1997 by afsadmin
     don't permit password reuse
```

The afsadmin identity has the ADMIN flag set, whereas user david does not. To increase security by delegating administration privileges, remove Kerberos ADMIN privilege from the shared afsadmin login and at the same time create new identities for the select few operators permitted to administer Kerberos.

It is simple to set the ADMIN flag.

```
$ kas -admin afsadmin
Administrator's (afsadmin) Password:
kas> setfields david.admin ADMIN
kas> examine david.admin

User data for david.admin (ADMIN)
     key (0) cksum is 1630388111, last cpw: Sun Mar 30 14:10:36 1997
     password will never expire.
     An unlimited number of unsuccessful authentications is permitted.
     entry never expires.  Max ticket lifetime 25.00 hours.
     last mod on Sun Mar 30 14:18:42 1997 by afsadmin
     permit password reuse
```

Now, when David logs in as david.kadmin, he can run Kerberos administration commands, such as account creation and deletion, but he does not have authority for other AFS operations, such as unlimited access to the file system, or authority to manipulate the AFS server processes.

As long as we have someone left who can administer Kerberos, we can take away ADMIN privilege from afsadmin.

```
kas> setfields afsadmin NOADMIN
```

Note that the ticket lifetime for david.admin is just 25 hours. Earlier, we gave David a personal credential lifetime of 168 hours, equal to one week. This extended limit made it easier for David to do general work all week long without having to reauthenticate with Kerberos. It makes sense to shorten the lifetime of ADMIN privileged tickets, even shorter than 25 hours, just to ensure that no long-lived ticket will accidentally be left around, encouraging dishonest use.

If, during outages or other administrative downtime, you need to turn off authorization setting, you can run the following command.

    $ **bos setauth db-one off**

This command inserts into the directory, /usr/afs/local, an empty file named NoAuth. Running server processes notice the existence of this file and from then on refrain from mutually authenticating the user with the server process. Without mutual authentication, there is no effective checking of who is permitted to run restricted operations such as creating and deleting AFS users. Obviously, turning off authentication is an extraordinary action to take and should be done only when you are installing the system or when there is a complete breakdown in use of AFS, as when the server's secret keys themselves are corrupted. If necessary, you can create the NoAuth file by hand.

Because the contents of the /usr/afs/local directories are usually not propagated among AFS servers, you may need to create this file on all file and database servers to turn off authorization checking cellwide. Additionally, to make sure that all RPC connections between the servers themselves will obey the lack of security, restart the AFS server processes.

    $ **bos restart db-one -all -noauth**

Here we appended one new option, -noauth. Most administration commands permit a -noauth option. This option instructs the command to use an unauthenticated connection to the servers. Because the connection is unauthenticated, no operations requiring restricted authority will be permitted. But if the authorization system is in NoAuth mode or is otherwise broken, using the -noauth option permits commands to complete successfully—as long as the operations are permitted to any user. Now that no authorization checks are being performed, you may see extraneous error messages displayed during the now useless authentication stage.

Cancelling authorization checking is a fundamental breach of the security system for emergency use only.

To turn authorization back on:

```
$ bos setauth db-one on
```

You must perform this operation on all the servers for which authorization checking was turned off. You should also restart all the AFS server processes to ensure that all of their connections are reset.

SERVER MANAGEMENT

In Chapter 3, we learned about the separate processes that run on server machines to create an AFS cell. The primary process is bosserver, a process that manages the real server processes. Through the bos command interface, you can query, shut down, restart, or create new jobs on any AFS server in any cells of your enterprise.

The configuration data for bosserver is kept in the file /usr/afs/local/BosConfig. Entries in this file are normally manipulated with bos commands to create or delete jobs. Though you'll rarely have to examine the file by hand, let's take a quick look at the format.

```
# cat /usr/afs/local/BosConfig
restarttime 11 0 4 0 0
checkbintime 3 0 5 0 0
bnode simple kaserver 1
parm /usr/afs/bin/kaserver
end
bnode simple ptserver 1
parm /usr/afs/bin/ptserver
end
bnode simple vlserver 1
parm /usr/afs/bin/vlserver
end
bnode simple buserver 1
parm /usr/afs/bin/buserver
end
bnode fs fs 1
parm /usr/afs/bin/fileserver
parm /usr/afs/bin/volserver
parm /usr/afs/bin/salvager
end
bnode simple upserver 1
parm /usr/afs/bin/upserver -crypt /usr/afs/etc -clear /usr/afs/bin
end
```

The contents start off with two lines specifying the restart time, that is, the time that all servers on this machine will be gracefully stopped and then restarted, and the checkbin time, the time at which new binaries will be checked and installed. These times are explained later in the chapter.

Next, several bnodes are listed. A *bnode* is a bosserver job entry in the file; it begins with the keyword bnode and finishes with the keyword end. On the line with the bnode keyword, the listed arguments indicate the type of the job, the name of the job, the number 1 or 0 signifying the status, and a final option if needed. A status number of 0 means that the process should not be started or monitored in the future; 1 means to start and continue monitoring.

In general, do not edit this file manually. Because the file is read into bosserver memory only during startup, any changes to the file would require a restart of the process. For normal operations, use the bos suite to contact the bosserver.

When the server is running, if you were to examine its standard UNIX process listing by logging onto the server, you'd see something like:

```
$ ps -ef
     UID    PID  PPID  C    STIME TTY     TIME CMD
. . .
    root   3680     1  0 04:00:45 ?      0:00 /usr/afs/bin/bosserver
    root   4138  3680  0 14:24:32 ?      0:00 /usr/afs/bin/kaserver
    root   4139  3680  0 14:24:32 ?      0:00 /usr/afs/bin/ptserver
    root   4140  3680  0 14:24:32 ?      0:00 /usr/afs/bin/vlserver
    root   4141  3680  0 14:24:32 ?      0:00 /usr/afs/bin/buserver
    root   4144  3680  0 14:24:34 ?      0:00 /usr/afs/bin/upserver
. . .
```

More usually, you would use the bos status command from any client to remotely check on any server's jobs.

```
$ bos status db-one
Instance kaserver, currently running normally.
Instance ptserver, currently running normally.
Instance vlserver, currently running normally.
Instance buserver, currently running normally.
Instance upserver, currently running normally.
$ bos status fs-one
Instance fs, currently running normally.
     Auxiliary status is: file server running.
Instance upclientetc, currently running normally.
Instance upclientbin, currently running normally.
```

The regular status listing, shown as the output to the first `status` command, is a terse description of each job and displays the job name and a status message. Here, all is running normally. For bos `cron` jobs, this output does not mean that the job is actually running, only that the scheduler is ready to run it when the time arrives. Other possible messages are:

- `temporarily enabled`—A job that was started via a `bos startup` command but is not configured to run automatically.
- `temporarily disabled`—A job that was stopped via `bos shutdown` or one disabled because of too many errors.

After this description, there may be another line of information:

- `has core file`—In this case, the job has crashed and `bosserver` has moved the core file to the `/usr/afs/logs` directory. If the job has been restarted successfully, this message will appear in addition to the "currently running normally" message.
- `stopped for too many errors`—The `bosserver` process restarted this job too many times in a short period of time and therefore assumes there is some system error.

File server jobs print out an additional status line, as shown in the second command output.

- `file server running`—The `fileserver` and `volserver` (file server and volume server) processes are running normally.
- `salvaging file system`—the `fileserver` and `volserver` have been disabled temporarily and the AFS partition check program, `salvager`, is running. Once the salvage is done, the `fileserver` and `volserver` are automatically restarted. The salvage process itself is described in the Chapter 10.

There is an additional status for `cron` jobs to indicate whether they are running now or whether they will run in the future:

- `currently executing`—The cron job specified is running.
- `run next Wed Mar 29 02:00:00 1996`—The time when the command is next scheduled to run.

The -long option provides more details on when the process was started, when it last exited, and exactly what command line was used to start the process.

```
$ bos status db-one -long
Instance kaserver, (type is simple) currently running normally.
    Process last started at Sun Mar 30 14:24:32 1997 (2 proc starts)
    Last exit at Sun Mar 30 14:24:32 1997
    Command 1 is '/usr/afs/bin/kaserver'

Instance ptserver, (type is simple) currently running normally.
    Process last started at Sun Mar 30 14:24:32 1997 (2 proc starts)
    Last exit at Sun Mar 30 14:24:32 1997
    Command 1 is '/usr/afs/bin/ptserver'

Instance vlserver, (type is simple) currently running normally.
    Process last started at Sun Mar 30 14:24:32 1997 (2 proc starts)
    Last exit at Sun Mar 30 14:24:32 1997
    Command 1 is '/usr/afs/bin/vlserver'

Instance buserver, (type is simple) currently running normally.
    Process last started at Sun Mar 30 14:24:32 1997 (3 proc starts)
    Last exit at Sun Mar 30 14:24:32 1997
    Command 1 is '/usr/afs/bin/buserver'

Instance upserver, (type is simple) currently running normally.
    Process last started at Sun Mar 30 14:24:32 1997 (2 proc starts)
    Last exit at Sun Mar 30 14:24:32 1997
    Command 1 is '/usr/afs/bin/upserver -crypt /usr/afs/etc -clear /usr/afs/bin'
```

Of particular interest is the number of times the job has been started during this invocation of bosserver and the times the job was last started and last exited. If the job exited abnormally, that time is printed separately.

A related set of subcommands controls bosserver jobs, as listed in Table 9-1.

Most of these subcommands can take one or more job names as arguments. But be careful with stopping database jobs (kaserver, ptserver, vlserver, and bakserver), the AFS system expects that a database server machine (i.e., a machine listed in the CellServDB file) will be running all database processes at once, and there's no way to configure one machine to run a subset of database jobs.

One recommended option to these subcommands, at least when they are run interactively, is -wait, which makes sure that the bos command—a client command to bosserver—waits for confirmation that the stop or start request has completed the operation. We used this option in Chapter 8 to shut down the database servers before archiving the database contents.

Table 9-1   `bosserver` Subcommands

Subcommand	Description
`shutdown`	Temporarily stops a job. The job gracefully shuts down but restarts normally when `bosserver` itself restarts or when the start or startup subcommands are issued.
`startup`	Restarts a job that has been shut down.
`stop`	Not only shuts down a job, but automatically edits the `BosConfig` file so that `bosserver` will not start the job on restarts or with the `startup` subcommand.
`start`	Starts a server job running and, like stop, edits the `config` file so that any future bos restarts will also start the job.
`restart`	Gracefully shuts down a job and then restarts it. The option `-all` causes all jobs on the specified server to restart; the `-bosserver` option causes even the `bosserver` process itself to begin anew.
`delete`	Permanently deletes the job entry from the `config` file. Should normally be preceded by a stop request.

Each AFS server process has its own log file located in the `/usr/afs/logs` directory. When a job is restarted, the corresponding log file for a server process is rotated. Unfortunately, the system does not keep more than one previous file in its rotation. For example, the fileserver log file, `/usr/afs/logs/FileLog` will be closed and renamed to `/usr/afs/logs/FileLog.old` whenever the fileserver restarts. The problem, of course, is that multiple restarts and their related log files will be lost. All that will be left after multiple crashes of a server are the current log file, which will report that all is well, and the previous log, which will report only the very last error and not the problem that precipitated the crashes in the first place.

In fact, the `bosserver` has its own log file. You can augment this log with information on all privileged commands run on a server. The file `/usr/afs/logs/BosLog` would thus provide an audit trail of AFS administration activities. To save this information, add the `-log` option to the `bosserver` command in the server's startup scripts.

As is usual for AFS, there is a bos subcommand that gets and prints out any log, so you need not manually log in to a server machine to read the log files.

```
$ bos getlog fs-one FileLog
Fetching log file 'FileLog'...
Sun Mar 30 14:24:33 1997 File server starting
Sun Mar 30 14:24:35 1997 Partition /vicepa:  attached 15 volumes; 0 volumes not attached
```

```
Sun Mar 30 14:24:36 1997 Partition /vicepb:  attached 7 volumes; 0 volumes not attached
Sun Mar 30 14:24:36 1997 Getting FileServer name...
Sun Mar 30 14:24:36 1997 FileServer host name is 'fs-one'
Sun Mar 30 14:24:36 1997 Getting FileServer address...
Sun Mar 30 14:24:36 1997 FileServer fs-one has address 0xc0a80315 (0xc0a80315 in host byte order)
Sun Mar 30 14:24:36 1997 File Server started Sun Mar 30 14:24:36 1997
Sun Mar 30 14:34:18 1997 fssync: volume 536870955 restored; breaking all call backs
...
```

The options to `getlog` are the server name and the log file name: `BosLog` for the `bosserver` process log, `FileLog` for `fileserver`, `VLLog` for the `vlserver`, `VolserLog` for `volserver`, `SalvageLog` for `salvager`, `BackupLog` for `bakserver`, and `AuthLog` for `ptserver`. However, you can retrieve any named file in the `/usr/afs/logs` subdirectory, so you can see any of the old log files or any other file if you've set up a system to rotate files over a longer period. Because the log files can grow large over time, you should periodically copy each to an archive, compress them, and start a new log.

Another feature of `bosserver`'s management of server jobs is to corral core files. When a UNIX process crashes due to inappropriate memory access, illegal instruction, or whatever, the kernel will create a dump of the process memory image in the process's current working directory and name the resulting file `core`. Since all AFS server jobs run in the `/usr/afs` directory, one process crashing after another would overwrite the core file of the previous crash. When `bosserver` notices that one of its jobs has crashed, it moves the core file to `/usr/afs/logs` and gives it a name based on the job that crashed. So, if `fileserver` crashes, you can expect to find a file `/usr/afs/logs/core.file`. Again, as with log files, `bosserver` retains only the last crash image. While there's not much that can be done with the core file by the average AFS site, if the crash is of unknown origin and not due to your own administrative actions (such as removing a disk while the server is on-line), you should make arrangements with Transarc to send the `core` file to their engineering staff for proper analysis.

Now's the time to more fully explain `restarttime` and `checkbintime`, the first two lines of the config file. Earlier versions of the AFS servers were prone to memory leaks; after running for several days, a server process would keep using up more and more memory in its user address space. To take care of this, `bosserver` was instructed to restart all of the server jobs at a specific time. By default, the restart time is every Sunday morning at 4 a.m. At that time, all running jobs are gracefully shut down, `bosserver` is reexecuted, and all jobs configured to run are restarted. This plan is supposed to keep the entire system more available by reducing delays due to job crashes. Of course, the solution itself causes a certain amount of server downtime. If you feel that this downtime is worth the peace of mind of not running out of process memory, at least stagger the default restart times for different servers so that all the servers don't bounce at the same time. Nowadays, though, the common wisdom is that the memory leak problems have been fixed, and many sites run `bosserver` with a restart time set to `never`.

More usefully, when new binaries are installed into the system, `bosserver` can be told when to check for them. `checkbintime` is the time at which the latest restart time of a server job is compared to the modification timestamp of the job's executable program file. If the file is newer than the server's last restart, then the process is restarted. By default, this check is performed at 5 a.m. every day. This binary check time can be set to any time and to either every day or any given day of the week. This feature is normally used as part of the automatic process of installing new binaries.

UPDATING AFS BINARIES

To help with the installation of new binaries, `bos` includes a subcommand that automatically copies over program updates and manages the process of deprecating the old versions. When given access to Transarc's file tree, the complete process looks like this:

```
$ cd /afs/transarc.com/product
$ cd afs/3.4a/sparc_sunos55
$ cd root.server/usr/afs/bin
$ bos install db-one buserver
bos: installed file buserver
```

Here, we use the global AFS tree to get at Transarc's product distribution area, then we change directory to a specific version of `afs` compiled for the Sun Solaris 2.5 platform. (We assume that we're authenticated as a user in Transarc's cell and are permitted access to that product.) There, we can see all of the files for the latest release and run the `bos` command to install specific files, in this case, new versions of the file server programs. The fact that we're getting the binaries directly from Transarc via AFS itself is simply showing off for this example. If the files were received on tape in the mail, we'd just as simply read them off the tape and install the programs from wherever they were unloaded.

The machine given as the argument to the `bos install` subcommand is chosen quite carefully. It is the binary distribution machine for the platform being installed, Sun Solaris 2.5. Recall the layout of our hypothetical cell as shown in Figure 3-2; the machine db-one was designated the binary distribution machine for Solaris and is running the update server process for the /usr/afs/bin directory, and the machines db-two, fs-one, and fs-two are its update clients. The machine db-three is the binary distribution machine for HP-UX executables and is also running the update server process for its /usr/afs/bin, and the machine fs-three is its only update client.

Use the bos install only to install new binaries into the /usr/afs/bin directory on running AFS servers. Of course, the binary that is presumably running still needs access to its program text, so it would not be appropriate to overwrite the file. Instead, bosserver renames the current program file and installs the new version with the correct name. Thus, when the binary check time (checkbintime) comes around, bosserver will notice the new version and restart the server. The renamed program file is still available as a backup in case the new version is drastically wrong. You can see the old version of the files in the /usr/afs/bin directory along with the new versions.

```
$ ls -l /usr/afs/bin/bu*
-rwxr-xr-x   1 root      staff        487516 Mar 30 14:52 buserver
-rwxr-xr-x   1 root      staff        487516 Jul  5  1996 buserver.BAK
```

This renaming scheme suggests that the backup version is kept around forever. In fact, when a new binary is being installed, any existing backup version is renamed as an old version and any existing old version is simply thrown away. Therefore, only the two previous generations of program files for a given process are kept. If you were to manually emulate the results of bos install, the process would be:

```
$ cd /usr/afs/bin
$ rm buserver.OLD
$ mv buserver.BAK buserver.OLD
$ mv buserver buserver.BAK
$ cp /afs/transarc.com/product/afs/.../buserver  buserver
```

Figure 9-1 shows the process graphically.

These actions permit the new version of fileserver or other server processes to be installed without disrupting the running of the current version. If you need to install new binaries immediately, you can run this install procedure and then follow it with an explicit bos restart command.

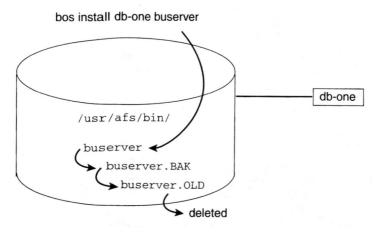

bos install db-one buserver

/usr/afs/bin/

db-one

buserver

buserver.BAK

buserver.OLD

deleted

Figure 9-1 `bos install` Process

If the binaries are installed on a binary distribution server, the update-server process will make similar changes to each of its configured update clients. Again, normally, at the next time to check for new binaries, the client machine's bosserver will restart the server processes. If you need to restart the processes immediately, run the bos restart command upon those servers but first make sure that the update process has finished distributing the binaries. The bos getdate command prints out the modification timestamps of selected binaries and any .BAK and .OLD versions of the binaries. When it is obvious by inspecting the times that the new version is available, it is safe to run the restart subcommand.

In case of a problem with the new binaries, you can use the bos uninstall command to roll back the transaction to the previous release. When the command is run, bosserver deletes the current program version, renames the .BAK version to the suffix-less file name, and renames the .OLD version to .BAK. Again, bosserver will discover the new program file at the binary check time and restart the process then; use the bos restart command to run the current version immediately.

This system is designed to be bulletproof and to provide the functionality needed to run a large, production cell. But the use of automatic restart times may seem a bit cocky to some. Even after testing the new versions of a program in a test cell or on an isolated file server, many administrators will feel squeamish about trusting a product turnover to an automated system. So remember that there's no need to use the system if you don't want to. If not, you can delete the upserver and upclient jobs and manually shut down file and database servers, copy over the new files, and restart the processes. In a cell with just a few servers, this choice is entirely reasonable.

If you use the automatic system, you may end up with many .BAK and .OLD files in every server's /usr/afs/bin/ directory. If these files take too much valuable disk space and you're confident that the server jobs are running correctly, you can use yet another bos subcommand to delete the previous versions of any program.

```
$ bos prune db-one -old -bak
$ ls -l /usr/afs/bin/bu*
-rwxr-xr-x   1 root      other      487516 Mar 30 14:52 buserver
```

As you can see, .BAK and .OLD versions can be deleted as needed. In this case, we're depending on the update server and client processes to take care of deleting the versions on the other machines.

To automatically delete core files from the /usr/afs/logs directory, you can use the -core option to the prune subcommand. Files in this directory are not managed by the update jobs, so you'll have to prune each server, database, and file individually, as needed.

To aid per-server management, the bos system has a built-in remote execution ability. Many organizations prefer to deny access to server machines for all users, allowing only console logins so as to increase the security of the system. The exec subcommand can be used by authorized users of AFS as follows:

```
$ bos exec db-one   /etc/reboot
```

The first argument is the server machine, and the second argument is a command to execute. The intention is to allow properly authenticated users to reboot the server or perform any other administration without their having to log on to the server directly.

JOB NOTIFICATION

When you are creating bosserver jobs, you can assign each a custom-designed notification script. If the job terminates, this script will run and can execute any commands that you desire. Most often, the script is used to send an e-mail or a beep to an administrator that the job stopped. As bosserver usually restarts any jobs which abnormally terminate, a single restart may just require a short e-mail notification; if the job is continually crashing, a more urgent alarm or beep could be sent.

The script is supplied as an argument to the -notifier option during the creation of the job.

```
$ bos create db-one kaserver simple /usr/afs/bin/kaserver -notifier /usr/afs/
bin/local-notifier
```

Information concerning the job that stopped is written to the standard input of the notifier program as a series of simple ASCII name-value pairs, one per line. Table 9-2 lists the available names with explanations of their meaning and an example value.

As the notifier program runs, it must read its standard input and store these names and values until the pipeline is closed by bosserver. The bosserver parent process will wait for the notifier to finish, so if any lengthy processing of the data needs to be done, it is best to execute a new process and allow bosserver to resume its monitoring job. A simple Perl language notifier skeleton looks like this:

```perl
#! /usr/local/bin/perl5

while (<>) {
        chop;
        s/://;
        my($name,$value)=split;
        next if ! $name;
        $JobInfo{$name}=$value;
}

$msg = $JobInfo{'name'}." was started again. ";
$msg .= "It exited with a return code of ".$JobInfo{'errorCode'};
system("echo $msg | mail afs-admins");

if ($JobInfo{'rsCount'} gt 5) {
        system("echo $msg | beep  on-call-admin");
}
```

This script is used to e-mail information about job restarts to a preset list of AFS administrators. If the job restarted more than five times, then the current on-call administrator would be beeped. While any unusual restart of an AFS server process needs to be investigated, the whole point of bosserver is that if a simple restart is all that is required, then bosserver can do that on its own and the administrators need not be beeped in the middle of the night.

Using the information prepared by bosserver, you can fairly easily determine if a job's termination is a serious event or not. And besides logging

Table 9-2 Names and Descriptions of Notifier Program Values

Name/Sample Value	Description
name: kaserver	The keyword name is used for the instance name of the bosserver job. This is not the name of the command, although for most jobs, the name is based on the job's command name.
rsTime: 859743005	The first time that the job was started during this run of bosserver. Like most internal time values in UNIX, this value equals the number of seconds since the start of day on January 1st, 1970. Most programming libraries have routines that can convert this value to a readable string of characters.
rsCount: 1	The number of times that the job has been restarted during this run of bosserver.
procStartTime: 859746941	The time that this job last started. Again, this is a UNIX epoch value.
procStarts: 2	The number of times that the job has been started. Note that this number, the total number of starts, can be greater than the rsCount; rsCount will not include starting up after a crash.
lastAnyExit: 1	The number of times the job exited for any reason.
lastErrorExit: 1	The number of times the job exited due to an error.
errorCode: -1	The return code of the process after its last exit.
errorSignal: 3	The last UNIX signal that terminated the process.
lastErrorName: fs	The name of the job that failed last.
goal: 1	Indicates whether bosserver was trying to keep the job running (a value of 1) or not running (a value of 0).
comLine: /usr/afs/bin/ kaserver	The complete command line used to run the bosserver job.
coreName: /usr/afs/ logs/core.kas	The name of the core file that was created, if any.
pid: 1433	The UNIX process identification number of the job when it was running.
lastExit: -1	The last return code from the process.
lastSignal: 3	The last UNIX signal that terminated the process.

appropriate information and sending messages to the on-call staff, the notifier script is a good place to try and save server log files through a longer rotation than the default of one restart.

KEYFILE MANAGEMENT

An AFS server key is essentially a password generated for use by the server processes themselves. These keys are initially created during the AFS installation phase and are stored in two places: in the Kerberos server database, under the principal name `afs`, and in a simple file on the server, `/usr/afs/etc/KeyFile`.

To keep things secure, neither the `KeyFile` nor the Kerberos database stores the plain text of the server password but stores an encrypted version. Because both the database and the simple `KeyFile` can be attacked by outsiders, it is crucial that all AFS servers be kept in secure locations and that they be isolated from sources of intrusion.

During a user's authentication process (through `klog` or Transarc's `/bin/login` program), a credential is created and associated with that user. When administrative commands or client file operations are executed, that credential is presented to a server for inspection. But this credential does not prove the user's identity simply with some clear text, which could potentially be forged. Instead, the identity is encrypted. A general AFS server has no way to read the credential to see what's inside; it can only pass the credential to a Kerberos server and request that the token be validated. A Kerberos server can do this only because it knows that the user credential was encrypted with a server key: a positive response from the Kerberos server therefore suffices to prove mutual authentication between the AFS server and the user.

It should be clear that the Kerberos database and the `KeyFile` must contain exactly the same encrypted key. This would not be much of an issue if the key never changed. But Transarc recommends that an administrator change the key regularly to reduce the window of opportunity in which an outsider could crack the encrypted version.

The authentication process uses DES 56-bit encryption. In 1997, thousands of workstations working collectively managed to crack a file that used this encryption—but that effort took several months. As long as you change your `KeyFile` more often than that, say, once a month, you should feel secure that your Kerberos systems (and therefore your cell) are safe from external infiltration.

The problem facing administrators is that as keys change, one or more servers could potentially have the wrong version of the key which, when presented to the Kerberos server would be assumed to be wrong, thereby denying access to files or procedures.

Following the correct procedures when changing keys is essential in keeping the kerberos server and `KeyFile` the same. To check if the keys are the same, run the following two commands (you must be authenticated as a user on the server's `UserList` and with Kerberos ADMIN privileges).

```
$ bos listkeys db-one
key 0 has cksum 553810536
Keys last changed on Sat Mar 29 08:36:16 1997.
All done.
$ kas examine afs -admin afsadmin
Administrator's (afsadmin) Password:

User data for afs
   key (0) cksum is 553810536, last cpw: Sat Mar 29 16:33:59 1997
   password will never expire.
   An unlimited number of unsuccessful authentications is permitted.
   entry never expires.  Max ticket lifetime 100.00 hours.
   last mod on Sat Mar 29 16:33:59 1997 by afsadmin
   permit password reuse
```

The two commands display the key's checksum rather than the characters that make up the key's encrypted string to further decrease the chance of attacks on the key. By comparing the checksums, you can see that the keys are the same.

The key encrypts certain pieces of data as the data travels on the network:

- The keys as they are installed with the `addkey` and `listkey` subcommands.
- Kerberos login and password changes.
- Kerberos administration commands. A `kas` interactive session is completely encrypted.
- The Kerberos database, which is encrypted during Ubik transfers and updates.
- Textual configuration files, during which the Update server encrypts transfers between servers. These are the files in `/usr/afs/etc`. The AFS product sold outside the United States of America does not permit this particular feature, although the other, purely authentication-oriented, encryptions are permitted.

CHANGING THE CELL NAME

An AFS cell name is normally used as part of the password encryption process. The name is not directly stored in any of the various databases, but if it changes, it is impossible to compare a user's password against the version in the Kerberos database. Thus, when changing a cell's name, you must assign new passwords to each user. Whether this is feasible depends on the size of the cell and the administrative or political control you have of your users.

If you choose to change the cell name, you will need to change the name in all the `CellServDB` and `ThisCell` files on all the clients and servers. It will be best to start with the servers: shut down all servers, make the change on the system control machine, install a new password for the `afs` principal (using NoAuth mode) and extract a new `KeyFile`, just as you did during the installation of the first server. You can then copy this `KeyFile` to all other servers along with the other configuration files, and then restart them.

Because the local cell name is copied into the kernel when a client cache manager starts, you'll also have to reboot each client after changing each `CellServDB` file to enable authenticated access to the new cell name.

Finally, if you're following the standard AFS cell layout, you'll have to replace your second-level path name: change `/afs/oldcell.com` to `/afs/newcell.com`. The implications of this procedure are that any external site that has mounted your cell via the public `CellServDB` file will need to have its remote cell mount point changed. And any absolute file names in your applications or administration scripts will have to be changed to use the new path.

As you can imagine, for large cells with many servers and users, this process is so laborious as to make the endeavor worthwhile only in special circumstances.

DATABASE SERVERS

Since there are usually only a few AFS database servers in a cell, their administration needs are modest. It's been suggested that these servers be distinct from the file servers so that administration of file servers can be done without interrupting database queries from clients. The hardware needed for a database server is minimal, in terms of processing power, although it's beneficial to have a sufficient amount of memory to permit the database processes to run at full speed.

When you are adding or deleting database servers, the only item to keep in mind is that the static `CellServDB` file must be updated on all database servers and eventually on all clients. You can use the AFS server's `upserver` and `upclient` processes to easily propagate this file to all servers, but you must individually restart each database process so that changes to this file are noticed. To restart the processes, simply run `bos shutdown` and then `bos` `restart` on the database servers. As a new Ubik election will normally be taking place, there will be an outage lasting a few minutes during which updates to the databases cannot be processed.

Because the databases are so important to the running of an AFS cell, once a computer has been set up to manage the database processes, you'll be tempted to just leave the machine alone.

Upgrading the operating system on these machines is not difficult, but you must take care to keep the databases intact. Let's next examine the steps needed to perform an operating system upgrade, say from SunOS 4.1.3 to Solaris 2.5.

1. Check that you have a copy of the AFS binaries for the new version of the operating system and the desired hardware platform. The version number of the AFS binaries should match the version running in the rest the cell.

    The release notes provided by Transarc with the binaries will discuss which combination of releases will work together, but you should reduce the risk of any incompatibility by using the same AFS version throughout the cell.

2. Run a `bos status -long` command to display exactly which AFS jobs are running. After the upgrade, you can use this information to recreate the cell's server infrastructure.

3. Assuming that there is more than one database server in the cell, issue `bos` commands to shut down the server.

    Because of the Ubik database protocol, the remaining server processes will notice the unavailability of this machine's databases, and, if necessary, elect a new master sync site.

4. While AFS database process can control which server is the master automatically, the update server, which makes sure that binaries and configuration files are kept up to date throughout the cell, is manually configured. Ensure that one of the remaining servers is an update server, specifically for the text-based configuration files. If necessary, reset the other update clients so that they understand the name of the new server.

5. Now, install the new operating system release on the server.

    There's no need to worry about saving the data in the AFS databases because that data is already replicated on the other servers.

6. Once the system has been upgraded, install the AFS binaries into the `/usr/afs` directory.

7. Just as you did during the initial cell set up, start the `bosserver` process and recreate the jobs previously installed on this machine.

First, restart an update client task. This task will automatically copy over the correct set of configuration files, such as the AFS secret Key-File, the `CellServDB` list, and the `UserList` file from the designated update server. It may take up to five minutes for this process to wake up and perform the file transfers. If you don't want to use the update client/server system, you can copy over these files manually.

When the configuration files are correct, restart the database processes. These jobs will start contacting the other database servers in the cell, so the database files themselves will be propagated from one of the other servers to the upgraded machine. Again, a Ubik election will take place and a new master sync site may be chosen, but these activities occur automatically and mostly transparently to users of the cell.

That's it. Because in this example the machine is just a database server, there was never any file service outage in the cell. At worst, there was only a short prohibition against write requests to the databases, such as adding or changing users or groups membership.

Here's another example. If, rather than upgrading the operating system, you are upgrading the hardware platform, the process is much the same. Again, you'll need to ensure that you have the correct AFS binaries for the new platform; the same caution concerning mixing versions of AFS applies. The luxury of a hardware upgrade is that you might be able to install the new hardware system alongside the soon-to-be obsolete system. If so, the changeover process could be much faster. You can copy the relevant configuration files over manually, turn off the old system, reset the IP address and host name of the new system, and then reboot the new system. When the database server processes and update client restart, the relevant data will propagate to the new system as detailed above.

The volume location database is also in /usr/afs/db and is the pair of files vldb.DB0 and vldb.DBSYS1. Unlike the protection, Kerberos, or backup databases, this database can be reconstructed from existing data. After all, it really is only a central repository for the information about which volumes exist on which servers. That information can be rebuilt by examining all of the file servers—indeed, that rebuilding is exactly what the vos subcommands syncserv and syncdb do. A fearless AFS administrator can use this fact to

restore a muddled database by simply deleting the existing database and running the volume synchronization commands.

```
$ vos syncvldb fs-one
VLDB synchronized with state of server fs-one
$ vos syncvldb fs-two
VLDB synchronized with state of server fs-two
```

FILE SERVERS

Usually an AFS cell will have many file server systems spread around the enterprise. Besides the general management of user requests, administrators will
want to spend some portion of their day making sure that these file servers are
working correctly and that they have the right set of volumes stored on them.

When you install a new hard-drive on the server, all you need do is use the
native operating system commands to mount it on a directory named /vice-
pxx, where xx is any one or two lowercase alphabetic characters in the range of
a to z and aa to iv. To make the fileserver notice the new disks, restart the
bos fs job.

The vice partitions managed by the fileserver and volserver processes contain standard UNIX file systems. That is AFS simply uses standard
mechanisms to store and manipulate data on the disk; the underlying disk file
system type could be almost any vendor-specialized file system. Some vendors support disk partitions of up to 2 gigabytes only. Other operating systems can handle larger partitions, or intermediary software may provide
virtual partitions on top of the disk surface. Sun's Online Disk Suite™ or
IBM's Journal File System™ can both be set up to deliver large partitions out
of smaller disks, and they additionally provide mirroring, striping, or other
RAID-style redundancies.

Although AFS supports vice partitions greater than 2 gigabytes, a single
file must be less than 2 gigabytes in size. Volumes greater than 2 gigabytes are
only partially supported: while residing on a large partition, a volume can grow
to greater than 2 gigabytes, but, at this point, several volume operations, such as
dumping, restoring, moving, or replicating the volume, are not supported.

Because the AFS file and volume server processes use the vendor's file
system as the basis for partition management, you can use other standard tools
to manipulate the disks. A classic UNIX tool, dd, is often used to move a vice
partition from one disk to another. This tool simply reads one file and writes to
another; if the files are disk devices, dd performs the equivalent of a disk copy.

To make sure that this operational hack works, you should ensure that the disk is quiescent by turning off the AFS servers, or better, by bringing the system into single-user mode. When trying to resurrect data from a dead disk, you may find that the command fails when reading a certain block. At this point, you may be able to use some options to dd to skip over a certain number of blocks during the reading and writing phases. When performing these operations, you'll have more success if the read-from and written-to disk partitions have the same geometries and are attached to equivalent operating systems.

When choosing disks and devices for file storage, it's probably best to stay one step behind the latest and densest drives. There's not much point in putting all of your file data behind a single controller, armature, and spindle, as opposed to purchasing a few smaller disks which will tend to spread out the load. And when partitioning the disks, it makes sense to have one partition for each spindle because AFS volumes perform their own logical division of the disk surface. Having more than one partition for a single disk may be useful in certain circumstances but more often will just add administrative overhead.

AFS volume replication takes care of redundant access to read-only data. Because of this (and the ever-present fact of client-side caching), the read-only copies need not be stored on particularly high-powered or fault tolerant hardware; on the contrary, second-rate or hand-me-down servers can prove extremely cost effective and yet still support a large number of clients. This is one of the scaling attributes of AFS. But we're still left with the read-write data—home directories, development areas, source repositories, and the masters for read-only volumes. These volumes should be grouped together when possible on hardware better designed to support precious data.

Either a software or hardware RAID solution works well for these read-write volumes. Software systems like Sun's Solstice DiskSuite™ or IBM's Logical Volume Manager enable administrators to mirror or stripe reads and writes to multiple disks. As for AFS, it will be given access to a metadisk and will dutifully record and report its data there, while in the background, furious activity will be taking place to duplicate the data. When a disk fails, the operating system drivers will keep the read-write data available with perhaps only a small performance penalty.

The problem with software solutions to highly-available disk storage is that it depends on a single, running operating system, more often than not, a single CPU. A hardware RAID disk may provide some better data availability characteristics but will be similarly dependent on a single AFS file server's reliability. Still, either software or hardware RAID is better than none.

Adding a file server to a cell is a simple process because the only dynamic configuration occurs when a volume creation or move command installs a file server's location into the volume location database. Unlike the case with database servers, there is no ongoing election process nor need to inform other servers or clients of file server addresses in the CellServDB file. Once you copy over the AFS binaries and static configuration files to a new file server, you can load the AFS kernel module and create a bos fs job so that the trilogy of fileserver, volserver, and salvager are available to run, and an upclient job, to enable configuration files to be updated on this file server.

Now, you can create volumes on the file server. This action automatically installs the volume's named and location in the volume location database. Once you mount the volumes into the enterprisewide AFS namespace, clients will query the VLDB to find the contents of the new volume on the new server.

Removing file servers is also easy. First, of course, you may want to delete or move the volumes stored on the file server's disks. Since the only connection to the server is a set of records in the volume location database to the file server, in extreme circumstances you can simply turn off the file server and delete the VLDB records one by one with the vos delentry command.

This description gives you a hint as to what must be done if you need to move disks around from one server to another to repair some machine disaster. After you move the survivor disks from the dead server to a living server, run the VLDB synchronization commands: syncserv to delete entries in the VLDB for the volumes no longer served by the dead machine and syncvldb to add in the entries for the disk newly added to the living server.

A more realistic sequence of commands for moving a disk from a dead server to another server is:

1. Stop the source bosserver jobs and halt the machine.
2. Remove the disk from the source file server.
3. Stop the destination bosserver jobs and halt the machine.
4. Install the disk.
5. Reboot the destination file server.
6. Ensure the fileserver job has restarted.
7. Salvage the newly installed disk if necessary to check that all the volumes are OK.
8. Run vos syncvldb to add in the new volume entries to the VLDB.
9. Run vos syncserv to remove volume entries from VLDB for volumes no longer on the source server.

This sequence of operations demonstrates the benefit of having database server processes on separate machines from the file servers; by separating the functionality, you can increase the uptime for the service as a whole. Although during the above command sequence, one file server was out of commission, all the database servers and file servers were still available for read and write operations.

Upgrading a file server's operating system is a process much like that described above for database servers. The additional issues are that during the installation of the new operating system, you should take the trouble to disconnect the AFS `vice` partition disks until you have completed the upgrade and replaced the vendor-supplied `fsck` program with the Transarc version. Once you're certain you have the correct `fsck` and AFS configuration files installed, reconnect the disks and restart `bosserver` and other jobs. Since the volume location data will be exactly the same as before the upgrade, the AFS cell should be able to function without a tedious series of VLDB synchronizations.

Retiring a server or its disks can be a much less troublesome affair. It's a simple matter to use the `vos move` command to move all volumes from the retiring system to other machines. Once all the volumes have been moved, there's no information in the VLDB or any other database pointing to the disk or machine. As we've seen, file servers aren't really attached to the cell by any intrinsic configuration—they've just been told by an AFS command to store a volume's set of files. Once the volumes have been moved off, no other cell management is necessary.

Unfortunately, unless you've been brutally strict with regard to volume location planning, it is easy to wind up with partitions containing all sorts of volumes. As you go through each volume in the disk or partition and consider how to move each type of volume, follow these prescriptions:

- If the volume is a read-write, it can be simply moved. If there was a backup volume on the source disk, it will be deleted. You will probably want to create a new backup volume on the new disk when the move is complete.
- If the volume has a read-only on the source disk, remove that version from the volume's list of read-only sites and add the destination site to the volume site list. Once the volume is moved, re-released it.
- If the volume is a read-only with no read-write on the disk, the site list for the volume must be updated. Add the new destination site to the list, re-release the volume to update the new site, and remove the old read-only site with the `vos remove` command. If the new destination site hap-

pens to be the location for the read-write master, make sure that there's no preexisting read-only volume—it should be zapped so that the re-release creates a read-only clone.

While the listed steps are wearisome to implement, for the most part there will be no loss of access to any data due to the implementation of volume moving and the AFS protocol for replicated data.

SALVAGER DATA

The salvager job is primarily used to recover from minor corruptions of the file server's vice partitions, but some other options that are available might be used more regularly to extract information from the server's volumes.

A common question asked by AFS administrators is, how do I find out where a volumes is mounted in the file system?. The somewhat surprising answer is that AFS does not explicitly track this information. The simple reason is that when an fs mkm command is run to create a connection between a file system path name and a volume name, this information is stored in only the file system itself, that is, on a disk attached to some AFS file server. Because of this, and because an AFS namespace is a usually quite broad, it pays to strictly enforce your volume naming and mount point conventions.

As the only place in AFS where this information is stored is in the file system itself, some command must read the entire namespace or vice partition data and report on any mount points encountered. As of AFS 3.4, the salvager has supported an option, -showmount , which logs a line to the SalvageLog file of all mount points it finds in a partition or volume. You can run the salvager in stand-alone mode as follows:

```
# /usr/afs/bin/salvager -showmounts -partition /vicepa -nowrite
# cat /usr/afs/logs/SalvageLog
@(#)Base configuration afs3.4 5.00
03/30/97 15:39:17 STARTING AFS SALVAGER 2.4 (/usr/afs/bin/salvager -showmounts -partition /vicepa)
03/30/97 15:39:27 Scanning inodes on device /dev/rdsk/c0t1d0s4...
03/30/97 15:39:40 In volume 536870912 (root.afs) found mountpoint ./hq.firm to '#root.cell.'
03/30/97 15:39:40 In volume 536870912 (root.afs) found mountpoint ./.hq.firm to '%root.cell.'
03/30/97 15:39:40 In volume 536870918 (root.cell) found mountpoint ./tmp to '#cell.tmp.'
03/30/97 15:39:40 In volume 536870918 (root.cell) found mountpoint ./user to '#cell.user.'
...
```

Since we're interested only in auditing the system, we add the -nowrite option to inhibit any attempted salvaging. See Chapter 10 for more details on using the salvager to debug AFS disk problems.

Another frequent audit request is to determine all the `setuid` or `setgid` executables in the system. You can use a `find` program for this task, but `salvager` includes an option, `-showsuid`, to report such files to the log just as `-showmount` displays the mount points.

NETWORKING SUPPORT

It is common now for computers, especially servers, to be configured with more than one network interface. Sometimes this configuration is done to permit alternate routes to the network, and other times, to provide different bandwidth capacities for different applications. These multihomed machines often cause problems with some software that assumes only a single network address per system. The current release of AFS, 3.4a, provides support for file servers with multiple interfaces, but does not support multihomed database servers. This is perhaps another reason to segregate the two sets of services.

Earlier versions of AFS relied on the one-to-one relationship between network addresses and servers by using the address as an index in several internal databases. With more than one address, that relationship would not work, so now each file server is provided with a new, AFS-only identity guaranteed to be unique. When the 3.4a version of the `fileserver` process starts up, it registers one or more local network interfaces with the cell's volume location database and then caches that data in a file, `/usr/afs/local/sysid`. The system can store up to 16 such interfaces.

This system identification file contains a unique magic number for the file server and a list of the network interfaces available. This file needs no particular administration because all the information is managed automatically. If any of the IP addresses on the server are changed, added, or deleted, a simple restart of the `fileserver` process is all that is needed to bring the multihome information block up to date. Managing address changes is an improvement on earlier versions of AFS which required an administrator to run the `vos changeaddr` command manually. Now, this change happens on restart and ensures that the VLDB knows all of the available interfaces to get to a file server's data.

Although this file is maintained by AFS, there were problems with early revisions of the 3.4a release: If the file `/usr/afs/local/sysid` was copied from one machine to another (for example, when one installed a new server by copying the files in `/usr/afs` from a running server), the registration process could cause corruption of the VLDB. The current releases no longer have these problems. Nevertheless, when administering file servers, do not copy any data in the /usr/afs/local directories between machines. If you suspect a problem, check the /usr/afs/logs/VLLog file on the volume location servers; the database server will log a message there if it finds a problem with duplicate IP addresses or other sysid file inconsistencies.

The result of this registration process is that the VLDB knows about all of the interfaces available on all of the servers. When a client is searching for file data and queries a volume location server, the volume location server sends not just a list of servers, but a full list of all the IP addresses from which the volume data (read-write, read-only, or backup) can be retrieved. The client cache manager then performs as it always has, by using that list to find an available server and getting at the file data.

Also, cache manager file server preferences work perfectly with this arrangement. If a volume is stored on a file server with two IP addresses, each address can be given its own numeric preference. For example, the client systems that archive volume data to tape can be told to prefer to use the high-speed interfaces of a file server. Not only will these systems then utilize an optimized connection to the server without affecting the rest of the network, but should the high-speed link fail, they will automatically fail over to any other available network.

From the server point of view, the fileserver process knows about its interfaces from the beginning, so if responses to a client's request on one interface fail, the server will use one of its other interfaces. Since clients now understand that servers can have multiple network connections, there will be no confusing different IP addresses with different servers.

Because of the robustness of the Kerberos-authenticated access controls in AFS, many organizations permit remote network access to their internal cell. AFS uses specific ports for different RPC requests. The UDP port numbers used are listed in Table 9-3.

For access to an AFS cell through a firewall, certain combinations of these ports must be opened up for network transfer. Since the underlying protocol, Rx, uses the UDP flavor of IP, any TCP packets or fragments on the above listed ports can immediately be discarded. An IP packet holds the value of the source and destination ports in its first few bytes. But these packets are susceptible to fragmentation during their transit across the Internet, so IP fragments that are part of a packet going to or coming from a selection of the above listed ports must be permitted through the firewall. You can be quite selective about the exact ports permitted through the firewall depending on the services you want to support.

Table 9-3 UDP Network Port Usage for AFS Processes

Port	Machine Type	Process
7000	file server	fs
7001	client	afsd (for callbacks)
7002	database server	ptserver
7003	database server	vlserver
7004	database server	kaserver
7005	file server	volserver
7007	server	bosserver
7008	server	upserver
7009	AFS/NFS gateway	–
7021	backup server	buserver
7025-7032+	backup tape coordinator	butc
7101	clients/servers	xstat

To support external clients accessing public (unauthenticated) areas of your AFS cell, you should, at a minimum, permit UDP protocol IP packets (and fragments) that access the following port pairs in either direction.

External Client IP Port	Internal Server IP Port	Purpose
7001	7000	File access
7001	7003	Volume location lookup

Authenticated access will require that the cell's Kerberos servers are visible:

External Client IP Port	Internal Server IP Port
7000-7009	7004

Other ports may be needed by various client programs, such as vos and pts, but are not necessary for straightforward file access.

NFS-AFS GATEWAYS

Clients for which Transarc does not offer a port of AFS can still access the file system via an NFS gateway. With the appropriately loaded kernel module on an AFS client (offered as a standard part of the AFS package), a client can export the /afs directory to NFS clients. So, using a sort of transitive property for file system protocols, an NFS client can request data from an NFS server, which, if it is set up as an AFS client, would then request the specific data from the AFS servers. The AFS protocol response would be repackaged as an NFS packet and then delivered to the NFS client. Figure 9-2 shows how the gateway acts as an AFS client and an NFS server.

Concerning file data access, this system works well and the machine in middle can even be an AFS server so long as it is also configured as an AFS client. However, problems arise with the need for authenticated access to the AFS system. Because the NFS client is, in this case, a system for which there is no AFS port, there is no AFS module that can be used as a store for the Kerberos tokens used as an authentication credential. Therefore, we must do some extra work.

The critical issue is whether the NFS client is one of the supported AFS architectures. Most likely it is not, for if it were, it would simply have the AFS

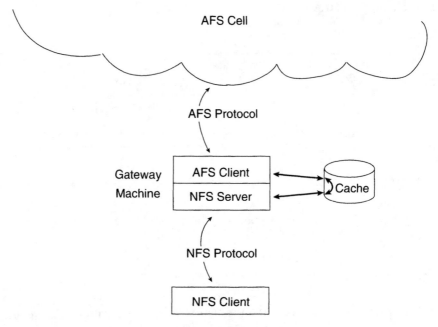

Figure 9-2   NFS-AFS Gateway Architecture

client code loaded at boot. If the client does have access to AFS command binaries of the correct architecture it may still need NFS-AFS gateway services. In this case, the translation and authentication issues are much simpler.

Either way, a couple of points about this system should be made: 1) only NFS client access to the AFS file namespace is supported; 2) there is no way for an NFS server to make its data visible anywhere under /afs on an AFS client. (Apart from not seeing NFS files in the /afs tree, an AFS client can access other NFS files anywhere else in its local namespace).

When dealing with NFS clients that belong to an unsupported AFS client architecture, you must ensure that the gateway is running NFS server processes and has /afs (or a subdirectory) in its list of exported file systems. Once AFS is running, use the exportafs subcommand to define some options.

```
# fs exportafs nfs on
'nfs' translator is enabled with the following options:
        Running in convert owner mode bits to world/other mode
        Running in no 'passwd sync' mode
        Only mounts to /afs allowed
```

You can set the following options:

- Mode bit conversion—Because AFS files are not concerned with the top six bits of the UNIX permission rights (these bits are overridden by the access control lists), the question remains how to tidy up the permissions as seen by the NFS client. The gateway machine can either convert (which means, make a copy of) the user permission bits into the group and other bits or not convert and leave them precisely as they are stored in AFS.
- UID check mode—Because the NFS client is obviously not running AFS client code, NFS users cannot authenticate to AFS on their desktop. To gain AFS credentials, the user must log in to the gateway and use the knfs command (described below) which associates a credential with the NFS client user's numeric identity. The problem here is how to perform the association if the NFS client has a mapping of users to numeric identities that is different from the gateway machine's mapping. If the set of users and their identities is the same, then the two password maps can be set to sync mode so that users can associate their own identity only with an AFS token. If the set of users or their identities are different, then users must be permitted to associate a credential with any numeric identity.
- Submounts—The gateway administrator can decide whether to permit

clients to mount on the NFS client machine either the /afs directory only or any subdirectory to which access is permitted.

The NFS client machine can then simply run the NFS client mount command to enable access. Here, a UNIX client mounts /afs from the gateway (which happens to be one of our AFS file servers) onto the local namespace:

```
# mount fs-one:/afs /afs
```

Users on the NFS client can now begin to access the AFS namespace.

```
$ cd /afs
$ ls
hq.firm  transarc.com
```

Although users can access the namespace, there is no credential on the local machine they can use to access secure areas of the file system. In this case, users authenticate by separately logging in to the gateway machine, obtaining normal AFS client tokens, for example with the klog program, and then exporting those tokens with the knfs command. This command associates particular Kerberos credentials with an NFS client. The association can either be fixed to a single UNIX identity on a single NFS client, or it can be assigned to all users on the NFS client. This latter case is most useful when the NFS client does not have a built-in concept of user identities, for example, personal computers running MS-DOS® or MS Windows.

```
$ klog david
Password:
$ knfs client2 -id 1235
```

Here, David obtains Kerberos credentials on the gateway and makes them available to user identity 1235 on NFS client client2. Any access from client2 by such a user will use those credentials when checking read and write permissions. When David wishes to destroy the token, he must again log in to the gateway and run knfs with the -unlog option.

Note that when a user accesses the AFS namespace in this manner, the user cannot use other client commands such as fs. The user must run any other queries, such as fs whereis or fs listquota, on the gateway.

With this configuration, the AFS path name element @sys will be translated according to the architecture of the gateway machine. If the NFS client is a different architecture, you can use the knfs command's -sys option to specify a different translation value. Here, the gateway machine of any hardware architecture is instructed to convert @sys path name elements into sun4m_412.

```
$ knfs client2 -sys sun4m_412
```

In the case where the NFS client is a system type that is supported by Transarc but for some reason cannot be made true AFS client, the situation is much better. First, on the gateway, run the AFS cache manager with the -rmtsys option. This option enables the gateway to perform a more direct mapping between an NFS client identity and an AFS credential. As before, the gateway must have the /afs directory declared in its list of exported file systems, and the NFS servers must be running.

Now, on the NFS client, you can make a normal NFS mount of /afs. Also, set up local versions of /usr/afs/etc/CellServDB and /usr/afs/etc/ThisCell and a file containing the name of the gateway machine. These items allow AFS client programs, like fs, to contact the gateway and return information much as if the NFS client were running AFS natively.

You can set the values for this configuration data in a variety of places to allow multiple users on the NFS client to manage their data themselves or for administrators to manage all client users at once. For the finest control, users can set two environment variables: they should set AFSCONF to a directory path name in which CellServDB and ThisCell files are stored, and they should set AFSSERVER to the name of the gateway machine. Rather than setting environment variables, users can store the same two values in two files in their home directory: .AFSCONF and .AFSSERVER. Lastly, to set defaults for all users on the client, an administrator can set the values in files in the root directory: /.AFSCONF and /.AFSSERVER.

With these values set up, a user can directly issue a klog command on the NFS client. The command will recognize that it is not an AFS client and so will try to use the configuration data to contact the Kerberos servers in the indicated cell and obtain a token. As the AFS namespace is traversed, this token will be used to check permissions. Similarly, fs commands will contact the appropriate servers to return correct AFS data. And when credentials need to be destroyed, the normal unlog command can be used.

ADMINISTRATION EXAMPLES

As with most system administration, it is important to construct and publish a well-thought-out set of management policies complete with the necessary implementation tools. The bane of distributed computing is not any architectural flaw but simply the proliferation of anything-goes operations. When different administrators (or a single administrator at different times) implement arbitrary practices, the likelihood increases that systems will fail, security will be broken, and poor decisions will turn into immutable legacies.

With the centralized administration model of AFS, such free-for-all behavior must be controlled from the beginning. Discipline of course, is difficult when bringing up one's first cell; even so, as administration experience is gathered and changes are made to the system, they should be made to the entire cell namespace , bringing everything up to the same level. In the cases where AFS has not been used to its best potential, the problems usually can be traced to a lack of resources and administrative discipline.

Administering user accounts and homes in AFS consists of coordinating four different databases: the Kerberos identity and password database, the protection group database, the volume database, and the file system's namespace itself. Consistent application of policies to all of these databases is essential to controlling a cell. While each site will wish to implement its own standards, a few examples should help to expose the details which need to be managed.

Adding a user to a cell is discussed in Chapter 6. Deleting a user from the system is simply the reverse. To start, look up the location for the user's home volume. Whether the volume is immediately deleted or is renamed and saved somewhere for staging before deletion depends on your policies. As always, make sure that you are authenticated as a member of system:administrators, that you are on the server's administration list, that you have the ADMIN flag set for the proper execution of Kerberos commands, and that you can read and write to the necessary portions of the file namespace. Once you are satisfied that you are properly authenticated, you can begin.

```
$ vos listvldb user.ethan
user.ethan
    RWrite: 536871000
    number of sites -> 1
        server fs-two partition /vicepa RW Site
$ vos remove fs-two a user.ethan
Volume 536871000 on partition /vicepa server fs-two deleted
$ fs rmm /afs/.hq.firm/user/ethan
$ vos release cell.user
Released volume cell.user successfully
```

This set of commands removes the user's home volume from the namespace, but the user still exists as an identity in the database. Before deleting the user identity, check to see what groups the user owns and determine which groups can be deleted and which ones should be reassigned.

```
$ pts listowned ethan
Groups owned by ethan (id: 6873) are:
  ethan:projectX
  ethan:friends
$ pts delete ethan:friends
$ pts chown ethan:projectX david
$ pts delete ethan
$ kas delete ethan -admin afsadmin
Administrator's (afsadmin) Password:
```

Ethan's personal groups can be deleted outright, but apparently ethan owned a development project's group. Rather than delete this, reassign the projectX group to another user. Now, you can delete the user from the protection and Kerberos databases.

Note that any access control lists which had entries for ethan or ethan:friends will now show an orphan numeric identifier rather than a string value when listed. Remove these orphan entries from ACLs with the fs cleanacl command. The ethan:projectX group will be properly displayed as david:projectX.

Changing a user's name is similar to deletion in that the difficulty is in modifying the user's groups. First, check for the groups that the user currently owns, rename the user, and rename the groups.

```
$ pts listowned bob
Groups owned by bob (id: 5321) are:
  bob:writers
  bob:readers
  bob:friends
$ pts rename bob robert
$ pts rename bob:friends robert:friends
$ pts rename bob:readers robert:readers
$ pts rename bob:writers robert:writers
$ pts examine robert:writers
Name: robert:writers, id: -208, owner: robert, creator: robert,
  membership: 1, flags: S-M--, group quota: 0.
```

As you can see, the new owner of the groups is the renamed user. Any ACLs in the file system will automatically show the new, correct names. Now you can delete the old Kerberos name and install the new name.

```
$ kas delete bob -admin afsadmin
Administrator's (afsadmin) Password:
$ kas create robert -admin afsadmin
Administrator's (afsadmin) Password:
initial_password:
Verifying, please re-enter initial_password:
```

While the bob principal is now deleted and a new principal, robert, has been created, the user identification number remains the same because it is stored in the protection database.

Once the identity information has been changed, you'll need to change the user's home volume name and mount point. This change is not strictly necessary, but if you have a policy that says that home volumes are named after the users, include the step.

```
$ vos rename user.bob user.robert
Renamed volume user.bob to user.robert
$ fs rmm /afs/.hq.firm/user/bob
$ fs mkm /afs/.hq.firm/user/robert  user.robert
$ vos release cell.user
Released volume cell.user successfully
```

Additionally, you may have to change the mount point name of any attached backup volume. And finally, you'll have to change entries in the UNIX password file or map.

E-MAIL, NETNEWS, AND THE WEB

Once the AFS bug has hit your administrators, it sometimes seems that all problems can be solved through appropriately named and access-controlled directories and files. Once a distributed file system is ubiquitous and trusted, everything from e-mail to NetNews newsgroups to Web pages is capable of being stored in AFS. Is this a good idea? The answer is, it depends.

Electronic mail systems have evolved over the years and now deal with many layers of software—from user agents, transfer protocols, and queueing systems—running on wildly different hardware platforms.

With AFS, a natural question is whether e-mail can be directly delivered to user's home directories; such delivery would reduce the disk contention and usage problems of a single mail spool server. Users who regularly leaves their spool file full of dozens of megabytes of unread mail will, with this scenario, affect only their own home volume quota rather than abuse everyone's shared spool area. This method has been used at several sites but requires a fair amount of hacking in to get the permissions just right.

If user mail is to be delivered to a file in the user's home directory, that delivery site, perhaps `/afs/hq.firm/user/david/Mail`, must have an ACL that permits writing by the mail deliver agent. Getting a correct Kerberos authentication credential for that agent is not trivial. Automatically obtaining credentials differs according to whether the agent is a a long-running or intermittent job. If the job is designed to start up and run for a long period, you can use the `reauth` command, which periodically refreshes tickets. But automatically running the `reauth` command requires that a principal's password be available, usually in a file on the mail delivery agent's disk. Transarc's public FTP site has a version of this approach implemented as `auth-sendmail`.

A better answer is the `kpop` client, which understands the Post Office Protocol. This protocol depends on a central mail spool area managed by a POP daemon, usually named `popper`. The `kpop` program is a client which can contact the `popper` daemon and retrieve new mail; this version has internal enhancements that understand Kerberos credentials. An authenticated user can contact the central daemon on the central mail server and, using the Kerberos protocols, prove his or her identity. The `kpop` system will then be able to retrieve any previously spooled mail to the user's mail directory. This method helps maintain a high level of security for mail, which is a good thing, but does nothing to address the concerns of overloading a central mail spool area.

One site tries to get the best of both worlds by making the central mail store an AFS client. Rather than having mail stored in a local disk spool area or directly into users' home directories, the central mail service uses AFS as the spool directory. The mail server is assured, by AFS machine ACL entries, that only it can have access to the spool area, but the spool can be managed via AFS volume commands. In one case, the spool area is divided into thirty different volumes spread over many machines; each volume is dedicated to a certain set of users. Since these are AFS volumes, they can be manipulated, moved, and secured with ease. Clients can then use a POP client or other protocol to talk to the secured server and retrieve their mail.

The anarchic NetNews system has similar problems and solutions but has perhaps fewer security concerns. Again, the normal architecture depends on a central machine receiving a news feed and delivering articles into any one of a thousand, or ten thousand, different directories. Users will contact the news server and request information on what news groups and articles are available and then download a particular article.

Again, the natural question is whether the news articles can be delivered directly into an AFS directory structure; such delivery would then permit users to read articles by accessing the shared namespace.

The trouble with replacing pieces of this system with AFS technology is that much of the bottleneck is simply on the Internet network connection which receives articles. In addition, complex indexing and threading applications often depend on their own protocols, which would be bypassed if clients accessed articles directly. The current Network News Transfer Protocol (NNTP) performs additional functions that would be lost if one were to simply list the news directories and read the files therein.

A reasonable use of AFS might be, as with e-mail, to deliver NetNews into AFS directories solely for the advanced management capabilities of volumes; users would still contact a regular, central NetNews server to retrieve articles. The drawback is that in addition to the network traffic needed to receive the news feed, writing files to AFS volumes imposes even more network bandwidth.

It may seem that with the advent of the World Wide Web there is less need for distributed file systems at all. Don't protocols like HTTP, SSL, CGI, and others, make AFS obsolete? On the contrary, AFS can improve the performance, security, and architecture of an enterprise intranet.

The beauty of the Web is that it is available on practically all platforms, including workstations, PCs, even set-top boxes, and connects installations worldwide whether they are connected by T1 networks or low-caliber modems. However, in an individual enterprise, there is usually a limited set of desktop architectures and a well-defined network topology. And, more importantly, there is a specific security model: all employees are members of a single administrative realm.

These natural limitations are recognized in the distinction between the Internet—everyone and everything connected any which way—and an intranet, a natural domain of control. The computing systems in an enterprise deserve not only their own Web of information using all of the power and utilities available, but also a unified file system. The new Web technologies should be embraced when they add value to an organization but an enterprisewide file system can be used with any and all of the legacy applications that merely read and write file data.

An intranet Web can use this enterprise file system for the distribution not only of production binaries, home directories, operating system components, and the like, but for all of the Web tools—the browser and builder executables—and also for Web pages and images with relatively static content. The benefit of using AFS for the support of most Web pages is the built-in benefits of replication, security, and caching.

A disadvantage of most graphical user interfaces, including file managers and Web browsers, is that they need a manual refresh operation to check whether the local cache is up to date. AFS, on the other hand, has a strong consistency model: any examination of file or directory data is guaranteed to obtain the latest, consistent view of the data. By using file-based uniform resource locators or URLs, browsers will be sure of getting the most recent data without having to use the unoptimized HTTP protocol to deal with data transfer and caching. AFS file-based URLs will automatically use a network protocol to grab the data from anywhere in the enterprise; in addition, the global namespace of AFS provides better location transparency because no geographic information, not even a server name, is embedded in the file name.

The security model of AFS provides much-needed functionality for enterprises. Users can be assigned to groups, those groups can be placed on directory ACLs, and a Web of information is immediately made secure; only certain people will be permitted to read certain data, and only certain others will be permitted to write that data. All without the need to enter additional user names and passwords because the underlying file system will use the user's already established Kerberos authentication token.

However, Web servers are not made obsolete with this enterprise file system. Many of the new protocols used by a browser need a server with which to communicate, and many Web pages will be generated on-demand rather than living statically in the file system. Yet even for Web servers, AFS provides benefits: because a ubiquitous file service will also be visible to the Web servers, any Web server will be able to distribute any pages from anywhere in the file system.

The best result of the Web hype of the late '90s will be to get everyone connected to the internet. Then, any of various protocols can be used to move information to the local processing and display unit. AFS helps create robust thin clients, supports Web browsing, and transparently works with all applications that read and write files.

THIRD-PARTY SOFTWARE

Management of third-party software is perhaps the greatest problem facing an AFS administration staff. Whereas servers, disks, and backups can be gradually shaped into a smoothly running system, new software products regularly demanded by users and developers are a continual source of problems. This issue is not new to AFS; sites using NFS or NetWare must also deal with troublesome software installs. Nor does AFS provide any special advantages, except that once installed, a package can rely on replication and robust security services.

The source of the trouble is the flexibility of our computing environments versus the assumptions software developers make regarding the layout of the file namespace. AFS encourages large areas of shared resources; this environment is often at odds with the environment used by software developers. Dealing with these differences occupies a large share of an administrator's time.

In the best case, you'd like to install a package by simply storing the application files in the AFS file system with no modifications made to the client's disk or set up. All desktops in the cell would be able to see this package at once, and users would simply run the application. In the worst case, you'll have to handcraft solutions to support multiple architectures, temporary write space, and hard-coded non-AFS path names.

Perhaps the easiest way to install a package into AFS is to first install it onto a local file system, the equivalent of an examination room, where the files and linkages can be examined. It is important to understand the structure of the package, its files, their types, and their sizes. By running the product through its paces and reading the documentation, you will come to understand its architecture, how the application processes find its resources, and where it stores temporary and permanent file data.

During the vendor's installation process, beware of running jobs as root; this login often masks changes made to a client's configuration or system executables. Often, there's no way to find out what's changed except by comparing files in the client's /etc or /bin directory with another client. Some vendors may expect that software will be installed on each client as needed; in this case, you can use the enterprisewide AFS namespace simply as a place to store the software image and then permit users to load the software onto their desktop by simply running the install program.

When your clients have migrated to the dataless model, you'll find that there are fewer desktop installations to perform. As an example, on any UNIX workstation, there's no reason for the graphical windowing software to be loaded locally. As long as the binaries are replicated there's no need to manually copy the desired programs down to a client—just let AFS the client grab the files as needed from AFS and cache them for the inevitable next use. This choice means that installing patches to the window system software involves copying the new files to the AFS server once and then releasing the replicas; clients will be informed of the changes and pick them up as they need them.

Usually, the biggest difference between a product's assumptions and AFS's reality is that products expect that the file server will also be the application server. AFS is unlikely to meet such expectations likely because it uses fewer total file servers and does not make its files servers available as application servers. Often, you can solve this by setting up separate servers to perform application services for multiple products. Also, software that expects to run on an NFS server may expect that the server view of the file system is different from the client view. In AFS, all AFS clients see exactly the same files with the same names. It may be necessary to change the installation process to fix this assumption.

Some of the quirks of AFS can also break applications: the inability to create hard links between files in different directories could cause an installation script to fail. Often, to fix the problem, you must laboriously track down the file names and replace the source file with a symbolic link or a full copy of the destination file.

Applications can take one of two approaches for dealing with multiple hardware types: the package is installed once per hardware type onto a different server, or all hardware types are installed into a single system and the application itself determines at run time which executable to run. The latter case works well with AFS because you can simply copy all the files into AFS as is and let the package manage itself. In the first case, you might perform multiple installations and write your own wrapper to distinguish which path to use for a given client. Or you can step through the application directory by directory and determine which pieces are architecture dependent, then create new directories for each architecture, and, finally, link the application directories to the per-architecture directories by using the AFS @sys path.

As an example, consider a hypothetical application available for Sun and SGI. It consists of a set of binaries in the bin directory and some man pages. After installing the two versions in two convenient directories, you can see the simple application layout.

```
$ ls /tmp/new-app-sun
bin      man
$ ls /tmp/new-app-sgi
bin      man
```

You could install these applications into AFS as a single package, where the bin directory is a link to the correct architecture's binaries.

```
$ cd /afs/hq.firm/apps/new-app
$ ls
bin      man      sgi_53   sun4m_54
$ ls -l bin
lrwxrwxrwx  staff   staff        bin -> @sys
```

When examining an application, watch out for assumptions that might break in a single, global file namespace. Perhaps resource files are expected to be stored in the installation area and yet remain writeable; this storage can cause problems when you replicate the package into multiple read-only volumes.

The separation of the namespace into read-only and read-write areas comes as a surprise to many applications. You may need to create read-write volumes that are mounted somewhere convenient so that applications running from replicated read-only areas can write into their data files.

Run-time read and write access can also present a problem. Using AFS ACLs and group entries, you can construct areas that only the correctly permissioned set of users can access. But if a setuid-root server process or a UNIX cron job expects to access that same area, it will probably fail because it has only anonymous credentials. After installing any package, run the application both with regular user credentials and then as an unauthenticated user to see where authorized file accesses are needed.

Another set of problems arises in building public software from source code. During the building process, some path names may be hardcoded into the product, either into compiled object modules or simply as text in files interpreted at run time. Automatic installation procedures may use this same path name as the installation location. This use is almost always wrong because the installation location will most likely be a read-write path, such as /afs/ .hq.firm/apps, whereas the run-time path should be /afs/hq.firm/ apps. You may have to fix this problem manually editing the install scripts or moving the products into AFS by hand.

PC software often comes with its own set of assumptions which make it onerous to install into an AFS cell. Beware of packages that insist on being located in the topmost directory: most packages in an AFS cell will be situated in directories three or four levels below the top. You may need to adjust your cell directory hierarchy to make such software more comfortable.

Even more often, packages for PCs assume that their installation areas are available for saving data as well as for simply storing the binaries. Again, you can use symbolic links in the AFS namespace to repoint directories used for scratch or per-user data over to special read-write volumes.

During the vendor's installation process, changes will often be made to a user's home directory. Much PC software seems to assume that the root directory of a local hard drive is the same thing as a home directory. To make such software work in a multiuser world, you'll have to study and capture the changes made to home directories and create mini-installation scripts that can be run per-user, when needed, to set up a given software package.

And don't forget that a lot of PC software is delivered as dynamic link libraries (DLL) which need to be installed in system directories. The continual management of these DLLs makes it hard to construct a dataless PC.

The latest releases of the differing Microsoft Windows operating systems include the Registry, a system database that stores desktop as well as user configuration information. After installing a piece of software locally, you should examine this registry to see what changes were made. You may be able to make the software available to others by just copying the package files into AFS and then updating another user's registry information, using a custom-built script.

Third-party software installation is not overly difficult, at least the first time when a certain intellectual challenge is involved. Yet as new releases and bug fixes are made available, the continual need to reexamine the same sets of files and to test the assumptions of each revision over and over again quickly becomes tiresome. And when releases for different architectures diverge or are delayed, you may need to revisit certain choices made to create an installation package.

Again, these problems are not specific to AFS; they are familiar to all shared, distributed file systems. But that does not make the process any easier.

OTHER ADMINISTRATION TOOLS

Managing server disk space is a large chunk of an administrator's job. With AFS, this job is made much easier because of the convenience and transparency of the vos move command. Because you can move volumes around without affecting any user jobs accessing those files, you may want to use a shareware tool to automatically move volumes among a set of servers and partitions.

Called balance, the command determines where all of a cell's volumes are located and also what size partitions are available. Then using some built-in and customizable rules, the tool moves volumes from one partition to another. You can customize the rules to balance volumes so that all servers have approximately equal free space available. Or, you can move all of the infrequently accessed volumes to less powerful backroom servers and disks. The public version of balance is available from Transarc's site of unsupported software.

Along with this automatic volume management, many sites would like tools to manually delegate certain AFS operations to groups of users. Just as AFS delegates certain group membership operations to a group or a user, so should an administrator be able to say that a nonprivileged user could, at times, create volumes according to certain predefined conditions.

One such tool is ADM. Once ADM is installed, a server process is started to listen to requests coming in from its client programs. As a user runs the ADM client and contacts the server, the server checks the authentication of the user, using the Kerberos mutual authentication protocol. If the user is permitted to run a privileged operation, the server forks a process that authenticates to AFS as a member of the system:administrators group and runs the request.

This system gains much of its power by not having a predefined set of internal policies or set of delegated users listed, but by using Scheme, a dialect of Lisp, to define all of its actions. When the server is run, it reads a file of Scheme expressions which add to its repertoire of operations and define the users and groups who are permitted to use the operations.

A client process can then contact the server and either request a prepackaged operation, for instance, make a user, or step through any available lower-level requests as desired. A tool of this sort makes a great deal of sense in a large organization because it permits administrative authority to be delegated. As an example, a development group manager could be allowed to create new project volumes as needed, but only on a specific subset of servers.

As for the standard operational toolchest, the AFS administration suite shows its decade-long history with its seemingly endless list of subcommands, choice of abbreviations, oddly formatted output and return codes, and hodge-podge of debugging features. By this point, given the large installed base of users, Transarc can hardly go back and rewrite the commands, but a rigorous reimplementation of the subcommands would be very welcome. Just such a rewrite is going on by a few citizens of the Net. The plan is to consolidate the AFS command functionality into a Perl module using that language's rich set of data structures to return information about AFS in a manageable fashion.

SUMMARY

AFS provides a large number of administration commands, some designed to be used piecemeal, others which can be used only according to the standard conventions of a cell management. If you are running a standard cell, most of these commands, such as mechanisms to install new system binaries, are beneficial. Any deviation from the norm may produce heartache. Again, AFS and Transarc are in the business of supporting policies to help maintain central file services, not in the academic world of atomic mechanisms for file manipulation.

As it is, the conventions do support a distributed file service extremely well. The `bos` command allows easy management of remote servers, to the point of controlling processes, binaries, restart times, and event notification. The drawback is that this system is specific to AFS; there is little appreciation for supporting more modern administration systems such as central logging through `syslog` or SNMP.

When running an AFS cell, it's easy to enlarge the administrative domain to include more and more files and directories that were formerly stored on local disks. But take care when attacking certain applications, such as electronic mail, the Internet NetNews system, or Web data. Some of the file data used by these systems is well suited to storage in AFS—especially their binary programs and any configuration data. But certain aspects of their implementations have been developed over the years with only local disk storage in mind. Installing other third-party software requires careful considerations of these same issues.

While the AFS command suite is large and time-consuming to master, there are a few public-domain tools available which can help. Don't forget that in addition to these systems there is a large on-line community to which you can post questions and share results: the `info-afs` mailing list regularly contains informative articles on real-world experiences from large and small sites.

Debugging Problems

A distinct disadvantage to AFS is a direct result of the success of its implementation. With more users dependent on fewer servers and with fewer administrators to watch over these servers, any problems which arise are likely to affect a large population. That being so, you should carefully plan and test any administrative tasks in an AFS cell before customers see poor performance or fret about unavailable data.

When any problems do arise, the best offense is a well-practiced debugging methodology. You should have a clear idea of exactly what systems in your cell should be performing what tasks—whether the systems are database servers, file servers, system configuration machines, or backup tape coordinators. Task assignments should be well defined and publicized.

The database servers in a cell should be completely listed in the CellServDB file on all servers and clients. Tape coordinators are listed in the backup database and can be displayed with a backup listhosts command. Update servers can be discovered by searching the bos jobs on servers and seeing where the upserver process is running. Interestingly, there's no definitive list of active file server machines in a cell. The best you can do is search the volume location database and find out which machines are currently being used to store volumes. A simple one-line UNIX command to do this goes like this:

```
$ vos listvldb | awk '/server/{print $2}' | sort -u
fs-one
fs-two
```

There's also no way to find out directly where in the AFS namespace a particular volume is mounted. Any volume can be mounted anywhere in the namespace, as many times as people may have desired. There's no problem with file access or security holes because of multiple mount points, but it does make it difficult to make sure that no one is using a volume if you'd like to delete it.

A reasonable policy is to mandate that volumes names must follow a strict naming convention and that the volumes will be supported only at a specific point in the tree. It then becomes easier to audit the VLDB contents and look for stray volumes that may have been created temporarily.

The VLDB is an important tool for investigating AFS management but the database keeps track only of a volume's basic statistics. You may find it useful to construct a parallel database (using either a relational database or simply a structured text file) to track other items of interest. For example, writing a wrapper to the `vos release` command which causes a brief record to be appended somewhere can help answer the question, when were the last few times the replicas were updated?

Other general tasks of AFS administration are as follows:

- Archive AFS databases regularly and store them on tape in convenient locations on disk for rapid recovery.
- Dump important volumes outside AFS: small dumps of many of the top-level volumes stored in out-of-the-way locations (even `/tmp`) of some file server will prove beneficial in emergencies.
- Be familiar with the log directory; rotate the log files so that new messages do not overwrite previous problems.
- Keep as much free space as possible on the disk on which you store the server's database files, log files, and potential core files. Usually, these files are located on the `/usr` partition.
- Know what release of the AFS binaries you're running everywhere.
- Have additional hardware available so that a new server or disk can be swapped in with as little downtime as possible.
- Reserve disk space on at least one file server so that volume operations or archival restores have a staging area in which to operate.
- Use a test cell to hone debugging skills and train new administrators.

You should test regularly to make sure that your administration processes work and that your staff is not rusty on the operations required. The time spent on testing will be repaid quickly when disaster strikes. Testing is also a good educational session for new administrators; for example, backups and restores involve many of the processes and databases which make AFS work.

FILE SERVER PERFORMANCE

When examining a file server for potential bottlenecks, start with the basics. Though AFS servers provide an integrated service, individually, they're fairly normal machines. Address performance problems with the usual tools: on a UNIX server, use commands such as `iostat` and `vmstat` to determine if the system is disk or processor bound. With the increased number of partitions available in AFS 3.4a, it may be easy to overload a file server's CPU.

Similarly, use the `netstat` command to see if there is an inordinate amount of network traffic. If so, investigate the volumes on the server with the `vos examine` command and the `-extended` option to see if certain volumes that are hogging the network could profitably be moved to other servers nearer their natural client users.

File server disk performance is as important to AFS as it is to any other database system. Any writes from a client to a server will come in large chunks of data. Each of these chunks will be received and then written to disk. Because the chunks are often large, these operations will normally be quite efficient, but any increase in disk performance will prove beneficial to clients and servers overall.

Any written chunks will still have copies available in the server's memory buffers. If a client read request asks for data just written, that data will be automatically served from the server's memory rather than requiring a disk read. This two-level cache is simply a consequence of standard operating system design. However, if a read request has not been satisfied by the client's own cache, the odds are that it won't be satisfied by the server's kernel cache either—client read requests are for files that the client hasn't read recently.

For this reason, it is still important to manage performance by spreading expected client loads among a number of file servers and a number of disk drives. With the goal of keeping the server CPU and disks busy. With AFS management tools to move volumes around and manage servers, there's not much need to invest in special-purpose servers or hardware accelerators; fast, cheaper workstations sold in server configurations are perfect for AFS servers. High-performance servers are usually needed only for servers running the backup processes.

The classic architectural difference between NFS and AFS is that the former attempts to be a stateless protocol and the latter stateful. AFS keeps track of myriad items of client information so as to provide a guaranteed consistency model while still providing efficient services. The penalty is that this state must be kept somewhere, so AFS servers often need more system memory. Exactly how much is used by an AFS file server can be adjusted through command-line arguments to the `fileserver` process.

In normal usage, the `fileserver` process is started with no options and is by default running a so-called medium-sized image. Using the `-S` option reduces the sizes of certain data structures, `-L` increases them. Among the structures that are affected are:

- The maximum number of lightweight processes
- The maximum number of directory blocks cached
- The maximum number of vnodes cached for tracking directory and file contents
- The maximum number of callbacks stored
- The maximum number of Rx protocol packets used
- The maximum size of the volume data cache

The `-S` option decreases these sizings to the minimum, in which case, the `fileserver` will consume approximately 751 kbytes of memory. When `fileserver` is run under the `-L` option, the defaults are raised to a reasonable maximum, using up about 1400 kbytes. With the systems now available from most UNIX vendors, the large size may be useful for most sites.

Several other options are available to fine-tune individual structures. The number of callbacks stored by file servers is of particular importance. Because a file server must track all read-write file accesses to be able to send messages about stale cache contents to the clients, each callback must be stored separately. This table is kept in memory; when it becomes full, the server flushes the oldest entries, sending a preemptive callback to the clients in question and then deleting the entry to make way for a new record. This feature ensures that the consistency guarantees are kept, albeit at the expense of having some clients checking the server to see if certain unchanged files are up to date. The small model allocates enough space for 20,000 callbacks, the default (medium) model has room for 32,000, and the large model, 40,000. Making this table even larger, by using the `-cb` option, is one recommended way to possibly increase large-scale system performance.

Another structure that can safely be made larger is the size of the volume data cache. This regular memory-cache increases performance of the server because it decreases repeated disk accesses to read volume data. In the small model, the volume cache is set to 200 volumes, in the default model, it is set to 400 volumes, and in the large model, 600. Use the `-vc` option to set this number higher.

Recall that the `fileserver` process is not run directly on an AFS server system but is managed as a job by the `bosserver`. In a very large cell, you may want to create this job with the large model flags and larger values for the callback table and volume cache.

```
# bos create fs-one fs fs "/usr/afs/bin/fileserver -L -cb 64000 -vc
800" /usr/afs/bin/volserver /usr/afs/bin/salvager
```

Whether this actually increases performance is another question. The first thing to check is the kernel memory usage of the file server system. As you've just drastically increased the memory requirements of the process, make sure that the system is not hogging resources needed by other processes.

Then, use the `afsmonitor` command, described later in this chapter, to check on client and server statistics to see if cache hits are greater and callbacks are more infrequent. If so, the result will be a much lighter load on the server.

FILE SERVER PROBLEMS

If a server goes down, you'll likely be flooded with calls from users who can't access the read-write volumes on that machine. You should have other monitoring systems—SNMP, etc.—on all server machines to check for hardware outages. If those haven't triggered and someone calls about access problems, you should suspect a problem with the file server and the `fileserver` process if:

- `vos examine` shows VLDB information but not volume header info.
- `bos status` shows that the `fileserver` process is running but the UNIX process table information on the server shows that the process is not actively using CPU.
- Running `bos restart` on the `fs` job doesn't appear to cause the `fileserver` process to restart.

If someone reports that a particular path is not responding to access requests, you should be able to deduce what volume underlies that path, based on your volume creation and naming policies. A first step is to query the `volserver` job on the file server machine with the `vos examine` command.

```
$ vos examine user.alice
Could not fetch the information about volume 536870921 from the server
Possible communication failure
Error in vos examine command. Possible communication failure

Dump only information from VLDB

user.alice
    RWrite: 536870921      Backup: 536870923
    number of sites -> 1
        server fs-one partition /vicepa RW Site
```

Here, the `volserver` is not responding to a basic query. The next question is whether the process is running at all. The `bos status` command or even a UNIX process status display on the server itself should tell you if the process is running or has crashed.

When an AFS server process appears to be running but doesn't respond to command requests, use the `rxdebug` program to see where the process is stuck. As the name implies, `rxdebug` connects to the Transarc Rx RPC layer in a remote server process; use the resulting output to determine if the process is completely hung or is simply busy with other processing.

In this next case, the `fileserver` process is suspected of being stuck. The arguments to `rxdebug` are, first, the address of the server, followed by the port number of the AFS service you want to query. Other options select debugging information you'd like to see displayed. Here, we choose to examine the statistics of the Rx protocol used by the `fileserver` process on `fs-one`:

```
$ rxdebug 192.168.3.21 7000 -rxstats
Trying 192.168.3.21 (port 7000):
Free packets: 328, packet reclaims: 0, calls: 0, used FDs: 8
not waiting for packets.
0 calls waiting for a thread
rx stats: free packets 0, allocs 9, alloc-failures(rcv 0,send 0,ack 0)
   greedy 0, bogusReads 0 (last from host 0), noPackets 0, noBuffers 0, selects
14, sendSelects 0
   packets read: data 3 ack 0 busy 0 abort 0 ackall 0 challenge 2 response 0
debug 2 params 0 unused 0 unused 0 unused 0 version 0
   other read counters: data 3, ack 0, dup 0 spurious 0
   packets sent: data 3 ack 2 busy 0 abort 0 ackall 0 challenge 0 response 2
debug 0 params 0 unused 0 unused 0 unused 0 version 0
   other send counters: ack 2, data 3 (not resends), resends 0, pushed 0,
acked&ignored 0
(these should be small) sendFailed 0, fatalErrors 0
```

```
   0 server connections, 4 client connections, 4 peer structs, 2 call structs, 0
free call structs
   0 clock updates
Connection from host 192.168.3.94, port 7003, Cuid ac769209/2351a28c
   serial 3,  natMTU 1472, flags pktCksum, security index 2, client conn
   rxkad: level clear, flags pktCksum
   Received 0 bytes in 1 packets
   Sent 60 bytes in 1 packets
     call 0: # 1, state dally, mode: receiving, flags: receive_done
     call 1: # 0, state not initialized
     call 2: # 0, state not initialized
     call 3: # 0, state not initialized
Connection from host 192.168.5.90, port 7002, Cuid ac769209/2351a290
   serial 4,  natMTU 1472, flags pktCksum, security index 2, client conn
   rxkad: level crypt, flags pktCksum
   Received 48 bytes in 2 packets
   Sent 16 bytes in 2 packets
     call 0: # 2, state dally, mode: receiving, flags: receive_done
     call 1: # 0, state not initialized
     call 2: # 0, state not initialized
     call 3: # 0, state not initialized
Done.
```

The output is designed to aid in the debugging of the Rx RPC layers themselves and is not well laid-out for AFS administrators. However, in the output you can see some hints about the state of the server: The number of calls waiting for a thread (in the third line of output) tells you how many outstanding requests are still waiting for processing; the number of calls (in the second line) tells you the total number of Rx calls; and the number of noBuffers is a measure of how many times Rx had to discard a packet because it did not have enough memory.

These numbers, though cryptic, can distinguish a broken server from a busy one. If the number of calls waiting for a thread is zero, and the total number of calls and noBuffers remains stable and greater than zero, the server is most likely simply overloaded and busy with current requests. There's little to do except to make sure there are no other non-AFS jobs running on the machine, wait for some spare processing time, and perhaps split some of the heavily used volumes among less burdened servers.

If the number of calls waiting for a thread and the number of noBuffers keeps rising but the total number of calls remains the same, these symptoms indicate a fileserver "meltdown," so called because the server process is most likely hung.

Of course, if there is no response whatsoever from the rxdebug program and the server process is using 100 percent of the system CPU, the job is clearly misbehaving.

In either of the last two cases, you'll have to force a `fileserver` restart. To aid Transarc in tracking down the server bug, you can send the server a signal to cause a core dump of the process image to be created. For the `fileserver` process, a good signal to use is SIGABRT. On a Solaris file server, the command sequence would be:

```
# ps -ef
    UID   PID  PPID  C   STIME TTY      TIME CMD
    root  548  248   0 16:24:38 ?       0:00 /usr/afs/bin/fileserver
. . .
# kill -ABRT 548
# bos status fs-one fs
Instance fs, has core file, currently running normally.
    Auxiliary status is: salvaging file system.
#
# cd /usr/afs/logs
# ls -1 core.file.fs
-rw-rw-rw-  1 root     root       3582580 Mar 30 16:27 core.file.fs
```

Note that `bosserver` has done its duty and restarted the `fileserver` and `salvager` processes immediately after discovering that the job had crashed. `bosserver` reports that also `salvager` is now running and shows that a core file exists. Changing the server log directory, we see a core file listed. Core files are all named with a `core.` prefix followed by the name of the job that crashed; in the case of the fs job, you may see either `core.file.fs` or `core.vol.fs`, depending on whether the `fileserver` or `volserver` daemon failed.

At this point, you can call Transarc product support and arrange to deliver to them the core file and any relevant log files. Note that the `fileserver` binary is delivered not stripped, that is, debugging information has been kept in the executable file. This information makes the program file bigger, but you'll be able to use your local debugger, such as `dbx` or `gdb`, to get a handle on where problems might be. (Other AFS binaries are delivered stripped.)

If you're lucky, you should be able to see the process stack trace from the core file, using `dbx`, `gdb`, or another general UNIX debugger. If you examine the output of the trace carefully, you should see some variable names such as `volid` or `volptr`; if you have access to the source, you would be able to determine exactly what those variables are used for. Otherwise, for debugging purposes, you'll just have to guess that any variables with names that include the string `vol` probably contain a volume identification number. By printing out the identification number, you will be able to compare it with the data in the VLDB and perhaps have a clue as to what the process was doing when it crashed.

Other variables may include the letters fid; these variables should contain a complete AFS file identifier, which includes the volume, vnode, and uniquifier numbers. Let's assume that the volume number is 536870921, the vnode is 6, and the uniquifier is 3. As before, you can search the VLDB to find out which volume was being accessed.

```
$ vos listvldb 536870921

user.alice
    RWrite: 536870921    Backup: 536870923
    number of sites -> 1
        server fs-one partition /vicepa RW Site
    Volume is currently LOCKED
```

As you can see, this is a user's volume and the volume is in the LOCKED state. This state usually indicates that some operation was being performed on the volume when either the client or server process crashed.

To find out exactly what file was being accessed at the time of the crash, we need to find out which file corresponds to the vnode in that volume. Transarc doesn't provide a tool for this function, but we do know the algorithm that is used to convert between volume and vnode identifiers and the UNIX inode number of the file. The uniquifier, the third numeric identifier in each FID, is not used when translating to an inode; instead, each AFS file appears in UNIX to have the same inode during its entire existence and only the AFS servers know about the unique version number of the file.

At Transarc's FTP site, you'll find a program, calcinode, that transforms a volume and vnode number into an inode. But the algorithm can be trivially performed in a few lines of Perl code or by any hexadecimal-enabled calculator. Here's a snippet of Perl code that performs the calculation for our particular data.

```
#  perl script to translate volume and vnode into inode
$volume = 536870921;
$vnode = 6;

#  take the low-order two bytes
$volume = $volume & 0xFFFF;
$vnode = $vnode & 0xFFFF;
```

```
#   check for an overflow
if ($volume >= 0x8000) { $volume -= 0x8000; }

#   convert into an inode
printf "%d\\n", ($volume<<16) + $vnode
```

Running this script answers our question.

```
$ perl5 calcinode.pl
589630
```

Once the UNIX inode is known, you can traverse the directories, starting at the mount point of the previously identified volume, to find the file. We'll use the find program, which has a built-in option to search for a specified inode.

```
$ cd /afs/hq.firm/user/alice
$ find /afs/hq.firm/user/alice -inum 589830 -print
/afs/hq.firm/user/alice/script1
$ ls -l /afs/hq.firm/user/alice/script1
589830 -r-xr-xr-x   1 alice     staff          29 Mar 29 16:57 script1
```

Knowing what file was involved during the crash might give you a clue as to its cause. Presumably, some user was processing that file, either reading or writing it. Of course, any reads or writes are not supposed to result in a crash. But perhaps this file can help track down who was using the file; perhaps it was on a client workstation with a newly ported version of the cache manager.

As you search for more information about this problem, consult the fileserver log file. As with other servers, the amount of detail stored in the file depends on the current debugging level. When tracking down repeatable bugs, you can increase that level by sending the fileserver process a SIGTSTP signal, or you can reset the level to basic process data with the SIGHUP signal. Here's how these signals work:

- First SIGTSTP (level 1)—fileserver logs Rx RPC calls received.
- Second SIGTSTP (level 5)—Also logs the return code of all Rx RPCs.
- Third SIGTSTP (level 25)—Also logs where the RPC call originated.
- SIGHUP (level 0)—Resets to base level.
- SIGQUIT—Gracefully kills the process.

At level 1, there's just enough detail to watch basic server processing:

```
# ps -ef
      UID   PID  PPID  C    STIME TTY      TIME CMD
      root  569   248  0  16:28:20 ?       0:00 /usr/afs/bin/fileserver
...
# kill -TSTP 569
#
# tail /usr/afs/logs/FileLog
Sun Mar 30 16:35:07 1997 Set Debug On level = 1
Sun Mar 30 16:35:27 1997 SAFS_FetchStatus,  Fid = 536870913.2.2811
Sun Mar 30 16:35:44 1997 SRXAFS_FetchData, Fid = 536870919.2.822
Sun Mar 30 16:35:44 1997 SAFS_FetchStatus,  Fid = 536870955.1.1
Sun Mar 30 16:36:10 1997 SAFS_CreateFile b,  Did = 536870985.1.1
Sun Mar 30 16:36:29 1997 SAFS_FetchACL, Fid = 536870985.1.1
Sun Mar 30 16:36:29 1997 SAFS_StoreACL, Fid = 536870985.1.1, ACL=3
0
system:administrators 127
system:anyuser 9
robert 127
Sun Mar 30 16:36:30 1997 SAFS_FetchStatus,  Fid = 536870985.1.1
Sun Mar 30 16:36:30 1997 SAFS_CreateFile b,  Did = 536870985.1.1
Sun Mar 30 16:36:30 1997 SRXAFS_FetchData, Fid = 536870985.6.405
Sun Mar 30 16:36:30 1997 StoreData: Fid = 536870985.6.405
#
# kill -HUP 569
# tail 1 /usr/afs/logs/FileLog
Sun Mar 30 16:38:02 1997 Reset Debug levels to 0
```

SALVAGING FILES

In AFS, a *disk salvage* is the process by which the internal structures of a vice partition are analyzed and any inconsistencies corrected. Because the system uses the native UNIX file system of the server's operating system, an AFS disk salvage is similar, in effect, to the vendor's file system check program but goes much further in examining and restoring the internal layout policies of volume headers and files.

The fileserver and volserver processes do their best to store coherent and stable versions of files and volume headers. But occasionally, if a server crashes or loses power or if a vice partition becomes corrupted, then inconsistent data may be written to disk. More infrequently, certain volume operations such as a vos move, if interrupted during execution by the administrator or by a network or system failure, can cause a similar problem.

When volserver is running, it keeps track of which volumes are in use at any given time. These are referred to as the active volumes. During a system crash, it is these active volumes that may be corrupted. The `salvager` process first checks these volumes for trouble, then pieces together any file data blocks or directories that appear to be disconnected.

A salvage is performed automatically when the `bosserver` process detects that the `fileserver` process has crashed, for example, after the reboot of a panic'd server machine, or when Transarc's `vfsck` program (as a replacement for the vendor's `fsck` program) deletes some level of corruption in a `vice` partition. When `fsck` detects a corrupted partition, it creates a file FORC-ESALVAGE, in the root of the vice partition. When the `fileserver` process first starts, it checks for FORCESALVAGE; if it exists, `fileserver` passes control to the `salvager`.

When the `fileserver` process starts, it writes a sentinel file, /usr/afs/local/SALVAGE.fs, which will be deleted during the normal shut down sequence. If `bosserver` detects the file on restart, it assumes that the server either panic'd or was brought down incorrectly, either of which cases means that the partitions may have been corrupted. One way to run salvages is to create the sentinel file by hand before starting AFS services.

Alternatively, administrators can manually instruct `bosserver` to run salvages to try to resurrect a specific volume, partition, or all partitions on a server.

An administrator can set two important options on the command line (or that of the `bos salvager` job).

- `-parallel` option, which raises or lowers the number of partitions `salvager` checks in parallel. The default is 4.
- `-tmpdir` option, which redirects temporary files written by `salvager`. Normally, the current partition is used for temporaries. In cases where little room is left on the disk, you can use this option to indicate an alternate workspace.

Salvaging, like most AFS actions, can be initiated from any machine in the cell. The `bos` suite has a `salvage` subcommand to run salvages on any of the file servers. The subcommand takes an option of `-all` to check all the partitions on a server, or a server name and list of partitions to check only a certain servers devices, or a server name, partition, and volume identifier number to check just a single volume. But beware when salvaging a whole partition: the `fileserver` process on that system will be shut down, causing a service interruption. Shutting down AFS makes some sense, especially because salvages are run after kernel panics or file server crashes. Yet during a salvage of just a single partition, it would be much nicer if Transarc would permit other partitions to still be available.

You may notice that `bosserver` creates a temporary job entry on the server that is being salvaged. During this operation, `salvager` writes information to the `/usr/afs/logs/SalvageLog` file; use the `-showlog` option to remotely display the file to the administration desktop.

```
$ bos salvage fs-one -all -showlog
bos: shutting down fs.
Starting salvage.
bos: waiting for salvage to complete.
bos: waiting for salvage to complete.
bos: salvage completed
SalvageLog:
@(#)Base configuration afs3.4 5.00
03/30/97 16:42:42 STARTING AFS SALVAGER 2.4 (/usr/afs/bin/salvager -f)
03/30/97 16:42:42 Starting salvage of file system partition /vicepa
03/30/97 16:43:32 Starting salvage of file system partition /vicepb
03/30/97 16:42:42 SALVAGING FILE SYSTEM PARTITION /vicepa (device=c0t1d0s4)
03/30/97 16:42:42 ***Forced salvage of all volumes on this partition***
03/30/97 16:42:53 Scanning inodes on device /dev/rdsk/c0t1d0s4...
03/30/97 16:43:05 CHECKING CLONED VOLUME 536870913.
03/30/97 16:43:05 root.afs.readonly (536870913) updated 03/29/97 12:32
03/30/97 16:43:05 SALVAGING VOLUME 536870912.
03/30/97 16:43:05 root.afs (536870912) updated 03/29/97 12:32
03/30/97 16:43:05 Salvaged root.afs (536870912): 5 files, 7 blocks
03/30/97 16:43:05 CHECKING CLONED VOLUME 536870919.
03/30/97 16:43:05 root.cell.readonly (536870919) updated 03/29/97 13:44
03/30/97 16:43:05 SALVAGING VOLUME 536870918.
03/30/97 16:43:05 root.cell (536870918) updated 03/29/97 13:44
03/30/97 16:43:05 Salvaged root.cell (536870918): 4 files, 5 blocks
03/30/97 16:43:05 SALVAGING VOLUME 536870921.
03/30/97 16:43:05 user.alice (536870921) updated 03/29/97 17:46
03/30/97 16:43:05 Salvaged user.alice (536870921): 9 files, 14 blocks
...
```

You should check that the server's volumes are all on-line.

```
$ vos listvol fs-one
Total number of volumes on server fs-one partition /vicepa: 15
cell.sys               536870960 RW      2 K On-line
cell.tmp               536870957 RW      5 K On-line
cell.tmp.readonly      536870958 RO      4 K On-line
cell.user              536870954 RW      7 K On-line
cell.user.readonly     536870955 RO      7 K On-line
root.afs               536870912 RW      7 K On-line
root.afs.readonly      536870913 RO      7 K On-line
root.cell              536870918 RW      5 K On-line
```

```
root.cell.readonly          536870919  RO          5 K On-line
tmp.sample                  536870973  RW      51202 K On-line
user.alice                  536870921  RW         14 K On-line
user.david                  536870976  RW       1026 K On-line
user.david.backup           536870978  BK       1026 K On-line
user.rob                    536870967  RW          2 K On-line
user.rob.backup             536870969  BK          2 K On-line
...
```

The SalvageLog output indicates which volumes were checked and updated and, occasionally, which volumes could not be salvaged. In these cases, attempt another salvage. If that salvage also fails, you'll have to resort to other strategies to resurrect those volumes: perhaps move all correctly salvaged volumes off the disk and move the disk to a spare server where more intensive disk repair tools can be used to discover the problem.

You can salvage a single volume without otherwise affecting the server.

```
$ bos salvage fs-one a user.alice -showlog
Starting salvage.
bos: waiting for salvage to complete.
bos: waiting for salvage to complete.
bos: salvage completed
SalvageLog:
@(#)Base configuration afs3.4 5.00
03/30/97 16:46:02 STARTING AFS SALVAGER 2.4 (/usr/afs/bin/salvager /vicepa 536870921)
03/30/97 16:46:12 Scanning inodes on device /dev/rdsk/c0t1d0s4...
03/30/97 16:46:25 SALVAGING VOLUME 536870921.
03/30/97 16:46:25 user.alice (536870921) updated 03/29/97 17:46
03/30/97 16:46:25 Salvaged user.alice (536870921): 9 files, 14 blocks
```

If bosserver is unavailable or other salvage options are needed, you'll have to start the salvage on the server machine and run the process via the command line. In this case, if salvaging one or more partitions, shut down the fs job before proceeding; if only a single volume is to be salvaged, the fs job should remain running.

Other options which may prove useful are:

- -force—Forces all volumes, rather than only the active volumes, on the partitions to be checked and salvaged.
- -salvagedirs—Forces all directories to be rebuilt. Normally, directories are reconstructed only when corrupt. Forcing all directories to be rebuilt is time consuming but can potentially relink files that are otherwise lost.

- `-blockread`—By default, the `salvager` reads multiple disk blocks at a time in order to be as efficient and quick as possible. But a physically damaged disk may cause a multiple-block read request to fail. With this option, only a single block is read at a time. While this method is time consuming, single-block reads can skip over damaged disk blocks and thereby salvage more of a `vice` partition.

During salvaging operations, the process must often create new versions of files, directories, or volume headers. Normally, these new files are created on the partition that is being salvaged. This practice can be a problem if the disk is corrupted or full. In these cases, use the `-tmpdir` option to supply an argument directing the `salvager` to create new temporary files on an alternate partition, such as `/tmp` or `/var/tmp`. The old versions of the file or directory blocks will be cleared from the partition being salvaged and the new version will then be moved back from the temporary location to the `vice` partition.

Finally, use the `-nowrite` option to bring online all undamaged volumes immediately, leaving any damaged volumes unsalvaged on the partition. With this option, undamaged volumes can be moved off of the partition and work can then continue on salvaging the damaged volumes, possibly limiting further unintended downtime for working volumes.

Volumes can become unavailable for a few reasons. One common reason is that a `vos move` operation was unexpectedly terminated. Moving volumes involves a number of steps, which AFS attempts to perform as a transaction. If an administrator interrupts the move, AFS will try to clean up any completed steps to the state that existed before the command was run. This is not always successful. The first indication of failure is that the volume is locked against further operations; `vos examine` will display this information.

The commonest problems are that the volume was being moved and now two versions of the volume exist, the original and the copy. To correct for this, follow these steps.

1. Manually unlock the volume.
2. Examine the volume location database to find out which server and partition contain the legitimate version.
3. Examine the volume headers on the server and partition to determine the state of the legitimate version.
4. If the preferred volume is reported to be unattached, then salvage it.
5. Once the volume is OK, run `zap` to delete the other version from disk.

6. Make sure that any temporary clone volumes are removed.

Because temporary clones do not show up in either the VLDB or the server's volume headers, you must salvage the entire partition by brute force. *At the next available maintenance period*, run the partition salvage (remember, partition salvages bring the file server down).

DATABASE SERVERS

If your database servers are also file servers, the sum total of the server jobs will take more memory and processing than if they were separated. But even a machine that is just a database server can have poor performance if it is the sync site, for then, that one server is the location to which all updates for all databases in the cell must be delivered.

If segregated from the file servers, the database processes only need a fast CPU and plenty of memory: any fast desktop workstation will provide excellent price/performance.

As long as there is sufficient processing power, users will only experience database outages due to a loss of network connectivity. If a command is run which accesses the databases (as do most administrative, authentication, and group management commands,) and the network is partitioned, the command will appear to hang as it looks for an available database server. If the command needed to perform an update and the issuer cannot transmit to the sync site, then the updates will fail.

Once running, the different database instances keep log files on the server in `/usr/afs/logs`. Because updates are sent to the database sync site (normally the lowest IP-addressed database server in the cell) for processing, the sync sites files usually contain the most relevant log data.

The `AuthLog` file, for the Kerberos server, is especially terse and does not log many messages unless there is a significant internal inconsistency. A typical functioning `kaserver` will simply log its initialization.

```
$ cat /usr/afs/logs/AuthLog
kerberos/udp port=750
kerberos5/udp is unknown; check /etc/services.  Using port=88 as default
Starting to listen for UDP packets
start 5 min check lwp
Starting to process AuthServer requests
```

The `BackupLog` file, used by the backup server, stores messages about dumps made and restored. You might be able to get a better overview of the cellwide backup activity by scanning this file with regular ASCII tools, rather than by using the backup database query commands.

```
$ cat /usr/afs/logs/BackupLog
...
03/30/97 12:30:05 Create dump users.full (DumpID 859743005), path /full
03/30/97 13:27:05 Create dump Ubik_db_dump (DumpID 859746425), path
03/30/97 13:29:48 Delete dump users.full (DumpID 859743005), path /full
...
```

For the volserver, a useful option is -log. Without this option, only certain operations are recorded; with it, all volume creation, deletion, and moves are logged along with the names of the users who initiate the operation. As with other file or database server options, this option needs to be added to the bos configuration entry for this process. This logging provides a very good audit trail of AFS management operations. But you must remember to rotate the logs manually and archive them yourself if you are to have a robust history of all AFS operations; the volserver overwrites the previous /usr/afs/log/VolserLog.old file every time it starts.

```
$ cat /usr/afs/log/VolserLog
Sun Mar 30 14:24:37 1997: Starting AFS Volserver 2.0 (/usr/afs/bin/volserver)
Sun Mar 30 14:34:18 1997: 1 Volser: Delete: volume 536870955 deleted
Sun Mar 30 14:34:18 1997: 1 Volser: Clone: Cloning volume 536870954 to new volume 536870955
Sun Mar 30 15:29:53 1997: 1 Volser: Delete: volume 536870993 deleted
Sun Mar 30 15:30:42 1997: 1 Volser: CreateVolume: volume 536870994 (user.helen) created
Sun Mar 30 15:31:12 1997: 1 Volser: Delete: volume 536870994 deleted
```

Few options are available to optimize the volserver process. To increase concurrency, it runs with nine threads of control. This number can be modified at startup via the flag -p given a value from 4 to 16.

The volume location server, vlserver, stores log information in /usr/afs/logs/VLLog; this file is new to AFS 3.4a. However, when started, vlserver by default does not log any information to this file. Three different levels of debug output are available:

- Level one—vlserver logs volume creations, deletions, change address operations, replacements, updates, volume locks and unlocks, and new volume identifier operations.
- Level two—in addition to the level one data, vlserver logs volume lookup by name or identification number, list attributes, get statistics, or get addresses.

- Level three—in addition to levels one and two data, vlserver logs other operations such as list entries.

To set the level of debugging, send UNIX signals to the vlserver process: the SIGTSTP signal increments the current level number, the SIGHUP signal decrements the level. (Note that this is different from the debugging protocol used by the fileserver.) There's no way to find out what the current level is, so either keep careful track or send some extra SIGHUP signals to ensure that the current level is level zero. The following shows how logging might be initialized.

```
# hostname
db-one
# ps -ef
     UID    PID   PPID  C    STIME TTY       TIME CMD
...
     root   1760  1309  0 15:32:19 ?         0:00 /usr/afs/bin/vlserver
...
# kill -TSTP 1760
```

The contents of the log file look like this:

```
$ cat /usr/afs/logs/VLLog
Sun Apr  6 17:01:08 1997 Starting AFS vlserver 4 (/usr/afs/bin/vlserver)
@(#)Base configuration afs3.4 5.00
Sun Apr  6 17:02:07 1997 Set Debug On level = 1
```

Like other server processes, the vlserver internally runs several threads of control to increase concurrency. In previous versions of AFS, four threads managed the volume location database; as of version 3.4a, the default number of threads is 9. This number can be increased to 16 via the -p option.

UBIK DEBUGGING

AFS databases replicate themselves automatically and reliably without any regular maintenance by administrators. When there are multiple database servers, each with its own dedicated hardware on which to run, there will be few problems with their operation. Because the architecture of the Ubik protocol is designed to overcome network problems and failed transactions, it is likely that users will never see an AFS database problem except in extraordinary situations.

Since AFS version 3.4a, data from any of the databases is still readable even when the servers have lost quorum and updates are rejected. Hence, if there are problems communicating with the security servers, you can manually choose to use a particular server with the `-server` option to the `klog` and `kas` commands.

```
$ klog afsadmin -server db-two
Password:
```

When tracking down database server outages situations, use `udebug` to query the status of each database server, determine which site is the master, and which site has an out-of-date copy of the data. To check the Ubik data of a running server, choose a port number appropriate for the database you want to check. Here, 7002 is the port for `ptserver`:

```
$ udebug db-two 7002
Host's 192.168.3.12 time is Sun Mar 30 16:51:23 1997
Local time is Sun Mar 30 16:51:23 1997 (time differential 0 secs)
Last yes vote for 192.168.3.11 was 7 secs ago (sync site);
Last vote started 6 secs ago (at Sun Mar 30 16:51:17 1997)
Local db version is 859748652.9
I am not sync site
Lowest host 192.168.3.11 was set 7 secs ago
Sync host 192.168.3.11 was set 7 secs ago
Sync site's db version is 859748652.9
0 locked pages, 0 of them for write
```

This output from a nonsync site shows only the local database conditions. When querying a sync site, you will see information on all known database servers (for that database process).

```
$ udebug db-one 7002
Host's 192.168.3.11 time is Sun Mar 30 16:51:29 1997
Local time is Sun Mar 30 16:51:27 1997 (time differential -2 secs)
Last yes vote for 192.168.3.11 was 10 secs ago (sync site);
Last vote started 10 secs ago (at Sun Mar 30 16:51:17 1997)
Local db version is 859748652.9
I am sync site until 49 secs from now (at Sun Mar 30 16:52:16 1997) (2 servers)
Recovery state 1f
Sync site's db version is 859748652.9
0 locked pages, 0 of them for write
Last time a new db version was labelled was:
         10035 secs ago (at Sun Mar 30 14:04:12 1997)

Server 192.168.3.12 (db 859748652.9)
    last vote rcvd 11 secs ago (at Sun Mar 30 16:51:16 1997),
    last beacon sent 10 secs ago (at Sun Mar 30 16:51:17 1997), last vote was yes
    dbcurrent=1, up=1 beaconSince=1
```

```
Server 192.168.5.13 (db 859748652.9)
    last vote rcvd 13 secs ago (at Sun Mar 30 16:51:14 1997),
    last beacon sent 15 secs ago (at Sun Mar 30 16:51:12 1997), last vote was yes
    dbcurrent=1, up=1 beaconSince=1
```

Having all machines in a cell know the same time is vital, especially for Ubik database servers. Each database process pings the others so each has an idea of how out of synchronization their times may be. If the "his time is n" line is greater than 10, this information indicates that the clock is more than 10 seconds off and could be the source of database election problems.

Votes for sync sites are performed every 15 seconds and are conducted by the sync site. Each database process keeps track of when the last vote was conducted; if no new vote is held for 75 seconds, then nonsync servers will initiate their own vote. The "Last vote for" line shows the Internet address of the server that the site queried voted for and how long ago that vote took place. If the server has just been restarted and has not voted for anyone, the Internet address is displayed as 255.255.255.255. This default address is also displayed for sites running a single database process because there is no need to vote for the sync site.

The database version number consists of a timestamp and a version number. The timestamp is the time at which the sync site was elected, and the version number is incremented after every update to the database. A database version of 0.0 means the database is corrupt (the file makes no internal sense) or can't be read.

The sync site also displays its recovery state. This is a 5-bit-wide status flag, where an on bit means OK. In hexadecimal, all 5 OK bits will display as recovery state 1f. If any of the following 5 bits is zero, there's a problem:

- bit 0 off—I am not the sync site.
- bit 1 off—Not all the database versions on the other servers are ok.
- bit 2 off—The sync site does not have the best database version.
- bit 3 off—The version number has changed.
- bit 4 off—I am the sync site, but my database has not been copied to any other database servers.

The sync site will display the status of any on-going writes, "n locked pages, n of them for write". The number of locked pages should usually be 0 because the updates take very little time to execute. If the numbers do not change, the database process could be hung.

Updates to an AFS database are sent from the Ubik sync site to the replicas as whole objects; rather than the entire database, only the complete object that was updated is sent. For example, when changes are made to group membership in the protection database, the new value of the group, that is, all the new and old members, is sent to each replica. Large groups can therefore present a problem: if thousands of users are placed in a single, updates to that group, such as adding or deleting a single person, will cause the entire group membership list to be transmitted. In such a case, the transmittal time may interfere with the on-going Ubik elections and therefore cause the `ptserver` processes to lose quorum.

If there is not enough room on disk to store the updates to a database, a sync site will return a failure to the client request. Disk shortages on a secondary will cause the secondary to disallow access until it is able to retrieve the new version of the entire, too-large database. Because the sync site must process all write requests, make sure that it has the most CPU, memory, and disk space.

If one database server process determines that its copy of the database is corrupt, it will initiate a transfer of the entire database from a working database server. You can use this functionality to your advantage: If you suspect a database is bad, you can simply rename the database files. In short order, the server process that controls the database will notice the missing database files and will get a new copy. This technique is preferable to copying over the database files via FTP or some other manual process because Ubik will correctly, lock the system from any updates. Thus the site retrieves a uniform version of the database. The process looks like this:

```
# bos shutdown db-two kaserver -localauth
# cd /usr/afs/db
# mv kaserver.DB0 kaserver.DB0.corrupt
# rm kaserver.DBSYS1
# bos restart db-two kaserver -localauth
# udebug db-two 7004
Host's 192.168.3.12 time is Sun Mar 30 16:55:57 1997
Local time is Sun Mar 30 16:55:57 1997 (time differential 0 secs)
Last yes vote for 255.255.255.255 was 80 secs ago (not sync site);
Last vote started 859758957 secs ago (at Wed Dec 31 19:00:00 1969)
Local db version is 859748656.8
I am not sync site
Lowest host 192.168.3.11 was set 14 secs ago
Sync host 192.168.3.11 was set 14 secs ago
Sync site's db version is 0.0
0 locked pages, 0 of them for write
```

Immediately after the restart of `kaserver` on `db-two`, you can see that the database version number is 0.0. Eventually, after perhaps a minute, you'll see that all is well.

```
# udebug db-two 7004
Host's 192.168.3.12 time is Sun Mar 30 16:56:14 1997
Local time is Sun Mar 30 16:56:14 1997 (time differential 0 secs)
Last yes vote for 192.168.3.11 was 0 secs ago (sync site);
Last vote started -1 secs ago (at Sun Mar 30 16:56:15 1997)
Local db version is 859748656.8
I am not sync site
Lowest host 192.168.3.11 was set 0 secs ago
Sync host 192.168.3.11 was set 0 secs ago
Sync site's db version is 859748656.8
0 locked pages, 0 of them for write
```

In a worst-case scenario, you can stop all the servers and restore a database from tape to the sync site. The other servers will then get their database copy soon.

If a database server crashes and will be down for some time, you may need to inform all client machines of the situation so they can work around the problem without interfering with other user operations. Use the `fs server-prefs` command to reset preferences for the database servers, as described in Chapter 5, or, more permanently, change a client's `CellServDB` file and/or kernel cell information.

Inform Transarc product support of any database corruptions that might have resulted from otherwise normal operations (as opposed to bad disk blocks or machine crashes). To assist them, save a copy of the correct as well as the corrupt database.

THE scout MONITOR

AFS file servers are naturally the focus of much administration. Transarc provides one tool, `scout`, designed for minute-by-minute monitoring of these file servers. Unfortunately, the monitoring facilities of `scout` are not integrated with other management systems such as UNIX `syslog` or the SNMP protocol. But its graphical interface does provide a good visual indication of the status of the cell.

When started from the command line, `scout` displays labels in the current terminal screen showing file servers, available space on each server's partition, number of active clients, and other information. Certain items can be flagged for alarm conditions; if the conditions are exceeded, the items are displayed in reverse-video. This terminal display capability is provided by the UNIX Curses library, which relies on the setting of the process's TERM environment variable. This set up is normally provided by your system administrator.

Any user can run scout, pointing it at any one or more servers in the cell. Since no administrative controls can be run from the program—only collective statistics are printed—access control is not an issue.

A typical use of scout in our example cell is:

```
$ scout -server fs-one fs-two
```

This command immediately clears the current terminal screen and displays information, as shown in Figure 10-1.

```
-------------------------------------------------------------------------
                                    Scout
Conn      Fetch       Store    Ws                    Disk attn: > 95% used
----      --------    -------- -----                 ----------
   5          15           2     2   fs-one          a:977036        b:1029484
                                                     c:1029519
   6           9           0     2   fs-two          a:259924


Probe 1 results
-------------------------------------------------------------------------
```

Figure 10-1 The scout Screen

The information includes the number of active connections, the number of fetch and store packets, the number of active clients, the server name, and then a set of numbers, one set for each partition on the server and the number of kilobytes still available on that partition.

In the first column, the number of active connections represents the number of active user sessions on all the workstations served from that file server. Since each workstation can support more than one user and each user can have more than one connection going at once, this number will likely be larger than the number of active workstations in the fourth column.

The second and third columns show the number of fetch and store packets sent to the server. The fetch packets include all get data, access lists, and status; store packets include all put data, access lists, and status. These numbers are reset to zero when the file server restarts.

The fourth column shows the number of active clients. Active in this context means that the client has communicated with the server in the last 15 minutes.

The fifth column displays the file server name. If the name is longer than 12 characters, it is truncated.

The last column contains a set of values, one for each of the partitions on that server and displaying the number of kilobytes still available. Each value set is composed of the abbreviated partition name, "a" for the partition on /vicepa, for example, a colon character, and the number of kilobytes. This column is headed by a label that shows the condition threshold beyond which the partition will be displayed in reverse video, indicating a low-space problem. By default, this condition is reached when the partition is 95 percent full.

At the bottom of the screen is a label that shows how many times the file servers have been queried by this instance of the scout process. The data is updated every 60 seconds by default.

In Figure 10-1, you can see that file server fs-one has 5 active connections from 2 active workstations.

Note that the file servers named on the scout command line do not need to be limited to the local cell or even be members of the same cell. File servers are only loosely coupled to their cells to begin with; there is no communication between file servers nor even a central configuration file for a cell's file servers. Thus, the servers must be specified individually on the scout command line. Because the load posed by the scout probes is quite small, you can use scout freely to monitor one or more file servers for one or more cells.

afsmonitor

A more detailed analysis of clients and servers is available with the afsmonitor utility. Much of this data will be of interest only to the implementors of AFS, but a few of the statistics help administrators to examine cache hit ratios or server load. Like scout, the program displays the results of regularly probing AFS servers. But in addition to probing servers, afsmonitor can query clients, highlight data that exceeds certain thresholds, and also run external programs when specified conditions are reached.

Like scout, afsmonitor is a Curses-based display program and so will run in any correctly configured terminal screen, either a dedicated monitor or a virtual terminal as provided by the xterm program. Also, all users are normally permitted to run the monitor; there are no access control issues and the burden on the servers or clients of a running monitor is quite light.

A typical session might start with:

```
$ afsmonitor -fshosts fs-one fs-two -cmhosts desktop1
```

This command begins probing two file servers and one desktop machine; it queries servers and clients separately to retrieve their unique information. The probes by default are triggered once every minute or as specified in a -frequency option.

When this command runs, it paints an overview page into the current terminal window. The page shows the machines indicated on the command line, summary statistics on the number of servers, clients, and errors, and the number of probes that have occurred. The servers are listed in a column on the left and the clients on the right. Any machine for which a statistic has indicated a problem will show the number of probes returned which have exceeded its threshold; if the machine has failed to answer the previous probe, the letters PF—probe failure—are displayed. Note well, in the upper right-hand corner, the current page number and total number of pages available are printed. Figure 10-2 shows the initial display from afsmonitor.

```
--------------------------------------------------------------------
AFSMonitor [Version 1.0]                     [System Overview, p. 1 of 1]

   2 File Servers monitored      1 Cache Managers monitored
   0 alerts on 0 machines        0 alerts on 0 machines

      fs-one                        client1
      fs-two




Command [fs, cm]?                  [probes 1(fs) 1(cm), freq=60 sec]
--------------------------------------------------------------------
```

Figure 10-2 The afsmonitor Initial Screen

During the run of the program, you can enter commands at the keyboard to navigate the many pages of information available. You can begin by entering either fs to display fileserver statistics or cm to display client cache manager data. Once the family of machines has been specified, a new page displays a large table of data showing results from the last probe. Each row displays information for one machine with each column devoted to a different statistic.

You can navigate back to the overview page by entering oview, to the other family of machines with either fs or cm, or move the table left or right by entering l or r. In the top right-hand column, again, you can see the number of available pages and columns. Figure 10-3 shows a snapshot of the file server statistics display.

```
--------------------------------------------------------------------
AFSMonitor [Version 1.0]           [File Servers, p. 1 of 1, c. 1 or 271]
         2 File Servers monitored, 0 alerts on 0 machines            >>>

                num      vcache    vcache    vcache    vcache    vcache
           PerfCalls   L_Entries  L_Allocs  L_Gets   L_Reads  L_Writes

fs-one             2       400          0       19         6         2

fs-two             2       400          0        9         2         0




Command [oview, cm, right]?                   [FS probes 2, freq=60 sec]
--------------------------------------------------------------------
```

Figure 10-3 The afsmonitor File Server Screen

When running afsmonitor, you will first notice the tremendous number of irrelevant statistics—and the column headers are practically indecipherable. See Appendix A of *AFS System Administrator's Guide* for an explanation of each column (271 for servers, 570 for clients). However, amid all the noise are many pieces of data that are of interest. Figure 10-4 shows the initial display screen for the client side statistics. You can use the statistics to extract some useful information on client performance.

- dlocalAccesses, vlocalAccesses—The number of accesses to file data and metadata, respectively, from the client to the local cell
- dcacheHits, dcacheMisses—The number of cache hits and misses for file data
- vcacheHits, vcacheMisses—The number of cache hits and misses for file metadata
- OutStandingMemUsage—The amount of allocated kernel memory
- fs_sc_numDowntimeIncidents—The number of times a file server was believed to be down
- vl_sc_numDowntimeIncidents—The number of times a volume location database server was believed to be down

```
---------------------------------------------------------------------
AFSMonitor [Version 1.0]              [Cache Managers, p. 1 of 1, c.1 of 571

        1 Cache Managers monitored, 0 alerts on 0 machines          >>>

            num                 numCells   numCells   dlocal     vlocal
        PerfCalls    epoch      Visible    Contacted  Accesses   Accesses

client1           6  859756168        1          1         47         28




Command [oview, fs, right]?                      [CM probes 6, freq=60 sec]
---------------------------------------------------------------------
```

Figure 10-4   The afsmonitor Client Screen

Figure 10-5 shows some of these numbers. These will be seen by typing the r key a few times to scroll the screen rightward, exposing the desired columns.

```
---------------------------------------------------------------------
AFSMonitor [Version 1.0]              [Cache Managers, p. 1 of 1, c. 13 or 571]

<<<         1 Cache Manager monitored, 0 alerts on 0 machines       >>>

            cache       cache
          MaxDirty    CurrDirty   dcache    vcache    dcache    vcache
           Chunks      Chunks      Hits      Hits     Misses    Misses

client1        926           0        41        13         6         27




Command [oview, fs, left, right]?                [CM probes 6, freq=60 sec]
---------------------------------------------------------------------
```

Figure 10-5   The afsmonitor Client Screen with Cache Hits

Detailed records are also kept for each client or file server's remote procedure calls. The details include total number of operations, number successful, sum of timings for all operations, minimum and maximum times for any given operation, and the number of server, network, and access errors. Figure 10-6 shows a selection of these statistics for our file servers.

```
--------------------------------------------------------------------
AFSMonitor [Version 1.0]        [File Servers, p. 1 of 1, c. 31 or 271]

<<<       2 File Servers monitored, 0 alerts on 0 machines            >>>

              rx          rx          rx          rx          rx          rx
          pktsRead      data         ack         dup       spurious   pktsSent
          SpecialCl*   PktsRead   PktsRead    PktsRead    PktsRead    RcvClass

fs-one             0          39          14           0           0          41

fs-two             0          53          11           0           0          61




Command [oview, cm, left, right]?                 [FS probes 5, freq=60 sec]
--------------------------------------------------------------------
```

Figure 10-6   The `afsmonitor` File Server Screen with Rx Statistics

Again, the meanings of these statistics are described in the *AFS System Administrator's Guide*. Table 10-1 lists information for some of these Rx remote procedure calls.

Table 10-1   Rx Remote Procedure Calls

RPC Statistic	Description
rx_dataPacketsSent	Number of unique data packets sent
rx_totalRtt_Sec, rx_totalRtt_Usec	Total round-trip time in seconds and milliseconds
rx_minRtt_Sec, rx_minRtt_Usec	Minimum round-trip time in seconds and milliseconds
rx_maxRtt_Sec, rx_maxRtt_Usec	Maximum round-trip time in seconds and milliseconds
rx_nRttSamples	Number of round-trip time samples
host_NumClients	Total number of clients seen by the server
host_HostsInDiffSubnet	Number of clients in different subnet than server

For file servers, statistics include the number of file server operations, successful requests, and minimum and maximum response time for all of the types of operations, as enumerated above for clients. Also, note that file server statistics are cumulative across all clients being serviced.

Besides total information on all Rx packets, these numbers are further broken down for each type of file system activity: fetch file data, fetch access control list, fetch file status, store file data, store access control list, store status, remove file, create file, rename file, create symlink, create hard link, make directory, remove directory, set lock, extend lock, release lock, get statistics, give up callbacks, get volume info, set volume status, get root volume, check token, get time, get volume info, and bulk status. In addition, afsmonitor reports the minimum, maximum, and sum of bytes transferred during data fetch and store operations.

This level of detail is far more than you will need for your daily work. But there will come a time when your engineering staff will need to understand exactly how certain pieces of client and server hardware are behaving, perhaps when installing new network segments or storage technology. You can then show these statistics as proof that the system works or fails.

In a production cell, once you've determined which pieces of data indicate potential problems for your site, you can set up afsmonitor to notify you when the threshold conditions are reached. First, construct a configuration file listing the file servers, cache managers, thresholds, and triggers. Each line of the configuration script must be one of:

- cm hostname—Adds a client to the list of monitored cache managers.
- fs hostname—Adds a server to the list of monitored file servers.
- thresh fs|cm column value [command preset-args]—
  Instructs the monitor to indicate an error condition when the specified
  file server or cache manager statistic exceeds a certain value. If a command is appended to this line, it is assumed to be an executable and is
  run when the threshold is exceeded. When executed, the command's
  arguments will be set to command fs|cm column value actual-
  value preset-args.

  When a thresh line comes after a cm or fs line, the threshold applies
  only to that single machine. If the line is before any named machine lines,
  it applies globally to all file servers or cache managers.
- show fs|cm column—Determines which columns are displayed. You
  can enter any number of show lines to customize the display. Take the
  name for the column argument from the list of statistics in Appendix A of
  the *AFS System Administrator's Guide*; alternatively, the argument could
  indicate a group or section of statistics, or all statistics for file servers or
  cache managers.

A brief example configuration file:

```
thresh fs rx_maxRtt_sec 1 logThresh
fs fs-one
fs fs-two
cm desktop1
thresh cm vl_sc_numDowntimeIncidents 10
```

Here, we set a global threshold for all file servers: when the maximum round-trip time for Rx protocol packets exceeds 1 second, the program `log-Thresh` will run. You could design this program to simply log the fact that a particular threshold was exceeded at a certain time and day; then later you can analyze and correlate the data with other network or system problems.

Next, we defined a selection of file server and clients. On the last line, we set a threshold for a single client (in this case, just `desktop1`) that exceeds 10 fail overs of volume location database servers. We did not designate a threshold program, so if the number of fail overs passes 10, only the visual display of the `afsmonitor` program will indicate this error.

To run `afsmonitor` with this configuration, add `-config` and the file name to the command-line invocation.

Additionally, `afsmonitor` can save all collected statistics in a data file. This way, hours', days', or weeks' worth of performance information can be stored away for later investigation. Simply add the `-output` option with a writeable file name as an argument.

Certain Rx packet statistics can stand on their own to warn of potential problems. Others can only make sense when compared as a percentage of the total number of packets. You should watch out for the warning signs in Table 10-2.

If you desire, you can even go one step further and write a customized program to probe a machine for any statistic you'd like; the entire data collection facility is provided as a programming library, `libxstat.a`. To realize the fullest benefit of this system, access Transarc's internal information, which explains the workings of the library. It is available on the Internet at `ftp://ftp.transarc.com/pub/doc/afs/xstat`.

Or, once you have AFS up and running, execute:

```
$ cd /afs/grand.central.org/pub/doc/afs/xstat
```

One nice statistic to calculate is the client cache hit ratio, the number of times that data requested from a file was found in the local cache. In the `afsmonitor` output, you can read the hits and misses for any client:

Table 10-2   Rx Statistic Warning Signs

RPC Statistic	Description
rx_noPacketOnRead	The number of times the Rx system tried to read a packet and discovered that nothing was available. This value should normally be 0 or other small number.
rx_noPacketBuffersOnRead	The number of packets read for which no buffer space was available to store the data. Any value larger than 0 indicates an out-of-memory condition.
rx_dataPacketsRead	Total number of packets read. This is a large number that increases over time on a healthy file server. Use this number to calculate the proportion of bad packets in the next few listed entries.
rx_dupPacketsRead	The number of duplicate packets read. Should be less than 2 percent of the total number of packets.
rx_SpuriousPacketsRead	The number of packets with inconsistent headers. It, too, should be less than 2 percent of the total number of packets.
rx_dataPacketsReSent	The number of packets that had to be retransmitted because of some failure. This number should be less than 2 percent of the total number of packets sent.

- dcacheHits, dcacheMisses—The number of times file data was found in the cache, and the number of misses that forced a request to be sent to the server.
- vcacheHits, vcacheMisses—The same statistics for file metadata.

Performing a bit of math produces the cache hit rates:

```
dcache hit ratio = dcacheHits / ( dcacheHits + dcacheMisses)
vcache hit ratio = vcacheHits / ( vcacheHits + vcacheMisses)
```

There's no particularly right or wrong value for the hit ratio because it depends on what the client has been doing and how large is its cache. You can use this value as a guide either to increase the cache size to raise the hit ratios or to reduce the cache if you feel that the larger sizes are not justified: there's not much sense in adding another 100 megabytes just to move from 98 percent to 99 percent.

In general, many sites have found that they can achieve hit rates of 98 percent for file data and 96 percent for file metadata without resorting to enormous caches.

Study these statistics to understand how a set of programs uses the file system or to get a feel for your standard environment. Different users and applications will tend to use or abuse the client cache in hard-to-predict ways. Even software developers, the target population for the AFS system, can either make extremely good use of their cache, if they are spending all day fixing bugs in a source file in a large project, or very poor use of the cache, if they are using many analysis tools and rebuilding many different packages in a short period of time.

To get a good snapshot of the numbers, reboot the client or server to make sure that the statistics are valid for the tests you run. You should collect the relevant statistics just before and after your test, check the total number of operations performed—create, delete, getattr, etc.—as well as the total number of bytes read and written and the callback activity generated. This data can help you decide how to change your client cache manager configurations, validate that AFS is performing as expected, or show that certain applications are trashing your cache.

AIX AUDITING

IBM's AIX operating system comes with an extensive built-in auditing mechanism that AFS can use to log significant file service events. To enable the auditing of AFS, add to each desired file server file, /usr/afs/local/Audit, which contains the single character string "AFS_AUDIT_AllEvents". Then restart all file server processes to cause the system to begin logging events to the AIX audit service.

You can use three other IBM system files for further configuration:

- /etc/security/audit/events—Describes the possible events that can be audited. The AFS file /usr/afs/local/audit/events.sample contains the data that should be added to the IBM configuration file.
- /etc/security/audit/config—Classifies the auditing events. The file /usr/afs/local/audit/config.sample contains examples of the six categories of AFS events.
- /etc/security/audit/objects—Defines the audit files. The file /usr/afs/local/audit/objects.sample has examples.

With this system, file service events, such as those listed in Table 10-3, can be completely monitored.

Table 10-3 AIX File Service Events for AFS

File Service Event	Description
AFS_VS_Start	The volume server has started.
AFS_VS_CrVol	A volume has been created. The host ID and volume name and number are recorded.
AFS_VS_DelVol	A volume has been deleted. Again, the host ID and volume number are recorded. Similar events for other volume server operations are audited.
AFS_VL_CreEnt	An entry in the volume location database has been created. Other volume location database server operations are also recorded.
AFS_BUDB_Start	The backup server has started. Most backup operations such as creating a backup dump, (AFS_BUDB_CrDump) are also recorded.
AFS_PTS_Start	The protection server has started. Again, protection database operations, such as creating or deleting an entry, are recorded.
AFS_KAA_Auth	An authentication operation succeeded. Other operations such as creating or deleting a user account and setting and changing passwords are recorded.
AFS_NoAuthEnbl	The server has been set to run in no authentication mode
AFS_BOS_StartAl	The bosserver process has been instructed to start all jobs.

Other operations such as shutting down all jobs, and adding or deleting names from the UserList are also recorded.

This auditing provides a good mechanism for tracking down administration problems or unauthorized access to the cell. But, of course, it records the event only after the action has been completed. This record can give an organization a tool to debrief administrators on what has occurred, but it does not replace proper security policy implementation.

CLIENT DEBUGGING

AFS clients will only rarely need debugging. Prior to AFS 3.4a, a debug subcommand of the fs suite enabled administrators to extract information on the status of a client cache manager. Now, a separate command, fstrace, performs this task. The information available is quite detailed and requires familiarity with the algorithms and implementation of the client. Note that it extracts immediate information on suspected problems; that is, it is not a long-running monitoring tool.

Most AFS customers will run this command only when requested by Transarc product support to provide the engineers with details of reported problems. Other AFS sites, especially those with source code, can run this command as desired, though the resulting information may be cryptic, if not even misleading. You must be root to run `fstrace` because tracing client operations will affect performance somewhat and because some of the information may be considered proprietary to users on the system.

This facility enables logging of a variety of client-side AFS events. When this debugging service is turned on, the cache manager records data about its operations into an in-kernel circular buffer. You can read this information directly from the kernel or save a snapshot into a file, You can even set the service to continuously save new data to a log file; in this case, be sure to set aside plenty of space because the amount of information logged can be quite large.

When researching problems, follow good debugging practices and restrict the problem set to as small an area as possible. If a large number of AFS operations are being performed on a client during this investigation, the `fstrace` log will likely have too much data in it, making debugging by either you or Transarc difficult at best.

To begin tracing, activate the facility and declare which set of operations to log; currently there is only one such set for the cache manager.

```
# fstrace setset -active
```

Activating the trace sets aside the in-kernel memory buffer for storing event information. This buffer is by default 60 kilobytes large. At times, logging information will wrap around the end and start again at the beginning. A message "Log wrapped; data missing" will appear on standard output if this happens before a snapshot of the data has been saved to a log file. A larger buffer may reduce the amount of missing data. To set the buffer to 100 kilobytes, use the `setlog` subcommand.

```
# fstrace setlog -buffersize 100
```

To toggle tracing off and on, you can issue options to `setset` to change the current state: `-inactive` temporarily stops tracing; `-dormant` stops tracing and deallocates the in-kernel memory buffer. An `-inactive` option confines the log information to just the operations surrounding the suspected problem area.

After activating tracing, the cache manager automatically starts logging its actions to the in-kernel buffer. You can then display the buffer contents with fstrace dump.

```
# fstrace dump
AFS Trace Dump -

   Date: Sun Mar 30 17:12:06 1997

Found 1 logs.

Contents of log cmfx:
time 266.962153, pid 0: Sun Mar 30 17:11:22 1997


time 266.962153, pid 793: RPC GetVolumeByName for 536870913
time 266.965527, pid 793: Analyze RPC op -1 conn 0x5095b278 code 0x0 user 0x489
time 266.986471, pid 793: Analyze RPC op 2 conn 0x5095b440 code 0x0 user 0x489
time 266.986496, pid 793: ProcessFS vp 0x5082a000 old len 0x800 new len 0x800
time 266.986520, pid 793: Gn_open vp 0x5082a000 flags 0x0 (returns 0x0)
time 266.986574, pid 793: GetdCache vp 0x5082a000 dcache 0x508da0b0 dcache low-version
0x16, vcache low-version 0x16
time 266.986625, pid 793: Lookup adp 0x5082a000 name hq.firm fid   1:536870913.2.2
811), code=0
time 267.001945, pid 793: Analyze RPC op 2 conn 0x5095b440 code 0x0 user 0x489
time 267.001966, pid 793: ProcessFS vp 0x5082a120 old len 0xb new len 0xb
time 267.002020, pid 793: RPC GetVolumeByName for root.cell
time 267.018888, pid 793: Analyze RPC op -1 conn 0x5095b278 code 0x0 user 0x489
time 267.018988, pid 793: Mount point is to vp 0x5082a120 fid (1:536870913.2.281
1)
```

If the output includes raw operation codes rather than textual description (such as RPC GetVolumeByName), check that the client has the file /usr/vice/etc/C/afszcm.cat installed correctly. This so-called catalog file stores the actual text of the messages in a standard format.

The times recorded in the log are the number of seconds relative to a timestamp logged to the buffer every 1024 seconds. To find the absolute time of an operation, you have to perform some math to translate the relative number of seconds to the most recent timestamp logged: in the above example, the second RPC GetVolumeByName, at time 267.002020, occurred 0.39867 seconds after the timestamp at 17:11:22.

For a continuous display of the in-kernel buffer, use the -follow option. Every 10 seconds, the latest contents of the buffer are dumped. To save this information in a file rather than have it scroll off the top of your terminal screen, use the -file option:

```
# fstrace dump -follow cmfx -file /tmp/fstrace.dump &
# tail -f /tmp/fstrace.dump
AFS Trace Dump -

  Date: Sun Mar 30 17:13:50 1997

time 266.962153, pid 0: Sun Mar 30 17:11:22 1997


time 266.962153, pid 793: RPC GetVolumeByName for 536870913
time 266.965527, pid 793: Analyze RPC op -1 conn 0x5095b278 code 0x0 user 0x489
time 266.986471, pid 793: Analyze RPC op 2 conn 0x5095b440 code 0x0 user 0x489
...
```

The cmfx argument to the -follow option specifies which kernel buffer
to use; the only available buffer is the cache manager's cmfx. Again, be aware
that this trace file can grow quite large, quite quickly.

To query the current state of the trace facility.

```
# fstrace lsset cm
Set cm: active
# fstrace lslog cm -long
Logs for set 'cm':
cmfx : 100 kbytes (allocated)
```

Rather than generate logs of operational messages, you may want to just
find out what a particular client is doing right now. You can use the cmdebug
("cache manager debug") program to display the current state of client operations. Here, we add the -long option to look at all cache entries.

```
# cmdebug client1 -long
Lock afs_xvcache status: (none_waiting)
Lock afs_xdcache status: (none_waiting)
Lock afs_xserver status: (none_waiting)
Lock afs_xvcb status: (none_waiting)
Lock afs_xbrs status: (none_waiting)
Lock afs_xcell status: (none_waiting)
Lock afs_xconn status: (none_waiting)
Lock afs_xuser status: (none_waiting)
Lock afs_xvolume status: (none_waiting)
Lock puttofile status: (none_waiting)
Lock afs_ftf status: (none_waiting)
Lock afs_xcbhash status: (none_waiting)
Lock afs_xaxs status: (none_waiting)
** Cache entry @ 0x5082a000 for 1.536870913.1.1
    2048 bytes  DV 22 refcnt 4
    callback 505ffd20    expires 859767116
```

```
      0 opens      0 writers
      volume root
      states (0x4), read-only
** Cache entry @ 0x5082a120 for 1.536870913.2.2811
      11 bytes     DV 1 refcnt 0
      callback 505ffd20    expires 859767115
      0 opens      0 writers
      mount point
      states (0x4), read-only
 . . .
```

A normally running client will show a small set of locks; over time, repeated runs of cmdebug will show a different set of locks. If you suspect that a particular entry is causing a problem, you should determine which file is being accessed. You can see the internal identifiers of the cache entry displayed as a quartet of numbers; in the first cache entry above, the quartet is 1.536870913.1.1. This number represents the cell number, the volume number, the vnode number, and the uniquifier or version number. You can find what volume is involved by running a vos command such as listvldb; based on the volume name, you should know where in the tree the volume is mounted. Then, use the calcinode algorithm to determine the exact inode for the file.

You can also see a line showing which server is holding a callback promise on which cache entries.

```
callback  c0a80315    expires 861438532
```

The number after the word callback is simply the Internet address, expressed in hexadecimal, of the server holding the callback: c0a80315 is separated into c0.a8.03.15, which is 192.168.3.21 in decimal. The expiration time is in seconds since the epoch January 1, 00:00 GMT 1970. Another unsupported Transarc program, calctime, can be used to translate the time in seconds into a readable timestamp. (Perl and other programming languages can perform this translation as well.)

Other information for each entry shows its size, how many processes have the file open or are writing to it, whether the file is a normal file, a mount point, or the root of a volume.

CACHE PROBLEMS

The heart of AFS is the client cache. Without the cache, there'd be little need for the complications of a stateful server. Because the AFS kernel-resident code package must be maintained across a variety of vendor hardware, problems can creep in, and occasionally you may see inconsistencies between client caches on two desktops. These problems usually arise with ports to new versions of operating systems or with hardware platforms unavailable for testing at Transarc. And sometimes, the inconsistencies are merely figments of users' imaginations. It is therefore important to learn how to determine that real, client cache inconsistencies exist and to help Transarc find the cause of the problem.

There are two general problems with client caches: either one client sees inconsistent or stale data that should have been updated automatically, or else the data is simply corrupt. You know you're seeing stale data when two clients have different versions of the same file. (Make sure you've got the exact same path; read-write volumes can be expected to have a newer set of files in them than their read-only replicas.) Stale data can be caused by missed callbacks on either the client or file server side.

While fixing a cache problem by using the fs flush command is trivial, it is very important—for both you and Transarc—to collect data about the problem and, if the problem is reproducible, to contact Transarc for help. Normally, the best strategy includes comparing the kernel structures of two clients and dumping the callback structures from the servers.

To compare client kernels, run the kdump program on the affected client and on a client that can see the correct version of the file. The printout will be somewhat unintelligible but will contain data that can be used by Transarc's technical staff to determine the exact state of the client system. Next, you can use some tools provided by customer support to track down exactly which V-files in the client cache hold this file, copy those files to a save area. Then, after fixing the problem by flushing the client cache, get a new kernel structure dump. Transarc can compare the before-and-after snapshots with the data from a "good" client to help determine the pieces of kernel state that made the inconsistent client think it had the right data.

On the file server, you can send a signal to the fileserver process to cause the job to dump a file detailing all the callback promises it is keeping. This is a list of all the read-write files that the file server's clients have read and cached; when a newer version of the affected file was written to this server, it should have contacted certain clients to warn them that their copy of the file data was inconsistent. There may be clues in this file that the server lost contact with the client or that a network problem might have caused the callback to be ignored.

A corrupt cache is often the result of a transient problem. If a file is composed of parts that are correct and parts that are garbled or composed of nulls, then the data that was stored in the cache was damaged somewhere in the transfer from the server to the client disk. When dealing with cache corruption, you'll be asked to retrieve all of the previous debugging information, and additionally, to qualify what kind of corruption has occurred:

- Is the incorrect data just a few bytes or is it large sections of the file? Is the size of the corruption related to the chunk-size of the cache?
- Is the incorrect data at the beginning of the file or in the middle? If in the middle, does it start at a particular chunk or page boundary?

These characterizations can point to either server, network, or client problems. There may be a bad disk on the server or client, or other processes on the client may be encroaching on the cache. Again, you'll be asked to retrieve kernel snapshots and copies of good and bad versions of the file. All of this data should be delivered immediately to Transarc support for debugging.

While it is time consuming to produce this debugging information, and quicker to simply flush the cache and get the user back to work, it should be obvious that without sufficient data Transarc will be unable to investigate the cache problem and improve their product. Happily, cache problems are rare and are usually associated with sites pushing AFS to the limits, either with extremely large WANs, new hardware or disks, or with overly customized cell and server configurations.

DISASTER RECOVERY

Previously, RAID or otherwise highly reliable disk drives were recommended as storage systems for master volumes because AFS does not implement any high-level, read-write data-mirroring mechanism, you're faced with a potential failure. Given what is essentially a single CPU and a single disk as the foundation for your writeable volumes—home directories, development areas, etc.—when disaster strikes, you're faced with two recovery modes: resurrecting an AFS server or resurrecting a disk.

If it is the disk that is damaged and the volumes on the disk are primarily read-write masters, you'll have to start recovering data from backup tapes. Any data in a home directory or a development area that was written after the time of the last archive operation will be lost.

If the read-write volumes in question are replicated, the data may be somewhat easier to recover. What's needed is a command that will simply turn one of the read-only volumes into the new read-write master. Alas, there's no such tool, but the process is straightforward. You'll use the volume dump command to temporarily save the data and then restore it to a new volume.

Here, we assume we need to recreate a read-write volume named sunos.usrbin from its read-only.

```
$ vos listvldb sunos.usrbin

sunos.usrbin
    RWrite: 536930451      ROnly: 5369304512
    number of sites -> 3
        server fs-one partition /vicepa RW Site
        server fs-one partition /vicepa RO Site
        server fs-two partition /vicepa RO Site
$
$ vos dump sunos.usrbin.readonly 0 -file /tmp/x
Dumped volume sunos.usrbin.readonly in file /tmp/x
$
$ vos restore fs-one a sunos.usrbin -file /tmp/x
The volume sunos.usrbin 536930451 already exists in the VLDB
Do you want to do a full/incremental restore or abort? [fia](a): f
Volume exists; Will delete and perform full restore
Restoring volume sunos.usrbin Id 536930451 on server fs-one partition /vicepa .. done
Restored volume sunos.usrbin on fs-one /vicepa
```

The listvldb command displays the information stored in the volume location database; this volume's read-write version is stored on fs-one with one read-only on fs-two. The vos dump operation saves all the data in the volume (because the timestamp option is 0) to a file. The subsequent restore operation reads that data and makes a new read-write volume on fs-two, vice partition /vicepa. The restore operation recognizes that the old read-write location information is being updated. The last listvldb operation shows that the system is back in synchronization.

The dump command stored the data in a file; you could easily attach the standard output of vos dump to the standard input of vos restore with a UNIX command-line pipe. Because no particular read-only volume was specified when dumping, the vos command has to query the database and choose to retrieve the volume data from one of the read-only volumes. There's no way on the command line to affect which read-only is used, so there may be delays as the command searches for one of the remaining available read-only volumes. You can use the fs setserverprefs command to temporarily bias the client toward getting data from one server versus another.

If the volume location database is still not correct after the restoration, you may need to run vos delentry commands to remove individual entries from the VLDB or `vos zap` commands to delete orphan volumes from disks. You can then follow these operations with `vos syncserv` and/or `vos syncvldb` commands to further synchronize the database with the actual contents of the disks.

CRASHING

If, or when, a server crashes, the system tries to make the effects as minimal as possible. Certainly, any client access to replicated files will automatically fail over to other servers. Also, any requests to read information from any AFS database will succeed because all database information is duplicated to other database servers.

If the machine that crashes is the database Ubik sync site, usually no updates can be performed until the site reboots and reestablishes mastery over the other sites. If the recovery process takes some time and there are sufficient other sites, a new sync site could be elected that would permit updates to occur. When the original server finally rejoins the cell, the other sites will recognize it, it will get a new copy of the latest database, and at some point, after a new election, it will again become the sync site.

File server crashes are more interesting. We've already discussed the salvaging process, but what about the state information retained by the `fileserver` process? What about all those callbacks? File servers maintain state on which clients have cached copies of read-write files they store and also on which read-only volumes are being accessed. After reboot and reattachement of disks and partitions, a file server knows that no new versions of the read-write files could have been retrieved or updated because it is the only repository for them. But the callback state is stored only in memory, so the server doesn't know who was using any of the files; if a file write request comes in immediately, the server won't be able to tell any clients that their copies are invalid.

To solve this problem, two tactics work.

First, clients probe servers periodically to see if they are alive. If a server is down, the server cannot respond to the probe, at which point the client will refuse to let any of its users use that server's read-write files.

Second, when the server comes back up, it will wait for the probe interval to pass before responding to any client requests for file data. After the probe interval passes, the server knows that any clients in the cell that have cached some of its file data will have attempted a probe to it and, receiving no response, learned that the server was down. So, after the interval passes, when any client contacts it, the server first responds with a message that effectively says it has just rebooted. Upon discovering this, the client will conclude that any read-write file it has stored in its cache from that server could be stale; so, it will recheck files, as they are used by applications, to see if newer versions exist.

When a client crashes and reboots, as far as the client is concerned, it will proceed as usual and any callbacks that come in will invalidate its cache. But since the client may have missed something while it was down, it checks all files against their server counterparts to make sure that the file is up to date.

Meanwhile, while the client was down, the server could well have noticed that a callback to that client failed. Servers that notice unresponsive clients will retry that client again in a few minutes; after all, it may just have been a transient network outage. If the callback RPC fails again, the server assumes that the client is actually down and deletes that client from all of its callback lists, because the client will be checking for those files anyway.

VERSION CONTROL

Some odd problems are caused simply by having different versions of AFS server or client code running in the same cell at the same time. There's no client command to determine the revision level of the various AFS servers, so you'll have to resort to some standard UNIX tricks.

```
$ what /usr/afs/bin/fileserver | grep Base
Base configuration afs3.4 5.13
$ what /usr/vice/etc/afsd | grep Base
Base configuration afs3.4 5.13
```

The UNIX what command reads through a program file and looks for ASCII strings that have been automatically embedded by the source code control tools used by the Transarc programmers. Though many such strings are placed into each AFS binary, only the string with the word "Base" in it (which is extracted with the grep command) signifies which release level has been installed.

As of March, 1997, the latest release number for AFS version 3.4 is 5.13.

If the what command is unavailable, use the UNIX strings command, which performs a more general search through a file for ASCII strings.

```
$ strings /usr/afs/bin/fileserver | grep Base
@(#)Base configuration afs3.4 5.13
```

Another technique uses the Rx protocol system.

```
$ rxdebug fs-one 7000 -vers
```

```
Trying 192.168.3.21 (port 7000):
AFS version: Base configuration afs3.4 5.13
```

The -vers option causes the rxdebug program to contact the server and query for the specified server on a given port, in this case, the file server on port 7000. The output has some good revision information, but not all servers will respond to the -vers request.

The version level of the Windows NT AFS client is stored in the system registry. Using one of the standard registry tools, such as Regedit, you should examine the value of the key HKEY_LOCAL_MACHINE\Software\TransarcCorporation\AFS Client\PatchLevel. The current patch is level 6.

When reporting problems to Transarc, be sure to include this revision number in your description. And make sure that you've installed the latest versions of the software on all servers in the first place.

Transarc's Web site provides access to their database of resolved trouble tickets. For nonemergencies, this is good place to browse issues raised by others. There are a host of mechanisms to jog the AFS servers and clients back into line; perusing the on-line troubles of others can provide some good clues as to how to go about fixing your own AFS issues.

SECURITY ISSUES

Kerberos provides a secure algorithm for the authentication of distributed systems, but the implementation raises certain security issues. Chapter 7 described the difference between MIT's file-based Kerberos tickets and AFS tokens that are associated with a process authentication group managed by the kernel. In general, a malicious user who obtained root on an AFS client can borrow file-based credentials and use them, though only on that host. PAG-based tokens are harder to borrow, but a dedicated hacker would eventually be able to use those as well.

As long as multiple users are not logged in to a single machine, the Kerberos network protocol provides very strong guarantees about process authentication. For this reason, some sites, such as MIT's campus environment, permit only a single login at a time on a workstation.

Once a token is obtained, it should be discarded when its use is over. PAG-based tokens are, like file-based ones, long lived. Users should unlog from AFS before exiting, or the logout scripts should include this functionality to erase all tokens at the end of a session.

On AFS clients, root users can also read all of the data in the client cache. Finding the data is more of a problem because the mappings of file name to V-file are stored in obscure places in the kernel.

Of course, a root user on a client can do additional damage and more subtly, can install Trojan Horse code on the system. These programs would look and, to some extent, act like local system or application software but would be used to steal passwords or other secure information from unwary users. This possibility is one reason why dataless or thinly installed AFS clients are suggested; it is much quicker and easier to reinstall the correct local system binaries.

It should be obvious that the AFS servers themselves are systems that, once infiltrated, are much more vulnerable to abuse by unauthorized superusers. For this reason, allow no BSD-style .rhosts trust model from clients to servers. And limit the servers to providing AFS file or database service alone, rather than supporting other applications such as e-mail or any other network-based service.

Root users on servers have enormous power to do damage. But besides arbitrarily shutting down the system or deleting data, root can read all vice partition data. This capability is not surprising because root has always had this ability on file servers. But don't forget about it; restrict access to file and database servers as much as possible.

Database servers have little information that is of use to malicious roots. The Kerberos database is completely encrypted and is therefore hard to crack; all password and authentication exchanges are also encrypted. However, a root user on the database servers can turn off authentication checking for the cell. Again, restrict access to the machine as much as possible. Recall that it is an explicit assumption of the Kerberos design that the database servers will be in locked rooms, highly secure, and unavailable to any general user except through the Kerberos protocol itself.

One piece of data which AFS does permit any user to read is the complete list of volume names. Since unauthenticated users are permitted to read (and write) data into appropriately permissioned areas of the tree, they are allowed to query the VLDB to discover name and location information. This permission includes listing the entire set of volumes. The security exposure here is that some confidential information may be extracted from the volume names themselves. If your cell is in the habit of naming user volumes after the login name of the user, this practice provides a way for anyone to collect a list of logins. Some sites may deem this inappropriate. It's a simple matter to obfuscate the names, at some small inconvenience to administrators: one tactic would be to name user volumes after user identification numbers instead.

When an organization is connected to other AFS sites on the Internet, there are obvious security issues when users run executables not stored in your local cell. AFS clients are normally configured to permit the running of setuid-root programs when these programs are retrieved from the local cell but not from other cells. Such programs must be configured to run on a per-cell basis.

With the growth of the Web, there has been much discussion of local sandboxes for remote executables. These sandboxes are environments wherein access to sensitive system resources—files, the window system, network interfaces—is restricted. This mechanism provides a measure of safety when users browse arbitrarily and run unknown code. But even when browsing, users can download any program, install, and execute it. And this is the AFS model: connected sites appear to each other as a shared file system.

When executed, any remote program will run under your own credentials. At worst, this means that a bad program from another cell can read or delete any files to which you can read or write. And any network ports that you can access can, therefore, be accessed by the programs you run.

Finally, there is always a potential for denial of service attacks by multiple users on the same desktop. AFS can do nothing about one user stealing processing cycles from another, but in addition, as the cache data is shared (though not the access rights) between users, one user who reads a gigantic stream of data will also adversely affect others' read and write throughput.

SUMMARY

The hodgepodge of debugging tools is another example where the long existence of AFS is a help and hindrance. There are so many different mechanisms for investigating the internals of the system that it can seem hard to know where to start. And some pieces seem destined never to change, such as the use of statically located log files rather than the more modern network system logging facilities or even SNMP.

However, the tools provided do cover most of the issues about which cell administrators are concerned. In particular, the `scout` and `afsmonitor` programs are available for periodic review of any server or client machine. While these programs are not particularly attractive compared to current graphical user interfaces, they make the necessary information easily available.

## CHAPTER 11

Large-Scale Management

I t's difficult to analyze the hardware requirements of an AFS cell before all the uses of that cell and its policy requirements are understood. The real difficulty is in deciding how small a cell can be and still be useful. Certainly, if you are dealing with an office of fewer than a dozen people and a single hard drive can store all the files, then the usefulness of AFS will be minimal.

The first point at which a site can truly realize benefits from AFS is when multiple servers are used to store shared binaries and data files such as program executables and group development areas. For executables, AFS can provide fail over characteristics to keep the organization running even when a server crashes; for group development areas, client caches provide an extremely effective way to reduce server and network loads while providing secure storage areas on servers. If the site is not geographically large, there may be more benefit in concentrating your scarce hardware resources on multiple file servers which, contrary to other suggestions in this book, are running the database processes concurrently.

When an organization has multiple, local area network segments installed with a variety of routers connecting many offices, additional database servers, separated from the file servers, will give much more flexibility to cell administration.

The maximum size of an AFS cell is impossible to quantify. This chapter contains some case studies of organizations with very large cells indeed: thousands of users and client desktops, tens of servers, and terabytes of storage. At some point, someone will suggest that introducing additional cells may help reduce performance or administrative burdens. That suggestion may be right, but multiple cells used in a single enterprise raise many issues.

Multiple cells are used for many reasons. Some organizations need more than one cell for the practical reason of internal politics. Rather than have a single entity in charge of authentication and volume manipulation, some groups or divisions would rather take matters into their own hands. Since AFS is a commercial product, which any group can purchase on their own, there's little that can or should be done to change this attitude. In many universities, individual colleges may trouble themselves with their own cell in an attempt to have more control over their file servers and namespace.

Others implement multiple cells to achieve a kind of redundancy. Read-only file sets can permit clients to get to any available set of binaries. But what happens if someone mistakenly releases a volume at the wrong time? Every client accessing those binaries will receive a message telling it to look up the file data anew. If that file data is bad, your entire cell will see a consistent view of the bad data. The initial reaction is to implement yet another layer of administrative testing. Yet, if you believe that no amount of testing is ever going to remove the possibility of a cellwide outage, you may decide to implement multiple cells to limit the effects of centralized misadventure. If so, be careful: often, multiple cells are organized in such a way that a single operation will cascade administrative functions throughout all cells; that situation ends up being no better than one cell to begin with. Perhaps a beta cell and a production cell are a good compromise—all binary and top-level volumes must be released to the beta cell and tested in an operational manner before being copied to the production cell.

Living in a multicell world is simple inasmuch as multiple cells are encouraged by the very design of AFS. When cell construction was described in Chapters 3 and 4, the mechanics of the operation were seen to be a natural part of cell administration. Multiple cells are expected to exist underneath the /afs connection to AFS; this is how most sites share information using this Internet-ready file system.

Some organizations, however, do not want to see the cell connections in every command or browser path name. Getting around such a demand is easy; for example, install a symbolic link on your desktop machines from /home to /afs/hq.firm/user. Everyday users can then access /home/alice rather than the admittedly more cumbersome /afs/hq.firm/user/alice. With

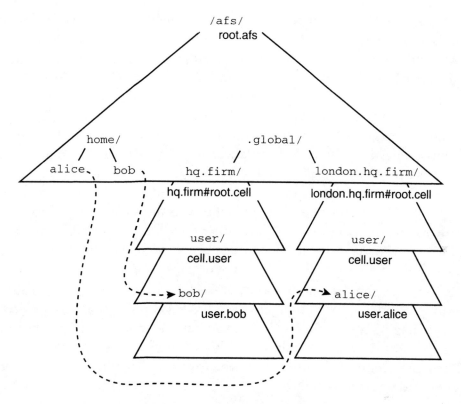

Figure 11-1 Alternative Construction of Top Levels for AFS Cell

such techniques, virtual top levels can be constructed to give any of various views of your namespace. Figure 11-1 shows an alternative construction for the top levels of an AFS cell.

For those trying to reduce the number of symbolic links, the connections to other cells can be buried in lower levels of the AFS namespace. By the use of default cell connections, common areas for all of an organization's cells can be maintained. In Figure 11-1, the root.afs volume contains regular directories with all of the organization's home directories available with short simple path names. The paths eventually lead to the correct cell, linked via a slightly less visible path name, and inside that cell to the actual home directory. When an organization has sites in different cities or campuses, such a scheme provides the illusion of a simple enterprisewide namespace by direct use of the wide-area coherence of AFS. The scalability of this solution has been proven by global companies serving home directories existing on servers in London, New York, and Tokyo.

One technical point to make about the linkages in Figure 11-1: the simple home directory paths, `/hq/home/alice` could have been a connection to the London cell's `user.alice` home volume but, instead, has been implemented as a symbolic link to `/hq/.global/london.hq.firm/user/alice`. If all of these home paths had been direct mount points, any directory listing of `/hq/home` would have caused many network transmissions across the WAN. While this scheme works in theory and practice, it is still a burden to the network, time consuming, and a potential bottleneck if all a user wants is a quick look at the user list. Because the symbolic link data is stored in the local cell, it can be read speedily and reliably from the local servers and the link values can be easily displayed. Then, because AFS symbolic links are cached, a desktop using such links more than once will not be adding to network or server loads. Once a user finds the right user name, the link can be followed over the cell in question without having to bother other cells in the organization.

Another reason for multiple cells arises when you need many AFS databases for redundancy or to mitigate slow links. Let's say you have one set of servers managing files for a few buildings, but one more building is behind a link that is very slow compared to the others. Volume releases will be delayed until the last volume has been updated. Invariably, that's the volume on a server behind your slowest link.

One other gotcha: the Ubik algorithms make each database process vote for the available server with the lowest IP address to be the database sync site. Too bad if, due to address assignments by the Network Information Center, your lowest network addresses are located at sites that are connected to the rest of the world via a slow link.

Once multiple cells are installed, however, users can share data among themselves through any application that can read and write files. Multiple cells look and feel exactly like one local cell, save for possibly longer network latencies and lower bandwidth. As such, there's no need to e-mail spreadsheets or documents back and forth; you can simply send the name of the file.

Getting authenticated access to multiple cells is supported with the `-cell` option to `klog`. A user token can store multiple credentials.

```
$ klog david
Password:
$ klog david -cell other.com
Password:
$ klog davey -cell another.com
```

```
Password:
$ tokens

Tokens held by the Cache Manager:

User's (AFS ID 2519) tokens for afs@another.com [Expires Apr 13 03:55]
User's (AFS ID 1026) tokens for afs@other.com [Expires Apr 13 03:54]
User's (AFS ID 1235) tokens for afs@hq.firm [Expires Apr 13 03:53]

--End of list--
```

As a client traverses a multicell file namespace according to the directions of a user, the cache manager will notice any cell crossings and, when in a particular cell, will establish an authenticated connection to that cell's servers, using the applicable credential obtained from the user's token.

To help with various user and administration tasks, many AFS utilities use the value of the AFSCELL variable in the user's current environment as the name of the cell against which to perform an operation. The environment variable overrides the setting of the ThisCell file. For example, the vos create command uses the value of AFSCELL, if set, as the name of the target cell, looks up the available database servers in the CellServDB file, and transmits the appropriate network requests to the listed servers. On the other hand, the fs mkm command must be directed to another cell via an explicit -cell option.

Remember that the cell is the domain of administrative control for AFS. Though certain commands can be made to affect different cells, these commands affect only one cell at a time. There are no provisions for multiple cell management.

Now is the time to expose a little white lie of AFS: there's no such thing as a cell. Unlike DCE's cells (or even Sun's NIS domains), there is no stable, system-wide definition of what composes an AFS cell. True, each database server machine will have to have a complete list of its peer servers, but each client is handed its own list of cell names and database servers and that list may not include all the database servers that actually exist in the cell. You could use this knowledge to restrict a client from ever contacting certain servers, though the server preferences value would be a more general mechanism for the same result.

Also, a client doesn't belong to an AFS cell in any real sense. While there is a default cell name in /usr/vice/etc/ThisCell, this is only a name that declares which servers should be used for default authentication, for certain administrative commands, and for finding the root volume of the AFS tree. Once the root volume has been contacted, all further traversal of the tree uses the current volume's cell until a foreign cell connection is crossed, as conventionally happens when crossing through the cells listed in the /afs subdirectory.

And more interestingly, file servers don't belong to a specific cell. As the system processes a create volume request, it assesses and updates the volume location database server of one cell, but the file server given as an argument could be any AFS file server on the Internet. File servers communicate only with client workstations, responding to requests for specific volume or file data. You could create and maintain on one file server volumes that are managed by different cells, but you'd have to be careful not to reuse volume identification numbers.

A common operational task is to list all the file servers in the cell. The only way to discover these servers is to read the entire volume location database and extract all of the file servers listed therein. No central database maintains information on a cell's set of file servers. One consequence of this attribute is seen in commands such as fs checkservers: This command can't contact all the servers in a cell because there's no place where that information is kept. Instead, the command can query only those file servers that the local cache manager has happened to contact in the recent past.

Just because AFS cells are more loosely connected than you might have thought, don't stretch the boundaries without good reason. On the contrary, if multiple cells are used, keep those boundaries clean and well known. But knowing how cells are used in the system can help you to understand the internal architecture of AFS and why the CellServDB file must be accurately and manually maintained on both the client and server sides. This deeper understanding can be particularly useful during disaster recovery or other administrative procedures. For example, because file servers don't know about the cell they belong to, you can import the volumes of an individual disk into an arbitrary cell. This operation is relatively benign because of the architecture of AFS and can be used (with care) as needed.

On the other hand, feel free to enjoy the ubiquity of AFS files to their fullest extent. It's amazing to think how many fewer client/server protocols would be needed if an enterprisewide, distributed, reliable, trustworthy file system were available. Do you need to disseminate regularly changing information to an unknown number of desktops? Think about putting that data in a file. Due to the highly available nature of the AFS namespace and the redundant access to data, the information can be easily, even trivially provided to clients on demand by simply writing it to a file. In this system, moderately sized NIS maps may be better served as straight files in well-known subdirectories. This process works equally well for small AFS sites as it does for global, multi-cell organizations.

Given this information, you should be able to design your own cell layout to exploit the strengths of the AFS cell architecture, with perhaps a few shortcuts taken for your particular site.

CASE STUDY: IBM

For many years, IBM has provided CMU with machines and expertise as the University developed a variety of interesting software systems, including AFS. During that relationship, several IBM sites began to use AFS for substantial portions of their file namespace. That use continues today, although some sites have moved on to embrace the successor technology, DCE/DFS. One site in particular, IBM's development center in Austin, Texas, has large-scale experience with both versions.

The Austin organization's job is, among other things, to support AIX operating system development, RS/6000 system engineering and manufacturing, and POWER CPU chip design. Three AFS cells supported all of this development until, a few years ago, the data was migrated to a single DFS cell.

The cell is now run on 12 file servers with an estimated two terabytes of storage used for all users and project development. This represents a user population of about 13,000 users; some 15,000 groups have been created to further control file permissions.

Like many sites, the Austin support staff created several customized tools to coordinate use of DFS with their particular administration polices. The human resources division has the authority to perform the tasks necessary for creating or removing a user and his or her home directory from the cell. Additional scripts are used by users to simplify the addition or deletion of a user from an ACL, and to show complete file storage information for any DFS file.

Users are also permitted to run a system application named TDISK. This program will create new, temporary space in the cell with a quota of up to one gigabyte for use only by the creator. The space can be used to unpack applications or store large files for a brief period. While seemingly free, the drawback is that the temporary space is destroyed, without question, after two weeks.

To manage the large numbers of volumes created to support all the users, projects, and systems, a relational database was originally used to track ownership, lifetime, backup and replication requirements. After much use, the database was eliminated in favor of a simple text file stored in DFS. Being a text file, the query tools are much simpler to create (using Perl or utilities like grep), finding and viewing the data is simple, and access is optimized through client caching.

Though the site was able to provide additional services at low cost, users were still hesitant to totally accept the file system. The organization's programming staff had previously been content to manage their software tools themselves, without worrying about the difficulties of sharing those tools with others. Developer's would typically store a version of a given tool on their local disk and keep that tool up-to-date at the needed revision level and optimized for their platform.

With the easily expandable namespace offered by AFS/DFS, the administrators are now able to offer all software packages at any needed revision levels and architectures to all developers. Each version is bundled into its own volume for administrative purposes and connected into the namespace. Developers can then link from their desktop's local file system into the shared namespace and seamlessly access the packages of their choice. This gives users the ability to control their software use while using the caching, distributed file system to centrally manage the storage.

Besides the administrative advantages of AFS/DFS, the standard caching policy provides an even more important service, enabling the organization to make much better use of their server and network resources. As an example, in the operating system group, all AIX binaries must be frequently rebuilt from the complete source tree. This process had previously taken several days to finish. Now that all data, source, tools, and object files are stored in DFS and cached on demand by clients, build turnaround times have been reduced to less than 24 hours. This is exactly the result the designers of AFS were aiming for a decade ago: developers generating a large amount of file read and write activity will see greater throughput through the use of aggressive client caching.

In addition to depending on AFS and DFS in a real-world day-to-day settings, IBM has also used the technology as the basis for their showcase Web sites, such as the 1996 Atlanta Olympic Games, the U.S. Open tennis tournament, and the Deep-Blue versus Gary Kasparov chess matches. The value that AFS adds to Web services are the high availability of production binaries and location-independent access to shared files, as well as the ability to replicate copies of files to geographically distributed Web servers.

Let's take a look at the specifics of the Atlanta Olympics site. In July of 1996, this Web site was the largest in the world, with coordinated servers located in four different countries, 24 hour-a-day service for the 17 days of the

Games, nine gigabytes of file data at the opening growing to 15 gigabytes by the closing ceremonies, and peak rates of 17 million hits a day.

All the content for this event was generated at the games in Atlanta but was immediately delivered to the primary administration site in Connecticut. From there, the data was massaged, formatted, and then replicated to the four main Web servers located in New York, England, Germany, and Japan. Each of these sites consisted of a major IBM SP2 cluster node.

To coordinate the distribution, a single DFS cell was used to encompass all of these computing centers. Each country's center had their own dedicated file servers but the three fileset location database servers (the equivalent of the AFS volume location database servers) were located only at the primary site. A little over once an hour, the newest files, consisting of anywhere from 20 to hundreds of megabytes were replicated to each read-only site.

Because no failures of the system could be tolerated, the hardware at the primary site included redundant disk controllers and mirrored disks. Of course, as the Web servers around the world were DFS clients and could fail over to any available read-only copy, each city was spared the expense of local RAID storage.

To produce the site's content, most data, however authored, was placed in a database specifically designed for Web objects. This web object manager stored all the information on the content, format, and meta-data needed to build any of the sites' HTML pages. One interesting feature of the manager is that while building any page, all embedded links would be automatically validated. The constructed pages would then be served via a built-in high-performance HTTP server.

With a dozen or so gigabytes of data available, each delivered Web page caused the server to access an average of 15 DFS files. Yet even with a DFS cache of only 250 megabytes, over 95% of file accesses were satisfied locally rather than requiring a file transfer from the server.

Some data could not be efficiently distributed to all replica sites. 38 video cameras captured images every ten seconds—an average of 21,0000 new images an hour—and stored the frames directly into DFS. Rather than ship this constantly changing information around the world, IBM relied on the single namespace of DFS to ensure that remote sites could always locate the images, no matter their physical location. As users requested new downloads, the latest images would be automatically downloaded (due to the consistency guarantees of DFS) and then inserted into a suitable Web page. Approximately

40% of the site hits were for these pages which accessed the single read-write master data.

IBM continues to use AFS and DFS at their corporate sites and as the basis for their Web services. This constant use and engineering has the important side-effect of providing IBM and Transarc developers important data points on the system's efficiencies. This scale of operation supports the contention that aggressive client-side caching, read-only replication, and the administrative tools of the system are uniquely suited for file services, including Web sites.

CASE STUDY: MORGAN STANLEY

Morgan Stanley is a financial services firm catering to all segments of the trading and asset management markets. It has over 10,000 employees with offices in every major city in the world, and its primary computing operations run continuously, everywhere.

Though Morgan Stanley's trades and accounting information are stored in relational databases, the production UNIX applications themselves are predominantly stored in AFS. And most UNIX clients are dataless: out of the box, they are quickly installed with a minimal kernel and AFS client code. Everything else—window systems, production binaries, home directories, and project development—is stored in AFS.

While the company sees a competitive advantage in having this highly tuned distributed file system, they are also concerned with the general success of Transarc and AFS. To their credit they have been quite open about their use of the system. You can read their LISA conference presentation (listed in the bibliography) for more information.

Several restrictions on cell sizing have had an effect on Morgan Stanley's rollout of AFS services. With each site needing quick and reliable access to volume location, group, and security information, many more than five or seven database servers need to be running to support the dozen or more cities around the world where Morgan Stanley has offices. Also, many more replicas are needed than the 11 possible read-only volumes; if any piece of the WAN goes down, each site still needs access to production code. And with certain sections of the WAN at drastically slower speeds than other sections, it is difficult for Ubik or the volume replication code to tell the difference between a slow link and an outage. Even with their huge investment in global WAN coverage, there is still a difference of an order or two magnitude in throughput and reliability between certain network routes.

To provide a higher level of availability for these services, at least one AFS cell per city has been implemented. Because most cities have offices in a single building, it's often one cell per building. And for New York, with its multiple offices, not only does each building have its own cell, but dual cells per building have been set up to provide the utmost in reliability. This is certainly an extreme approach, but the design of a central cell could introduce the risk of a single point of failure; if the root.afs volume were to become corrupt and released to all replicas, every AFS client in the cell would be unable to get at critical production applications. With dual cells in a building and every other client bound to one or the other cell, only half of the desktops would be affected by an AFS outage.

Servers are typically Solaris machines; globally, about 1.4 terabytes of disk storage are available, and about 1 terabyte is actively used. Legato Networker with BoxHill's vosasm utility is used to back up the file data.

The namespace is optimized for corporate operations and is quite different from the usual generic, public AFS namespace. Rather than many cells located underneath /afs, the local cell root.afs volume is mounted at /ms, and the other Morgan Stanley cells are mounted underneath /ms/.global. Several directories under /ms create a virtual view of the entire namespace; symbolic links are set up from the virtual area leading to the actual cell-based location of the data.

For instance, all users home directories can be found underneath /ms/user. You'll recall from Chapter 5 when we set up home directories, we mentioned the problem of finding one home among many thousands. Morgan Stanley uses the convention of locating a home directory in a subdirectory based on the first letter of the user's login name. A user Alice would therefore have a home directory path of /ms/user/a/alice; this path name is actually a symbolic link to wherever Alice's home is geographically located; if her desk is in Tokyo, /ms/user/a/alice points to /ms/.global/tokyo/user/a/alice. With this system, it is trivial to find each user's directory. Once you find it, you can either directly descend into the directory or examine the value of the link to determine if the user's data is on a distant, slow network.

Group directories are handled similarly: a bond project's home directory could be found at /ms/group/it/bond, which is a link to the New York office cell's /ms/.global/newyork/group/it/bond.

Two other top-level directories are dev and dist. Under dev are project development areas, again, using symbolic links to point to the read-write home for the data. The `dist` subtree is different in that it is guaranteed to be a local copy of the standard, globally distributed set of read-only production binaries. There is a careful correspondence between the naming of the directories in the `dev` and `dist` area, so that for any given piece of production code, the current set of source that was used to produce it can be found—anywhere on the planet.

A specially written Volume Management System keeps the global set of read-only volumes up to date. This client/server system has processes running as root on AFS servers. These processes can use the `-localauth` option to perform privileged commands on behalf of properly authorized users. When, for example, a developer is ready to distribute a new version of an application, the developer runs a simple command to contact a VMS process, and, if the user's authentication checks out, the VMS process carriers out a series of predefined AFS operations.

When asked to propagate a volume globally, VMS determines the authority of the user to perform the operation by checking directory ACLs and protection group memberships. If the developer is authorized, VMS dumps the volume containing the new release of the code, then restores the volume in each remote cell. The decision as to where binaries are to be distributed is kept, along with other volume metadata, in a separate administrative database. The binaries are thereby distributed worldwide efficiently and quickly. However, any interruptions or problems with the WAN can cause a volume not to reach certain cells; these problems must usually be corrected manually.

VMS is also used to set up users into the global namespace or even to move a user from one location to another. With this system, developers and administrators do not directly manipulate volumes or cells; they simply request that certain predefined actions are initiated. Because of the multiple cells, and the large number of volumes, a nightly audit volume location databases and `vice` partitions ensures that the database and the disks are in synchronization, that there are no off-line volumes, and that selected volumes are correctly replicated at all designated sites.

All database servers in all cells are also checked regularly to make sure that the Ubik system in each cell has a quorum, a valid sync site, and that all server `CellServDB` files are correct. Any restarted `bos` jobs and AFS program core dumps are also reported.

The existence of multiple cells raises the question of how authentication is managed. Luckily, Morgan Stanley had implemented a single, global Kerberos version 4 realm based on standard MIT sources a few years before AFS was introduced. The standard AFS `kaserver` was therefore never run. Improvements to the MIT Kerberos system permitted multiple, redundant servers to run without the usual limitations on the number of Ubik servers. More recently, Kerberos version 5 has been introduced.

Administration of this system simply requires creating or deleting users at the master Kerberos site with propagation automatically copying the changes out to remote servers. All of the user login programs have been modified so that with each entry into a machine, Kerberos 4 and 5 tickets are granted, as are AFS tokens for all cells. (Morgan Stanley has many other applications that use Kerberos authentication). Thus, after login, each user has credentials that will be recognized anywhere in the file system to permit reading, writing, or deleting of file data where authorized.

Transarc's protection server databases must still be used to contain all user identities and group membership. But each database holds information valid only for a single cell, and so, because of the multiple cell layout, most `pts` commands are replaced with a wrapper that performs read-only queries against the local cell. The wrapper performs any update operations first against a designated primary cell to serialize and verify the operation, then against the local cell, where the information is immediately needed, and then, in a background process, against all other remote cells.

This is a cumbersome, error-prone operation, so, again, an audit process runs regularly to synchronize all `ptserver` databases. The AFS libraries provide only a few remote procedure calls to extract and inject information to the databases; most of the work is done by laboriously running `pts` commands against the various cells and comparing the textual output.

Some other large-scale problems are due to Transarc's limited resources and market focus: Ports of AFS to the latest operating system versions must be available before a platform can be used effectively. Until the port is ready, the NFS-to-AFS gateway must be used as a stopgap. And while very large scale symmetric multiprocessing systems with their very high I/O throughputs and multiple network interfaces could be useful for certain applications, AFS is not optimized for them.

AFS's traditional missing functionality—no hard mounts across directories, group and other permission bits made obsolete—are a nagging problem that needs regular attention. Newly installed software must be checked carefully to make sure that there are no unforeseen AFS incompatibilities.

But the nagging problems and cumbersome cell layout are issues that are dealt with behind the scenes. What traders and managers see is a global enterprise file system: almost every UNIX desktop is identical to all others, users can log in to any workstation in any Morgan Stanley office and see their home directory; all other users, groups, and project directories for the entire corporation are visible as needed, and applications can be distributed and made reliably available everywhere with delegated control to developers.

CASE STUDY: UNIVERSITY OF MICHIGAN

The University of Michigan is one of the larger public universities in the United States. In the late '60s, the University installed a large IBM mainframe to support its educational and administrative needs resulting in a powerful, shared computing resource for the entire campus. During the '80s, the proliferation of thousands of PCs, Macs, and hundreds of departmental minicomputers increased the useful computing power but devalued the easy sharing of data.

By the late '80s, the University established a research project to use the mainframe computers as the backbone to a campus-wide, distributed file system based on AFS. With the chilling title of the Institutional File System, the project spawned a service organization that offered IFS to the campus in 1991. After a few years, IFS has become a de facto storage location for file data at the University; like the local phone service, it is ubiquitous, visible on all major client platforms, and supports sharing of data across the city-sized campus.

In terms of scale, a terabyte of disk space is available, with almost 700 gigabytes in current use; there are 138,000 principals in the AFS Kerberos databases, and some 65,000 home directories are installed.

The namespace is based on the conventional AFS layout with remote cells—especially dozens of other academic sites—available underneath /afs. Under the local cell, /afs/umich.edu, there are areas for system binaries, group home directories, class homes, and users. The user namespace makes use of the two-letter convention: a user with the login name of alice will have her home directory located at /afs/umich.edu/user/a/l/alice. The virtues of this path name are that it breaks the multitudes of home directories down to manageable sizes which can be retrieved quickly by file browsers and that the intermediate directory names can be simply derived from the login name itself. For the users, this convention has been accepted without undue problems.

The original hardware proposal was to use the legacy mainframes as the primary storage device for IFS. The research project completed the port successfully and the system is being used for some cell services, but IFS is currently using ordinary IBM RS/6000™ servers for database and file services. Even with over 100,000 principals and upwards of 100,000 volumes, only three database servers are needed to support the entire campus.

For file services, a total of 15 servers are installed. Because of the security concerns of having each server store the current AFS file service key, `/usr/afs/etc/KeyFile`, all of these servers and their disks are located in one building on campus. This strategy makes it easier to ensure that access to the servers is restricted to the minimum number of people. Even though the total number of servers is quite small for this large cell, data transfers among them use a separate FDDI ring for increased throughput.

The file server disk drives are standard SCSI drives used even for the read-write volumes. Many sites have chosen hardware RAID systems for this precious nonreplicated data, but the University, which for all its size does not have unlimited resources, still has questions about the performance and reliability of RAID. The downside is that disk crashes on partitions housing read-write volumes cause a considerable amount of work as files are retrieved from backup tapes.

The IFS project's initial charter was to port AFS to new hardware and to investigate areas where intermediate caching or other mechanisms would be needed to support the campus. As the University of Michigan is about 10 times as large as Carnegie Mellon University, the project tested the limits of AFS is scalability. It turns out that the implementation scaled more than enough. For example, while many sites use the MIT Kerberos server because of the slightly more standard interfaces offered by it, the University of Michigan chose to use the AFS `kaserver` because of the much better replication characteristics of the CMU-built and Ubik-based distributed database.

The one nonstandard extension provided by IFS concerns the protection server. AFS provides a significant enhancement over normal UNIX group management by encouraging user-managed groups. Since the University has access to the AFS source code, they improved upon this idea by permitting AFS groups to contain other groups as members. This hierarchy of group membership further eases the management of the large number of principals. For example, there is a `university:members` group that consists of the subgroups `university:employees`, `university:student.registered`, etc. Each of these subgroups may contain further subgroups, until, finally, there are groups containing actual principals.

Without subgroups permitted as members of groups, whenever a student registers or graduates, many dozen groups would have to be modified. And, of course, at the University of Michigan, about 10,000 new students enroll over the summer, and some 10,000 others graduate each June. The `university:mem-`

bers group does not have to change at all during these population shifts, so this arrangement reduces AFS management a great deal.

Now that a manageable group like university:members is available, it is used on ACLs that control permissions to many pieces of licensed software. You are free to browse the public areas of /afs/umich.edu, but unless you are a student at the University, or a staff or faculty member, you will not be able to use the software products purchased for use only by members of the University community.

Joining this community is an interesting exercise in modern computing. The University's data systems unit manages all new personnel and student registrations by storing their data in a large relational database. This data is used for construction of each person's University identification card—a smart-card/cash-card which is used for identification, as a debit card for local merchants, to check out library materials, for dormitory meals, or as a cash card to access facilities such as vending machines or discount long-distance telephone services.

The IFS administrators regularly extract the personnel data and add or delete principals from the various AFS groups which they maintain. New users must use a facility called uniqname which makes sure that all principals have a name and numeric identifier to uniquely describe the individual across all campus computing sites.

All new users are entered into the Kerberos database so that authenticated access is possible. Users are then able to subscribe to any of various services such as a dial-in service, e-mail, Lotus Notes, or IFS. For certain services, students receive a subsidized account balance; others have to apportion their budgets themselves. The IFS service provides entry into the standard password database, a home directory volume, a path name, and an on-line backup volume for a total cost of $0.09 per megabyte of stored data per month.

IFS supported workstations include all of Transarc's client ports. In addition, Macintosh users can attach to one of nine dedicated IFS clients which speak the Mac's AppleShare® Filing Protocol and translate those requests into IFS file accesses. As with all gateways, the difficult part is to securely enable authenticated access for each Mac user. This support was another important product of the IFS research project.

For every one of the native AFS clients around the campus, the CellServDB file must be copied over as needed from a centrally maintained copy. Similarly, for UNIX systems, a single /etc/passwd file is available with the complete set of current users and their home directory paths. Finally, login services have been replaced with a version that checks an auxiliary database to see if a user is permitted to log in to that workstation. For users not affiliated with any other computer resource, 20 Sun machines are maintained as login servers for general use; their system binaries are maintained and replicated in IFS.

The usual sore spots of AFS management do not present much of a problem at the University. While many sites have to fight the mismatch between UNIX and Kerberos authentication as users access remote machines, IFS users rely on the easy availability of file data across the campus; there's not much need to pass credentials over to a specific machine when the machine you're logged in to can access all the data it needs. For long-running jobs, you can request a new Kerberos service ticket which you can use with products such as reauth to keep process credentials fresh.

And while some have found inadequacies with Transarc's backup system, IFS uses the AFS archive system as delivered for the backup of the entire system every night.

The original research project team charged with investigating large-scale distributed file services chose AFS for many of the same reasons that CMU researchers wrote the system in the first place. AFS was five years old at that point and the University of Michigan was much larger than CMU, so the project team expected that significant work would be needed to make AFS feasible. The big surprise is that the production IFS services are running a fairly stock AFS cell with only minor improvements such as AFS protection subgroup membership and support for AppleShare.

CASE STUDY: MULTIRESIDENT AFS

A final case study is devoted not to a particular site but to a version of AFS used by the Pittsburgh Supercomputing Center. The PSC was faced with managing an ever-larger amount of data and making it available to any of their researchers on any of their special-purpose computers. Their total storage needs at the time, about 2.5 terabytes, was growing at over 3 gigabytes a day.

A typical project at the center involves animating a natural phenomenon. One or more of the supercomputers will create many directories containing hundreds of files of data totaling 100-200 megabytes each. All of the files must then be processed by other computers to create ray-traced animation frames. Each frame must further be converted into a common graphical format and then rendered into a final picture.

After beginning with a regular NFS installation, the PSC became concerned that there were inherent limitations with their set up. They investigated

AFS and became convinced that it provided a superior solution. In their experience, on similar server hardware, NFS servers became saturated more quickly and were more difficult to manage than were AFS servers. And while AFS was somewhat proprietary, the source code was available and the technology was being used as the basis for an industry-standard implementation, DFS.

Since 1990, AFS has provided a secure caching file system and global namespace to 100 PSC computers, including training, graphics, and staff workstations, and each of the center's supercomputers. The staff has since extended AFS to meet a variety of mass storage needs, including a flexible, hierarchical file system.

The name *multi-resident* describes how MR-AFS adds additional functionality to AFS. Files in a standard AFS volume are permitted to exist on only a single file server. MR-AFS permits each file in a volume to be stored at a different site. These additional sites are permitted not only to be other disk drives but to be optical storage devices or tape drives. In this model, a volume is now a container for a variety of data, some of which may be accessed quickly, and some of which especially large data sets on serial storage, would be accessed slowly. For example, an 8mm data tape can hold approximately 5,000 files of about 1 megabytes each.

Additionally, each file can reside on multiple storage devices. This feature not only provides redundancy for all AFS file data but also allows automatically maintained archival versions of all files to be stored on a tape drive.

This new model of volume containment helps alleviate one AFS administrative concern: How big should a volume be? AFS volumes are normally restricted to a single file server's `vice` partition. As the file data in the volume grows, administrators either have to move the volume from one machine to another or break up the volume by potentially copying some portion of it into a new volume and then mounting one inside the other. In MR-AFS, a volume is still stored on a partition, but the volume contents can reside on any of several storage systems, and the total size of the volume is almost immaterial.

This model is implemented with yet another replicated database to store information about the available storage devices, including the device's priority level, the computers supporting the device, and desired file sizes. A data migration facility uses this information to move or copy data from one storage device to another, either to move frequently accessed files to faster media and less frequently used files to slower media or to free up space on overused systems. By use of the size distribution information in the database, files are migrated to a medium that is optimized for its size. Naturally, all of these moves are made transparently to users of the files.

The critical design issue with this system is how to maintain the consistency of multiply-resident read-write files. The goals of the supercomputing center are important to recall: overwhelmingly, files are written once and then read once or a few times; only very rarely are files randomly accessed and written. In fact, according to PSC statistics, almost 70 percent of files (containing about 50 percent of the data) are written but never read from the file server. If that data is read back at all, it is read back while it is still in an AFS client cache.

The solution to the consistency problem is that, when written, all other residencies for a file are immediately freed. The system will at some point attempt to reconstruct the desired residencies, but that attempt is only an administrative concern. Any files that have a heavy write access pattern are therefore not given multiple residencies to slow media.

It is also possible to use MR-AFS to introduce file data on existing media into AFS without a laborious copy operation. Given a piece of hardware with large amounts of data already on it, that data location is simply installed as a new residency for some volume's files. As if by magic, the pre-existing data thereby shows up in the AFS namespace.

Also, file servers can make use of a remote server's I/O devices by using a new RPC service. In this way, one file server can use the disks belonging to another. And therefore, hardware systems to which AFS has not been ported can still provide AFS storage services; all that is needed is for the remote I/O RPC service to be installed on them.

Clients access MR-AFS files in the same way as with standard AFS. They follow the volume location database's pointer to the file server that contains the volume; the `fileserver` process there retrieves the file, though in this case, any of the residencies for the file can be read. In the case where the file exists only on a serial device, an additional residency is created on a disk, the data is spooled onto the disk, and the file is delivered from the spool to the client.

The resulting system enables the visualization process outlined above to take place with no intermediate file transfers and with the data being stored on an appropriate storage device, automatically managed by the data migrator and residency database.

Now that multiple residencies of files are available, PSC uses this facility, rather than the coarse-grained, read-only volume replication, to make data delivery reliable. When read-only replicas are desired, a further enhancement permits read-only volumes to point to the same set of file residencies as the read-write files. Thus, the volume headers are readily available via AFS, and the file data, via MR-AFS.

If you recall that the file server's `fs` job consists of three processes, you'll be wondering how MR-AFS deals with salvaging. The `salvager` needed many enhancements to understand the multiple residencies of files and to understand that not all storage devices would be available at all times. If a device is not available because it is either down or busy, `salvager` must not remove files which it can't see.

Besides the PSC, several other sites use MR-AFS. While some of these sites are similar in storage needs to PSC, others use MR-AFS just for the additional location functionality. In the mid-90s, PSC and Transarc discussed folding some of these features into the commercial AFS offering, but nothing ever came of it. For now, MR-AFS is available only as a set of source-code changes to AFS; because sites can purchase source from Transarc for a very reasonable price, this burden is not too heavy.

The MR-AFS sites necessarily provide their own support for the product and help each other with features and issues which inevitably crop up. Currently, The Computing Center of the Max-Plank-Gesellshaft and the Institute for Plasma Physics in Germany has brought MR-AFS up to date with AFS version 3.4a.

MR-AFS is included here as another example of how many academic and research institutions are using AFS. Like the University of Michigan, the PSC needed to find a solution to their distributed file system needs. Their particular scale was not merely the number of users or desktops, but the size and location of file data. Though they have modified some fundamental aspects of AFS, their changes really add to many of the design assumptions of the system. As a production tool, their version of AFS provides unmatched functionality. And, it is hoped, at some point that functionality will find its way into standards work supported by the Data Management Interfaces Group (DMIG) and future versions of DCE/DFS.

SUMMARY

In this chapter, we examined some large-scale uses of AFS. As you can see, the primary goal of AFS, support for ever-increasing numbers of desktops and users, has been achieved without the need for advanced hardware or networks. A shared, common, file storage medium can be a central part of the data processing environments in many organizations.

AFS succeeds not only with its ability to efficiently use a WAN and cache files locally, but with additional features which delegate group management and provide flexible access controls to users. That way, administrators can concentrate on providing seemingly omnipresent and highly reliable file services.

Though AFS certainly scales up, you may wonder if it is right for small sites. Given the state of the computing market, there probably are no small sites, at least in the long term. Certainly anyone who has had to bring down a server to replace a disk or who has had to manually replicate most system files onto the desktop should appreciate the functionality available in AFS. The learning curve and initial investments are clearly higher than for bundled or shareware services, but the payback as additional desktops are brought on-line is potentially enormous.

Implementing AFS

After so many chapters on administering, using, and debugging AFS, you may have forgotten the reasons for looking into this distributed file system in the first place. Certainly, few managers will purchase the system without making a clear business case for the system. And once the decision is made, any prudent engineer or administrator will take the necessary steps to ensure the success of the system. After all, the whole point of your enterprise is not to use the most technically interesting tools but to produce some product or service. Demonstrating the positive effect that AFS will have on your business is not easy as the benefits are often seen only at medium to large implementation scales. Based on several sites experience with bringing in AFS, here are some suggestions as to how to make that case.

THE BUSINESS CASE

The first place to look when investigating AFS is the successes it has had at other organizations. Transarc, of course, tells many success stories in its regular marketing literature. Most importantly, these stories are based on real enterprises with good administration staffs that simply can't keep up with their file storage problems with the usually available tools.

The published data shows that AFS has permitted a given organization to support 5 to 10 times more clients and users than with other file systems. The classic business case can then be made that this organization will need 5 to 10 fewer file servers and, almost as importantly, as many fewer system administrators. As technical companies today rapidly expand, this reduction in the number of administrators is more than made up for in future expansion, and AFS becomes a way to permit the existing staff to support many more desktops without an increase in resources.

Taking a conservative estimate of 5 times fewer servers and administrators for a particular-sized company, we can easily work out the math: 2,000 desktops needing, say, 50 servers now will need only 10 AFS servers of the same hardware configuration. The 40 servers left over are 40 computers either not purchased or converted into new desktops. And rather than perhaps 5 administrators for 50 servers, only 1 administrator would be needed strictly for file storage administration. For some commercial organizations, the savings in administration costs can easily outpace savings due to reduced hardware. As the user population grows, these savings will accumulate year-in and year-out. This back-of-the-envelope calculation suggests savings for moderately large organizations of millions of dollars per year. Even taking into account the initial software purchase and training for AFS, most companies will be saving an enormous amount over traditional file services.

Smaller companies will certainly not see such savings, and the idea of an initial investment in resources and education may appear to be a drawback to AFS. But there are no static organizations: change and growth is inevitable. As more and more file data needs to be managed even at a small site, there will be benefits in using AFS to create a more flexible infrastructure that can be easily expanded or modified as needed. And AFS's cost benefits will still permit savings year after year.

On the other hand, try not to get bogged down in unnecessary cash-flow details. If, as in many other companies, few projects are subjected to a complex business analysis, you should feel free to wonder if this exercise is intended to prove the viability of the project or just to delay it. Almost certainly, larger projects at your company with heavier up-front costs have gotten the go-ahead based on nothing more than buzzwords and good feelings. Your business case must make clear that of moving into AFS is constructed from proven technologies providing *built-in security, high-availability, remote manageability*, and *long-term scalability*. And those rewards surely outweigh the risks of spending capital to bring in a new infrastructure.

AN AFS PROJECT

The cost savings and technical advantages should not be taken on faith by managers; you must demonstrate the system and show regular progress before you can fully integrate AFS into an organization. There are usually three distinct phases to any organization's introduction to AFS: research, pilot tests, and rollout.

In the research phase, you establish contact with Transarc and the AFS community to bring the system in house and demonstrate its workings to engineers, administrators, and management. Once a demonstration period has been agreed to, you should bring up two or three servers. For the research phase, these may as well be desktop systems in an engineering group; all that may be needed is to scrounge a few extra disks to use as storage partitions.

More than one server is essential because one of the primary benefits of the system is its fail over characteristics. Once the servers are set up, create volumes that house examples of writeable home directories and replicate volumes containing directories of read-only binaries. Now you can write simple scripts to prove the ability of the system to move volumes between servers while remaining on-line to user reads and writes. And you can run long-lived executables while the file servers are brought up and down. These demonstrations by themselves will sell administrators and managers on the virtues of AFS more than any business case ever could.

If direct access to the Internet is available, don't forget to install a `CellServDB` file to enable contact with the hundreds of other publicly visible AFS sites around the world, especially Transarc's home site. If it's ever possible that your organization will need to pick up patches from Transarc or connect distant office sites together, this demonstration will convince management that globally connected information systems can be a reality.

Demonstrating the scalability of AFS is, however, more difficult. By its nature, scalability can only be seen with large numbers of clients. For a valid experiment, write a set of scripts that create, read, write, and remove hundreds of files of various sizes to simulate the effects of the real working sets of an everyday client. Then run these scripts simultaneously on one to at least six clients at a time. This test is, in effect, what is done during the Andrew Benchmark as run and reported by CMU and Transarc, or what happens during the SPEC organization's SDET benchmark. (It is to AFS's disadvantage that a robust, standard benchmark has not been designed to describe the performance of large-scale distributed file systems, for it is not too difficult to unwittingly bias a naive script to perform an odd mix of operations that will not show the advantages of AFS in the best light).

If your site uses NFS, one way to create a fairly decent test script begins with the `nfsstat` program. This program reports the number and percentage of each operation carried out on an NFS server and client. You can then write a script that attempts to duplicate that mix of operations. Once written, run the script repeatedly on an NFS client and reread the NFS statistics to make sure that the proper proportion of operations has been executed. This script can then be run on AFS clients and the total execution time, system time, and megabytes of network traffic can be compared to the NFS scenario. Most importantly, run the script on multiple clients simultaneously. Typical conclusions for tests run on six clients are that AFS cuts network traffic by 60 percent, server load by 80 percent, and execution time by 30 percent.

One note about the publicly available nhfstones benchmark: It is written exclusively to benchmark NFS server performance. Internally, it incorporates code that triggers specific NFS operations and constantly monitors the server to make sure that the correct mix of these operations is being maintained. And it reports its results in number of NFS operations per second within a certain millisecond latency. This is intriguing information for designers of NFS but cannot be used to compare user loads versus AFS.

When the research phase has demonstrated the administrative and technical benefits of the system, a pilot project is the next logical step. At this point, commission the initial server hardware and install a select population of user's desktops with AFS client code. The pilot phase ensures that client desktops, users, and administrators are comfortable with the system.

Every organization using distributed computing devises its own mechanisms for creating desktop machines. Some desktops are constructed as exact duplicates of each other; others are permitted to vary as needed. As detailed in the chapters on client configuration, not much needs to be done to connect to AFS, but that which is done must be done exactly right. The pilot phase enables the administration staff to make sure that each client in the current population is configured correctly. This task includes ensuring that the operating system is running at the correct level; that the local CellServDB file is up-to-date; and that the login program performs both local and AFS authentication. While a client can have any decently sized cache it can find on its local disks, it would be best to find several dozen megabytes at the very least, and preferable to put that cache on its own partition so it won't be disturbed by other uses of the disk.

This interim phase is also the time to begin training users with the few facts they will need to know in day-to-day operation: how to check their authentication credentials and reauthenticate if necessary; what ACLs are and how they affect privileges; how to manage their own groups of users; and how to check the disk space and quota allotment of their volume. Luckily, while this information is not too onerous for savvy users, those less adept at computers will not need to know too much for day-to-day use. Write up clear and simple Web-based materials to explain the most common commands.

The purpose of this phase is to introduce everyone, especially the administration staff, to AFS. Now you can start putting together the typical operational scripts used by cell managers: automate client configurations as needed; install a system to copy updated `CellServDB` files from some central repository to the local desktop; and write some tools customized for your customers to ease their use of the system. Most importantly, now is the time to formulate policies that deal with volume names, replication schemes, file server locations, backup strategies, and administration privileges.

Also, you will gain experience as to what size of server you should use for a certain number of your users. AFS's load on the hardware and operating system of a server is quite different from that of other systems, so take the time to stress-test your particular vendor platforms to find out which should be delegated to read-write, read-only, database, or other services.

To reduce the risk of switching to AFS, start making available to clients your heavily used production binaries. It may seem odd to recommend production use of the system as a way to reduce risk, but because your other distributed file system (perhaps NFS or Novell) will most likely still be in place it is trivial to redirect a client back to the old system if problems arise with client configurations or server availability. Meanwhile, users will be seeing the benefits of the global namespace and client side caching. And because the binaries will probably have access controls that give them wide visibility, there will be fewer problems with authentication issues. Lastly, with the original binaries still stored in another system, you can test the backup system on a large scale without hazarding the loss of newly written data.

This strategy promotes the widest use of AFS as early as possible with little risk so that the organization can get up to speed quickly. By the time you're ready to tackle putting users home directories, development areas, and other read-write data into the AFS tree, you'll already have several months' experience under your belt.

Begin the final rollout phase by making all desktops clients of AFS. In parallel, copy users home directories into personal volumes along with other read-write data sets. In the long run, this operation will free up disk space on the old servers; you can wipe those disks clean and add them to the AFS server systems. Convert the old servers or simply turn them into desktop systems. The key to this stage is providing well-thought-out backup and recovery procedures. If you've followed a strategy of segregating read-only from read-write servers, you'll be able to rely on the automatic fail over of AFS clients to replicated volumes. So, the most important data, the read-write master volumes, can be concentrated on fewer machines and backed up accordingly.

As important as it is to create your policies, scripts, and procedures, don't allow this process to delay use of the system. Certainly, the replication and caching features of AFS provide many advantages over other systems. And if your organization is like most others, your current file system will not have a complete set of procedures in place to handle every contingency. Rather, current procedures have evolved from past ones as the client/server configurations have changed. AFS will not be any different; with time new and different procedures will need to be designed to care for changing environments.

OPERATIONAL BUY-IN

When bringing in AFS to an organization, perhaps the most important issue is to make sure that management is behind the project and has made its success a specific goal of the operational staff. In the long run, it is the administrators who will be crafting and using the scripts used for daily system administration. Naturally, most operators will rightly complain that they have no extra time to work on the small-scale pilot phase versus the immediate problems of the current system. This perception can easily lead to AFS being left in the backwater of interesting projects on which no one has the time to work.

From the start, AFS must be viewed as a way to solve critical problems faced by your organization. The AFS solution is designed not only to save systems from disaster but to save real money as well. Once the efficacy of AFS is demonstrated, management should make prudent implementation of AFS a high priority for the entire enterprise. After all, AFS isn't free: while the system is not outrageously expensive, someone will have to pay for it. Only a fully implemented AFS project will be able to justify and pay back that expense.

After AFS has been demonstrated, train as many operational staff members as possible. Though the training is lengthy—the standard administration course from Transarc is three full days—the content is important and must be learned by a majority of staffers. It's important at this point to make sure that the information on how to make AFS work be easily available. Although AFS is a large system, none of its technologies require administrative gurus for operation. It seems strange that, given the pace of change in the computing industry, some people will insist that they are too busy to learn about AFS. But if AFS is not the chosen solution to distributed file storage management, whatever else is chosen will have its training requirements as well.

Once staff are trained, management must make available the appropriate resources to test and implement a stable solution. AFS is a complex system with many interrelated components; these components work together to provide seamless access to all file data. If components begin to fail, the potential for site-wide outages increases. These risks are easily mitigated only when the proper infrastructure has been planned for and implemented without kludges, stop-gap fixes, or scrounged hardware. The biggest problems are seen at AFS sites that do not enforce appropriate procedures for file system maintenance, relying merely on ad hoc support efforts. Proper procedures are a management problem, pure and simple, and require up-front investment and continual follow-through to ensure success.

Again, the operational staff must be the ones to roll out the final implementation. It's far too easy for senior engineers to develop AFS solutions that are not understood by administrators. Even such a simple task as server installation should be done by those who will be running the system—when you've installed the files and processes yourself, an AFS server will cease to be mysterious and begin to be an ordinary part of the enterprise. By now, AFS has been around a long time; it doesn't need obscure development efforts to make it work in most organizations. What it needs is experienced administration, which, of course, can come only through actual use of the system by those who run the day-to-day operations.

After the right staff has been recruited to work on implementing AFS, the next item is to prioritize your client base and decide which desktops should be connected to AFS first. This is a key decision, and its success will encourage all parties to continue the rollout. If these clients are important to your organization, they can be the perfect showcase for the best features of AFS, such as automatic fail over from unavailable servers, transparent movement of files from server to server, and lighter network loads. By publicly demonstrating these benefits, not only will you gain needed acceptance of AFS, but the entire project can gain closure: AFS ceases to be a research project, the up-front expenses have paid off, and the system can become part of your dependable infrastructure.

There will come a point in the adolescence of AFS use when the system will perhaps become a victim of its own success. Presumably, AFS was brought in to solve a set of distributed systems problems. As more time and effort are put into AFS to make it a regular part of the computing environment, more and more individuals—administrators and managers—will begin to see it as a potential solution for their immediate crises. And more than likely, they are exactly right. It then becomes a delicate balancing act for the AFS project to grow at a reasonable pace without incurring too much risk at one time; by prudently expanding its administrative domain as solutions are implemented and not before.

At the other end of the scale, the AFS project could wind up as a niche solution for just certain desktops or certain files. Because AFS offers many solutions to many disparate problems, its learning curve is somewhat steep and its implications for a computing environment are many; the best way to amortize those costs is to spread them out over as much of your computing population as possible. If every client in the organization gets access to AFS, administrators can work toward putting most of the file data into AFS and then stop administering desktops one at a time. Otherwise, instead of introducing a technology designed to solve problems, AFS will simply double the amount of work.

The centralized administration model and global visibility of files guaranteed by AFS works best when the system is ubiquitous. When everyone can get to all files all the time, when anyone can walk up to any desktop—potentially from anywhere in the world—and still access their home directory and mail with ease, then AFS will have repaid the effort put into it.

ONGOING WORK

Though use of AFS is supposed to be transparent to most users, there are several ways that the underlying distributed file system can affect people's jobs in ways that will raise criticisms of AFS itself.

One such issue is the perception by users that they have less control over their files. A multitude of loosely administered servers has now become a small centralized cell; user's may have been permitted to create directories and projects with whatever names and structures they wanted. With the single namespace of AFS, there will probably be stricter policies on the top-level path names permitted. A reasonable response to this is to create alternate views of the AFS namespace according to user's suggestions. And you can also emphasize that, although the namespace structure is under somewhat tighter control, it is guaranteed to be visible 24 hours a day to all clients in the enterprise.

Another issue is that as a smaller number of administrators take on responsibility for a larger user population, it may take longer than usual for simple tasks to be completed. This delay should not be the case: AFS provides a rich set of tools to manage its cell efficiently, often with no disruption to normal file service. So, to make sure that changes to an administrative organization does not result in perceptions of inefficiency, implement procedures to ensure that user requests are fulfilled quickly.

Once AFS is implemented, individual AFS operators will find that their workload has not been much reduced; rather, it has simply changed. Regular file system administration will take a smaller bite out of the day: rather than fighting disks, partitions, and servers, an administrator will be able to single-handedly manage many more users and desktops. Perusal of the entire file tree and underlying volumes is trivial, and therefore hour-by-hour maintenance is straightforward. Because users are insulated from the physical disks by AFS's layer of indirection, operators can manipulate and tweak the namespace with hardly a bother to anyone.

Instead, administrators will find their time is filled up with maintenance of the backup system and the installation of software packages. Transarc's backup system provides the necessary tools to manage the archiving of volume-based data, but only through the slightly laborious process of naming volume sets and labelling tapes. Judicious use of the automation features can allow handling of the majority of cases. However, some cases will always need watching. For example, while the tape error logs can provide indications of failure, you'll have to either manually watch over their content or write a script that extracts useful information and e-mails or beeps someone if a problem develops.

Third-party software installations are the bane of AFS administration. Many more sites are based on NFS and Novell than on AFS, so it stands to reason that installations are geared toward the many rather than toward the few. But NFS-style installations are still primarily local installations which just happen to be visible to a select few machines. To put such a package into AFS, you are well advised to install it on a local desktop to see the entire shape of the software package. Through a seemingly file-by-file examination of the software, you can discover those portions that are read-only versus read-write and apportion these to the appropriate volumes in AFS. Happily, once installed, AFS guarantees that all desktop systems in the organization will see the package without further ado.

If different architectures are supported, you must examine them, too, to find the files that are system neutral versus those that are not. You can copy the neutral files (such as man pages and shell scripts) a single time into an AFS volume; copy the architecture dependent files into multiple directories and use the `@sys` path name element construct a single file name to them.

Spending the time to make a multiple-architecture package fit into AFS is sometimes not worth the bother, so you can simply copy the entire package into its own volume, one volume per architecture. But when replicating those volumes, you must still take care of paths that the package binaries expect to be writeable. On UNIX based AFS servers, yet another symbolic link usually takes care of the problem.

As part of the education and training of new administrators, run regular disaster recovery drills. These drills should include testing the failure of read-only volumes, recovering single read-write volumes from backup tapes, recovering whole disks, and recovering the AFS databases themselves (volume location, Kerberos, protection groups, and backup).

You should allocate a small set of servers to a test cell so that you can try out new scripts and unload and check out new releases of server binaries. This test cell is also the obvious arena in which to let loose new administrators. As long as trainees are given only the password to the administration group of the test cell, they can experiment without fear of disrupting the main production cell.

One final aspect of AFS administration is to be ready to investigate the inevitable complaints—some justified, some not—with which you will be faced during the transition. It seems that computer users are quite conservative when it comes to the commands they use and the responsiveness of the system. Though users may run dozens of commands a day, AFS introduces a few commands of its own; to many people this is a burden. The only way to reduce this frustration is through early, swift training sessions geared towards the commonest scenarios while saving the more complex user issues (such as individual group membership management) for those persons who need it.

One of the simplest issues raised by users of AFS is that path names to many files become longer. As a consequence of the single namespace visible underneath `/afs`, many directories that have been haphazardly mounted on a variety of names or drive-letters are now mostly accessed through the wellknown, top-level directory; this single namespace can lead to longer paths. Your response: Although the paths may be longer, all computers in the organization always see exactly the same set of paths. Once this point is clear, the benefit versus other systems with per-client views, each more likely than not to be different from the other, becomes quite clear.

With AFS's aggressive use of caching, most file accesses will appear to be almost as quick as if the files were local. Yet the first access will, of course, necessitate a trip to the server. Unlike other systems with their rather predictable responsiveness, it is somewhat easy to feel when your desktop computer has a file cached and when it hasn't. This fact inevitably leads users to request that certain files be stored locally for faster speeds. You should point out that while some accesses feel slower, overall performance has increased and manually caching certain files locally will only lead to less local disk space for truly transient files (like cache and swap) and inevitable mismatches between versions on one desktop and another; the resulting administrative nightmare is just the situation that was solved with AFS.

Similarly, users, during their first skirmishes with access control permissions and volume quotas, will tend to blame problems on bugs with AFS. As with all user queries, give due attention to these reports. In practically all cases, the problem does not lie with AFS system software. But, explaining to a frustrated user that something which seems to be a bug is in reality a feature of the system is difficult at best.

AFS FUTURES

To be honest, while AFS provides much needed functionality, an organization's first experiences with it will not be trouble free. Especially when dealing with the unexpectedly strong authorization scheme proscribed by Kerberos and ACLs, using AFS can at times seem more trouble than it is worth. After all, goes the criticism, aren't distributed file systems easy? The answer is, of course, no. And just because we have grown used to the problems of other systems doesn't mean that those technologies don't present their own sets of ongoing issues that must be overcome.

Yet when compared to other systems, AFS does appear burdensome. While providing certain features of undeniable benefit, there's a certain lack of completeness and integration for which we all end up paying extra. For AFS, being able to transparently move pieces of the file system around a distributed environment is a brilliant tool to solve practical problems. But the constant hacking at backup scripts, juggling token lifetimes, and repackaging third-party software adds much friction to the system's efficiencies. Though most competing file systems don't even try to solve similar problems, they nevertheless coexist with existing infrastructures, if for no other reason than that NFS or NetWare is probably used at other sites, whereas AFS is not.

Perhaps a better analogy is to call AFS the Macintosh of file systems. It may be prettier, easier, and have a cult of diehard believers, but will it ever become mainstream? Certainly, the major innovations from CMU, such as caching, replication, fail over, and location transparent namespaces, are being adopted by competing systems. And while purists will argue, perhaps rightly, that these add-ons to existing protocols are never as good as the original, all that matters is that the result is good enough. And if good enough is available for a better price on more platforms with superior integration, the winner will be obvious.

Nowadays, it appears that the market mechanisms have subverted price-performance questions into simple demands for free services, at least on the client side. Even though AFS is not exorbitantly expensive, it does require a purchasing decision; that process in itself is so fraught with nontechnical issues and politics that the successes AFS has had is an unbelievable achievement in itself. Given that Transarc does not charge a per-client fee, the question for Transarc is, is there a better business model that will transform this product (or DFS) into a de facto standard, at least for a certain segment of the computing industry?

Worse, no truly significant advances have been made to the product in the last few years. Transarc is so busy working on ports to never-ending new releases of hardware operating systems that any significant features seem to be years away. And AFS could stand some real improvements: How about a better interface to AFS functions with real return codes and structured, informative output? Higher availability through shorter fail over periods? Use of emerging hardware cluster standards to provide fail over for mirrored read-write volumes? The ability to export non-`vice` partitions or even CD-ROMs into the AFS namespace? Finally providing support for hierarchical storage systems as was promised long ago? Although DFS has improved write-consistency semantics, it doesn't provide any of these features, either.

The more optimistic viewpoint is that while AFS solves some issues and raises others, many hundreds of large commercial sites around the world have chosen to invest in AFS because it has proven itself to possess needed functionality that translates into persuasive cost benefits. More importantly, distributed file systems are like programming languages: there's no reason to use a few different solutions as long as they can interoperate. The more significant change to an organization will not be in the bit-by-bit wire protocol used but in a change from distributed to centralized management of the enterprise's file storage.

Choosing a distributed file system technology from the available products is not a trivial task. That's not unusual for an industry seemingly based simultaneously on vaporware and legacy systems. Trying to decide on different technology to support an organization's infrastructure is a gut-wrenching process. It would help to have unambiguous direction statements for AFS from Transarc, a hope perhaps doomed by the fact that Transarc also sells DFS, the most technically advanced competitor to AFS.

But as of late in 1997, there is no indication that work on AFS will end any time soon. Enhancements for the product up to the turn of the century are in the works. AFS 3.5 is planned for release in early 1998. Among the features intended for inclusion are:

- Multihomed support for database servers and clients
- Selective use of network interfaces for file servers
- On-line salvage operations to permit volumes and partitions to be available while corrupt volumes are being fixed
- Better support for third-party backup systems
- Integration of user authentication with other login systems such as the Common Desktop Environment

The recent AFS client port to Windows NT is being upgraded to NT version 4.0. This upgrade will necessitate replacement of the integrated File Manager operations with the newer Explorer interface. Other enhancements on the todo list include:

- Support for NT Universal Naming Convention file path names
- Performance improvements
- A true disk cache
- More support for other AFS client commands such as the `pts` suite, password changing, and server preferences

Clearly, these on-going improvements suggest that AFS will continue to have a lifetime longer than the computing market's event horizon. Looking beyond that is a risky proposition. But it is hard to conceive of a moment in time when AFS is truly dead: far too many organizations have source code licenses and can support AFS on their own; the University of Michigan and the Pittsburgh Supercomputing Center are prime examples of this. Until all AFS sites have migrated to DFS (or some other equally scalable and efficient system), users and administrators should not worry too much about the end of AFS. Indeed, it would probably be beneficial to all if, at the end of its life cycle, AFS were released into the public domain; AFS source code has, after all, been available to many universities for years. Such a release would probably increase the number of sites using AFS, Transarc could focus solely on DFS and other products, and sites that wanted more and better-supported functionality could go straight to DFS.

However, even when Transarc's support of AFS is dropped at some far future date, that doesn't mean that implementing AFS now is a waste. The difference between AFS and other solutions is really a difference in management infrastructure and not a technical battle over protocols. For users, the difference between sites before and after AFS is introduced has to do with the efficiencies of AFS's central administration model and the transparency of file access across the enterprise. As far as can be determined, any other future distributed file system could be installed in place of AFS without much fanfare; administrators may need to learn new support tools, but users and developers will still be browsing and creating data in directories and folders as before.

DCE AND DFS

Toward the end of the '80s, in order to thwart an imagined power play by Sun Microsystems to control the future of UNIX, several competing workstation vendors—Digital Equipment Corp., IBM, Hewlett-Packard, Bull, and others—combined resources to form an independent software institute chartered with the creation of a new operating system and related tools. This institute, the Open Software Foundation, put out a request for technology to provide a distributed environment with directory services, security, remote procedure calls, and a distributed file system. This request was answered through a collaborative effort by many of the OSF founders as well as Transarc with a suite of specifications for what became the Distributed Computer Environment and the Distributed File System—DCE and DFS.

DCE enables an application writer to specify the interfaces to a client/server system in a high-level language. This interface definition can then be turned into real code to which can be added the actual application logic. When run, servers can register themselves with the DCE directory services such that clients can find the servers without the need for location-dependent configuration data. The security services can then be employed to confirm the identity of client and server through a system of mutual authentication and also to encrypt all data packets.

Most of these technologies were based on existing implementations rewritten to add more functionality such as replication and redundancy. DFS itself was produced by Transarc as a rewrite of AFS. In some respects, DFS can be thought of as simply a new version of AFS that attempts to solve some of the following outstanding problems of the system.

- DFS generalizes the server callback model into a token-passing system. When a client wishes to read to a portion of a file, the client must first request a read token for that portion. Similarly, when writing data into a file, the client must obtain a write token. Since the DFS servers manage all token transitions, this system allows for almost perfect emulation of standard UNIX file semantics. No longer do distributed applications have to wait for file closes to synchronize data, as in AFS; all clients should see all reads and writes as they occur anywhere in the system.

  The drawback is that the server must maintain yet more state and, of course, during server recovery, a more complicated scheme ensures that consistency is maintained. And, in order to implement the token-passing system, more data packets must be passed between clients and servers. Nevertheless, with local file caching as in AFS, DFS is able to provide similarly high performance and scalability with predictable file behavior.

- On the administrative side, DFS and AFS are very similar. Though much of the terminology has been changed—volumes are called filesets, `vice` partitions become aggregates, the `vos` command is now the `fts` command with a different selection of subcommands—most of the basic workings are the same. You can still create filesets at will, attach them to the file namespace, and move them around with full location transparency. One change that seems trivial will come as a relief to many AFS administrators: fileset names can be 106 characters long. Other changes seem somewhat arbitrary: an AFS volume quote of 0 means that the quota is turned off, whereas in DFS, 0 means a quota of 0 bytes.

  But in general, much regular DFS administration should be completely familiar to AFSers. Even the volume (that is, fileset) backup system is practically the same.

- Desktop administration is different because clients of the cell must be configured as DCE clients. DFS client caches are located in a different place but are otherwise treated similarly, though the implementation is much changed. Most interestingly, there is no `CellServDB` file to be maintained. All server information is registered with the DCE directory services, and clients query DCE to determine where to find the fileset location database servers and the security services.

- Regarding security, access control lists can be attached to all objects in the DCE cell. Such objects include all of the administrative DCE services as well as all DFS files and directories, as opposed to just the directories in AFS. Having ACLs on each file in a directory is touted as a good thing. With files ACLs, you can implement fine-grained permissioning schemes, but more importantly, there is a strong linkage between the DFS ACLs and the standard UNIX permission bits. When permission bits are modified, such as with the chmod command, the corresponding ACL entry is changed; when a specific entry (such as the owner entry) is edited, the permission bits reflect the new controls. This is another example of how DFS more closely emulates POSIX semantics.

    On the other hand, DFS ACLs are more difficult to read and internalize. Making sure that all files in a directory have the same DFS ACL or any non-trivial access pattern, is a task fit for automation only and not casual visual inspection. And because multiple groups can be added to an ACL but those group entries must be reflected in the single UNIX group permission, DFS ACLs include a group mask entry which seems to magically change to ensure POSIX conformance.

- The DCE Kerberos server can be replicated, but it does not use the Ubik protocol, so there is only a single, immovable master site.

- Transarc has produced a port of DFS to Windows NT which includes not only client access but the server side as well. It's remarkable to have an organization's file data be moved between UNIX and NT servers while UNIX and NT clients of the cell continue to access the same data no matter where it comes from.

    Significantly, the server port comes with a graphical user interface so that most DFS administration tasks can be accomplished through a few mouse clicks. At the very least, the interface helps train administrators in DFS operations with its visualization of servers, aggregates, filesets, and services. Even better, the DFS system interface is provided as a set of ActiveX objects so that customized tasks can be custom built into your own administration suite.

The conclusion in many people's minds is that DFS is an adequate competitor to AFS but there is no overriding reason to choose one over the other. The reasons favoring AFS are its greater maturity and simpler administration model versus DFS's closer POSIX semantics and potential ability to support other DCE applications.

Others will argue that DCE and DFS provide a better bridge to systems such as CORBA and that it is the only production-grade distributed environment supporting an integrated set of security, naming, and network transactions. Certainly such support makes DFS compelling if an organization is moving towards DCE anyway.

In fact, one particularly good reason to introduce DFS services is to make DCE available to all desktops. Generally, a programming group that wishes to use the DCE RPC for an application will install DCE on just the few machines in their territory. Cajoling other divisions or the entire organization to use DCE becomes a political battle more often lost than won. A central IT group, however, usually has a specific mission to support widespread infrastructural technologies such as file and directory services. Putting DCE on all computers to gain access to DFS files will automatically enable other DCE applications to be built and rolled out with relative ease.

If AFS is already in use, a migration path to DFS is available: AFS clients can connect to a DFS cell through a gateway. Given a DFS cell, you would add the list of DFS fileset location servers to an AFS client's `CellServDB` files and then run a gateway process, `adapt`, on the DFS servers. This process converts AFS client requests into DFS protocol packets. The migration path would then be to introduce a DFS cell into an AFS site and allow AFS clients to see both the AFS and DFS namespaces.

In this scenario, you can use a Transarc utility to transform AFS volumes into DFS filesets. Administrators could then gradually move data from cell to cell as the opportunities arise. As the last volumes are moved over into DFS filesets, the AFS cell can then be turned off. Naturally, the security systems of both cells will have to be coordinated and users may need to know both AFS and DFS command suites for some time, for instance, to manipulate ACLs. In theory, the migration can be accomplished with less interference in day-to-day operations than the introduction of AFS services in the first place.

If desired, a given desktop client can even run both the AFS and DFS protocols simultaneously. The only drawback to this model is that DFS is not currently available for quite the range of client platforms as is AFS. One significant omission is lack of support for SunOS 4.1.3; you may want to keep AFS installed on these clients and use the AFS-to-DFS gateway.

However, the strangest aspect of DCE/DFS is not technical at all but political: Who's in charge of the product? While Transarc is nominally the expert provider of the DFS system, OSF is a member-supported consortium. Yet of the original members who are hardware vendors, only IBM provides full support for DFS client and server on their UNIX platform. HP has only recently started to release DFS servers with full replication support for their hardware. And DEC supports basic DFS services only on their UNIX system and have failed to provide client support for VMS systems. It's fallen to Transarc to provide the most complete implementation for some of these platforms.

In 1996, OSF combined with the open standards-setting organization X/Open, forming The Open Group, an umbrella group to manage many of the computing industry's practices. The good news is that the technology has a more organized promoter; the bad news is that innovations to DCE and DFS have to pass through many hands before becoming standardized, a process that must be streamlined to ensure that the system continues to improve at a rapid pace.

THE COMPETITION

Meanwhile, back at Sun, work on the future of NFS has been proceeding faster than ever. As of 1996, Solaris 2.5 included much-needed improvements to their `automount` daemon and a caching file system layer that could be used for either remote files or CD-ROM data. This release also included Version 3 of the NFS protocol, which favors TCP connections rather than UDP datagrams, provides for some protocol optimizations, such as returning attribute information even when it wasn't specifically requested, and supports 64-bit file offsets.

In 1997, Sun released Solaris 2.6, which, as far as distributed file systems are concerned, provided support for large UNIX files and client fail over between NFS servers. Previously, fail over was available only at the moment of a client's initial mount of an exported file system. Now, fail over of read-only files can occur at any time. These are welcome innovations and will prove useful.

But the combination of features is not the same as the integrated system provided by AFS. For example, while fail over between read-only file systems is supported, there's no mechanism to ensure that the read-only file systems are equivalent.

Worse, you cannot both cache and allow fail over for the same file system. So, the files that might benefit most from caching, such as on-line documentation or often-used binaries, won't have the protection that fail over offers. Assuredly, later versions of Solaris will improve the performance and functionality of these capabilities. But unlike Transarc's ports of AFS to multiple platforms, few other vendors have shown an interest in supporting these advanced features.

Though NFS Version 3 is only a year or so old, Version 4 of the protocol is in development. This version is based on work done to help NFS deal with the World Wide Web; the early versions have been called WebNFS™. One of its features is its ability to be incorporated directly into a Web browser. A Uniform Resource Locator with the prefix nfs: would result in use of the NFS protocol to fetch a desired file from a given server. The major innovation here is the disappearance of the heavyweight mount protocol.

(Strangely, while the Network Computer reference profile mandates the use of NFS, it does not include cachefs or fail over, technologies that would make network clients and servers much more reliable and efficient.)

Novell's NetWare and Microsoft's NTFS and CIFS are also going full steam ahead. All are bringing a certain amount of robust fail over and caching efficiencies to the desktop. This implicit acknowledgement of the rightness of the AFS technologies would be heartwarming to Transarc if the fear of being steamrollered by the marketing of these competitors wasn't so chilling. But let's not forget that the real winners will be the organizations who use the best technology to support their users.

SUMMARY

In the world according to UNIX, everything's a file. The operating system promises to maintain this illusion, and we pretend to play along. Even things that aren't files, such as window systems, e-mail, and client/server computing, have been, at one time or another and with little or more success, treated as files. But as some systems move toward distributed objects and others to network computers, we still find that the general paradigm of files—a stream of bytes able to be read and written—is where most of our data resides. After all is said and done, Java™ bytecodes, most of the Web's content, the interface definition language for CORBA objects, and relational database executables are all stored in files.

For the most part, local file systems raise very few concerns among users or administrators. Bringing AFS into any established computing culture might therefore generate a shock. To those that wonder why anyone should bother with a technology that appears only to complicate something solved years ago, just take a look at what the competition is up to.

There seems to be general agreement that many of the issues AFS is trying to address are worth the added complexity. The relaxed security model of trusted hosts is giving way to cryptographically provable authentication. Fixed, small-scale permissioning schemes are being replaced with fully generalized access control lists. Overused networks are having throughput freed up through aggressive client caching. And one-at-a-time administration of innumerable desktops is being replaced with global, centralized management methods.

Make no mistake, this is still distributed, client/server computing. But rather than each individual client bearing the burden of this paradigm, the servers are now working together, behind the scenes, in a coordinated system to keep alive the illusion that everything's just a file.

These trends did not begin nor will they end with AFS. Yet this product has had a decade of experience with its implementation and has a multitude of large sites that can demonstrate its success. Understanding this, some organizations will want to aggressively push AFS to as large a population as possible as quickly as possible; the risk here is that the user and administrator training can be shortchanged, resulting in more problems than solutions.

Others organizations will implement a research project to investigate the product, insisting on a completely detailed project plan before proceeding. Here, the risk is that the large-scale implementation schedule will be used only as a make-work project for middle managers, resulting in endless planning meetings.

The successful plan will naturally evade either extreme and focus on the best parts of the system and the greatest needs of the organization. Showing early and sustained success is vital to this project, as it is to any project. And getting all interested parties signed on and invested in the long-term success is most important of all.

While the transition to AFS is not trivial, the bottom line is that a networked file system can be a ubiquitous resource, omnipresent and dependable. With this in mind, it's hoped that your organization will find good use for AFS. It will undoubtedly complement and enhance your distributed computing environment. Like most other users and administrators who use AFS daily all over the world, you'll quickly wonder how you ever did without it.

AFS Command Suite

The AFS command suite has grown over the years so that it currently includes about 50 commands and processes. Each command and option is described in the AFS manual set in detail. But in this book, some commands and even many subcommands have been only briefly noted as a compromise to allow a more generous description for the more common administrative and user tasks. This appendix lists all files and commands that make up AFS and also shows where each is stored in the local or distributed file system.

This information is based on version 3.4a of Transarc's AFS product.

COMMAND PARSING

All of the utility commands use the same command-line argument parser, so their behavior is quite predictable. Using the fs command as an example:

```
$ fs
fs: Type 'fs help' or 'fs help <topic>' for help
$ fs help
...
listacl         list access control list
listcells       list configured cells
listquota       list volume quota
lsmount         list mount point
...
$ fs help listquota
```

```
fs listquota: list volume quota
aliases: lq
Usage: fs listquota [-path <dir/file path>+] [-help ]
$ fs listquota -help
Usage: fs listquota [-path <dir/file path>+] [-help ]
```

The single subcommand help lists all subcommands. Following help with a particular subcommand prints out a simple sentence describing the command's purpose. Using -help as an option to a subcommand displays the complete syntax of the command.

Arguments enclosed by square brackets are optional; otherwise the argument is mandatory. When typing a command which has mandatory arguments, you can drop the actual option name as long as the arguments are presented in the order displayed. When writing scripts or programs that run AFS commands, you should include the option in full. Not only does this practice produce somewhat self-documenting code, but it allows for possible changing of option order in future releases of the system.

In almost all cases, subcommands and option names can be abbreviated to the shortest, uniquely identifying prefix: fs listquota could be typed as fs listq but not fs list because that term might mean either listquota or listacl.

The help output for a subcommand might also display an abbreviation: lsq is an acceptable abbreviation for listquota.

Another standard subcommand is apropos. Running fs apropos key searches the subcommand help text for the word key and prints any subcommands for which there is a match.

```
$ fs apropos quota
listquota: list volume quota
quota: show volume quota usage
setquota: set volume quota
```

Transarc provides traditional on-line UNIX man pages for only a selection of commonly used commands. Because of the large number of subcommands, the main page lists the available subcommands with other pages available for each subcommand, rather than single man page for the entire command. As an example, for the fs command suite, the fs man page would contain a pointer to subcommands such as listquota; to see listquota information, you would read the man page for fs_listquota.

In the sections that follow, the most common AFS administration commands are listed with all of their subcommands and a brief description of their use. After the description, a quick key indicates any special permissions needed to run the command:

- `root`—The command must be run as UNIX root.
- `anyuser`—Any user, authenticated or not, may issue the command.
- `authuser`—Only authenticated users may issue the command.
- `R, L, I, D, W, K, A`—Read, list, insert, delete, write, lock, or administer rights on a given directory.
- `administrators`—The user must be authenticated as a member of the group `system:administrators`.
- `UserList`—The user must be authenticated as an individual or member of a group listed in the file `/usr/afs/etc/UserList` on the AFS server. Only used for the `bos` command suite.
- `localauth`—The command can automatically be run under `system:administrators` privileges if it is run on an AFS server machine as root.
- `Kerberos ADMIN`—The authenticated principal must have the ADMIN flag set in the Kerberos database.
- group owner—The owner of the protection group entry.
- privacy flag value—Many protection group commands require a specific value, encoded as a letter or hyphen, of a given privacy flag. These flag values can be displayed with the `pts examine` command.

THE bos SUITE

The `bos` commands control the AFS processes running on the servers. They make sure the right jobs are running, restart failed jobs, circulate log files, and manage security information on the server. Note that many of these commands are provided as a formal mechanism to retrieve information without requiring administrators to log in to a server. Table A-1 lists `bos` subcommands.

Table A-1 bos Subcommands

Subcommand	Description	Authorization
addhost	Adds a host name to a server's CellServDB database. The database servers should be restarted so that they notice this change.	UserList or localauth
addkey	Adds an encryption key to a server's KeyFile database. New keys are stored with a specified version number. The highest-numbered key is the one used in normal operation. All servers in a cell should have the same value for their keys.	UserList or localauth
adduser	Adds users to a server's UserList, the list of users permitted to issue the bos command suite.	UserList or localauth
create	Adds a new job to a server's basic overseers task list. Jobs must be specified by giving a server, a job name, a job type, and a complete path name and argument list.	UserList or localauth
delete	Removes a job from the task list of a server's basic overseer. The job should be stopped before deletion.	UserList or localauth
exec	Runs arbitrary jobs on an AFS server. Intended for security-conscious sites that do not permit remote shell execution on trusted servers.	UserList or localauth
getdate	Prints out the last modified timestamps for a given executable in /usr/afs/bin. This printout is used to check that a server has the most up-to-date version of a server binary.	anyuser
getlog	Displays the contents of a server's log file. The log file name must be specified exactly. Because the file is often large, the output should be redirected to a local temporary file or a file browser program.	UserList or localauth
getrestart	Displays the time defined by bos to automatically restart all the AFS server processes on a server and the time set to check if new versions of the server binaries have been installed.	anyuser
install	Copies executables into a server's /usr/afs/bin directory and rotates the current version into a file named with a .BAK extension. This command will not immediately restart the server process; instead, the server checks for new versions at the specified restart times.	UserList or localauth
listhosts	Prints out a server's CellServDB file listing the set of data server machines configured for the local cell.	anyuser

Table A-1   bos Subcommands *(continued)*

Subcommand	Description	Authorization
listkeys	Prints out information on the server's KeyFile. When server authorization checking is on, as is usual, the output is just a checksum of the key's character string. This value can be compared to the checksum of the key for the AFS Kerberos principals. If authorization checking is turned off, the octal characters making up the key string are displayed.	UserList or localauth
listusers	Displays the set of users authorized to run bos commands on a server as configured in the UserList file.	anyuser
prune	Deletes old files from a server machine. These files include any server executables in /usr/afs/bin with a .BAK or .OLD extension and any core files in the /usr/afs/logs directory.	UserList or localauth
removehost	Removes a particular machine from a server's CellServDB file. The database servers should be restarted so that they notice the change.	UserList or localauth
removekey	Deletes a key from a server's KeyFile database. This command should be used only to remove obsolete keys from the file.	UserList or localauth
removeuser	Removes a user from the UserList file.	UserList or localauth
restart	Shuts down a running server process and restarts it cleanly. This command can be used to restart all processes including the bosserver coordinator itself.	UserList or localauth
salvage	Runs an AFS salvage process on a server's vice partitions. This command is used when corruption of a disk is suspected. Verbose output listing the volumes encountered can be specified.	UserList or localauth
setauth	Turns on or off authorization checking on a server. When checking is off, the file /usr/afs/local/NoAuth is created as a flag for further tasks. Turning off authorization checking is a grave security risk and is usually only done for the installation of the first AFS server or during catastrophic cell outages.	UserList or localauth
setcellname	Sets up a CellServDB and ThisCell file on a server. This command is used only during initial installation of first AFS server.	UserList or localauth
setrestart	Configures the times at which a server will restart its jobs or the times at which it checks for new binaries.	UserList or localauth
shutdown	Shuts down a currently running server process.	UserList or localauth

Table A-1 bos Subcommands *(continued)*

Subcommand	Description	Authorization
start	Configures a server process to run and starts it up. Any future restarts of the server will cause this process to run.	UserList or localauth
startup	Starts a server process running without configuring it to run in the future. When the server is restarted in the future, this process will not be automatically restarted.	UserList or localauth
status	Displays the status of all jobs that AFS is overseeing. The output includes information on how many times each job has been restarted and whether any core files were produced.	anyuser
stop	Stops a server process and reconfigures the job to not run in the future.	UserList or localauth
uninstall	Backs out of a previous server executable installation by replacing the binary file with its .BAK version. Should be followed by a restart command.	UserList or localauth

THE fs SUITE

The fs suite contains a variety of subcommands. Some are intended for everyday use by all users, and others are AFS administration commands requiring membership in the administration group or UNIX root privilege. Most are intended to modify the client view of AFS, either the file namespace or the local cache manager process. Table A-2 lists the commands in the fs suite.

Table A-2 fs Subcommands

Subcommand	Description	Authorization
checkservers	Checks connectivity to a cell's file servers. This command probes each file server that it has contacted previously to see if it is still responding to AFS requests. Because the probe may take some time (to distinguish between servers that are down instead of simply being slow), the command can be run in the background or with the -fast option, which prints only the latest status information. The -interval option resets the interval in seconds between automatic probes of the file servers.	anyuser root
checkvolumes	Instructs the local client's cache manager to invalidate its list of volume names and identification numbers. The result is that any new file data accesses will force the client to issue a fresh query to the database servers.	anyuser

Table A-2 `fs` Subcommands *(continued)*

Subcommand	Description	Authorization
cleanacl	Removes obsolete entries from an AFS directory's access control list. Entries for users or groups which no longer exist are deleted.	A rights on the directory. Administrators and the directory's owner automatically have this right.
copyacl	Copies an ACL from one directory to another. This function is useful because it is otherwise easy to make small mistakes in ACL editing that result in incorrect permissions.	L rights on the source directory. A rights on the target directory. Administrators and the directory's owner automatically have this right.
diskfree	Displays the name of the volume that stores a named file or directory and the amount of disk space used and available for the `vice` partition that houses that volume.	anyuser
examine	Displays information about the volume that stores the named file or directory. The data includes the volume name, the volume identification number, any messages set on the volume by an administrator, the volume quota and current size, and the disk space on the server's vice partition.	anyuser
exportafs	Enables this client to export the AFS file namespace to other machines. Generally, this command allows a client to become an NFS server and allows other non-AFS clients to mount AFS files.	root
flush	Instructs a client to ignore any cached information about a given file or directory. On the next read access, the data will be reread from the server.	anyuser
flushvolume	Instructs the client to ignore any cached information about any files or directories stored in a given volume. The volume is specified by a path name.	anyuser
getcacheparms	Prints the size of the client cache and the current amount of cached data being used.	anyuser
getcellstatus	Shows whether UNIX `setuid` programs stored in AFS are honored by this client. Such programs can be honored on a per-cell basis.	anyuser

Table A-2   fs Subcommands *(continued)*

Subcommand	Description	Authorization
getserverprefs	Returns a listing of all file server machines that this client has contacted and a number indicating which servers are preferred over others for the same read-only volume. Lower numerical preferences indicate a stronger preference.	anyuser
listacl	Prints the access control list associated with given directory.	L on a directory, or L and R on a file.
listcells	Displays the client's in-kernel version of the list of cells and database server machines. The client CellServDB file holds a static version of cell information; this file is read by the cache manager on startup.	anyuser
listquota	Prints the volume name, volume quota, and amount of storage currently used for the volume that stores the named file or directory.	reader
lsmount	Displays the volume name connected to a given directory name. If the volume name is preceded by a # character, then the directory is a regular volume mount point and the client will access either the read-write or read-only version depending on its current path preference. If the volume name is preceded by a % character, then the directory is an explicit link to the read-write version of the volume.	anyuser
messages	Controls whether various cache manager messages are written to the console device and/or the user's controlling terminal.	root
mkmount	Creates a connection between an AFS directory path name and a given AFS storage volume. This command is used to construct the complete AFS file namespace out of volumes stored on AFS servers. Note that access to data beneath the mount point directory depends on the access control list at the topmost directory in the volume. While this operation is referred to as making a volume mount point, the operation does not result in a UNIX-style heavyweight mount; this mount is an AFS-controlled association between a path name and a volume. The connection information is stored in the AFS file system itself; any such changes are immediately visible to all clients.	I, A rights on the directory

Table A-2 `fs` Subcommands *(continued)*

Subcommand	Description	Authorization
monitor	Enables information about the client cache manager actions to be written to a separate monitoring computer. This command is useful only when used in conjunction with the free utility `console` from Carnegie Mellon University.	anyuser
newcell	Adds a new cell name and list of database servers to a running cache manager or modifies an existing entry. The cache manager's in-memory version of these entries is distinct from the `CellServDB` file.	root
quota	Reports briefly on the percentage of storage space quota available for a volume housing the specified file or directory.	reader
rmmount	Removes the connection between an AFS directory and its underlying volume.	D privilege in the parent directory
setacl	Sets or modifies an AFS directory access control list.	A rights to the directory. The directory's owner and `administrators` automatically have this right.
setcachesize	Resets the size of the cache used by the client manager. This command does not change the size stored in the file `/usr/afs/etc/cacheinfo`.	root
setcell	Enables or disables the promotion of user identity through the use of a setuid program in a given cell.	root
setquota	Changes the quota associated with the volume that stores a specified file or directory.	administrators
setserverprefs	Assigns a numerical preference for a given file server or database server. Lower values indicate a more preferred server; the value can be thought of as a distance or cost—nearer or cheaper is better.	root
setvol	Sets various per-volume attributes: the volume quota, a message-of-the-day for the volume, and a message displayed when the volume is off-line.	administrators
storebehind	Reconfigures a client to return from a file `close` operation before all bytes are written to the server.	root

Table A-2   `fs` Subcommands *(continued)*

Subcommand	Description	Authorization
`sysname`	Displays or changes the client's value used when interpreting `@sys` path names.	root, to set; anyuser, to display
`whereis`	Displays the file servers that are currently storing the file or directory. Prints a list of file servers the file or directory is available from multiple read-only volumes.	anyuser
`whichcell`	Shows in which cell a given file or directory is stored.	anyuser
`wscell`	Prints the name of the client's default cell.	anyuser

THE vos SUITE

The `vos` commands, listed in Table A-3, are primarily used by administrators to manipulate the AFS volumes that store the file data and directory listings of the file system.

Table A-3   `vos` Subcommands

Subcommand	Description	Authorization
`addsite`	Adds a file server as a potential site for storage of read-only versions of a given volume. The volume will not be replicated until a release subcommand is performed.	UserList on the specified server or localauth
`backup`	Creates a snapshot volume based on a read-write. The backup volume has the same name as the read-write master with a `.backup` extension added. This volume does not duplicate the file data; it merely copies pointers to the original volume's data. As such, backup volumes cannot be moved to other disks independently of their read-write master.	UserList or localauth
`backupsys`	Creates en masse backup volumes for all read-write volumes that match a given pattern. The pattern can be a simple regular expression for the volume name or a given server or partition name.	UserList or localauth
`changeaddr`	This command is obsolete as of version 3.4 or later. Changes the IP address for a server that is in the VLDB. The VLDB maps each volume to a set of servers that store that volume. Because the servers are identified by IP address, if any servers' addresses need changing, the address must be changed in the VLDB via this command.	UserList or localauth
`create`	Creates a new read-write volume. This command introduces an entry into the volume location database and makes a volume, initially consisting of just an empty directory, on a given server and partition.	UserList or localauth

Table A-3   vos Subcommands *(continued)*

Subcommand	Description	Authorization
delentry	Deletes a specific entry from the volume location database. The entry can refer to a read-write, read-only, or backup volume. This command does not delete an actual volume on a server's disk.	UserList or localauth
dump	Reads all the data in a volume and writes the data out into a portable ASCII format. Either a full dump or all data changed after a specified data can be dumped.	
examine	Displays information contained in the volume location database and in the volume header on disk.	anyuser
listpart	Displays the available vice partitions on a given server.	anyuser
listvldb	Displays information in the volume location database for all or one particular volume.	anyuser
listvol	Displays information on volumes stored on a server. This command does not show any data from the VLDB.	anyuser
lock	Locks an entry in the volume location database. Once the entry is locked, no AFS operations can be performed on the volume.	UserList or localauth
move	Performs all the work necessary to move a volume from one server and partition to another. During the move operation, user access to the volume is still permitted. AFS ensures that all reads and writes will work during this operation.	UserList on the source and destination server or localauth
partinfo	Displays the storage space currently available on the partitions of a given file server.	anyuser
release	Duplicates all file data in a master volume to each of its read-only replicas.	UserList or localauth
remove	Deletes a given volume from the volume location database and erases the data from the disk. Read-write, read-only, or backup volumes can be removed.	UserList or localauth
remsite	Deletes a file server's registration as a volume's replica site from the volume location database. This command does not delete any data from the server's disk.	UserList or localauth
rename	Changes the name of a read-write volume. Volumes are associated internally with an identification number, so this command automatically changes the names of any read-only and backup volumes.	UserList or localauth

Table A-3   vos Subcommands *(continued)*

Subcommand	Description	Authorization
restore	Recreates a volume from data previously stored from a vos dump operation. The data can be restored into a new volume if desired.	UserList or localauth
status	Shows whether there are active transactions in a volume server process. If there are, the output will be of interest only to AFS programmers.	anyuser
syncserv	Reads the volume location database and checks each entry's presence on disk. If the entry does not exist on the specified disk, the command deletes the entry from the VLDB.	UserList or localauth
syncvldb	Scans the disk partitions of all known servers and adds to the volume location database any volume entries that are missing.	UserList or localauth
unlock	Unlocks a locked entry in the volume location database.	UserList or localauth
unlockvldb	Deletes all locks held on any entries in the volume location database.	UserList or localauth
zap	Deletes a volume from a server's disk. The cell's volume location database is not updated. This command can be used to bring the servers back into synchronization with the location information in the VLDB.	UserList or localauth

THE kas SUITE

The kas command suite, described in Table A-4, manages the Kerberos database. Almost all of its commands require that the issuing user be authenticated with the Kerberos ADMIN flag set; there's no -localauth option, so even a UNIX superuser on the AFS Kerberos server needs to be authenticated.

Table A-4   kas Subcommands

Subcommand	Description	Authorization
create	Creates a principal for a user or service in the Kerberos authentication database and assigns an initial password.	Kerberos ADMIN
debuginfo	Useful only to AFS gurus. This command connects with the Kerberos server and attempts to perform authentication. It prints out copious debugging as it does so, and thus can aid debugging.	anyuser

Table A-4   kas Subcommands *(continued)*

Subcommand	Description	Authorization
delete	Removes a user from the authentication database.	Kerberos ADMIN
examine	Displays the internal information about a principal stored in the authentication database.	Kerberos ADMIN. Users without the ADMIN flag may examine only their own entry.
forgetticket	Deletes any tickets stored for the issuing user by the server. This command is similar to the unlog command.	anyuser; only the issuer's tickets are deleted.
getpassword	An obsolete command used during the upgrade from AFS version 2 to 3.0. It displayed the octal value of the encryption key, was similar to the examine command, and required a specially compiled authentication server.	
getrandomkey	Creates a new, random encryption key. Usually used only for testing.	anyuser
getticket	Gets a Kerberos ticket for a user similarly to the klog command. Used primarily for debugging.	anyuser
interactive	Runs an interactive, authenticated session with the AFS kaserver process. This command permits just the subcommands to be entered rather than requiring manual entry of individual kas commands.	anyuser; subsequent subcommands require more restrictive authentication as required
list	Displays all entries in the database. For all entries, either the name only or full information can be printed.	Kerberos ADMIN
listtickets	Displays all tickets owned by a user. Similar to the tokens command.	anyuser
noauthentication	Discontinues use of the user's authentication credentials. Used only in interactive mode.	anyuser
quit	Returns to the normal UNIX command prompt. Used only in interactive mode.	anyuser

Table A-4 kas Subcommands *(continued)*

Subcommand	Description	Authorization
setfields	Changes various flags and fields in a user's authentication database entry.	Kerberos ADMIN
setkey	Sets a principal's key in authentication database. This command is provided as a mechanism to reset a server's key. Because a key is an encrypted form of the password string, setting a user's key to some value with this subcommand is not useful, as there is no mechanism to convert the key to the password that would match it.	Kerberos ADMIN to change a server key.
setpassword	Changes a principal's password. This command is normally used by administrators to change server's keys. Users will generally use the kpasswd command to change their own passwords.	Kerberos ADMIN, to change a server key; authenticated users can change their own passwords.
statistics	Shows various statistics for a given AFS kaserver process.	Kerberos ADMIN
stringtokey	Causes the AFS string-to-key function to change a character string into its encrypted key form. The resulting key is displayed only; it is not stored in any database. Used only for diagnosing problems.	anyuser
unlock	Enables authentication for a principal after the account was locked out because the maximum number of failed authentication attempts was exceeded.	Kerberos ADMIN

THE **pts** SUITE

The protection database stores information linking an authenticated principal to an AFS user account and also user membership in AFS groups.

The privilege for certain commands is complicated because groups can delegate some administration to others. Mostly, this delegation depends on the group's privacy flags.

As with the kas suite, the -localauth option cannot be used. Table A-5 lists the pts commands.

Table A-5   pts Subcommands

Subcommand	Description	Authorization
adduser	Adds a user (or machine) to the given group membership.	See the individual group's ADD privacy flag: -, only group owner or administrators can add; a, any group members; A, anyuser
chown	Transfers a group's ownership to another user or group.	group owner or administrators
creategroup	Creates a new group. Authenticated users can create groups only with prefixes named after their login name. Only administrators can create groups without prefix names. In addition, a user must not have created more groups than the quota permits.	authuser or administrators
createuser	Creates a new user (or machine) entry	administrators
delete	Deletes a user, machine, or group from database. Deleting users or machine entries requires administrator authorization. Groups can be deleted by their owner.	owner or administrators
examine	Displays internal information about a protection database entry.	See the entry's STATUS privacy flag. s, group members and administrators may examine this entry; S, anyuser
listmax	Displays the value of the GroupMax and UserMax internal counters. These counters determine the values for the group or user identification numbers that are automatically assigned for new entries.	anyuser
listowned	Displays groups owned by an entry. Both users and groups can own AFS protection groups. This command also displays those groups that are orphans, that is, owned by users or groups that have been deleted.	See the entry's OWNERSHIP privacy flag: -, user, group owner, and administrators can list; O, anyuser

Table A-5 pts Subcommands *(continued)*

Subcommand	Description	Authorization
membership	Prints out the complete membership of a group or the groups in which a user is a member.	See the MEMBER-SHIP privacy flag: M, anyuser can list the membership; m, administrators or, for groups, group members; -, user, group owner, or administrators
removeuser	Deletes a specific user from a group.	See the REMOVE privacy flag: -, group owner and administrators can remove; r, group members and administrators
rename	Updates the name that specifies a given protection group. Because an identification number is used internally on access control lists, changing the name causes the new name to be seen immediately when ACLs are displayed.	group owner or administrators. Only administrators can rename user entries or change a group to a name without a prefix.
setfields	Sets various internal states for group or user entries. This command changes the privacy flags and the group creation quota.	user or group owner or administrators. Only administrators can change group quotas.
setmax	Resets the current value of GroupMax or UserMax used to automatically assign identification numbers to new groups or users.	administrators

THE backup SUITE

The backup database stores information on the dump levels, collections of volumes called volume sets, and a list of all dumps made, the volumes contained in the dump, and other data.

Most of the `backup` subcommands manipulate this database directly, while the `dump` and various `restore` subcommands perform the actual writing or reading of data to archive media. The `-localauth` option was added to this command as of AFS version 3.4a. Table A-6 lists the commands.

Table A-6 `backup` Subcommands

Subcommand	Description	Authorization
adddump	Adds a new dump level to the abstract dump hierarchy.	UserList or localauth
addhost	Informs the backup system that a new tape coordinator process is available at a specified port number.	UserList or localauth
addvolentry	Adds a new entry to a volume set. The entry is a pattern for the server name, vice partition, and volume name. This pattern is expanded into all valid volume names during the backup process.	UserList or localauth
addvolset	Creates a new, named volume set in the backup database.	UserList or localauth
dbverify	Performs an integrity check of the on-line backup database.	UserList or localauth
deldump	Deletes a dump level from the dump.	UserList or localauth
deletedump	Removes the record of a dump from the backup database.	UserList or localauth
delhost	Removes the pointer to a tape coordinator from the system.	UserList or localauth
delvolentry	Deletes an entry from a named volume set.	UserList or localauth
delvolset	Deletes an entire named volume set from the backup database.	UserList or localauth
diskrestore	Attempts to restore all the volumes residing on an AFS file server partition. An operator is prompted to insert all the tapes on which each volume was dumped.	UserList or localauth
dump	Creates a full or incremental archive of a set of volumes. The information about which volumes are dumped at what level is stored in the backup database.	UserList or localauth
dumpinfo	Displays information about dumps stored in the backup database.	UserList or localauth

Table A-6 backup Subcommands *(continued)*

Subcommand	Description	Authorization
interactive	Starts an interactive session. Only subcommands and their options need to be entered.	UserList or localauth
jobs	Lists running jobs. Only available in interactive mode.	UserList or localauth
kill	Stops a running or pending dump.	UserList or localauth
labeltape	Writes an identifying label to tape and records the information in the backup database.	UserList or localauth
listdumps	Prints the entire abstract dump hierarchy.	UserList or localauth
listhosts	Displays all hosts configured to run a tape coordinator.	UserList or localauth
listvolsets	Shows all volume sets and their volume entry patterns.	UserList or localauth
quit	Exits interactive mode.	
readlabel	Reads the label written on a tape and prints it.	UserList or localauth
restoredb	Reads a copy of the backup database from tape.	UserList or localauth
savedb	Stores a copy of the backup database on tape.	UserList or localauth
scantape	Reads archive tapes to reconstruct missing information from the backup database.	UserList or localauth
setexp	Assigns the expiration dates for a given dump level.	UserList or localauth
status	Finds out what a given tape coordinator is currently doing.	UserList or localauth
volinfo	Displays all the dumps known to have been made of a volume.	UserList or localauth
volrestore	Determines which archive tape has stored a dump of a volume, prompts for it to be inserted in the tape drive, and then recreates the volume from that data.	UserList or localauth
volsetrestore	Performs volrestore operations for a set of volumes.	UserList or localauth

PROGRAMS FOR ALL SYSTEMS

The entire AFS command suite is generally made available to all systems through the distributed file system itself. Typically, a machine will contain a link from /usr/afsws to the area where these programs are stored, somewhere in the local cell. The @sys path name is a convenient mechanism to use to make sure that each system reaches the appropriate set of binaries for its particular architecture. Commonly, the link is from /usr/afsws to /afs/hq.firm/system/@sys/afsws; administrators or users would then put /usr/afsws/bin into their PATH environment variable.

Table A-7 lists the programs in /usr/afsws/bin.

Table A-7   AFS Utility Programs in /usr/afsws/bin

Program	Description
afsmonitor	Displays statistics about client and server Rx RPC and cache
bos	Suite of tools to manipulate AFS server jobs
cmdebug	Debugging tool to display internal state of client cache
compile_et	Compiles a table of external messages
fs	Suite of utilities to manipulate AFS files and client cache
klog	Authenticates to AFS
klog.krb	Same as klog but uses MIT Kerberos protocol
knfs	Associates AFS tokens with a specific client for use with NFS
kpasswd	Changes a Kerberos password
kpwvalid	Utility to check the strength, length, etc. of new passwords
login	Replacement login that authenticates with Kerberos
login.krb	Same as login but uses MIT Kerberos protocol
pagsh	Starts a shell in a new process authentication group
pagsh.krb	Same as pagsh but uses MIT Kerberos protocol
pts	Suite of utilities to manipulate users and groups
rcp	Uses current credentials when copying files remotely
rsh	Connects to another AFS client and maintains authentication
rxgen	Uses interface definition to generate client and server stubs
scout	Displays file server statistics such as disk space available

Table A-7   AFS Utility Programs in `/usr/afsws/bin` *(continued)*

Program	Description
`sys`	Reports `@sys` value
`tokens`	Displays current Kerberos credentials
`tokens.krb`	Same as `tokens` but uses MIT Kerberos protocol
`translate_et`	Converts an error message number into text
`udebug`	Queries and displas internal state of AFS database processes
`unlog`	Deletes current Kerberos credentials
`up`	Recursively copies files and directories including ACLs
`washtool`	Used to help build AFS
`xstat_fs_test`	Tests the statistics gathering tool against a file server
`xstat_cm_test`	Tests the statistics gathering tool against a cache manager

Table A-8 lists the programs in `/usr/afsws/etc`.

Table A-8   AFS Utility Programs in `/usr/afsws/etc`

Program	Description
`backup`	Suite of tools to manage backup system
`butc`	Tape coordinator process that manages archive devices
`copyauth`	Copies a ticket to a remote cell
`fms`	Determines the space available on an archive device
`fstrace`	Starts, stops, and dumps cache manager debugging info
`ftpd`	An FTP daemon that performs Kerberos authentication
`inetd`	Service daemon that understands Kerberos remote authentication
`kas`	Suite of utilities to manipulate the AFS Kerberos database
`kdb`	Prints entries logged to the authentication log
`kdump`	Dumps internal state of AFS kernel module
`kpwvalid`	Checks the strength, length, etc., of new passwords
`makepkgfiles`	Used with the package system to set up a client image
`ntp`	The network time protocol daemon

Table A-8   AFS Utility Programs in `/usr/afsws/etc` *(continued)*

Program	Description
`ntpdc`	Network time protocol control program
`package`	Manages the creation of standard volumes and files
`package_test`	Checks for errors in package system files
`rxdebug`	Displays statistics of the Rx RPC system
`uss`	Creates all volumes, files, credentials for a new user
`vldb_convert`	Brings previous release of volume location database up to date
`vos`	Suite of tools to manage AFS volumes
`vsys`	Low-level command to interface with AFS system calls

Bibliography

Preface

Transarc Corporation
`http://www.transarc.com`

Richard Campbell
`http://www.netrc.com`

Chapter 1: Architectural Overview

"Scale and Performance in a Distributed File System"
John H. Howard, Michael L. Kazar, Sherri G. Menees, David A. Nichols,
M. Satyanarayanan, Robert N. Sidebotham, Michael J. West
ACM Transactions on Computer Systems, Vol. 6, No. 1, February 1988, pp. 51-81.

"A Survey of Distributed File Systems"
M. Satyanarayanan
Carnegie-Mellon University, Computer Sciences Department Technical Report
CMU-CS-89-116, Februrary 1989

"Synchronization and Caching Issues in the Andrew File System"
Michael Kazar
USENIX Conference Proceedings, Dallas, January 1988, pp. 27-36.

"A Usage Profile and Evaluation of a Wide-Area Distributed File System"
Mirjana Spasojevic, M. Satyanarayanan
USENIX Conference Proceedings, San Francisco, January 1994, pp. 307-323

On-line references

AFS-FAQ
`http://www.transarc.com/afs/transarc.com/public/www/`
`Product/AFS/FAQ/faq/html`

Linux-AFS FAQ
`http://linux.wauug.org/umlug/linuxafsfaq.html`

Chapter 2: AFS Technology

"Rx: A High Performance Remote Procedure Call Transport Protocol"
Bob Sidebotham
Information Technology Center, CMU, February 23, 1989

Chapter 3: Setting Up an AFS Cell

Ubik
Philip K. Dick
Vintage Books, 1991

Chapter 6: Managing Users

"Kerberos: An Authentication Service for Open Network Systems"
Jennifer G. Steiner, Clifford Neuman, Jeffrey I. Schiller
Usenix Conference Proceedings, March 1988

"Using Encryption for Authentication in Large Networks of Computers"
R.M. Needham, M.D. Schroeder
Communications of the ACM, Vol 21(12), December 1978, pp. 993-999.

Chapter 8: Archiving Data

"The AFS 3.0 Backup System"
Steve Lammert
LISA IV, Proceedings of the Fourth Systems Administration Conference,
October 1990

Chapter 11: Large-Scale Management

"An AFS-Based Mass Storage System at the Pittsburgh Supercomputing Center"
Nydick, D., et al.
Proceedings of the Eleventh IEEE Symposium on Mass Storage Systems,
October 1991

"An AFS-Based Supercomputing Environment"
Jonathon S. Goldick, Kathy Benninger, Woody Brown, Christopher Kirby,
Cristopher Maher, Daniel S. Nydick, Bill Zumach
Pittsburgh Supercomputing Center

"Institutional File System at the University of Michigan"
Ted Hanss
In *Distributed Computing: Implementation and Management Strategies*
Raman Khanna, Editor, Prentice Hall, 1993

"Morgan Stanley's Aurora System: Designing a Next Generation Global Production UNIX Environment"
Xev Gittler, W. Phillip Moore, and J. Rambhaskar
LISA IX, Proceedings of the Ninth Systems Administration Conference,
September 1995, pp. 47-58.

Index